Islam and Peacemaking in the Middle East

Islam and Peacemaking in the Middle East

Nathan C. Funk and
Abdul Aziz Said

Viva Books

New Delhi | Mumbai | Chennai | Kolkata | Bangalore | Hyderabad | Kochi | Guwahati

First Indian Edition 2010

VIVA BOOKS PRIVATE LIMITED

- 4737/23 Ansari Road, Daryaganj, New Delhi 110 002
  E-mail: vivadelhi@vivagroupindia.net, Tel. 42242200
- Plot No. 76, Service Industries, Shirvane, Sector 1, Nerul, Navi Mumbai 400 706
  E-mail: vivamumbai@vivagroupindia.net, Tel. 27721273, 27721274
- Jamals Fazal Chambers, 26 Greams Road, Chennai 600 006
  E-mail: vivachennai@vivagroupindia.net, Tel. 28290304, 28294241
- B-103, Jindal Towers, 21/1A/3 Darga Road, Kolkata 700 017
  E-mail: vivakolkata@vivagroupindia.net, Tel. 22836381, 22816713
- 7, Sovereign Park Apartments, 56-58, K. R. Road, Basavanagudi, Bangalore 560 004
  E-mail: vivabangalore@vivagroupindia.net, Tel. 26607409, 26607410
- 101-102 Mughal Marc Aptt., 3-4-637 to 641, Narayanguda, Hyderabad 500 029
  E-mail: vivahyderabad@vivagroupindia.net, Tel. 27564481, 27564482
- First Floor, Beevi Towers, SRM Road, Kaloor, Kochi 682 018, Kerala
  E-mail: vivakochi@vivagroupindia.net, Tel: 0484-2403055, 2403056
- 232, GNB Road, Beside UCO Bank, Silpukhuri, Guwahati 781 003
  E-mail: vivaguwahati@vivagroupindia.net, Tel: 0361-2666386

Published by arrangement with

Lynne Rienner Publishers Inc.
1800 30th Street, Boulder,
Colorado 80301
USA

ISBN 978-81-309-1221-9

Published by Vinod Vasishtha for Viva Books Private Limited, 4737/23, Ansari Road, New Delhi - 110 002. Printed and bound by Anand Sons, Delhi - 110 092.

To Meena and Elena, our magnificent spouses,
and to Mikael, whose arrival has brought
everything into focus

Contents

Acknowledgments

The idea for this book was originally conceived in spring 2000, at a time when the world looked somewhat different than it does today. Though the events set into motion after September 2001 forced us to revise several passages of the text more than once, the rationale for *Islam and Peacemaking in the Middle East* remains the same as it was on that fine spring day when its seed was first planted during a luncheon at American University. We are convinced that there is a profound need for knowledge not just about the roots and manifestations of religious militancy, but also about warrants and precedents for peacemaking in Islamic thought and historical experience.

Animated by the premise that peace in the Middle East and in the larger context of Islamic-Western relations depends in no small part on the activation of rich resources within the Islamic tradition, we have sought to challenge misconceptions about the world's second largest religion and develop an account of the many ways in which Muslims in the Middle East and beyond are capable of working for peace and responding to positive overtures.

Authors of books on Islam and the Middle East face many dilemmas, among them the problems of transliteration and translation from Arabic into English. Whenever possible, we have used a simplified *International Journal of Middle East Studies* system for Arabic transliteration, making adjustments on occasion for maximum accessibility and consistency with popular usage. Most transliterated Arabic words are presented in italicized font, except for proper nouns and terms that can be found in most English dictionaries. Quotations from the Quran are based primarily on translations by Yusuf Ali and Ahmed Ali, which we have adapted as needed.

This book could not have been completed without assistance and inspiration from a great many persons. We would like to acknowledge profound intellectual debts to Şerif Mardin, Mohammed Abu-Nimer, George Irani, Mubarak Awad, and Chaiwat Satha-Anand, all of whom have influenced our thinking about Islamic approaches to peacemaking. We would like to thank

Hani Farsi and Mohammed Said Farsi for their constant support of the ideals of life-affirming Islam, cross-religious discourse, and cooperative global politics. John Kiser and the William and Mary Greve Foundation contributed greatly to our ability to complete this project.

Numerous individuals aided our research and editing efforts in substantive and much-appreciated ways, including Adel Ait-Ghezala, Shannon Beuthe, Peter Corcoran, Karim Douglas Crow, Shanna Edwards, Zen Hunter-Ishikawa, Ben Jensen, Maria Jessop, Steve Jones, Ayse Kadayifci-Orellana, Lynn Kunkle, Nawal Mustafa, Elli Nagai-Rothe, Ana Carmen Neboisa, Carole O'Leary, Geoff Orens, Betty Sitka, Robbie Wellington, and Jim Zanotti. A special debt of gratitude is owed to Marilyn Grobschmidt, Bridget Julian, and Karen Williams of Lynne Rienner Publishers, and to copyeditor Jason Cook, for their patient support and encouragement throughout the editorial process.

The encouragement, feedback, support, and suggestions of many others—including family members and friends as well as students and coworkers—have been invaluable. Conrad Grebel University College and the American University School of International Service provided collegial institutional homes for us as we worked to bring this project to fruition.

Islam and Peacemaking in the Middle East

1

Introduction

Studies of public opinion in the Arab world and in the United States since September 2001 suggest that, in recent years, alienation between Arab-Islamic and American cultures has become painfully acute. Throughout the Middle East, views of the United States have gone from bad to worse. In April 2002, 76 percent of Egyptians claimed to hold the United States in low regard, whereas by July 2004, 98 percent expressed a negative opinion. In Morocco the trend was much the same, moving from 61 percent negative in 2002 to 88 percent negative in 2004.[1] The event generally held responsible for this deterioration—the decision to invade Iraq in March 2003—has reinforced widespread perceptions that US policy is biased against Arabs and Muslims, and that the "war on terror" is really a war on Islam.

The data from North American polls are also troubling. Since 2001, increasing numbers of Americans have reported that, in their view, Islam is an inherently violent religion.[2] As American beliefs about Islam harden, so too do attitudes about the use of force to protect national security. Current trends appear particularly unsettling when considered in light of a December 2006 poll by the University of Maryland's Program on International Public Attitudes. In their responses to the poll, Americans were significantly *less* likely than citizens of the world's most populous Muslim-majority countries to categorically condemn "bombing and other attacks intentionally aimed at civilians."[3]

Trends in public opinion, of course, can be highly volatile, and not all of the polling news is negative. Recent surveys by the Pew Global Attitudes Project, for example, reveal significant declines in the number of individuals in Muslim-majority nations who are willing to justify suicide bombings as a valid means of defending Islam.[4] Despite ongoing political violence in Iraq, Afghanistan, Israel-Palestine, and Somalia, and the continuing threat of a new clash between the United States and Iran, fatalism would appear both unwarranted and premature.

This book is founded on the proposition that a time has come to consider new approaches to conflicts within and with the Islamic world, particularly but not exclusively in a Middle Eastern context. To develop these approaches, diplomats, policymakers, activists, and engaged academics will need far more than familiar platitudes asserting simply that "Islam is a religion of peace" or that radical Muslim groups threaten international security. They will need well-researched information about the many different ways in which Muslims are capable of thinking about conflict, peace, and peacemaking. Contemporary conflicts are indeed about much more than Islam, but unless Western and especially US actors find a way to engage Muslims in a manner that affirms religious beliefs and identities, opportunities to foster new dynamics will be missed.

Given the damaging character of the allegations non-Muslims are raising about Islam and the profound importance of Islamic identity and values for Muslim communities, there is a vital need for nonsuperficial approaches to dialogue and engagement, with a special emphasis on ways in which Islam—a source of sacred meaning to approximately one-fifth of the world's people—can contribute to global peace. Muslims and non-Muslims alike need to transcend the simplistic assumptions that underpin contemporary debates, resulting in portrayal of Islam as a victim or perpetrator. Both need to penetrate beyond media images and suspend the temptation to settle arguments through selective and isolated references to historical events, actions of adversaries, and passages from religious texts.

In writing this volume, we have dedicated ourselves to the search for new ways of understanding the richness and complexity of the Islamic cultural and religious heritage as it relates to peace and peacemaking. We offer a framework that is intended to facilitate understanding of diverse currents in Muslim politics, and to identify values and practices that can be invoked to further the cause of coexistence. Our primary intention, however, is not to refute those who make sweeping judgments and forecast inevitable conflict. Instead, our purpose is to move beyond simplistic arguments about Islam's inherent character to reveal the many different ways in which Muslims have thought about peace and conflict resolution. In the process, we hope to provide a basis for rethinking what may be possible in Islamic-Western relations, and to provide an inventory of resources for potential peacemaking initiatives that appeal to shared and complementary values.

Beyond September 11

For most North Americans, the starting point for discussions about Islam and peace is September 11, 2001—a calendar date that is so laden with symbolism that it signifies not only a tragically destructive event but also the advent of a new phase in modern history. What happened on that day brought death to thousands, and profound distress to millions more. Simultaneously, this date signified the beginning of a new and rapidly shifting reality, a time of danger, challenge, and uncertainty.

In the United States, the immediate reaction was utter shock. For one entire day, the nation's attention was fixed on a single, terrible drama, and Americans spent the following weeks grappling with a troubling set of questions: Why did this atrocity happen? Who were the perpetrators? Was there something that Americans had done to provoke anger and inspire hatred, or was the United States under attack simply because its values differ from those of its enemies?

Halfway around the world, in the Middle East and other predominantly Islamic contexts, September 11 brought forth an even more widely divergent set of responses. Some, it is true, welcomed the attacks on the World Trade Center and the Pentagon. Others refused to believe that their co-religionists were morally or technically capable of committing such grave atrocities. Most observers, however, were both shocked and saddened by the scenes on their television screens. In Iran, large numbers of people participated in candlelight vigils. In Jordan, people left flowers at the US embassy in an expression of sympathy. Elsewhere, there were widespread expressions of dismay about the harm done to civilians. Many were shocked by the destruction of universally recognized icons symbolizing the boldness and dynamism of American aspirations. Vocalizations of concern were conditioned in no small degree by a sense of foreboding: What would come next? Would the United States seek retribution? Where would this all end?

The questions that Americans and Muslims asked immediately after September 11 were both legitimate and important. Concerned first and foremost with the nature of the threat posed by actual as well as perceived adversaries, these questions were preoccupied with a search for appropriate defensive measures. They were authentic responses to a situation of profound distress. They continue to invite serious deliberation and demand straightforward answers. These questions did little, however, to illuminate the context of September 11's fateful events, nor did they concern themselves substantively with opportunities for improving the intercultural relationships that are now viewed as sources of security threats. Focused as they were on the problem of achieving security *from* the "other" rather than security *with* the "other," these questions were not conducive to conflict transformation or intercultural cooperation between Islam and the West.

Since September 11, much has changed. The United States has gone to war in Afghanistan and Iraq, and now appears to have entered a period of heightened tensions with Iran. The conflict in Israel-Palestine has deteriorated markedly in recent years. Bombings and other acts of terrorism have shaken South and Southeast Asia as well as Spain, Saudi Arabia, North Africa, and

England. A new politics of international security has emerged, resulting in profound challenges for the global human rights movement.[5] With each new crisis in international affairs—including controversy over Danish cartoons, indignation over Papal comments on Islam, and outrage over an Iranian Holocaust conference—distrust has deepened, together with defensiveness, righteous indignation, and cultural insularity. The rising tensions in our world must give us pause: Have opportunities to foster deeper understanding been missed?

Though Muslims have been grappling with the impact of Western values and practices on Islamic culture for decades, events following September 11 have pushed Western analysts to engage with Islam at a deeper level than in the past. Many now realize that Islamic culture is dynamically contested. Diverse formulations of Islamic precepts have profoundly different implications for social and political practice, and Western policies have a significant impact on the outcome of debates among Muslims. Most Muslims reject terrorism as an aberration that contradicts religious norms, yet many also maintain that Western policies contribute to the appeal of radical views. Thoughtful Western commentators recognize that true security will prove elusive unless such claims receive due consideration.

Our goal is to take policy discussions one step further, toward direct consideration of resources for intercultural and interreligious peacemaking that can be found within the context of Middle Eastern Islamic culture. The time has come for active efforts that seek, through cultural and religious understanding as well as through concrete political initiatives, to "make peace with Islam." Through an exploration of different paradigms of interpretation and practice, we seek to identify opportunities for creative peacemaking partnerships. By keeping our focus primarily on the Middle East, we examine bases for constructive change in the region of the Islamic world that has most often been affected by conflict with the West.

The Middle East: Where the West and Islam Meet

Like "Islam," the term "Middle East" is richly evocative. From a North American or European perspective, it is a strategic region. Though afflicted by conflicts such as the decades-long Israeli-Palestinian confrontation and the ongoing war in Iraq, the Middle East remains a vital repository of world petroleum reserves and a gateway to the Far East.

For those who reside in this region, however, the appellation "Middle East" is viewed with discomfort. Many contest the use of the term because it was invented by the British to define a particular theater of operations during World War I—the region between the Nile river in North Africa and the Oxus river in Central Asia.[6] In its actual application, the label is notoriously imprecise. When used narrowly it denotes the eastern Arab states, Iran, and Israel, yet in many contexts the term "Middle East" signifies a swath of territory stretching from Morocco to Pakistan. It should therefore come as no surprise that many who live in core "Middle Eastern" countries prefer to project their regional identity in other terms, in relation to a broader Arab or Islamic world.

Despite the fact that few—if any—people are passionately committed to a Middle Eastern identity, the Middle East does have a measure of coherence as an analytical construct. In political analysis, discussion of the region often includes references to the Arab states of North Africa and Southwest Asia as well as to Israel, Turkey, and Iran. It is an area that has been defined as much by the conflicts that beset it—for example, modern conflicts between Arab nationalism and Zionism, among rival claimants to Arab and Islamic leadership, and among various seekers of its vast oil wealth—as by overarching cultural and geographical unities. Yet the term "Middle East" is commonly used by Arab and Israeli as well as Persian analysts. Some Afghans and Pakistanis also view themselves as participants in a broadly defined "Middle Eastern" milieu, and although events and traditions of Afghanistan and Pakistan are not a primary focus of this book, they are invoked on occasion as they relate to happenings elsewhere.

Internal divisions notwithstanding, the "greater Middle East" retains a politically significant cultural history. Anyone who is concerned about contemporary tensions between Islam and the West must take notice of a rough correspondence between the region comprising the Middle East and North Africa, and what was historically a core region of Islamic civilization, a region administered variously by Arab, Persian, and Turkish (especially Ottoman) rulers. This region has never been homogeneous, nor have its boundaries been fixed. In modern times it has contained majority Christian and Jewish states (Lebanon and Israel, respectively),[7] and significant segments of its population—for example, the Kurds—are ethnically distinct minorities without states to call their own. Taken as a whole, this region is acknowledged by most Muslims as the historical "heartland" of their faith. This Islamic heartland faced encroachment by dynamic and expansive European neighbors in the nineteenth century and fragmented into a large number of distinct nation-states during the twentieth century, yet a majority of the region's people continue to share common historical narratives. Most affirm the central role of religion in shaping their cultural identities, while also highlighting the ways in which colonial-era boundaries, oil geopolitics, and the Arab-Israeli conflict have shaped their political horizons and lived realities.

Recognizing the Middle East as the historical—and in the eyes of Muslims, beleaguered—heartland of Islam in no way detracts from the importance of major Muslim cultural and population centers in South Asia, Southeast Asia, sub-Saharan Africa, or post-Soviet Central Asia. Some of the largest concentrations of Muslims in the world may be found in states that are not

Middle Eastern, including Indonesia, India, and Nigeria. Indeed, with over 200 million Muslim citizens, Indonesia is home to more followers of Islam than any other country. Still, as the traditional core of Islamic civilization, the Middle East—especially the Arab world—has had and continues to have a tremendous impact on Islamic social norms and religious thought. Approximately one-third of the world's 1.3 billion Muslims reside in the Middle East and North Africa, and the Arabic-speaking peoples who are concentrated in this area played a historically decisive role in propagating Islam. The crucial importance of the Arabic language in religious texts and interpretive discourse cannot be underestimated. Moreover, all the world's ritually observant Muslims turn to the Arabian Peninsula each day for prayers, and hope for the opportunity to visit Mecca and Medina through rites of pilgrimage.

In the present international system, the Middle East is the region in which conflict between Western (especially US) strategic objectives and popular Muslim aspirations is most strikingly evident. To a considerable extent this region and its conflicts—in Iraq, Israel-Palestine, and many other locales—mediates Western images of and relations with Islamic civilization as a whole. Middle Eastern tensions with Western powers such as the United States, in turn, affect the way in which a decisive segment of the Muslim world perceives the West.

When focusing on the Islamic dimension of Middle Eastern politics, it is important to emphasize that religious culture is by no means an independent factor driving processes of conflict or peacemaking. Any effort to reduce conflicts within the region or between regional and external actors to their religious component results in caricature rather than sound analysis, by excluding consideration of economic and political realities that shape the daily experiences of people in the region. Nonetheless, religion remains a profoundly important dimension of the social and cultural environment of the Middle East. As the region's predominant religious tradition, Islam plays a powerful role in shaping both collective identity and the values to which governments appeal in their search for political legitimacy. Protagonists of change utilize the language of Islamic beliefs and values to galvanize potential supporters, while many of their adversaries draw upon the same language in an effort to maintain the status quo. Though important nonreligious voices and movements exist, the Middle East remains a place in which religion matters.

For reasons of geography as well as geopolitics, the Middle East is a region of Islamic civilization that has long experienced strained relations with Europe and the West. Strictly speaking, none of the major conflicts in the region are purely internal or "Middle Eastern." For decades, the actions of foreign powers have exerted a decisive impact on regional processes and outcomes, and external pressures and influences have often provided impetus to Islamic movements as diverse as Egypt's Muslim Brotherhood, Lebanon's Hezbollah, and Turkey's Justice and Development Party. Middle Eastern social and political processes cannot be understood without reference to global cultural and intellectual currents, and to the policies of extra-regional actors toward Middle Eastern states and peoples.

Because the problems of the Middle East and the problems of the West are shared problems, much can be gained from efforts to experience North American–Middle Eastern and Islamic-Western relations in new ways. In particular, there is a need to leave behind the notion that Middle Eastern Islam is somehow strange or "an exception" among the religious cultures of the world. As we emphasize in this book, we believe that Westerners who investigate Middle Eastern culture in a spirit of fairness and genuine interest are likely to find much to respect and much that is familiar. They will notice that many of the problems currently faced by predominantly Muslim countries of the Middle East are not alien to the Western experience, and that political uses and abuses of Islam are often reminiscent of historical interactions between religion and politics in Europe and North America.

Approaching Middle Eastern Islam with an eye to its distinctiveness *and* an eye to the familiar permits nuanced responses to the "Islamic factor" in Middle Eastern politics. Rather than framing Islam primarily as a basis of radicalism, this approach recognizes Islam as a system of social values with relevance to peacemaking—a system that is internally contested, and that is neither diametrically opposed to prevailing Western values nor equivalent to them.

The Clash of Symbols

Representing dynamics of Islamic-Western conflict is a delicate and perilous endeavor, especially when one considers that intellectual constructs are capable not only of reflecting the world, but also of shaping it. A prime example is Samuel Huntington's now-famous "clash of civilizations" thesis, which predicted that in the post–Cold War era, geopolitical conflict would be dominated by civilizational identity rather than by state-centric nationalism, with new threats to Western culture and alliance systems emanating particularly from the Islamic and Confucian cultural spheres.[8] Huntington's argument soon entered popular discourse, because it was easily grasped, dramatic, and linked to a phenomenon that had already become quite perceptible: the increasing salience of ethnic and religious identity in world politics following the eclipse of communism.

Because the role of culture and religion in international affairs is easily sensationalized in ways that mask the complexity of human motivation, many scholars reacted to the "clash of civilizations" thesis quite critically, by pointing away from cultural and religious factors. In response to arguments raised by Huntington and others about the Middle East and the broader Islamic world, detractors asserted the primacy of politics. Some, for example, argued quite forcefully that religious militancy in the Islamic world cannot be understood in isolation from several decades of US geostrategic policies that have contributed to popular discontent.[9] Others proposed that the "turn to Islam" in Muslim opposition politics was more strategic than religious; from this standpoint, religious language can be used instrumentally to galvanize resistance against repressive regimes that frustrate popular aspirations for political change.[10]

One of the more important challenges for contemporary analysts of global politics is taking the cultural and religious dimensions of conflict seriously, without enshrining these factors as independent and autonomous causes of strife. Given the extent to which culture and religion have become "securitized," it is now vital for analysts to explore multiple perspectives on the subject of cultural difference in international relations. Samuel Huntington was neither the first nor the last commentator to broach the subject of "civilizations" in world politics.[11] Whereas Huntington's framework begins and ends its analysis of culture with traditional military security concerns (and, indeed, represents external and internal cultural diversity as the new security threat to Western democracies), other frameworks manifest a more hopeful preoccupation with the challenge of fostering global solidarities as a basis for facing shared humanitarian concerns. Such approaches are premised on observations concerning the internal diversity of civilizations and cultures, the limited explanatory power of civilizational identity relative to other factors that can influence political behavior,[12] and the existence of common spiritual values that might facilitate the pursuit of superordinate goals by members of different cultural groups.[13]

Current Western-Islamic tensions testify not only to divergences in the objectives pursued by various Western and Islamic states, but also to a condition of mutual ignorance and estrangement that has deep historical and political roots. Where there is ignorance and estrangement, hostile stories find ready ears. Imprisonment in hostile narratives, in turn, makes resolving basic conflicts of interest extremely difficult. Peace becomes equated with the implementation of one's own cultural and political values; cultural difference becomes a security threat. Furthermore, superficial approaches to observing the "other" tend to become fixated on clichés and stereotypes.

In the Middle East and other predominantly Muslim cultural areas, stereotypical "Westerners" are recognizable not only by anticipated linguistic and racial markers, but also by the manner in which they dress and carry themselves; in North America and Europe, stereotypical Muslims are believed to be identifiable from a distance through the head scarves worn by women and the beards or mustaches of (presumably Arab) men. These are standard profiles through which Western-Islamic relations are experienced, the symbolic referents within which more abstract ideas about "us" and "them" are framed.

The problem with stereotypes is that they are both superficial and misleading. They are superficial because they fail to penetrate beyond the outward, symbolic forms of culture, and misleading because they overgeneralize—often in pernicious ways—from particular cases. In reality, there is no such thing as a "typical" Westerner or Muslim. Millions of Muslims may be found within the West, and many of them trace their origins to South Asia or sub-Saharan Africa rather than to the Middle East. Middle Easterners themselves are highly diverse religiously and ethnically (including Muslim and Christian Arabs, Armenians, Berbers, Circassians, Ashkenazi and Sephardic Jews, Kurds, Persians, and Turks) as well as culturally (compare, for example, modes of religious expression in Turkey and Saudi Arabia). Although we often find that we are pushed by language or by popular preconceptions to speak as if this were not so, our words distort the subject matter when they fail to accommodate diversity. Middle Eastern Muslim women in "modest dress," for example, may wear spandex at home and harbor fondness for Western pop music, and a less conservatively dressed Western woman might happen to be an avid reader of bestselling poetry by Rumi and Hafez, Muslim poets who wrote hundreds of years ago and are still cherished in the Middle East today. When trapped by stereotypes, we lose sensitivity to such "anomalies," and our thoughts become preoccupied with a "clash of symbols."

In addition to stereotypes that prevent deeper engagement, peacemaking is also hindered by the historical legacy of unequal power relations. For the past several centuries, the West has been dominant in its relations with the Islamic world, and Western thinkers have not generally felt a need to investigate conceptions of peace emanating from the Middle East and other predominantly Muslim regions. By default, Western policies affecting Muslims have been formulated without engaging Muslim conceptions of a peaceful, just, and desirable international order. Instead, colonial-era Western policies toward Muslim lands were driven both by the realpolitik of imperial competition among great powers (a reality that most Muslims experienced quite directly) and by faith in a "civilizing mission." Western powers such as France and England believed that they were bringing their own values—and indeed "peace"—to peoples who were perceived as having little to offer in exchange.

Such acts of moral presumption are by no means unique to the modern West. Unfortunately, the tendency to equate one's own cultural and political order with "peace" appears to have been nearly universal in human history. In every age, ascendant powers have sought support for their practices by claiming—and sometimes genuinely aspiring—to either keep the peace or teach it to others. The colonial era has ended, yet Earth's peoples have only just begun to initiate forms of cross-cultural and interreligious dialogue that might someday yield a more widely shared set of understandings about bases for global peace.

There is of course resistance to such dialogue. Unsurprisingly, contemporary Muslim reactions to Western predominance have been marked by defensiveness. Many Muslims find it difficult to acknowledge ways in which their cultures have been enriched by contact with the West, and focus instead on incompatible social mores and rivalries in the domain of international politics.

This emphasis on differences helps to maintain a clear sense of identity and a basis for fighting against perceived injustices and intrusions, but at the cost of allowing oneself to be defined negatively through contrasts to the "other" rather than positively and autonomously, on the basis of affirmations. The predominant Western approach to Islamic-Western relations also seeks differences and reinforces them, viewing Islamic culture through the lens of security threats and seemingly exotic practices. An essential task of all those who would seek new and creative options is to subject stories of Islamic-Western confrontation to critical analysis and evaluation, both by clarifying the ways in which religion and culture enter into the politics of conflict and peacemaking, and by demonstrating the relevance of cultural traditions that affirm the possibility of peaceful coexistence.

A Prospective Approach to Peacemaking

At a time when the rift between Islamic and Western cultures appears to be growing, it is crucial to take note of common values, among the most significant of which is a simple desire to live in peace. Because understandings of peace are culturally inflected, however, understanding the diversity of thinking about peace is an essential prerequisite for intercultural cooperation.

In many respects the most important conflicts in the world today are being played out *within* rather than between civilizations, among divergent ways of articulating what "peace" actually means.[14] Most cultural and religious traditions include multiple paradigms for defining, understanding, and pursuing peace. A student of cultures and religions, therefore, should not be surprised to find divergent subcultures within any macro-cultural tradition, with differing understandings of history's lessons and of the manner in which sacred values are to be embodied. In some subcultures, history is remembered and texts are read to support the notion that peace depends first and foremost on military strength, and is largely reducible to an absence of war or a cease-fire. In others, peace is idealized as much more than a simple absence of war, and is understood to depend less on military prowess than on human solidarity in efforts to advance values such as human dignity and ecological balance. Still other subcultures highlight the spiritual significance of peace, as a state of integration, harmony, or wholeness.

Both in the West and in the Islamic world, there are many who regard peace as a distant goal—as a temporary absence of violence or as an ethereal value that cannot guide practical politics. Among those who adhere to this "minimalist" understanding of peace, military assertiveness in confrontations with adversaries is a primary basis for maintaining moral and political order. Yet each tradition also encompasses more actively pacific tendencies, within which peace is understood as a value that pertains not only to ends but also to means. For those who embrace this "fuller" understanding, peace is not only an absence of war and violence but also a presence of justice and conditions for human flourishing.[15]

Which conceptions of peace will prevail? The answer to this question depends not only on the imagination and energy of Muslims and Westerners, but also on the extent to which common ground is sought and established across cultural and religious boundaries. Recent years have been characterized to a considerable extent by a cycle of confrontation and mutual reinforcement between Westerners and Muslims who underscore the importance of military means for establishing peaceful conditions. Post–September 11 efforts by the United States to extend military, cultural, and economic influence in the Middle East have been met by rising activism among Muslims who believe that Islamic values can only be protected and advanced through armed struggle against external adversaries. The voices of Westerners as well as Muslims who are skeptical of "peace through war" thinking have too often gone unheard, even though their struggles continue. A central task of this book is to draw increased attention to bases for active peace-seeking within the Islamic world and, in the process, to identify ways in which Western Christians and Jews as well as secularists and followers of other traditions might reach out to engage Muslims in collaborative peacebuilding ventures.

Peacemaking between the Islamic Middle East and the West requires willingness to face both intellectual and practical challenges. Intellectually, the challenge is to find terms of reference that empower constructive actions, and that do not promulgate stereotypes or conflate appearance with substance. New and creative ways of thinking about the Middle East and its role in global politics are needed, starting with a new set of questions. These questions should emerge from a clear, positive vision of the desirable (peace, social justice, political participation, cultural diversity, broad-based economic development, and ecological sustainability), and not only from a negative vision of threats and fears (terrorism and political violence). How can peaceful coexistence be established, both in the Middle East and between Middle Eastern Muslims and Westerners? What, exactly, does Islam teach about peace, and how do Islamic standards for peacemaking relate to Western ideas and traditions? How do Western peace paradigms speak to paradigms that may be characterized as Middle Eastern or Islamic? What combinations of steps, unilateral as well as collaborative and reciprocal, might address root causes of war and terrorism, building upon the *best* that is to be found in Middle Eastern Islam and in the West rather than bringing out the worst?

In practical terms, Islamic-Western peacemaking means working to "make the world safe for diversity." This objective depends in no small part on discovering ways to strengthen peace processes through *prospective* research with an explicit purpose: to identify consequential debates within Middle Eastern societies that have a bearing on possibilities for peaceful change and coexistence.

To respond to this challenge, we seek to provide an academically based yet accessible text that clarifies the diversity of Islamic understandings of peace, and that offers examples of how these peace traditions have been and *might be* used to advance peacebuilding within and beyond the Middle East region. In our present time, in which the West perceives Islam as a hostile and alien force and Muslims feel that they are under siege by the West, it is vitally important to recognize resources for peace within the Islamic tradition. This book therefore aims to explore various Islamic principles, precepts, practices, precedents, and paradigms that can inform peacebuilding, utilizing a mode of inquiry that could also be applied to other religions.

It is not the goal of this book to demonstrate that Islam is intrinsically either more peaceful or less peaceful than other religious traditions. In our opinion, too much ink has already been spilled in arguments concerning the innate peacefulness or nonpeacefulness of the Islamic tradition. While we are predisposed to agree with Assad Ali, a prominent scholar of Islam at the University of Damascus in Syria, that in its purest form the religion of Islam is a "*fatwa* [command] of peace," we do not in any way wish to deny that this spirit has not always been expressed in Muslim thought and practice. Sadly, many misdeeds have been committed in the name of Islam, and in the names of the world's other major religious and ideological systems. Misdeeds, however, are not the primary subject of this book. By exploring the many meanings of peace within Islamic culture—from strict order to spiritual universalism—we hope to provide readers with inspiration for their own engagement with Islam, whether that be as non-Muslims interested in reaching out to Muslims in an appeal for new beginnings, or as committed practitioners intrigued by a view of their tradition through the lenses of peace and conflict resolution studies.

Despite the fact that Islamic and Western cultures have been interacting with each other for centuries, cultivating a history of shared experiences and values, the common ground shared by Islam and the West remains easy to overlook.[16] Although voices of exclusivity and confrontation have not succeeded in silencing all other voices, they have proved quite successful at defining the parameters of public discussion. The exact details of contention vary, but several themes resurface with disconcerting regularity. The common discourse is that Westerners and Muslims—especially Middle Eastern Muslims—share few, if any, common values. "Our way of life" (be it "Western" or "Islamic") and "their way" are incommensurable. "Our way" is more civilized, peaceful, and true than "their way." Discord is inevitable, at least so long as "they" do not hold sacred the values "we" esteem.

Are such claims justified? Insofar as Islam and the West constitute distinct and separate civilizations (and this is, in fact, debatable), each civilization is commonly understood to prioritize a somewhat different response to perennial dilemmas of human social life, such as individual autonomy versus communal authority, personal interest versus collective interest, and free exercise of practical reason versus transmission of traditional wisdom. The word "civilization" can indeed provide a convenient way of referring to such broad cultural patterns of value differentiation and, when used appropriately, neither glosses over the rich internal diversity of subcultures and traditions nor draws attention to differences at the expense of those similarities in human values that make civilizations "civil." It is unfortunate, however, that most contemporary discussions of civilizations draw far more attention to differences than to similarities, or to ways in which multiple cultural heritages have cross-fertilized one another throughout human history.[17]

Islamic and Western cultures embrace remarkable internal variation, and each is distinguished more by allegiance to shared symbols and by broadly patterned value priorities than by allegiance to a pure and unique conception of how to lead a "good" human life. Furthermore, differences in value priorities are no more fundamental to the genesis of most conflicts than competing material claims. Sadly, strategic *manipulation* of culture and identity—the use of sacred symbols to justify actions that may constitute their antithesis—has sharpened conflicts to the point where a spirit of confrontation threatens to develop autonomous dynamism.

Rather than focusing narrowly on retrospective assessments of "what has gone wrong" in Islam or in Islamic-Western relations, this book is primarily intended to stimulate prospective thinking about how Muslims and non-Muslims might work together to "make things right." While conducting our research on Islamic teachings about and experiences of peacemaking, we have sought to identify *resources* within Islamic religious and cultural experience—some of which are rooted in the past, and others emergent among contemporary interpreters—that can be tapped to support present efforts. In the Islamic tradition as in other religious and cultural traditions, precept and practice are rarely a perfect match, and often there are serious divergences as well as disagreements even among those who believe themselves to be pursuing the same goals. The cases we present here reflect these human tendencies, but in our view they also challenge us to imagine scenarios in which conscious effort could bring about a closer alignment of ideals and actions.[18] We hope that readers will feel inclined to join us in thinking prospectively, with critical openness to new possibilities and relationships as well as with awareness of challenges that remain to be faced.

Looking Forward

In the emerging twenty-first-century world, much depends on positive Islamic-Western relations, and on the development of constructive ways to engage the cultural, political, and spiritual aspirations of Muslims within the context of a pluralistic and still fragile world community. To meet this challenge, Westerners and Muslims alike need a clear understanding of Islamic resources for peace, and of their relevance to peacebuilding challenges within and beyond the Middle East.

Because the issue of Islam and politics is an immensely important and also sensitive issue, we begin our investigation with an overview of contending narratives about Islamic-Western relations. In Chapter 2, we propose that present difficulties in relations between Muslim-majority and predominantly non-Muslim (especially North American and European) societies are the product both of a tragic historical legacy and of the ways in which this legacy is continuously recycled and recast by decisions that we make today. Reframing relations between Islam and the West by making the challenge of peaceful coexistence a central priority is crucial for achieving a more harmonious post–Cold War, post–September 11 era.[19]

We regard this focus on remembered history to be vital, because in the transformative period that lies ahead we will need to carefully distinguish between two types of narratives: narratives of inevitability and narratives of possibility. Narratives of inevitability are based on simple extrapolations from retrospective thinking about past conflicts. They tell us that what we do today is of little consequence, or can at best enable us to "manage" the conflict we are fated to experience in our dealings with current adversaries. Narratives of possibility are inherently open to prospective thinking about ways in which we might break free from past patterns. They remind us that, as participants in an unfolding human drama, we have the freedom and responsibility of choice.

In Chapter 3, we place our investigation of resources for peacemaking within Islam in a theoretical and comparative context, and attempt to distill some of the most central precepts of Islam as they pertain to peace and conflict. We note that, though there is broad consensus among Muslims on essential religious precepts, the Islamic tradition as a cultural and historical phenomenon has developed considerable internal diversity as a result of the many ways in which Muslims, motivated by conviction and by the need to respond to a range of worldly challenges, have sought to apply Islamic values.

A basic conceptual differentiation between "Islam" and "Muslims" is vital for any study of Islam and the politics of peacemaking. As a religion that is concerned with all aspects of a believer's life, Islam offers its adherents both a bonding culture of ideal precepts and a concrete set of received practices and examples. It is at once a theological doctrine that finds its reflection in such affirmations of faith as *Allahu akbar* (which translates literally as "God is greater," and connotatively as "God is greater than any obstacle, and beyond any human concept or image"), and a historical dynamic with multiple, emergent syntheses that have been shaped by the interpretations of Muslims. In principle, Islam is a singular religion, but in the lived experiences of Muslims it takes many forms.[20] This becomes particularly apparent in situations of conflict, and as a result Islam has developed multiple paradigms for peacemaking: Muslims have heard different overtones in their religion's call to peace.

We outline the diversity of Islamic peace paradigms in Chapters 4 through 8: peace through coercion, peace through equity, peace through conciliation, peace through nonviolence, and peace through universalism. Each of these paradigms conveys a distinctive Muslim response to foundational texts, to specific types of problems, and to historically accumulated experiences and precedents.

By using this five-paradigm template, we seek to clarify common patterns in Muslim understandings of peace, and of the means by which peace can be realized. Differences among paradigms can be quite dramatic. For those who stand within the "peace through coercion" paradigm, peace is preeminently to be sought as an absence of war secured through power or force to compel and protect. Those who object to this minimalist approach to peace and instead emphasize the demands of justice evoke a "peace through equity" paradigm, which relates Islamic understandings of peace to the advancement of a more just and cooperative world order. Another peace paradigm, "peace through conciliation," has developed historically among those who have been entrusted with resolving disputes and preserving communal equilibrium through mediation, arbitration, and rituals of reconciliation. The "peace through nonviolence" paradigm provides an Islamic framework for resisting oppression without violence, and has been expounded by those who seek to make traditional injunctions against both bloodshed and unjust rule speak to contemporary demands for political participation, self-rule, and human dignity. Still others, drawing upon Islam's spiritual traditions, have contributed to a "peace through universalism" paradigm that regards peace as an all-encompassing harmony in which human beings can participate when they correctly perceive their relations to Creator and creation, and implement Islamic prescriptions for coexistence.

Although most of these paradigms are not mutually exclusive—many Muslims have, at one time or another, subscribed to views that incorporate aspects of more than one paradigm—categorization is useful for understanding different orientations toward peace that derive their legitimacy from Islam and from the historical experiences of Muslims. While some pundits would question the Islamic credentials of one approach or another, each has been advocated by Muslims on the basis of religious precepts, and all five represent ongoing conversations as well as fields of experimentation in theory and practice.

Exploring the multiple ways of imagining and pursuing peace on an Islamic basis—some adversarial, and others deeply committed to cooperation and respect for differences—can become a vehicle for transforming the legacy of modern conflicts. The concluding section of the book relates our findings to a positive imperative of our times: enabling Muslims and Westerners to bring out the best in their respective traditions rather than provoke the worst. More nuanced understandings of Islamic perspectives on peace and conflict can enhance intercultural dialogue and strengthen cooperative efforts—starting with applications in the Muslim Middle East and with redoubled Western policy initiatives.

Chapter 9 reviews the five Islamic peace paradigms to examine their suitability for this task of transforming conflict, identifying multiple points of contact and complementarity between Islamic and Western cultures as well as core principles for intercultural engagement and rapprochement. In Chapter 10, we seek to pinpoint crucial issues for addressing root causes of Middle Eastern and Islamic-Western conflict, and provide a set of recommendations for Western policy initiatives that might improve Islamic-Western relations and support peacemaking in the Middle East.

This book is premised on the notion that relations between the Middle East and the West have become precarious in no small part because Muslims and Westerners understand each other too superficially. Dialogue premised on a respectful search for understanding has occurred too infrequently, and without sufficient persistence, participation, and purposefulness.[21] The dominant framework for intercultural relations, which we call a "story of confrontation," is predicated on an assumption of uniformity within cultures and on a presumption that conflict between them is inevitable. Such thinking leads to programs of conquest at worst or to agendas of peaceful assimilation at best, but rarely to authentic dialogue.

As authors, we write with the conviction that the ultimate significance of the present turbulent period has yet to be determined. Will Westerners and Muslims seek to transcend their immediate, emotional reactions to violent and painful events, or will they withdraw into more deeply ethnocentric and aggrieved frames of reference? Will they aspire to gain more authentic knowledge about their counterparts' fears and aspirations, or will they allow their mutual perceptions to become more polarized, partisan, and self-serving? Will they move toward broader and more humane understandings of their respective cultural and political traditions, or will they amplify belief systems that deny the virtues of tolerance and cultural pluralism? Such questions are vitally important, and only a prophet could presume to answer them with any certainty.

What is clear, however, is that we need not remain prisoners of the stories we once told about one another. We have the opportunity to create a *new story* by moving beyond the scripted tropes that have been recited too often in relations between Islam and the West. We may lack perfect freedom to choose our future, but it is our fundamental responsibility—to this generation as well as the next—to capitalize on the degrees of freedom that *are* available to us as we make conscious choices between war and peace, isolation and engagement, pessimism and hope.

Notes

1. Linzer, "Poll Shows Growing Arab Rancor at U.S.," 2004.
2. Deane and Fears, "Negative Perception of Islam Increasing," 2006, p. A1.
3. Ballen, "The Myth of Muslim Support for Terror," 2007.
4. Pew Global Attitudes Project, "Global Opinion Trends 2002–2007." Such findings are obviously welcome, especially when considered in relation to C. Christine Fair and Bryan Shepherd's survey on Muslim attitudes ("Who Supports Terrorism?" 2006), which found belief that Islam itself has come under attack to be the most significant predictor (not social class, gender, or level of education) of willingness to justify suicide bombings and other attacks against civilian targets.
5. Mertus, *Bait and Switch,* 2004.
6. Eickelman, *The Middle East and Central Asia,* 1998, p. 5; Hodgson, *The Venture of Islam,* 1974, pp. 60–61.
7. Lebanon, when it emerged as an independent state in 1943, was a majority-Christian state. At present, however, Muslims constitute a majority of Lebanese citizens.
8. Huntington, "The Clash of Civilizations?" 1993; Huntington, *The Clash of Civilizations and the Remaking of World Order,* 1996.
9. See, for example, Zunes, *Tinderbox,* 2003; Khalidi, *Resurrecting Empire,* 2004; Mamdani, *Good Muslim, Bad Muslim,* 2004.
10. Hafez, *Why Muslims Rebel,* 2003.
11. Bozeman, *Politics and Culture in International History,* 1960; Galtung, *Peace by Peaceful Means,* 1996; Havel, "The Divine Revolution," 1998; Segesvary, *Dialogue of Civilizations,* 2000.
12. Fox and Sandler, *Bringing Religion into International Relations,* 2004, pp. 118–125.
13. Havel, "The Divine Revolution," 1998.
14. Said, Funk, and Kadayifci, *Peace and Conflict Resolution in Islam,* 2001.
15. Although peace as an "absence of war" is a primary usage in the field of international relations, the field of peace research devotes particular attention to the practical implications of "fuller" conceptions of peace that include conditions such as a presence of social justice and other bases for human well-being. For further discussion of the distinction between "peace as absence" and "peace as presence," and of the internal diversity of peace definitions within Western and Islamic cultures, see Chapter 3.
16. Western observers and Muslims alike tend to paint with broad brushstrokes when they make generalizations about "Islam and the West." So perilous is the effort to compare Islamic and Western civilizations that many intellectuals have rejected efforts to frame problems in North American or European relations with the Middle East in cultural terms. We recognize these dangers, and do not in any way wish to deny that labels such as "Western" and "Islamic" can distort more than they clarify. For further exploration of these challenges, see Chapter 2.
17. We use the term "civilization" to refer to complex cultural conglomerates that, through shared historical narratives and symbols, provide a sense of bounded identity and cultural authenticity for those who claim membership within them. In offering this definition, we recognize that de facto cultural norms and value systems of civilizations are much more variegated than their members tend to recognize. A civilization is, to use a term Benedict Anderson coined for the study of nationalism, an "imagined community" in which membership is determined by perceptions of belonging and by shared symbolic reference points rather than by a singular, authentic set of cultural values and traits. In contrast to Samuel Huntington, who describes a civilization as the "broadest

level of identification with which [a person] intensely identifies" ("The Clash of Civilizations?" 1993, pp. 24, 44–45), we believe it is important to acknowledge that, in the current world historical context, a small but growing number of people intensely identify with a global or "human" sense of identity, and even with the idea of a single, emergent global civilization. Moreover, the differences within civilizations can be every bit as divisive as differences between them (take, for example, relations between Sunni and Shia Muslims in many contexts, and historical Western clashes between groups divided by religious, economic, and nationalist ideologies). Hence we will refer to "Islamic and Western cultures" more frequently than "civilizations," to avoid attributing a misplaced concreteness and uniformity to phenomena that are, in real terms, diverse. There are multiple Islamic and Western cultures, and though bonds of affinity within each cluster of cultures tend to be stronger than relationships that cut across symbolic boundaries, we do not wish to contribute to totalizing discourses and to the divisive politics that go with them. We use such labels as "Muslim" and "Western" as a matter of necessity—they are terms that reflect real patterns of culture and identity—but concur with those analysts who argue against static and overgeneralized conceptualizations of human differences.

18. As constructivist thinkers have argued, the social world is a domain of collective intentionality and its institutions and practices do not exist independently of human analysts. Institutions and practices are woven on the latticework of deeply embedded ideas and meanings, and by the mere act of choosing to explore these ideas and meanings the researcher becomes at least to some extent a participant in the social processes studied. Although analysts should not uncritically adopt "categories of practice" (the meanings of everyday life) as academic "categories of analysis" (Brubaker, *Nationalism Reframed,* 1996, pp. 15–16, 22), close and respectful academic engagement with cultural meanings and forms can generate new opportunities for public reflection and dialogue.

19. We place quotation marks around "other" and, in many cases, around such terms as "the West" and "Islam" to acknowledge the intrinsically problematic nature of these terms when they are used to suggest boundedness and homogeneity across time and space. What is considered "other," "Western," or "Islamic" varies historically and geographically, and human cultures are inevitably more complex and dynamic than the overarching categories within which we perceive them.

20. Readers seeking deeper treatment of theological issues raised by our exploration would be well advised to explore some of our references or to delve into one of the many accessible primers on Islamic beliefs and values.

21. In stating that there is a need for greater commitment to dialogue, we do not in any way wish to discount serious initiatives that have been under way for many years. See, for example, Kung and Kuschel, *A Global Ethic,* 1993; Herzog, *Preventing the Clash of Civilizations,* 1999; Tehranian and Chappell, *Dialogue of Civilizations,* 2002.

Part 1

The Context: Transformations in Islamic-Western Relations

2

The Need for a New Story

Insofar as the Islamic world and the West appear to be mired in an intensifying cycle of political and cultural conflict, one of the more significant drivers of this rivalry is the profoundly unsettled state of US relations with the Muslim Middle East. On both sides of the troubled relationship between the United States and the Middle East, there is deep anxiety and a growing belief in the futility of communication. When asked to explain these difficulties, many commentators are quick to link present disputes to seemingly distant epochs and rivalries. The popularity of catchphrases such as the "clash of civilizations" attests to the mood of pessimism and apprehension that now surrounds discussions of international conflict.

As they analyze the complexity of Islamic-Western relations, social scientists face a dilemma: How can they make the cultural aspects of conflict more intelligible to policymakers and to the public without reinforcing stereotypes or deflecting attention from more conventional political issues that also demand attention? Analyses of cultural differences at an international or global level are arguably even more prone to overgeneralization than traditional discourse on international politics, which is marked by an inclination to treat states and nations as monolithic, unitary actors. Yet studies that focus on political and economic factors alone can offer only a partial set of prescriptions for rapprochement.

In light of recent world events, denying the significance of culture and religion in international affairs has become increasingly untenable. These factors clearly matter. In any situation of intense conflict, there is a tendency among disputants to become trapped inside their own frames of reference, telling stories about threatened values, justified fear, and unjustifiable suffering. Refusal to take cultural estrangement seriously results in a misunderstanding of what is at stake for disputants. However, accepting partisan stories and their often exaggerated claims at face value is equally problematic. In cultural and identity conflict, as in political and economic rivalries, there is no substitute for critical analysis.

As practitioners of mediation recognize, it is often more useful to help each disputant in a conflict dyad become more conversant with their counterpart's unique perspective on events than it is to seek the truth adversarially by managing a process of debate. The task of the interpersonal mediator is to highlight points of convergence between narratives, to help the parties understand and if possible respect divergent claims, and to elicit "unstoried experiences" of past cooperation or even mutual affinity that might enable antagonists to shift from "conflict-saturated" narratives to stories that permit the formation of a new relationship.[1] Such an approach applies to intercultural mediation as much as it does to interpersonal mediation, and holds out the promise of mitigating conflicts in which Islamic and Western identities have been activated. Listening to stories, and encouraging rivals to reflect on unquestioned assumptions in their own stories while giving more weight to the narrative of the "other," provides a valuable basis for building trust and finding ways in which adversaries might cease to work at cross-purposes.

Attentiveness to the stories being told by the many peoples who identify with the West and with Islamic culture—and, more specifically, by Americans and Middle Eastern Muslims—reveals an increasing salience of deeply polarized, conflict-saturated narratives about cultural conflict. At the popular level, narratives of intercultural rivalry are already dominant, and more innocuous stories about "what went wrong" are clearly at a disadvantage. To escape the narrow confines of the dominant stories, we need to examine critically the contents and origins of polarizing narratives, while also giving serious consideration to the insights that can be found in counternarratives of intercultural compatibility or complementarity.

The Power of Narratives

According to Marc Howard Ross, an influential theorist of cultural factors in conflict management, narratives may be defined as "frameworks for action" through which members of particular identity groups "understand the social and political worlds in which they live, and explain the conflicts in which they are involved."[2] Narratives are the stories that members of social and political groups tell about themselves and their relations with selected "others," to create or reinforce a sense of collective identity and shared purpose. Dynamic rather than static narratives bind individuals together within an active and adaptive community, and change in response to traumatic events and new challenges. While dynamic and changing, narratives still tend to manifest internal consistency over time because group members draw upon a shared stock of cultural symbols and historical experiences (for example, Pearl Harbor, the Crusades, or September 11) to create meaningful bonds, shared goals, and maps of the world that are infused with emotion and metaphor.[3] Though contested by rival factions and leaders within a group, the narratives that come to dominate public discourse are often those that serve most effectively to give definition to in-group identity and values through reference to an out-group. Such narratives provide authoritative, commonsense understandings about the nature of perceived threats to the in-group and its values, while connecting the fears, insecurities, and problems of the moment both with past tribulations and with a favored political program.

Analysis of narratives can provide considerable insight into conflict situations. First, narratives play a causal role in conflict dynamics, by ruling certain political options either "in" or "out" for communal groups and for those who claim to advance their interests. Narratives that promote exclusive in-group loyalties, negative images of adversaries, and escalatory conflict moves can easily exacerbate tensions, while narratives that highlight common ground shared by disputants can make resolution of conflict more likely. Second, narratives provide invaluable information about the understandings that disputants have concerning the nature of their conflict and the driving motivations of each party. They manifest the emotional fears and visceral threats experienced by conflict protagonists, and therefore provide criteria for effective settlements. An essential part of the search for constructive responses to conflict, Ross notes, is "the development of *new* narratives—narratives that do not directly challenge older ones, but reframe them in more inclusive terms that de-emphasize the emotional significance of differences between groups and identify shared goals or experiences."[4]

Reexamining narratives about "the West" and "Islam" is essential for contemporary peacemaking efforts. Prevailing narratives on each side of the cultural divide exhibit remarkably similar tendencies toward polarization of identity issues, adversarial framing of historical relations, and rejection of shared responsibility for contemporary conflict. Similarities between counternarratives that may be found on each side are even more marked—exhibiting not only resemblance in form and style but also substantial agreement on matters pertaining to intercultural relations and historical memory. The existence of such positive narrative themes cutting across the lines of conflict provides insight into resources available to those who wish to "tell a new story" that aspires toward intercultural peace.

The Story of Confrontation

North American and European relations with the Muslim Middle East are mediated by images that each side has formed of the other. These images, in turn, are embedded within narratives about the history of cultural conflict between "Islam" and "the West." When Americans and Arab Muslims interact, for example, the significance of the interaction is not limited to the manifest, external appearance of a political discussion or an economic transaction. The significance of the occasion is a function of the meaning that the protagonists give it.

Adversarial Narratives and Images

Dominant narratives about relations between Islam and the West define the two civilizations in opposition to each other and place particular emphasis on putatively irreconcilable differences. Though the narratives differ with respect to their invocation of historical facts, their overarching themes are so similar that we may refer to them as constituting a single "story" of intercultural confrontation.

Despite centuries of relations defined as much by commerce in goods and ideas as by intermittent warfare and strife, historical memories and imaginings of Islamic and Western civilizations tend to emphasize adversarialism. Conceptions of the "other" as an inferior rival or shadow of the "self" have led to dehumanizing stereotypes as well as to habits of selective perception in which negative interactions are remembered while more positive encounters are forgotten.[5] In the present context of acrimonious relations, memories of violent excesses—from the wholesale slaughter of the Muslim and Jewish inhabitants of Jerusalem by the Crusader army in C.E. 1099,[6] to the terrorist attacks that destroyed thousands of lives at the World Trade Center—easily displace recollections of "normal" intercultural relations.

Narratives of competition between Islamic and Western civilizations derive their subject matter both from the geopolitical tensions of the present and from the cultural legacies of the past. For European Christians who were developing a sense of collective self-consciousness amid tumultuous internal rivalries, the idea of an Islamic "other"—be it "Saracen," "Moor," or "Turk"—provided a basis for articulating a shared identity, a set of common values, and at times a common political program. The more recent notion of a struggle between "the West" and "Islamic civilization" is a transmutation of this older theme, with terms of reference that have been redefined by secularization of the Western Christian public sphere, and by the simultaneous definition of a broader "East" or "Orient" against which Europeans and their descendants might come to recognize their own contrasting distinctiveness.[7] Likewise, Muslims in the Middle East and beyond have developed a greater sense of their own identity and values through competition with "Frankish" (i.e., "Crusader"), "Christian," and now "Western" "others." The "other," then, is integral to the way each cultural grouping has understood itself. The preferred label for the present-day "other" is applied retroactively, conjuring up images of continuity over time.

Although the term "Middle East" is of relatively recent provenance, it evokes rich and varied associations in what we may refer to as the "collective imagination" of Western cultures. These associations are laden with vivid and often contradictory images: peaceful desert oases and enormous oil refineries, fabulous newfound wealth and interminable religious conflicts, luxury vehicles and camel caravans, scimitar-bearing Arabs in traditional Bedouin dress and military leaders in starched khakis, silent veiled women and sensuous belly dancers, world-changing prophets and fanatical charismatic leaders, shrouded saints in sandals and tyrants in palatial estates. While more romantic and colorfully exotic images often prevailed during the colonial era, when European superiority was unquestioned, the return of Islamic discourse to the international political stage since the Iranian Revolution of 1978–1979 and the eclipse of Cold War ideological rivalries in the late 1980s have cast these images in a darker hue. Though diverse, the images are united by the same idea of "otherness" that has haunted Europe's past relations with the eastern Mediterranean and northern Africa, painting the Muslim Middle East as a land of harsh extremes. For many Americans and other Westerners, the Middle East is a part of the world that may justifiably be considered strange and even arbitrary—a place that runs in accordance with unfamiliar rules that only learned historians and foreign policy experts can understand.

If Americans and others who identify with the West are tempted to regard the Muslim Middle East as a foil—as a means of defining themselves in relation to everything that they hope they are not—Middle Eastern Muslims frequently manifest a similar attitude toward a Western "other." This attitude comes complete with an array of images and associations that most Westerners would not regard as flattering, particularly in the areas of sexual morality, family life, crime, and public safety. Like Western ideas about the Muslim Middle East, the images have at least a provisional basis in reality, but are often more representative of Hollywood than of day-to-day life.

In the dominant "self/other" perceptions of Westerners and Middle Eastern Muslims, real cultural differences are exaggerated and distorted. Each side experiences the world of its counterpart vicariously; commercial television programming and political discourse mediate encounters with the "other" by accentuating the strange, the sensational, and the shocking, with a minimum of interpretive context. Middle Eastern programming, for example, tends to provide grist for the mill of defeatist theories about unchangeable US and Western foreign policies, while Western media productions reduce the complex disputations among Muslims on rights of women and non-Muslims to a simple "moderate versus extremist" dichotomy, typically leaving the impression that the "strict" and disturbing interpretations of Islamic values made by such groups as the Taliban and Al-Qaida are the most authentic and widely accepted. The beliefs and practices of nonmilitant Muslims have been left largely unexplored, leading the casual viewer to conclude that so-called moderates are compromisers, and that Islam as a religion is uniquely susceptible to the contagion of militant fundamentalism. Middle Eastern Muslim media commentary, in turn, does little to correct the misguided ideas about Western culture that viewers pick up while watching satellite television.

Without necessarily resorting to the outright fantasies and fabrications that can emerge in times of intense conflict, prevailing narratives in both the West and the Middle East neglect common ground and context in favor of events and arguments that symbolize the preconceived ideas about incommensurable, deeply opposed cultural value systems. Profound "otherness" is taken for granted, even at the level of basic preferences for violence or nonviolence. The "other" is inherently unstable or overbearing, while the "self" is by nature pacific yet placed on the defensive by adverse circumstances.

Muslims and Westerners who narrate the story of confrontation seek to place Islamic-Western relations within an "us versus them" framework that posits continuous historical antagonism from the rise of Islam in the seventh century to the present day. They project a world of protracted conflict between incompatible civilizations defined by religious allegiance, cultural affinity, and historical bonds. To underscore the allegedly violence-prone character of boundaries between civilizations and explain current tensions between the United States and contemporary Muslim movements, they highlight instances of conflict between key members of each camp—the Arab tribes versus the Byzantines in the seventh century, the "Saracens" versus the Franks during the era of the Crusades, and Ottoman Turks versus European empires in more recent times. To support speculations concerning the future volatility of cross-cultural relationships, conflicts *between* groups identified with each civilizational camp are emphasized at the expense of more numerous conflicts *within* civilizations.[8]

As distasteful as crude enemy images may appear to the moderate and largely apolitical majorities in both cultural regions, sensational accounts of perennial confrontation and irreconcilable cultural divergence have a very real impact on public perceptions, particularly when they appear to correspond with televised portrayals of intractable, violent conflict. Narratives of inevitable confrontation offer a simple explanation of two Gulf wars (1991 and 2003), the attacks of September 11, and the escalation of Israeli-Palestinian violence that followed the breakdown of the Oslo process. They encourage observers to take competition and violence for granted as part of the natural state of things, rather than regard them as problems worthy of fact-finding and soul-searching investigation. All who would seek to understand conflict between Middle Eastern Muslims and the West must therefore face widespread and powerful perceptions that "our reality" and "their reality" cannot meet, and that authentic security is to be found in cultural retrenchment combined with vigorous efforts to repress, repel, or convert the adversary.

When conflicts between identity groups intensify, discussion of competing interests and areas of possible compromise gives way to a reframing of conflict in terms of opposed values and essences. "Our values" and "their values" are deemed mutually exclusive, and the latest frictions become yet another episode in a centuries-old chronicle of untoward events. Militant Muslim groups liken US hegemony over the Middle East to Crusader occupation and cite Western speculations concerning a "clash of civilizations" as proof of hostile intent.[9] For their part, influential American pundits have often floated references to the notion of an irreconcilable "clash of civilizations" before proposing that a World War II or Cold War analogy is more strategically appropriate: the appeal of militant Islamic ideologies and the capabilities of extremist groups signal a need for policies similar to those used to "roll back" fascism and communism.[10] Rather than engage their counterparts in dialogue to probe for underlying sources of tension, powerful voices in both cultural camps utilize strained historical analogies to argue that the necessary lessons for dealing with contemporary problems are to be found in epic struggles against the adversaries of times past.

Three decades after the Iranian Revolution, American doubts concerning the ability of Middle Eastern Muslims to govern themselves, and Muslim mistrust of American intentions, appear to be interacting in a more precarious manner than ever before, and the perceptual gap has widened.[11] Middle Eastern Muslim analysts, on the one hand, tend to view militant groups such as Al-Qaida as byproducts of foreign hegemony, distorted change, and the defeat of secular Arab nationalist movements in the Arab-Israeli conflict. American commentators, on the other hand, are inclined to view extremist groups as evidence of inherent backwardness—cultural intolerance and an associated inability or unwillingness to assimilate into the international system by adopting Western liberal models of thought and governance.[12] Where Muslim thinkers argue that cultural and political change proceed best when people are allowed to learn from their own trial and error process, without external manipulation or control, a majority of American analysts call for tighter controls on Middle Eastern governments and societies, with some advocating forceful regime change in countries such as Iraq, Iran, and Syria. The manifest assumption behind such policy convictions is that Middle Eastern Muslim populations lack indigenous resources for democratic reform, understood in Western liberal terms. Change, then, must be exported to the region—first by combating subversive regimes and movements, and second by encouraging authoritarian leaders to adopt gradual economic and political reforms.[13]

The Construction of Enduring Differences

To understand narratives about confrontation between the West and Muslim peoples, we must be attentive not only to history and contemporary politics, but also to subtleties of human psychology and intercultural relations. As analysts of ethnic conflict recognize, members of communal groups tend to define their identity not only through the affirmation of positive qualities that are said to be manifest among their group's members, but also through *contrasting* these positive qualities with the putatively inferior traits of out-group members.[14] This creates a sense of bounded identity, reinforces in-group solidarity, affirms shared values, strengthens individual and collective self-esteem, and facilitates cooperation to achieve common purposes. In short, "others" provide the collective "self" with a means of defining its own qualities and boundaries. The bonding culture that unites members of a group is formed by defining both "existential *otherness*"—*what* is normatively bad and therefore rejected in interactions among group members—and also "existential *others*"—*who* is, at best, outside the embrace of the community and, at worst, a threat to the in-group.

This is another way of saying that, in intergroup relations, self-perception plays a role in conditioning the way the "other" will be perceived. Although down-to-earth material issues and interests play a decisive role in any significant intergroup conflict, cultural differences powerfully affect the way conflict is symbolized and conducted. Culturally charged perceptions influence the *meaning* that estranged groups give to their conflict, and the meaning that groups give to their real and imagined differences defines the quality of relations between them. Similarly, *actual history*—to the extent that we are able to reconstruct it—plays a far less powerful role in shaping relations between communal groups than *remembered history:* the history that the record-keepers, politicians, and storytellers of a community define as pertinent to challenges the group faces today. The way we remember the past—what it says about who "we" are, who or what our adversaries are, and what lessons we should apply to our present affairs—affects the way we construe the present, and vice versa.

Because Islam appeared on the stage of world history shortly after the rise of Christianity to political prominence within the Roman and Byzantine empires, Islam has been a factor in the formation of Western identity for centuries, consistently playing the roles of political "rival" and theological "other." Islam's sudden breakthrough in Arab conquests of Byzantine and Persian lands, not to mention Spain, presented early Christians with a profound challenge, and gave rise to the conception of Islam as a "religion of the sword." European Christians did not, however, immediately conceive of Islam as a source of religious ideas that could compete with Christianity on a level ideological playing field. From the beginning, their images of Islam were colored not only by the vicissitudes of relations between Muslim and Christian groups, but also by internal cultural and political preoccupations. The "Islamic other" was defined through largely ethnic distinctions—as "Moor," "Saracen," or "Turk"—and used as a foil in debates about Christian virtue.[15]

Traditional Western images of Islam were based as much on imagination and presumption as on knowledge. In the Middle Ages, when the greatest hazards to Christians were political anarchy and failure to live up to religious ideals, European Christian writers represented Islam as a force of chaotic and violent passions of the flesh. At the time of the Crusades, Christian chroniclers referred to the "Saracens" as idolaters who worshipped the sun and Muhammad rather than as fellow monotheists; yet during the Protestant Reformation and the Counter-Reformation, characterizations of Islam shifted to accentuate theological deviation, heresy, and corruption—the same sins that Protestants and Catholics were vigorously attributing to each other. By the time of the Enlightenment, a newer and more familiar Islamic "other" began to appear. This time it embodied fanaticism, intolerant backwardness, and obscurantist despotism in the face of rational faith and liberty. More recently, images of Islam have been shaped by the perception that Islamic culture represses women, encourages intolerant fundamentalism, and incites terrorism. Although the emphasis has differed in accordance with the salient issues of the day, the idea of Islam as "other" or as an "exception" to Western standards has remained constant. This idea grows in cultural prominence during times of direct political conflict, when Islam is viewed as alien, intrusive, and aggressive.

Like Western impressions of Islam, Muslim images of the West have varied in accordance with cultural and political circumstances. Prior to the Western expansion in the modern age, Muslim thinkers lacked elaborate notions of a "Western other," and indeed appeared to take little interest in their European neighbors. In contrast to initial Western ideas about Islam, which were shaped by insecurity in the face of a theological and political challenge, early Islamic ideas about Europeans developed within a context of political success and cultural self-confidence. Muslims, after all, interpreted the rise of Islam to world historical prominence as a sign of divine favor, just as Christian interpreters of Islam viewed the good fortunes of their counterparts with great existential discomfort. For Western chroniclers, the defeat of Muslim forces at Poitiers by Charles Martel in 732 was a watershed moment, while for most Muslims it was a relatively minor setback in a remote region of world. For medieval Muslims, then, the European "other" was perhaps a confirmation of relative Islamic greatness, just as Jews and Christians living under Islamic administration were viewed as generally nonthreatening "people of the book" who no longer possessed the divine mandate to rule in accordance with the word of God. Such, at least, was the state of affairs when Muslims, jeopardized far more by marauding Mongols emerging from Central Asia than by Europeans, felt secure in their worldly status. The principal exception to this sense of security (some might even say complacency) vis-à-vis the West was the Crusades. Memories of invasion by Christian armies from the eleventh to the thirteenth century have provided Middle Eastern Muslims with a major narrative motif for representations of modern colonialism.

Muslim self-confidence vis-à-vis the West began to diminish with the loss of Spain in the late fifteenth century and, more significantly, with the collapse of Ottoman rule over a large swath of eastern Europe. Americans remember 1492 as the year Columbus, sailing under the Spanish flag, "discovered" the New World. Contemporary Arabs and Muslims remember the year 1492 not for the voyage of Columbus to America, but rather for the fall of the kingdom of Granada, the last Arab Islamic presence in the West. In retrospect, this year marks the beginning of an era in which Islam receded to the East—to the periphery of an increasingly dynamic European state system—to become a non-Western phenomenon. With the Treaty of Karlowitz in 1699 and later the Treaty of Kuchuk Kaynarji in 1774, the Ottomans retreated from Europe and Muslims were reduced to passivity in world politics, leaving for European states the task of shaping the modern world. As Muslims see it, they were excluded from history; their destinies were now determined by increasingly intrusive Western powers.

To this day, the experience of Western imperialism remains the overarching framework within which Muslims reconstruct their memories of the past. A widely shared impression among present-day Muslims is that Islam is struggling to regain its international stature after a prolonged eclipse associated with Western colonial expansion. From the hills of Algeria to the islands of Indonesia, European powers such as France, Great Britain, and the Netherlands succeeded in conquering indigenous Muslim populations and extracting resources from the new lands that came under their control. As a result, the West came to resemble what Islam had represented for early European Christians: a serious political and cultural threat. Particularly in the Middle East, this perception has remained acute even with the passing of colonialism, in no small part on account of Cold War geopolitics, Western oil interests, and protracted Arab-Israeli conflict.

Recent decades have witnessed the slow and often painful reemergence of Muslim peoples in world politics. The end of colonialism brought Muslim "nation-states" into existence for the first time, but many of these states have faced great difficulty establishing political legitimacy. Challenges to the legitimacy of Muslim states have arisen not only from the cultural and ethnic diversity of their subject peoples, but also from Islam's traditional subordination of principles of nationality, ethnicity, and territoriality to the bonds of religious solidarity. Especially in the Arab Middle East, the legitimacy of postcolonial states has been undercut both by long-standing Islamic affinities and by the crosscutting ties of ethnic and national feeling. Division among Arabs has frequently been attributed to the Western colonial legacy, and to the narrow self-interest of ruling elites.

Middle Eastern Muslim images of the West are colored simultaneously by envy and fear, admiration and suspicion. Western technological, economic, and political achievements are appealing, while the assertion of Western military, political, and economic power creates feelings of distrust, humiliation, and resentment. Pervasive Western cultural penetration generates deep ambivalence, in which attitudes of curiosity and even enthusiasm are coupled with a residual sense of inauthenticity or scandal associated with Western popular culture. Overall, Western civilization is seen as an example to be copied; but when Muslims of the Middle East examine Western culture through the lens of television and cinema, they see cultural decadence in the forms of sensuality, individualism, and materialistic disregard for religious values. From a Middle Eastern perspective, Western families have become atomized and fragmented because there are too few brakes on individual self-interest. Muslim societies, in contrast, are seeking to meet the hardships of economic transformation while maintaining the traditional family as the cornerstone of their social system.

While Muslim critics who look to the West see moral decay and a disintegration of family values, Western pundits accentuate the value of individual freedom in their critiques of contemporary Islam. In the Islamic world, they suggest, the individual is subordinate to the collective and to clerical or charismatic leadership; in the West, freedom of the individual from political, religious, and cultural coercion is enshrined in a social system that limits arbitrary abuses of personal power.[16] In response to such criticism, contemporary Muslims locate freedom at the level of the community and argue that the West has become estranged from itself, placing expediency ahead of all other values. These critiques of the "other" are deeply intertwined with political conflict, and frequently discolored by the taint of hypocrisy. Western rhetoric on freedom and democracy, for example, has often accompanied support for repressive leaders, just as invocations of Islamic values have been used to defend actions that appear contrary to their spirit.[17]

Although there is not a single, static image of the West in the Muslim Middle East, adversarial images move from the background of awareness to the foreground when political disputes become acute. For example, most Arab Muslims differentiate between the United States as a land of technological accomplishment, political freedom, and economic opportunity, on the one hand, and the United States as a great power that exercises hegemonic influence over the Middle East, on the other. Whereas the former is a country worthy of admiration and respect—perhaps even a country that relatives living abroad claim has treated them well—the latter is a source of frustration, confusion, and righteous indignation. When relative calm prevails, these two images of the United States—dominant power and land of opportunity—compete with each other in the public mind. At times of violent conflict, however, all things American and Western—from English courses at the local American Language Center to the latest Hollywood release—lose much of their appeal.

As conflict escalates, memories of religious wars and of colonialism are awakened and cited as a basis for distrusting Western motives. Images depicting the deep suffering of Arabs and Muslims at the hands of non-Muslims circulate, and a climate of defensiveness and moral outrage builds. The United States becomes a great power that can be courted by politicians but not influenced as it implements policies favoring a stifling political and economic status quo: oil flows freely from the wells of wealthy regional monarchs, Israeli settlers build new compounds on Palestinian land, and advocates of change fear for the safety of their families and loved ones. Political resentment feeds a generalized disenchantment with the West, reinforcing fears that foreign influences will induce Muslims to sacrifice not only their dignity but also their faith.

Such is the climate in which the militant groups that Westerners describe as "fundamentalist" have become established, often garnering considerable sympathy for assertions that change in the Middle East can only be accomplished by confronting a politically overbearing and morally suspect West. Unfortunately, the categorical "anti-West" or "anti-America" refrains of these movements, which purvey the idea that "Western" and "Islamic" are incompatible terms, tend to be heard much more loudly in foreign capitals than the voices of those who offer focused critiques of political and military policies that evoke Muslim concern. Lack of Western responsiveness to nuanced criticism reinforces the appeal of militant discourse.

Whereas middle-class Muslims tend to encounter the West in multiple ways—through education, images of popular culture, and news of politics—the average Westerner or American experiences the Middle East and the Islamic world primarily through media reports on political, military, and terrorist events. He or she is not routinely exposed to Islamic culture and is easily influenced by decontextualized images of radicalism, which predominate over all other images of Islam that circulate in the popular media. These images are conjoined with unsettling messages of anger, which cause Westerners to retreat into defensiveness rather than seek the reasons for passionately held Muslim views. On the basis of the most readily available (albeit superficial) information, it becomes plausible to believe that Islamic and Western cultures are irreconcilable.

Because the media gives priority to dangers posed by extremism and terrorism, the words and deeds of moderate and peaceful Muslims rarely capture headlines. In effect, Islam becomes known through news of intolerance and violence, as well as through simplistic political distinctions between "good Muslims" (pro-Western or secular) and "bad Muslims" (anti-Western or militant).[18] The governments of Muslim countries often play into this latter notion when soliciting economic and military support from Western sources.

The dominant image of Islam in the West conveys the idea that the religion of approximately one-fifth of humanity is rigidly intolerant and prone to violence.[19] Instead of taking critical analyses of Western attitudes toward Islam and the Middle East seriously, many who claim knowledge of the Islamic world focus overwhelmingly on threads of hatred and fear articulated through religious discourse. Though religious radicalism is indeed a legitimate and important focus of scholarly attention, much of the popular writing on this subject fails to account for the complex and deeply conflicted situations in which militant religious sentiments emerge.

To a considerable extent, Islam has come to represent the "irrational" for Westerners—a symbol for that which cannot be understood. The Muslim world becomes known first and foremost as a security threat, and as a set of forms and images that in essence appear contrary to Western ideals, goals, and values. This can generate a temptation to recoil from all things Islamic, and to protect a self-image of superiority that affords little scope for acknowledging moral complexity. From such a standpoint—by no means universal among Westerners, yet influential in the political sphere—dialogue receives support as a public relations strategy, but not as a framework for political problem solving.

Exclusive Moral Claims and Double Standards

Why do they hate us? Ironically, this question, which has been raised with increased frequency in the United States, echoes what a visitor to the Islamic Middle East is likely to hear from a wide cross-section of Muslim interlocutors—from taxi drivers to college students, accountants, and bazaar merchants.

In the dominant approach to framing Islamic-Western relations, the actions of the "other," whether Western or Islamic, are explicable only in terms of an antipathy that is presumably alien to one's own experience. According to this view, the problem is not miscommunication or misguided policies of governments and insurgents, but rather the innate hostility of the adversary, whether it is conceived as an entire culture or as a set of manipulative agents within an opposing social and political system. The problem, in other words, has very little to do with "what we are doing," and almost everything to do with the adversary's intrinsic motivation—for example, hate, greed, jealousy, or antipathy toward our values. They are *different* from us; we value reasonable, peaceful approaches to problems, while they seek to impose their own culture by force. The conflict is about identity, not policies—about opposed values but not about concerns, interests, and needs that often overlap.

In the end, the story of confrontation organizes historical images and metaphors in a way that permits actions based on double standards: one standard of morality may be applied for in-group members, and another for relations with dehumanized out-group members, be they "Muslim fanatics" or "Western hypocrites." The "authentic other" has become a security threat or an insult to one's dignity and must be conquered, repelled, or persuaded to accept in-group values, standards, and policies. Such are the implications of the dominant narrative frame for conflict between the Muslims and the West.

The Story of Compatibility

Fortunately, alternatives to narratives of confrontation exist, and have found expression in Western and Middle Eastern Muslim consciousness alike. The most common manifestation of these inclusive narratives is what we may characterize as a "second story" of compatibility. According to the narrators of this story, whose numbers include academics and diplomats as well as diverse protagonists of intercultural understanding, value differences between Western and Islamic civilizations do not predispose Muslims and Westerners to inevitable conflict. Insofar as both the West and Islam partake in a common human heritage of "civilization," they share many values that provide a basis for cooperation. These values include respect for learning, desire for peace, esteem for toleration, and affirmation of human dignity.

Shared Heritages

For narrators of the story of compatibility, the existence of shared values is a result of historical relationships that protagonists of confrontation overlook. Not only is Islam an Abrahamic monotheist tradition in the same family as Judaism and Christianity; it is also a stakeholder in the classical tradition of ancient Greek learning. Medieval Islamic civilization, after all, was constructed out of Arab, biblicist, and Hellenic cultures, and Europe benefited from knowledge garnered through interaction with Muslim lands.[20] To speak of Islam and the West as perennial rivals distorts the actual historical record. In the words of historian Richard Bulliet, "The past and future of the West cannot be fully comprehended without appreciation of the twinned relationship it has had with Islam over some fourteen centuries. The same is true of the Islamic world."[21]

Islam's Hellenism was mediated primarily through Eastern Christian intellectual circles, and Muslim philosophical and scientific thought still remains an understudied field linking Late Antiquity with the Renaissance. Islamic contributions went far beyond mere preservation of the classical legacy, as is testified by the efforts that 'Abd al-Rahman Ibn Khaldun made to tutor an Andalusian prince after the model of Plato's *Republic,* or by the Heliocentric planetary theories that entered the scientific milieu of Copernicus by means of Arabic manuscripts. Culturally and intellectually, Islam formed a bridge between East and West, and generated a broader cultural synthesis by integrating Persian and Central Asian as well as Indian influences. Europeans were willing recipients of much that it had to offer; Islamic civilization, in turn, profited from trade with Europe. The ubiquity of these linkages persuades narrators of the story of compatibility that Islam as a civilizational force has been an integral part of the Western tradition.

While pointing out these bases for mutual appreciation, the compatibility story warns against polarizing misapplication of cultural labels. "Islam" and "the West" are heterogeneous categories; the diversity of each cultural region means that conflicts within civilizations are as significant as conflicts between them, and conflicts between particular Muslim and Western states or groups need not escalate to draw in entire civilizations. In a very real sense, Islam is present in the West through large immigrant communities, and the West is commercially and culturally present in the Islamic world. Western models for higher education have been widely disseminated in the Muslim world, and many Muslim elites have been educated at Western universities.

Because Islam and the West partake in common bonding cultures, they can coexist so long as a clash of *symbols* is not mistaken for a clash of *substances.* Preventing this cognitive error is possible, provided that spokespersons for Muslims and Westerners emphasize cultural commonalities while accommodating differences, and differentiate between constructive and destructive means of redressing grievances. Demystifying conflict is also important, because many problems in Muslim-Western relations have much less to do with religion or culture than with nationalism, gaps in levels of development, historical disadvantages of Muslim countries, and protracted rivalries over territory and natural resources.[22] Such gaps can be bridged through goodwill, dialogue directed toward understanding, and practical problem solving.[23]

Problematic Asymmetries

Advocates of the story of compatibility seek to place a check on forms of cultural hubris and fanaticism that exaggerate differences, instill fear, and provide justification for misguided policies.[24] With regard to cultural hubris, narrators of this story are particularly attuned to dangers of "civilizing missions" and presumptions of moral superiority that produce insensitivity to the protests and objections of others. When a nation or culture becomes too self-confident in its unique goodness, policies that humiliate or antagonize adversaries become easy to rationalize. While acknowledging that, from a historical perspective, both Middle Eastern Islamic and Western cultures have indulged in such self-referential moralizing, they propose that present tensions are complicated by the highly asymmetrical nature of relations. These relations have produced a dominant and a subordinate culture.[25] The persistence of this asymmetry, combined with a failure of Western leaders to internalize urgent feedback from Muslim spokespersons, has placed countries such as the United States on a collision course with contemporary Islamic movements.

Whereas the confrontation story seeks to trace the roots of conflict overwhelmingly to cultural differences, the compatibility story attempts to combine cultural and political analysis. It proposes that Middle Eastern Muslims and Westerners are enmeshed in a complex, multidimensional conflict. On the one hand, the West remains unrivaled in terms of political, economic, and military capability. In the absence of a superpower competitor, the United States has become more deeply entwined in the politics and culture of the Middle East than ever before, alternately supporting or marginalizing various regimes and movements while also generating foreign satellite television images that are beamed into middle- and upper-class households on a daily basis. On the other hand, the increasingly pervasive US role in the region has engaged the political passions of Muslim activists, many of these activists hold the United States responsible, through sins of commission and omission, for the status of the Palestinians and the Iraqi people, as well as for the corruption and incompetence of regimes that defer to Washington while resisting democratic participation and accountability.

According to the compatibility story, cultural contact in a global context of unequal political and economic relations blemishes the exchange between Islam and the West, leaving the latter insensitively assertive and the former defensive and insecure. Many contemporary Muslims feel deeply threatened by what they perceive as an attitude in Western civilization that holds out the European and North American experiences of economic, political, and cultural development as models for the entire world. While most Muslims accept the idea that Western innovations in technology can be a source of great benefit for Muslim societies, many do object to what they view as the pretentious notion that the essential substance of democratic governance, development, human rights, and cultural enlightenment is embodied in the current practices of Western states and in the international norms these states have played a disproportionate role in shaping. Muslim doubts are reinforced by the perceived "unwillingness" of Western great powers to resolve outstanding conflicts in Israel-Palestine, Iraq, Kashmir, Chechnya, and other regions. Given the scope of Western influence around the world, the idea that the West in general and the United States in particular might be incapable of solving these problems is not generally perceived as valid.

Because of the current economic and political standing of Western countries, the West is often seen to control symbols of legitimacy and status. Elites in non-Western nations seek to acquire these symbols through degrees from Western educational institutions as well as through consumer goods and regular "eavesdropping" on Western entertainment and sports programming. Western films are marketed throughout the world, helping to transform Western cultural dreams into more universal aspirations. Through a variety of intentional and unintentional mechanisms, Western "soft power" shapes the way the world is run. Many Muslims long to acquire status and standing within the Western cultural sphere, while others take umbrage at what they perceive as insurmountable barriers and a lack of sympathy for Muslim stories and perspectives.

Since the last quarter of the twentieth century, the assimilation and diffusion of Western technology within the Islamic world has begun to redress the imbalance between these two cultures, and the development of new satellite networks (e.g., Al-Jazeera, Al-Arabiya) and Internet forums has provided Muslims in regions such as the Middle East with enhanced means of "telling their own story" without relying exclusively on state-controlled media outlets. These technological factors, combined with a determination not to submit any longer to the cultural humiliation of judging oneself by Western standards, has contributed to the growth in a tide of greater self-consciousness as Islamic peoples in the Middle East and other regions have sought to rediscover the inherent worth of their own cultures. Probably the most dramatic example is the Islamic revival, which is called Islamic "fundamentalism" by Westerners.

Differentiating Between Revivalism and Terrorism

While the story of confrontation attributes the political attitudes of militant factions to cultural and ideological factors, the story of compatibility proposes that mundane, political inspiration drives much of what is done in the name of Islamic or Western values. Contemporary Islamic movements, for example, have assimilated the modern anti-imperialist discourse pioneered by early socialist and nationalist movements in colonized countries. While a religious vocabulary for justice and injustice has been revived as well, the widespread appeal of Islamic movements depends heavily on political issues such as governmental corruption, autocracy, and apparent subservience to foreign masters. Likewise, Western policies toward Muslim and Middle Eastern countries have drawn more inspiration from Cold War geopolitics than from the Crusades, and have cast purportedly illiberal Islamic movements in the same mold as the communist insurgents of previous decades. Such perceptions underlie the increasingly popular idea that the Islamic world is gripped by a uniformly intolerant and militant ideology that must be contained and forcibly defeated.

In addition to highlighting the contemporary political context within which the drama of Islamic-Western relations is unfolding, narrators of the compatibility story actively seek to differentiate between moderates and hardliners in each cultural system.[26] With respect to Islam, they point out that those who argue for forcible defeat of Islamic activism often fail to differentiate between *Islamic revivalism,* a movement to renew the Muslim communities from within through public reaffirmation of Islamic values, and *terrorism,* the use of indiscriminate violence for political purposes. Whereas Islamic revivalism manifests a constructive concern with matters of social justice, political participation, and cultural authenticity—that is, with the practical challenge of constructing an "Islamic future"—terrorism channels feelings of crisis, besiegement, and despair into destructive and counterproductive acts. Where revivalism seeks to heighten the role of Islamic symbols and values in the public sphere, terrorism invokes a worldview of zero-sum identity conflict, in which Islam is under direct and deliberate assault by a powerful enemy against whom any means of combat are legitimate.[27]

As narrators of this second story observe, Islamic revivalism has far greater popular appeal than terrorism, and has become a broad-based social and political movement. First and foremost, it is a response to a widely felt malaise that has left Muslim societies weak and unable to meet the modern world on their own terms.[28] Although its manifestations are remarkably widespread, Islamic revivalism is not a monolithic movement, nor is it equivalent to the militant fundamentalism and terrorism that capture most media attention. It is based in no small part on a widespread feeling among Muslims that, in comparison to such other historical centers of human civilization as China and Japan, they have not reversed the decline in their global status. Beset by a failure of secular nationalist movements to restore a sense of dignity and self-respect to the Islamic world, Muslim peoples of diverse nationalities have turned to Islamic revivalism as a way of defining who they are. Under conditions of cultural, economic, and political marginalization, large numbers of people have returned to deeply embedded religious discourses as they search for authentic values and alternative means of responding to their problems.[29]

The issues that motivate Islamic revivalism are similar to those that provide impetus to popular revival movements in other religious and communal contexts. In fact, the tension between secular nationalism and alternative religious solidarities in the Islamic world bears a similarity to splits in Israel, India, and even the United States. In an increasingly "globalized" world, latent dissatisfaction with what materialist, consumer-oriented society offers has become remarkably widespread. When national governments are perceived as failing to offer their peoples more than a medley of technical "fixes" that amount to tinkering with inefficient political, social, and economic institutions, this sentiment comes to the forefront of cultural and often political life.[30]

Adherents of the compatibility story rightly note that contemporary Islamic revivalism is better understood as an attempt to "Islamize" modernity than as a backward-looking rejection of the modern world.[31] Instead, revivalists frame their advocacy as a strongly felt expression of cultural identity and as an ideological critique of domestic as well as international political orders. Representing Islam as a deeply embedded aspect of culture, they emphasize that it is natural for the idiom of politics in the Middle East and other predominantly Muslim regions to bear the imprint of Islamic symbols and values. Islam provides a language that addresses politics as well as social relations and worship; Islamic revivalism equips Muslims with a vocabulary through which they may affirm their identity, project themselves politically, and protest conditions that they recognize as root causes of instability—social exclusion, maldistribution of resources, and absence of legitimate, accountable, and participatory governance. In this respect, the role of Islamic revivalism in the modernization process of predominantly Muslim countries lends itself to comparison with the role of religious movements such as Calvinism in the West during the Reformation and Industrial Revolution.[32]

Extremism in the Islamic world should not be viewed as an autonomous phenomenon, but rather as a reaction to genuine political, economic, and cultural contradictions. Many contemporary Muslims feel that they are adrift in the modern world, cut off from the past by colonialism and yet also devoid of a hopeful future toward which they might confidently aspire. Many Western observers, unsettled by the broad appeal of Islamic slogans and failing to grasp the context of political action, have made the mistake of tarring all Muslim political movements with the same brush.

When policymakers fail to discriminate between Muslim movements or recognize possibilities for them to play a positive role, there is a danger of sanctioning repressive actions that exacerbate conflict and radicalize opposition. This drives the impulse of revivalism into narrower channels born of pain, frustration, and hopelessness.[33] Particularly in the Middle East, the lack of political space for the expression of dissident views is a leading source of radicalization; often the only "safe" space for dissent is the mosque. Opening political space and taking actions that ameliorate key grievances can help to correct this problem by providing a sense of political efficacy that inspires creative thought and action. The primary barrier to democracy in the Middle East is not an absence of desire for it, but rather a lack of opportunities for democratic practice.

Fundamentalism as a Shared Problem

From the standpoint of the story of compatibility, Islam and the West are dangerously out of touch with each other. Misperceptions and mistrust have led to an ever-deepening estrangement in which each civilization has transformed symbols of the "other" into receptacles for their own collective fears. A form of psychopathology is operating at this symbolic level, in which self-referential systems of meaning are constructed around images of "self" and "other," without reference either to material conditions that heighten conflict or to common aspects of the Abrahamic spiritual heritage. Muslims are equating Western media productions with the substance of Western culture, while failing to recognize such subtle manifestations of Western morality as regulations requiring accommodation for the handicapped; Westerners are reducing Islam to a set of fundamentalist practices that denigrate women and reject religious tolerance. The result is a relationship based on competition and rivalry, accompanied by cultural insularity, retreat, and a tendency to denounce the "other's" lack of positive values.[34]

While fundamentalism is usually understood to have an exclusively religious denotation, the compatibility story suggests the possibility of a broader definition of this term that accounts for intellectual rigidities on both sides of the Islamic-Western relationship. Many conflict analysts have noted that groups in conflict tend to "mimic" one another, not merely by adopting similar strategic behaviors but also by adapting their collective belief systems to facilitate in-group cohesion and the exclusion of outsiders. In the midst of conflict, inclusive understandings of shared values often give way to narrow formulations insisting on intellectual closure. In the process, the ability to hear and communicate with others shuts down. Thus do identity groups react to repeated external challenges by reducing previously complex belief systems to minimalist sets of "fundamentals" that can be used to reassert uniformity and organize in-group members to fight and protect themselves. Each embattled community takes a subset of basic tenets from their tradition and, either under pressure of insecurity or in the pursuit of political dominance, uses these symbolic values and doctrines to seal off others or maintain control.

For Middle Eastern Muslims, fundamentalist tendencies take on an explicitly religious coloration (religion being a genuinely indigenous framework, in contrast to past experiments with Western derivatives such as nationalism and socialism). These tendencies reject foreign influences and seek to mount a defensive cultural and political campaign to repel outside intrusions. To ensure authenticity, all cultural practices, past or present, must be reexamined for correspondence with a current understanding of Islamic correctness. For Americans, a fundamentalist impulse may be seen not only in the uncompromising attitudes of an assertive religious right, but also in a hegemonic outlook that views the export of a particular Western approach to democracy and free market economy as the key to promoting security. Both tendencies are willing to part with humbler and more flexible traditions in the service of "urgent" political objectives, and deny responsibility for humiliation or insecurity that others have experienced. Neither can imagine the adversary's behavior as a response (however morally problematic) to their own, and both doubt that a more inclusive formulation of their own values might help defuse the confrontation. In each case, the world is divided into two opposing camps, with rival parties representing their own practices as righteous, authoritative, and final.[35]

Significantly, both of these "fundamentalisms" project a triumphalist vision of their own culture and values. It is arguable, though, that Western thinkers should be particularly concerned that, given existing power asymmetries, cultural confrontation places non-Western traditions on the defensive. This pushes Muslims and other groups to conceive of their options dichotomously, as a choice between "authenticity" and "soulless" adaptation to practices defined by others. If it could be affirmed that non-Western cultures have something substantive to contribute to the advancement of peace and human solidarity, more constructive and mutually beneficial forms of dialogue would likely develop.

As they manifest in the story of confrontation, attitudes of fundamentalism project the idea that goodness, truth, and beauty are scarce and unevenly distributed values. From this assumption it is only a short step to the conclusion that those who are not allies are in fact enemies. Because the virtue of the in-group is presumed to be self-evident, reflective self-examination becomes unnecessary, and listening to sift through the surprising and uncomfortable claims of others appears superfluous. The complexity of global politics is reduced to a morality play.

Narrators of the story of compatibility suggest that destructive conflict between Muslim movements and Western states is not the result of cultural essences.[36] Rather than a "clash of civilizations," it is a "clash of ignorance"[37] or a failure to appreciate the best values in each tradition.[38] If Muslims were to hold themselves accountable to their tradition of ethical monotheism and Westerners were to adhere to democratic values in foreign as well as domestic policy, cultural and political tensions would be much less severe. Moreover, if dialogue were preferred to coercive measures, areas of convergence could be found.

The story of compatibility questions the comfortable, self-exculpatory assumptions of the story of confrontation, and seeks to counteract misperceptions as well as double standards. This means replacing moralistic "self"-images and monochromatically negative "other"-images with images that are closer to the complexity of reality, and also requires putting brakes on habits of contrasting one's own cultural ideal (be it "freedom" or "faith") with the other's practice. One need not abandon particularity or preference for the value system of one's own community; all that is necessary is recognition that developing a realistic and constructive relationship with the "other" is impossible without cultural empathy and a desire to know the ideal and the existential reality of the "other" on their own terms. Vartan Gregorian, president of the Carnegie Corporation in New York, describes the challenge in the following terms: "History teaches innumerable lessons about ideas and beliefs that at first seemed frighteningly 'other' and impossibly different, but with time became part of the complex tapestry of culture and practice that we now accept as an integral part of our world, even as we continue to hold to our own traditions and religions."[39] As Gregorian suggests, Islamic-Western relations need not be considered a zero-sum game.

In addition to reconsidering perceptions of "self" and "other," the compatibility story speaks of a need to reassert shared values and interests, in order to impose limits on conflicts and prevent the provocations of militants from expanding them.[40] When groups in conflict respond to provocations without giving weight to shared values and interests, they allow a narrow contradiction to define an entire relationship. To prevent runaway conflict escalation, both words and deeds must communicate cooperative and constructive intent to deal with shared problems on the basis of common standards. Fundamentalism implies a refusal to listen to the "other." Yet a return to the larger frame of a culture and its humane values, always present if sought for, can open up the space for understanding, cooperation, or at the very least, mutual respect.

Where the story of confrontation narrows options to coercion/resistance and assimilation, the story of compatibility focuses attention on ways of coping with conflict more effectively. The confrontation story—the dominant story in political and strategic analyses—informs us of tensions that do in fact exist, but it neglects the truths of the compatibility story: significant areas of compatibility and deep resonance between Islamic and Western civilizations exist, and many problems in Islamic-Western relationships have as much to do with politics as with culture. Where the first story portrays dialogue between the West and Islam as an exercise in futility, the second story provides a hint of what can be gained by moving beyond facile, stereotypical language and judgments.

Toward a Story of Complementarity

Although the story of compatibility offers hope and a less culture-bound frame of reference for understanding conflict, its appeal to shared values and aspirations may not be adequate to overcome the present impasse. As we have seen, much conventional discourse on "Islam and the West" is deeply laden with presuppositions of irreconcilable "otherness." Implicitly, Western and Muslim narrators of the story of confrontation argue that "we" cannot work with "them" until "they" become like "us." "Islam" and "the West" are regarded as exclusive, static categories, and cultural or religious factors are obstacles to peacemaking, not resources. In arguing that these differences can indeed be transcended, the story of compatibility tends not to provide an in-depth response to questions about how Western models for political and economic development might be reconciled with intense Muslim desires for authenticity and distinctiveness. The second story escapes what Gregorian describes as the "unwarranted support for prejudice and false generalizations" that can be found in stories of confrontation,[41] but offers only limited guidance with respect to the process through which Westerners and Muslims might come to accept that their similarities are at least as important as their differences. Islam and the West may well be compatible, but how, for example, might non-Muslim Americans come to know Middle Eastern Muslims more deeply? What might make the necessary engagement and perceived risk worthwhile?

To escape the present impasse, we need a way of thinking about relations between Islam and the West that frames cultural and religious difference not only as a challenge but also as an *opportunity*. Leaders on both sides of the Islamic-Western divide have much to gain from moving beyond preoccupation with tired images, symbols, and postures, and toward genuine openness to a new experience of the "other." Narrow attachment to preconceived images, inflexible doctrines, and fixed political positions prevents dialogue. Most important for both communities at this time is the need to move beyond reactionary impulses triggered by symbols. To fixate on symbols that trigger an "us versus them" mentality is to endure a profoundly limiting psychological condition. This confusion of symbolic form with substance is precisely what drove the terrorists who struck at the World Trade Center and the Pentagon: the United States is not a series of buildings that can be brought down, and destroying external forms does not necessarily damage the spirit that built them. Similarly, Arab and Muslim attitudes toward the United States and US foreign policy cannot be transformed simply by eliminating leaders such as Osama bin Laden or Saddam Hussein. Preoccupation with defeating adversary leaders can lead to a self-defeating foreign policy—no matter how unsavory those leaders may be. Only active engagement through sustained dialogue can help us to transcend the fear, anger, and insecurity that foster conflict escalation, and discover the common humanity that these emotions conceal. And we are only likely to commit ourselves to such dialogue if we can begin to narrate a new story, *a story about complementarity.*

Moving beyond reactionary attitudes and symbolic positions requires that the West and Islam know each other. Instead of retreating into deep subjectivity and strengthening the position of confrontationists, Muslims and Westerners need to develop processes of communication that generate new insights. There is an opportunity to develop awareness of experiences, practices, and visions according to which people operating within one cultural or religious framework are able to enrich and support those living within another, enhancing the quality of human life through cooperation rather than detracting from it through destructive competition.

The current estrangement between Islamic and Western cultures is unsustainable. The events of September 11 and the subsequent US military campaigns have left Muslims and Westerners increasingly distrustful both of each other and of the more humanistic and life-affirming values within their respective traditions. Rather than encounter in Islam a distinctive patterning of human life that enriches Western understandings of how cultural pluralism might be accommodated,[42] Westerners are responding to political conflict with Muslims by reconsidering past experiments with cultural diversity. Muslims, in turn, are increasingly experiencing Western calls for greater political pluralism as a threat rather than as an opportunity to develop their own political systems.

At the same time, there are many in both the Islamic world and the West who recognize that remaining true to their own best values will require both political and cultural coexistence. Westerners are finding that they cannot retain a fully "Western" way of life without peaceful relations with Muslims—insofar as the term "Western" is intended to evoke respect for democracy, human dignity, and human rights. Likewise, many Muslims are discovering that they cannot fully realize the potential of their faith tradition as long as they find themselves defining Islam in opposition to a "Western other."[43] Such relations empower extremist factions who are willing to jeopardize the rich and diverse heritage of Islamic civilization in their pursuit of an elusive ideal of cultural purity.

Because the world no longer affords scope for authenticity in isolation or security through empire, Muslims and Westerners need to experience themselves "in relationship" rather than "out of relationship." They have an opportunity to find meaning in the common tragedy of their estrangement as well as in the possibility of reconciliation. They can also reconsider traditional ways of construing the values that divide them in dichotomous terms—individualism versus community, reason versus revelation, science versus faith, materialism versus spirituality, efficiency versus relationships, freedom to do versus freedom to be. When cultures view these sets of values as polarities rather than as complementarities, they are more likely to find themselves in conflict with those who have different priorities. Recognizing that seemingly opposed values can actually reinforce each other opens new possibilities both for intercultural relations and for full development of the human personality.

Establishing peace in the present climate of mutual recrimination will not be easy. Dominant American and Middle Eastern narratives are remarkably similar in the ways they construct enemy images through selective appropriation of history; Westerners and Muslims in other contexts may be less directly involved in active contention but have also internalized many assumptions from the same story of confrontation. As the story suggests, war appears natural when parties to conflict remain barricaded in reactive and defensive states of awareness. Peacemaking, in contrast to war-making, is proactive and requires deliberate efforts to move from the superficial to the essential, from morbidity to creativity, from defensiveness to openness, from a competitive focus on the negative to a cooperative affirmation of positive possibilities, and from the politics of fear and projection to a politics of hope. Positive change requires full engagement of the "self" with the "other," together with an awareness that Islamic and Western cultures bear within themselves not just the burdens of past conflicts but also resources for change in the present.

Notes

Some material in this chapter has been adapted from Funk and Said, "Islam and the West," 2004.

1. Winslade and Monk, *Narrative Mediation,* 2000.
2. Ross, "The Political Psychology of Competing Narratives," 2002, p. 303.
3. The equation of September 11 with the Japanese attack on Pearl Harbor during World War II (December 7, 1941) is a clear example of how experiences of one traumatic event can become the basis for stories about a new trial.
4. Ross, "The Political Psychology of Competing Narratives," 2002. p. 304, emphasis added.
5. For analysis of how images of "self" and "other" affect intergroup conflict, see Kelman, "Social-Psychological Dimensions of International Conflict," 1997; Stein, "Image, Identity, and the Resolution of Violent Conflict," 2001.
6. Armstrong, *Holy War,* 1991, pp. 178–179; Maalouf, *The Crusades Through Arab Eyes,* 1984, pp. 50–51.
7. Neumann, *Uses of the Other,* 1999.
8. As the Cold War waned, historian Bernard Lewis proposed that Islam would become the next major rival of the United States and of Western civilization in general. He predicted a "clash of civilizations"—"the perhaps irrational but surely historic re-

action of an ancient rival against our Judeo-Christian heritage, our secular present, and the worldwide expansion of both" ("The Roots of Muslim Rage," 1990, p. 60). Political scientist Samuel Huntington embellished on this prediction in his much-debated 1993 article "The Clash of Civilizations?"

9. Huntington, "The Clash of Civilizations?" 1993. Huntington's credentials as a Harvard University professor and an adviser to past US administrations inclined many to view his thesis as indicative of American perceptions more generally.

10. Goldberg, "A New Cold War," 2001.

11. Halliday, *Two Hours That Shook the World,* 2002.

12. Lewis's arguments in "The Roots of Muslim Rage" (1990), "Islam and Liberal Democracy" (1993), and *What Went Wrong?* (2003) are exemplary.

13. Zakaria, "How to Save the Arab World," 2001.

14. Cohen, *The Symbolic Construction of Community,* 1985; Northrup, "The Dynamic of Identity in Personal and Social Conflict," 1989; Stein, "Image, Identity, and the Resolution of Violent Conflict," 2001.

15. Daniel, *Islam and the West,* 1993.

16. Lewis, "Islam and Liberal Democracy," 1993.

17. Tavakoli-Targhi, "Frontline Mysticism and Eastern Spirituality," 2002.

18. Mamdani, *Good Muslim, Bad Muslim,* 2004, p. 15.

19. Fallaci, *The Force of Reason,* 2006.

20. Avicenna (Ibn Sina), Averroes (Ibn Rushd), and other Muslim thinkers made notable contributions to the Western intellectual tradition in a range of fields that included medicine, philosophy, and chemistry. See Morgan, *Lost History,* 2007; Saliba, *Islamic Science and the Making of the European Renaissance,* 2007.

21. Bulliet, *The Case for Islamo-Christian Civilization,* 2004, p. 45.

22. Canadian commentator Rick Salutin implicitly invokes the "second story" in his critique of the "clash of civilizations" idea as a totalizing concept that distracts attention from specific political conflicts that deserve our focused attention: "I think you can deplete your brain spelling out details and causes for them, without invoking grand civilizational clashes. There's no need to, there are too many causes for them already. A clash of civs is just a big cartoon to get your mind off your headache from thinking about what's really out there" ("Muslims 'R' Us, Not Them," 2006, p. A15). For a related argument, see Halliday, *Islam and the Myth of Confrontation,* 1996.

23. Ansari and Esposito, *Muslims and the West,* 2001.

24. Esposito, *The Islamic Threat,* 1999.

25. Falk, "False Universalism and the Geopolitics of Exclusion," 1997.

26. Moussalli, *Moderate and Radical Islamic Fundamentalism,* 1999.

27. As studies of popular opinion in the Arab world have indicated, the belief that Islam is under attack is a factor that correlates strongly with support for terrorism. See US Institute of Peace, "Support for Terrorism Linked to Feelings of Threat," 2006; Fair and Shepherd, "Who Supports Terrorism?" 2006.

28. Esposito, *Islam and Politics,* 1987.

29. Voll, *Islam,* 1994.

30. Juergensmeyer, *The New Cold War?* 1993.

31. Euben, *Enemy in the Mirror,* 1999.

32. Weber, *The Protestant Ethic and the Spirit of Capitalism,* 1930; Walzer, *The Revolution of the Saints,* 1969.

33. Gerges, *America and Political Islam,* 1999, pp. 231–232.

34. In "The Clash of Civilizations Is Really One of Emotions" (2006), Dominique Moisi provides a quite compelling explanation for these dynamics, characterized as they are by superficial jingoism and increasing hostility: "In our globalized age, we

have lost the privilege—and, paradoxically, the virtue—of ignorance. We all see how others react, but without the minimal historical and cultural tools necessary to decipher those reactions. Globalization has paved the way to a world dominated by the dictatorship of the emotions—and of ignorance."

35. Ali, *The Clash of Fundamentalisms,* 2002; Euben, *Enemy in the Mirror,* 1999, p. 19.

36. Eickelman and Piscatori, *Muslim Politics,* 1996, pp. 162–163.

37. Edward Said, "The Clash of Ignorance," 2001.

38. In *What's Right with Islam* (2004), Feisal Abdul Rauf offers the following formula: "What's right with America and what's right with Islam have a lot in common. At their highest levels, both worldviews reflect an enlightened recognition that all of humankind shares a common Creator" (p. 282).

39. Gregorian, *Islam,* 2003, p. 118.

40. Gerges, *America and Political Islam,* 1999, pp. 241–242.

41. Gregorian, *Islam,* 2003, p. 115.

42. Said and Sharify-Funk, *Cultural Diversity and Islam,* 2003.

43. Said, Abu-Nimer, and Sharify-Funk, *Contemporary Islam,* 2006.

3

Religious Resources for Peacemaking: Engaging Islam

Popular discourse on Islamic-Western relations offers lively debate on a wide range of topics, but deals with the subject of cultural difference rather one-sidedly. Protagonists of narratives about confrontation between civilizations underscore and maximize differences—resulting in a highly politicized understanding of cultural values, and a portrayal of political differences as insoluble—while advocates of gradual Islamic adaptation to Western cultural, political, and economic frameworks tend to minimize differences.

The absence of well-developed principles for managing the coexistence of different cultures within a pluralistic global society becomes particularly apparent when we take a closer look at the "end of history" versus "clash of civilizations" debate that inspired considerable foreign policy debate in the United States throughout the 1990s. In this debate, advocates of Francis Fukuyama's popular "end of history" idea contended that Western liberal (capitalist) democracy represented the best possible political and economic formula for all states and societies—a formula that most non-Western societies were likely to emulate.[1] Those who sided with Samuel Huntington replied that, despite its merits, the Western model held limited appeal. Western democracies would soon find themselves in conflict with other civilizations that espoused different assumptions about the relative merits of individualism vis-à-vis political and communal authority, and about the role of religion in the public sphere.[2] In other words, Western universalism would not prevail, leading to geopolitical competition with non-Western civilizations embracing modernity on the basis of their own values. Taken together, these two arguments framed much academic and popular discussion: Would the world become Western, or would the West face new threats from "the rest" as a result of modernization without Westernization?

Since 2001 the "end of history" vision has declined in popularity, but the corresponding rise of the "clash of civilizations" concept has offered little hope for a more harmonious world. History, many now argue, has returned after a brief "end of Cold War" respite, bringing with it the promise of continued international, interethnic, and interreligious rivalries. From this perspective, September 11 was not an exception to the norm—it was the "new normal."

Coming to terms with the complex global interactions of the twenty-first century requires new conceptual frameworks—frameworks that are attentive to both differences and similarities between world cultures, that recognize ways in which cultural and political differences can become mutually reinforcing, and that highlight cultural as well as political pathways to peace. Cultural differences can and do lead to misunderstandings, yet they do not inevitably produce violent conflict. The distinctiveness of a particular culture can indeed become a source of challenges to other cultures, but we need not regard religiously justified warfare as "normal" for the twenty-first century. Cultures—even cultures constructed on different religious premises—can also enrich one another by providing diverse models for organizing human relations, by focusing creative activity, and by offering unique perspectives on the human condition and on the ultimate values toward which societies aspire, including peace.

Within the context of Islamic-Western relations, this means that the complexity of each macro-cultural system is a blessing. When patterns of difference are highlighted at the expense of similarities and internal variations, destructive conflict seems inevitable. When common values and cultural complexity receive acknowledgment, Muslims and Westerners are freer to draw upon their diverse internal resources in ways that support peacemaking and mutual accommodation. Awareness of common values makes peace conceivable; recognition of the complexity of one's own cultural and religious heritage permits fresh interpretive and practical efforts.

No cultural or religious system is a monolith. Every major cultural heritage provides a complex set of resources that can be used to reinforce both peaceful and combative behaviors. Similarly, any cultural community with deep historical roots is likely to discover multiple precedents for relations with outsiders, some of which are more inclusive and collaborative than others. "Islamic culture" writ large is no exception. Muslims, like Westerners, engage their intertwined cultural and religious traditions in diverse ways, finding resources both for confrontation and for the maintenance of peaceful relations with others.

Viewing culture as a resource provides the basis for a dynamic view of intercultural relations predicated on the principles of coexistence, complementarity, and conflict transformation. By freeing advocates of peaceful relations to "seek the best" within their cultures and engage religious as well as secular traditions, this approach creates scope for empowerment through critical reappraisal of traditions, reappropriation of life-affirming values, and active participation in dialogue. "Seeking the best" within the context of Middle Eastern Islamic culture may seem counterintuitive to Western audiences who are much more familiar with political Islam than with more peaceful manifestations of religious culture and identity, but applying a "culture as resource" framework facilitates the recognition of opportunities for creative engagement.

Islam: Part of the Solution

Admittedly, such talk of coexistence may appear difficult to apply in the present historical context, in which grave insecurities persist and protagonists of polarization seek to reduce the "essence" of each culture to those practices that appear most offensive to out-group sensibilities. Mutual appreciation cannot be imposed by fiat, nor can challenges in the contemporary Middle East—a flashpoint between Islamic and Western cultures—be resolved simply through appeals to common and complementary values. Nonetheless, intercultural and interreligious distrust have become powerful barriers to political problem solving, and peace proposals that fail to affirm threatened identities and foster culturally "authentic" modes of conciliation seem unlikely to succeed. Islamic approaches to peacemaking can make vital contributions to cultural empowerment for change, and to the reeducation of Westerners about Islam's potential dynamism.

It is crucial for observers of Middle Eastern affairs to recognize that Islam plays many roles in society and politics. Sometimes "Islamic correctness" is claimed by governments, and often by the opposition. At times Islam is utilized as a banner by partisans of revolutionary change, yet Islamic culture also provides justifications for defenders of the status quo and for advocates of gradual reform. In his classic study, *Modern Islamic Political Thought,* Hamid Enayat underscores this reality of Muslim diversity: "Muslims do not have a unified and monolithic perception of their faith, any more than the followers of other great religions. However much the orthodox dislike it, different groups of Muslims interpret the Qur'anic injunctions and the Prophetic sayings differently—each according to its historical background, and to the realities encircling it."[3] As Enayat suggests, Islam is present in the language that accompanies many political and social as well as religious activities and, together with local cultural wisdom and modern secularism, contributes to the framework of meaning that ordinary as well as powerful individuals draw upon as they negotiate with one another in day-to-day life. Belief that a behavior is consistent with Islam does much to reinforce its legitimacy; convictions that an action or policy is contrary to Islam are rarely without consequence.

Students of Middle Eastern politics would be gravely mistaken to conclude that, because Islam is contested, there is no point in becoming familiar with religious discourses and interpretations. Islam is central to Middle Eastern identity and politics, and engaging the Middle East without a nuanced understanding of Islamic politics increases the likelihood of misunderstanding and of perceived disrespect for religious culture. When powerful external actors recognize that Islam must be *included* rather than excluded from problem-solving efforts in the region, they increase prospects for respectful intercultural relations and for partnership in processes of social change. As we argue in subsequent chapters, Middle Eastern Islamic culture carries within itself a basis for tolerance toward other religious cultures, as well as precepts that are compatible with development and democracy. Although consensus is elusive in Islamic politics, the events of recent decades suggest quite emphatically that Islam must be an integral part of any solution to regional problems.

Islam can be part of the solution for two reasons. First, Islamic precepts provide a coherent and affirmative position on the desirability of peace for human flourishing. Second, Islamic culture provides not one but multiple paradigms through which efforts to translate these precepts into reality may be pursued.

The first point, that Islamic precepts affirm peace, is the principal topic of this chapter, within which we explore the Islamic "peace vocabulary" and begin to compare it to culturally Western ways of "speaking about peace," secular as well as religious. While both Muslims and Westerners value "peace," they construe the meaning of peace in different ways. However, these differences need not signify inevitable conflict. Contrasts between conceptions of peace are strongest when secular Western conceptions of a smoothly functioning social order are compared to Islamic understandings laden with religious conceptions of social solidarity and justice; comparing Islamic understandings of peace with Western Christian and Jewish understandings reveals greater common ground.

The second point, that Islamic culture contains multiple approaches to peacemaking, means that the Islamic peace vocabulary can be—and has been—employed in diverse ways, through different syntheses of precept and practice. Like all religions, Islam is *singular* from the standpoint of the practitioner and *many* from the standpoint of the observer. Because Muslims in the Middle East and other regions differ in their understandings of what peace is and how it is made, there is no single Islamic approach to peacemaking. Diverse paradigms of interpretation and application result in varied ways of using a religious vocabulary to talk about peace. Part 2 of this volume explores these varied ways of understanding peace as it relates to Islamic precepts, and to contemporary practices of power politics, global multilateralism, communal conflict resolution efforts, nonviolent activism, and appeals for human unity. Though some of the associated paradigms may strike the reader as more "authentic" than others, we seek to demonstrate how Islamic precepts, filtered through history, human personalities, and political contingencies, have resulted in such a rich range of interpretations and warrants for different types of behavior. By highlighting diversity, we attempt to move beyond conventional framings of the "Islam and peace" topic, which postulate a simple dichotomy between radical and "moderate" interpretations. Coercive understandings of the prerequisites for peace do indeed exist, yet the range of interpretations is much richer than conventional approaches suggest.[4]

Islamic precepts and symbols provide considerable scope for peacebuilding efforts and for Western initiatives to collaborate across cultural lines on the basis of shared values.[5] As we argued in the previous chapter, "Middle Eastern Islam" and "the West" are macro-cultural units of analysis, notable as much for their diverse manifestations and expressions as for their coherence and uniqueness. Both the coherence and the diversity deserve serious attention, and in this chapter we seek to provide an analysis of the most commonplace and well-established Islamic and Western understandings of peace—understandings of peace in public life and mainstream culture—as a prelude to investigating specific paradigms for peacemaking that have emerged within a Middle Eastern Islamic context.

Religion, Politics, and Peacemaking

The rising prominence of protracted ethnic and religious conflicts has convinced many scholars and commentators that dominant models of human and social development are insufficient for the twenty-first-century world. Clearly, the cultural and religious aspects of human behavior must be taken seriously; some of our contemporary misunderstandings and miscommunications can be explained through the simple observation that what works in Washington or Ottawa often does not work in Cairo, Ankara, or New Delhi. Even mundane interactions among persons from different cultures can be greatly expedited through consideration of cultural norms, meanings, and identities, or significantly impeded when these factors are neglected. Deep consideration of such factors becomes all the more necessary when the stakes are higher, and when material and nonmaterial sources of tension become intertwined.

To "make sense" of tensions between groups that come into conflict, we need to know not only how the communities define what is "at stake" (e.g., territory, resources, identity, honor), but also how constituencies within each group square the realities of their conflict with shared communal values and aspirations, including cultural conceptions of peace. Across religions and cultures, ideals of peace signify the most worthy and desirable objectives and conditions of human life. They signpost what is taken to be morally desirable and provide benchmarks for determining "what has gone wrong" in instances of conflict. They offer a standard for prescribing what should change if harmony is to be restored, and point to spiritual and ethical resources for reconciliation.[6]

Raimon Panikkar, an eminent scholar of comparative religion, has noted that peace is "one of the few positive symbols having meaning for the whole of humanity."[7] Cultural conceptions of peace provide a normative compass for group behavior, and may be found in belief systems concerning the idealized ends and means of routine social behavior.[8] Virtually every major system of faith and belief, whether religious or secular, has propounded some form of agreed standard for defining what constitutes a "disturbance of the peace," and has promised peace as a result of faithfully implementing its precepts. While the exact content and character of each ideal differs, definitions of peace typically appeal to valued conditions of security and harmony as well as justice and human dignity. Although peace is at times construed narrowly, to denote a simple *absence* of war and tumult, most languages offer a peace vocabulary laden with broader connotations, implying a *presence* of social, spiritual, or ecological harmony. In international relations and global politics, peace serves as a normative standard analogous to health in medicine.

Although peace is arguably one of the world's most widely appreciated values, precisely what *constitutes* peace is a subject of debate among partisans of diverse philosophical, cultural, and religious orientations. In the field of international relations, exponents of realpolitik define peace in minimalist terms as stability or order, while advocates of change identify "real" peace with conditions that embody social justice. A more culturally significant example may be derived from the Israeli-Palestinian conflict. Among Israelis, the word for "peace," *shalom,* signifies many things, including wholeness and safety. One of the most compelling connotations of the word for Israelis today, however, is "quiet"—that is, an absence of the threat of violent conflict or of renewed warfare with Middle Eastern Arabs and Muslims. In contrast, Palestinian discourse on "peace" *(salam)* brings forth a different set of meanings. Palestinian conceptions such as "the peace of the brave," for example, are heavily laden with overtones suggesting a desire for dignity, justice, and honor. Although these two conceptions of peace may well be reconcilable, failure to expose the full range of meanings implicit in each formulation can contribute to frustration, disappointment, and an exacerbation of tensions when a "peace agreement" fails to deliver "peace" as understood by each community.[9]

Far from consigning us to endless conflict, disagreements as to what constitutes peace signal the need for dialogue. In the contemporary, culturally pluralistic world, a diverse heritage of peace ideals is actually an asset to humanity. In a global age, cultural concepts of peace provide a basis for critically examining the value systems within which such goals as development, democratization, and conflict resolution are selected, defined, and pursued.

Every cultural tradition possesses a repertoire of peace-related precepts and practices that shape their responses to problems of social and political life, which are ultimately problems of human coexistence. Politics itself may be defined as the process through which human beings negotiate the terms of their coexistence within a context of social and cultural values. Whether this context is an ethnically homogeneous nation-state with a taken-for-granted framework of cultural norms or the enormously diverse international system defined by a more modest set of conventionally accepted value parameters (national sovereignty, nonintervention, diplomatic immunity, collective response to terrorism and gross human rights abuses, etc.), politics remains a value-driven process. Even decisions to favor coercion over persuasion or elevate principles of private gain over ideas of the public good presuppose a preexisting system of values or ideal standards through which this course of action may be justified and represented as legitimate. The fact that formulations and interpretations of this preexisting system of values may be disputed only underscores the importance of investigating the ethical systems invoked in the course of political action and their relation to concepts of peace.

Religion and Culture

Explicitly as well as implicitly, religion plays a powerful role in shaping the values and norms upon which social order is based. R. Scott Appleby, a scholar of religion and peacebuilding at Notre Dame University, has defined religion as "the human response to a reality perceived as sacred"—culturally speaking, a communal affirmation of what is deemed most valuable in human life—that encompasses a "creed" or basic system of beliefs and values, a "cult" (i.e., a set of ritual and devotional practices), a "code of conduct" with norms for moral behavior, and a "confessional community."[10] Thus, religion may be described as a common "bonding culture" shared by members of a group. This bonding culture derives its coherence from a set of shared doctrines, symbols, value priorities, and illustrative stories. While religion is directly concerned with realities experienced as spiritual in their significance, the *communal* dimension of religion distinguishes it from spirituality as such. Spirituality may be defined as a search for truth and sacred meaning that, though typically informed by a confessional commitment, seeks personal, unmediated contact with the realities to which religious symbols refer.[11]

In many societies, religion provides a powerful basis for communal identification, together with a framework within which ideals and social practices are evaluated. Religion is thus an important element in the fabric of group and individual identity, and in some societies, including contemporary Muslim societies, a shared religious identity is commonly understood to exert claims rivaling those of more modern ideologies such as nationalism. The foundational affirmations of religions enable individuals to imbue their existence with order, meaning, and a stable sense of social identity and purpose.

As an interconnected system of symbolic values, religion plays a major role in defining the content of what peace theorist Johan Galtung calls "deep culture," the largely subconscious frame of reference or cosmology through which people define what is real and unreal as well as good and bad, and interpret the rightness or wrongness of events.[12] Religions, of course, are far from static, and the same set of basic symbols and texts can yield diverse interpretive and practical syntheses. No culture, secular or religious, is uniform; each contains multiple paradigms within which basic symbolic affirmations and injunctions are given specific practical meaning, intellectual significance, and ethical content. While we may speak of overarching tendencies in interpretation and even of "dominant paradigms" that guide practice at the social or political level, we must always remain aware that "meaning making" is an open-ended process.

By including religious creeds and codes in our analysis of conflict between cultural groups, we gain access to a more profound understanding of the categories of meaning within which the most powerful human experiences are understood. In the process, we develop new insight into how "self" and "other" are construed, into the values that are believed to be at stake, and into the symbolic as well as normative requirements of a less conflictual order. We also begin to uncover discourses and practices that diverge from the terms of reference provided by dominant paradigms, in ways that break down stereotypical simplifications and overgeneralizations.

Religion speaks to the most profound mysteries of human existence—quite literally to matters of life and death—and while religious belief plays a more powerful and direct role in the day-to-day life of most Islamic societies than in the West, it is arguable that in a North American or even a European context, discussions of war and peace are often infused with religiously resonant symbolism. Religious categories connect with powerful currents in human psychology, and equip communities with a common stock of values, symbols, and narratives. These values, symbols, and narratives, in turn, bond group members with one another and provide a vocabulary through which shared standards may be established. Even avowedly atheistic ideologies, such as millenarian communism, have depended upon religiously evocative, archetypal imagery to motivate the masses and call forth willingness to sacrifice for a higher ideal. More politically settled societies also seek to appropriate a measure of the power of religious commitment and belief in what is sometimes referred to as "civic religion." The modern nation-state itself may be viewed by the patriot as a covenanted community bound by a sacred constitution, and guided by heroic figures modeling shared values in much the same manner as traditional prophets and sages; contemporary states infuse their national institutions, edifices, histories, and flags with a measure of the sanctity that traditional religious cultures ascribe to their own shared objects of devotion.

To understand a culture, analysis of historical as well as contemporary religious influences is indispensable. In a situation of conflict, awareness of cultural and religious dynamics can greatly facilitate efforts to improve relations between communities. Religious and cultural understanding are vital if one is to refrain from actions that aggravate relations by causing offense, and can also enhance the effectiveness of positive initiatives intended to build mutual confidence. Engaging the "other" with a sensitivity to meanings that are central to collective identity can provide a basis for shifting energies away from paradigms presupposing exclusion, injustice, and war, toward modes of thought and action that favor inclusion and just peacemaking.

Religion and Peacemaking: A Fresh Look

Misuses of religious symbols and institutions to promote intolerance and belligerence have led to considerable reluctance on the part of many thinkers to regard religious values as a resource for peacemaking. Undeniably, the symbolic language of religion can be a powerful tool in the hands of authoritarian leaders, ambitious clerics, and extremist groups. The European Enlightenment generated a powerful reaction to political abuses of the sacred, leading to efforts to circumscribe the role of religion in public life and develop secular criteria for gauging government performance and accountability. The discipline of international relations itself derives its normative bearings from the Peace of Westphalia after the Thirty Years War, a period of bloody strife in which religious differences among Protestants and Catholics provided pretexts for military interventionism and crude power politics. Such ignoble legacies gave impetus to the Western idea that matters of war and peace should be left exclusively to secular authorities, for the good of religion and for the good of the state. To mix religion and politics is to risk providing scope for sectarianism, absolutism, and fanaticism.

The prevailing Western attitude toward religion and politics is based both on valid historical experiences and on partial truths that have been rigidly formulated.[13] While Western arguments against the political exploitation of religion and religious sentiment reflect hard-won experiences that should not be dismissed, dogmatic secularism (as manifest in the French, Russian, and Chinese revolutions) also has a mixed historical record. The simplistic contention that public religion is harmful to social peace impedes deeper and more profound understanding of the role of religious and other cultural factors in conflict and peacemaking. Though symbolic religious forms can be abused by political opportunists and ideological extremists to polarize communities and incite violence, the religious impulse remains at least as profoundly related to peace as to conflict.

Taking religion into account as a factor in politics allows analysts to ground discussions of conflict and peace in an extended conception of the human psyche that is not limited to the calculating "homo economicus" or "rational man" with which modern social scientists have become familiar. While the forms that religious expression takes are culturally specific, the archetypal appeal of religious symbolism has deeper human roots that transcend cultural differences. The implication is that sidelining the *forms of religion* (i.e., separating religious and political institutions, curtailing open statements of religious belief in public spaces) does not eliminate the impact of the *religious impulse* on politics. As scholars of comparative religion such as William James, Rudolph Otto, and Mircea Eliade have maintained, the religious impulse is primordially human and, presumably, innate.[14] While some may find traditional religious loyalties and beliefs more palatable than others, basic categories such as "the sacred" and "the profane" can take on multiple guises, some of them secular in form.

Wary of the abuses that often follow from concentrated power—particularly when exercised on the basis of a divine claim or birthright, without checks and balances—Western political thinkers have sought to replace traditional doctrines such as the "divine right of kings" with modern, pragmatic bases for authority, such as a "social contract" that is, in principle, revocable. In the process, they have sought to reduce religious authority in the public sphere, separate church and state, replace religious decrees with positive law, and alternately personalize and nationalize ideas of ethical accountability. Many of the results of such policies are undeniably salutary, as they have unmasked traditional abuses of power, releasing the intellect from dogmatic constraints and human energies from repressive social arrangements. However, to propose that the West has succeeded in ridding the public sphere of mythology would be profoundly mistaken. When the kings and bishops were driven out of politics, new claimants to absolute authority often followed, propounding totalizing ideologies based on new absolutes of class or nation. Twentieth-century totalitarianism is only the most glaring evidence that when secular authority is not subjected to critique and counterbalancing forces, new "absolutes" emerge.[15] The power of such anti-liberal ideologies as Marxism and fascism derived not only from the ruthlessness with which protagonists sought to implement these ideologies, but also from the absolute moral claims they asserted on behalf of aggrieved, mistreated, or marginalized peoples and against oppressors and scapegoats. Even celebration (some might call it "canonization") of the "invisible hand of the market" by economic theorists reveals an almost mystical faith in markets and in the principle of minimally regulated competition. Modern thought does indeed construct impressive models disciplined by empirical measurement, but in the domain of practice mythic themes persist. Even the most well-founded beliefs about society and politics are easily reduced to ideological shorthand through metaphor, captivating imagery, and grand stories about the goals of history. Human beings, it would seem, find it difficult to live on rationalism alone.

Politics is never driven solely by rationally calculated interests; cultural ideals and deeply held belief systems exert an often-subtle yet always significant impact on human outcomes. Politics remains saturated with symbolic content and with ideological "truths" that are neither self-evident to cultural outsiders nor universally shared by all human groups. Rather than ignore the human need for symbolic systems of meaning, those who hope for progressive change could do far worse than to explore ways in which the religious impulse might contribute.

The religious impulse's capacity to motivate activism for peace should not be underestimated. The etymology of the word *religion* (from the Latin *re-ligio,* "to link again," or reconnect and integrate) speaks of a deeply rooted quest for wholeness. This human quest for wholeness is most vulnerable to political manipulation when not subject to open reflection and dialogue, which can occur under both theocratic *and* dogmatically secularist forms of governance. Although institutionalized religion can provide a basis for factionalism and communal strife, religious sentiments also possess the capacity to link peacemaking efforts to powerful and perennial human needs for bonding and sacred meaning. It is arguable that even apparently "secular" concepts of peace have been shaped to some degree by religious traditions, insofar as they embody and build on the highest moral and ethical principles of a given society, engage nonrational (but not necessarily "irrational") elements of the human psyche, evoke powerful motivating images (e.g., "beating swords into ploughshares"), and define terms and conditions for individual and social harmony.

Implicitly, arguments that frame religious commitment primarily as a source of conflict appeal to the idea that a universally valid (and presumably rationalist) framework for peace and the resolution of conflicts already exists. This notion not only presents a rather one-sided perspective on the relation of religious commitment to such political "evils" as absolutism and fanaticism, but also effectively rules out the possibility that non-Western cultures can contribute to peacemaking on their own terms.[16] A zero-sum conflict between "more" and "less" religious cultures is created, at the expense of creative thinking about constructive responses to shared problems.

But are all cultures and religions equal in their capacity to contribute to peace? Are not some religious cultures more peaceful than others? Can we place different religions at various points on a "peace and war" continuum? Most certainly, differences among religions are significant, yet in the domain of historical practice and application the world's religions have much in common. In reality, no major religious culture has proved itself immune to violent fanaticism, and few religions are without subcultures that have affirmed active nonviolence as a basis for winning over adversaries. To explain widely divergent expressions of the same system of belief, it is important to recognize that doctrines are subject to multiple interpretations, and that interpretations are influenced by the life circumstances of the interpreter. In many cases religious extremism can be explained just as readily through reference to the traumas from which it is born as to the dogmatic assertions with which it is justified.

The struggle between Chechen insurgents and Russian forces during the 1990s provides a telling example. Traditionally, Islamic practice in Chechnya was known for its generally "Sufi" character, and for its divergence from the puritanical interpretations of Islam that have become common among Muslim militants in other regions. The widespread destruction wrought by wars of secession from Russia, however, has dramatically increased the appeal of puritan doctrines and radical Islamist ideologies. By the late 1990s, the tendency of Chechens to draw upon religion as a source of strength and solidarity produced a comparable reaction among Russian soldiers, who became more conscious of their largely Christian Orthodox character, to the extent that cries of

Allahu akbar! ("God is greater!") among Chechen partisans were at times countered with Russian proclamations that "Christ is risen!" (a traditional Orthodox Easter greeting). In this case, as in many others, the rise of religious passions has sharpened conflict and altered the parameters of ethnic and nationalist identity within which it is waged, yet the root sources of opposition arguably pertain much more to cultural pride and a history of geopolitical rivalry than to religion as such.

The more a conflict escalates into a "life or death" struggle, the more the parties find themselves in need of ultimate justifications for the risks they run and the actions they take. Yet the same experiences that drive one individual to embrace a militant, exclusivist doctrine may inspire another person to adopt an ethical stance predicated upon aversion to violence. Moreover, a decline in hostilities that mitigates the existential dimension of a conflict can also reduce the appeal and plausibility of more apocalyptic ways of "reading" strife. Religion, then, provides a vocabulary and a set of symbolic values through which conflict is experienced and interpreted.

To understand how and why religious symbols, slogans, doctrines, and narratives stoke or extinguish the flames of violence, we must move beyond simplistic generalizations to examine the multiple *paradigms* of religious interpretation and practice available both to would-be peacemakers and to those seeking to deepen hostilities between estranged groups. By recognizing the diverse roles that religion plays within every society—traditional as well as modern—we can gain deeper insight into ways in which the religious impulse can be interpreted and instrumentalized, used and abused.[17]

Cultural Cosmology and Conflict Resolution

Analyzing how the religious dimension of culture and identity can be mobilized either for conflict or for peace provides new insight into why nations and communal groups go to war, as well as guidance on how estranged groups might ultimately become reconciled to one another. Understanding what people *hold sacred*—be it land, honor, justice, national security, a particular concept of divine guidance, or cultural "authenticity"—is essential for understanding how peace can be preserved or restored.

In addition to providing us with a deeper grounding from which to understand conflict processes, appreciating the religious dimension of culture also enables us to recognize that peace and conflict resolution are both universal and particular; similar as well as divergent approaches derive form and vitality from the cultural resources of a people. Religious belief systems help to shape basic convictions about why conflict occurs and how it can be resolved, as well as ideas about how to live an "authentic," ideal life—the life of inner and outer peace.

At the cross-cultural level, different religious traditions view conflict resolution through their own unique lenses, and prioritize some values and ideals over others. Different perceptions and preferences are in turn reflected in the peacemaking strategies a given society evolves over time. Since cultural values, ethics, norms, and goals are influenced by religious belief systems, conflict resolution approaches need to speak directly to the highest ethical models of transformation found in the cultural and religious traditions of parties to conflict.

In short, religious cultures help to provide both meaning and moral guidelines for individuals and groups. They convey overall understandings about the nature of conflict and the preconditions required for "resolution" to take place. They also are bound to differ on significant points, which means that in conflicts between members of different religious groups, special effort to bridge gaps and foster mutual understanding is a necessity. For example, in Western Christianity, acute interpersonal conflict is often recognized as a phenomenon that demands inner transformation. Significantly, Christianity is the most unequivocal of the monotheist traditions in encouraging unilateral, personalized methods for resolving conflict, based on such principles as confession, repentance, and forgiveness accompanied by personal transcendence and new beginnings. In both Islam and Judaism, such approaches are not altogether absent, yet reciprocal or other social arrangements are more strongly emphasized. This may result in granting greater relative weight to communal interests, through third-party efforts seeking to ensure that collectively accepted standards are applied. Whereas Christianity conceives of forgiveness as a moral and religious imperative, Islam affirms forgiveness as a noble course of action, as a social good, and as a source of heavenly reward, but places less theological emphasis on its redemptive, transformative significance for the individual and society.[18]

Activation of religious and cultural resources for conflict resolution supports empowerment at both practical and motivational levels. Understanding how the higher moral values of communities are at work within a particular cultural style of conflict resolution is beneficial to external third parties as well as to communal members. For example, Islamic conflict resolution approaches highlight the role of a community and its leaders in achieving acceptable solutions to shared problems, in which individuals and families (responsibility for wrongdoing is more collective than in Western cultures) are asked to forgive offenses in the name of a greater moral good. Forgiveness in traditional rituals of reconciliation is typically accompanied by some form of symbolic compensation and enhanced social prestige. Any effort to set up the functional equivalent of a "truth and reconciliation commission," with the intent of achieving closure and renewed civic vitality after a period of strife, would have to adopt a different approach than those used in predominantly Christian countries, where traditions affirming individual confession, repentance, and forgiveness have their own distinctive theological underpinnings.

Religious beliefs can influence preferred conflict resolution approaches directly, by presenting idealized actions and guidelines for moral conduct, as well as implicitly, through "taken for granted" understandings, principles, and values. Faith-based conflict resolution, then, encourages participants to look to the guidelines and moral exemplars of their own cultural and religious tradition, while also drawing upon personal spirituality as they seek to recognize legitimate claims, take responsibility for a share of the conflict situation, and reconsider assumptions about self and other. In situations where belief systems differ, parties to conflict may find exemplars of moral conduct within their own traditions who challenge preconceptions about the possibility of respecting divergent truth claims.

Peace in Islam

To speak of the role of religion in politics is to recognize that religion is not merely a set of ritual practices and doctrines pertaining to a compartmentalized aspect of life, but rather an integral part of a cosmology that plays a profound role in constituting the identity, historical narrative, perceptions, and normative preferences of those who are raised within it. The way we define peace depends not only on our formal learning and immediate life experiences, but also on background cultural assumptions that inform our worldview. Although no cultural cosmology is invariant or immutable—a central theme of this book is that religious systems are pluralistic and dynamic, providing multiple "paradigms" for interpretation and action—what makes a belief system significant is its power to shape human consciousness and generate deep commitment to social values.

Islam plays a powerful role in Middle Eastern politics precisely because it is not only a set of theological propositions but also a historical dynamic that has shaped and been shaped by the experiences of Muslims for generations. As a theological statement Islam is an abstract ideal, but as a historical dynamic it is an emergent, contemporary practice through which Muslims seeks to approximate the ideal within the immediate context of daily life. Comprehension of Islam as an ideal system without knowledge of Muslims and their efforts to realize the values of this system is partial at best. In many respects, the visible ferment in the Middle East today is evidence of this tension between theory and practice, as Muslims strive to make Islam relevant to their immediate circumstances and vice versa. Through tension between the real and the ideal, as well as between expectations and achievements, contemporary Muslims are arriving at their own particular understandings of what is essential and life-affirming in Islamic tradition, and what is nonessential or derivative.

To be sure, Islamic practices often fall short of Islamic ideals, and Western thinkers may have a legitimate point in arguing that there is much Muslims can learn through careful study of Western struggles to establish buffers between church and state, if for no other reason than to prevent the abuse of religious forms by those who exercise political and economic power. Yet the Islamic insistence on abiding by one's own moral compass is not easily dismissed, and reflects the concerns of self-critical Westerners who argue that separation of church and state has far too often been accompanied by a "lowest common denominator" effect, through which spiritual values (including noninstrumental, ecumenical commitments to peace, social justice, and the ecological integrity of our world) have been eclipsed in the public sphere. For the foreseeable future, it appears likely that most Muslim-majority societies will continue to draw extensively upon the moral vocabulary of Islam in their efforts to define a cultural future.

Particularly in our present historical context, it is crucial to initiate examination of Islam and peace with a clear and fair-minded portrayal of the ideal as most Muslims define and experience it. Subsequent chapters deal with precept-practice tensions in far greater detail; first, however, we must briefly review the vocabulary of faith found in the Quran and in other foundational Islamic sources.

One of the first things a devout Muslim is likely to tell a non-Muslim about his or her religion's understanding of peace is that "Islam *is* peace." Though the assertion sharply contrasts with non-Muslim concerns about terrorism and other forms of political violence that have been committed in the name of Islam, this expression of faith has a theological and linguistic basis. As Muslims are quick to point out, both Islam and the Arabic term *salam* ("peace") derive from the same trilateral root, *sa-li-ma,* "to be safe, secure, free from any evil or affliction." As a noun derived from this root, *salam* denotes a condition of peace or safety while also connoting "freedom from faults and defects." For Muslims the related term *Islam,* conventionally translated as "surrender or submission to the will of God," suggests a state of peace and security that comes through renunciation of willfulness and resignation to a higher power.

For the practicing Muslim, the Quranic revelation is understood as a call to integration and wholeness through surrender to the divine. Submission to God through following revealed guidance brings authentic peace and well-being not only to the individual believer but also to his or her community. We see the Islamic understanding of peace displayed quite directly in the *taslim,* or exchange of salutations (*al-salam 'alaykum,* or "may safety and peace abide with you"), by which Muslims greet one another. This greeting may also be rendered, "I will not do to thee anything disliked or evil." It is an assurance of security and of freedom from all harm. Peace in the highest sense, however, is to be found with God alone, for according to the Quran, God Himself is known as Al-Salam (literally, "The Peace," or "The Author of Peace, Safety, and Security"), one of His "most beautiful names" (59:23). God (Allah) is the ultimate source of refuge and well-being, and is by His nature flawless and free from all imperfections.[19]

From a Muslim theological perspective, life in the world often involves conflict, yet the ultimate objective of life's struggles is peace. Peace in the world reflects higher realities, for peace is the greeting, language, and condition of paradise.[20] God calls believers unto the abode of peace *(dar al-salam),*[21] and the yearning for peace derives from the innermost nature, or *fitra,* of humankind. As the Quran constantly exhorts its readers to aspire toward virtuous conduct and knowledge, it also affirms a positive view of human nature, insisting that—despite tendencies toward forgetfulness and misdirection—the original human constitution *(fitra)* is intrinsically good and "muslim" (in a universal sense) in character.

This characterization of Islamic values is likely to appear unfamiliar to many non-Muslims, who are better acquainted with militant calls for *jihad,* a word that has frequently been translated as "holy war." While it is true that, in the politics of contemporary Islam, jihad has often been reduced to a call for religiously sanctioned armed struggle, the word itself has a much richer history and usage. 'Ali Gomaa, the Grand Mufti (highest religious authority) of Egypt, emphasizes the diversity of meanings encompassed by the term:

> Within Islam the term jihad refers to a large category of meanings. . . . For Muslims, jihad is much more than armed struggle against an enemy from the outside, for it includes constant struggles within both oneself and one's own society. . . . Once, upon returning from a battle, the prophet Muhammad said to his companions, "We have returned from the lesser jihad to the greater jihad; the jihad of the soul." This is referred to as the greater jihad since people spend their entire lives struggling against the base desires within them. Jihad is also used to refer to the pilgrimage to Mecca. . . . The term jihad is also used to refer to speaking truth to those in power, so in Islam government oversight is a form of jihad.
>
> In addition to these meanings, the term jihad refers to the defense of a nation or a just cause. These characteristics . . . are summed up in the Koran, "Fight in the way of God against those who wage war against you, but do not commit aggression—for, verily, God does not love aggressors" (2:190). . . . As for suicide bombing, Islam forbids suicide, it forbids the taking of one's own life. Attacking civilians, women, children and the elderly by blowing oneself up is absolutely forbidden in Islam.[22]

Linguistically, the most essential and basic meaning of *jihad* is not "holy war," but rather "striving" or "struggle." Although rendered by early Islamic jurists as a form of just war to defend or extend the "abode of Islam" (*dar al-Islam,* a non-Quranic term that could be rendered as "pax Islamica"), references to jihad in the Quran pertain to moral and spiritual exertion as well as to the struggle of the early Islamic community to survive in a hostile environment.

According to Gomaa, the crimes committed in New York, Spain, and London represent an abasement of jihad, and contravene its fundamental principles.[23]

Throughout history, mainstream Islamic tradition has upheld the distinction mentioned by Mufti Gomaa between the "greater jihad" *(al-jihad al-akbar),* the inner struggle to purify the self and behave in an exemplary manner, and the "lesser jihad" *(al-jihad al-asghar),* the outer, armed struggle to defend Muslim communities and values. While self-sacrifice in defense of the community and sacred values is recognized as a noble act of great merit, esteem for the greater, or inner jihad derives from the understanding that it is necessary to bring peace and integrity to the soul and to the personality. As a struggle within the heart of each individual, it is both the most fundamental form of struggle and the ultimate basis for spreading virtue and justice within society. Calls for behaviors consistent with this inner, nonviolent struggle—that is, for individual and collective jihad to realize Islamic values and advance a worthy cause—are commonplace in Muslim social life.[24]

Though notions of "preemptive defense" against presumably hostile non-Muslim lands have indeed been considered by Muslim religious authorities, modern commentators on military jihad underscore its nonoffensive nature. The comments of Grand Ayatollah Muhammad Hussein Fadlallah of Lebanon are broadly representative:

> [Military jihad] is the fighting movement that aims at preventing the enemy from forcing its hegemony over the land and the people by means of violence that confiscates freedom, kills the people, usurps the wealth and prevents the people's rights in self-determination. Therefore, jihad is confronting violence by means of violence and force by force, which makes it of a defensive nature at times and a preventive one at others. . . .
>
> In the light of this, jihad is no different than any human and civilized concept of self-defense. It expresses the innate human nature of self-defense, or preventing the others from building the ability for a sudden aggression. There is also the case of defending the downtrodden who are prosecuted by the arrogant and who have no means of defending themselves.
>
> As for those suicidal bombers who kill innocent people, as well [as] those who accuse others of unbelief, just because they differ with them in some sectarian views even within the same religion, or those who explode car bombs, killing women, children, elderly and youth who have nothing to do with any war of aggression. To those we say that their inhuman brutal actions have nothing to do with Islam whatsoever, and that what they are doing will lead to God's wrath and not His satisfaction.[25]

Fadlallah, like most Middle Eastern Muslims, argues quite firmly for a Muslim right of self-defense against armed aggression, while condemning acts of mayhem perpetrated in the name of religion. Based on the testimony that he and many other Muslim jurists offer about jihad, it is arguable that Western moral debates about just war differ far less from Muslim discussions about military jihad than is generally assumed. First, both traditions have clear—but not always respected—standards for "justice in war," with an emphasis on safeguarding noncombatants. Second, both argue that war should be defensive in nature, while creating allowances for "humanitarian intervention" and "preemptive defense." Finally, though both traditions have at times become subject to political contestation and disturbing misappropriations, they are intended to impose limitations on who is theoretically entitled to declare war, placing this right firmly in the hands of those deemed "legitimate" on the basis of political and religious authority. The fact that Muslims and Westerners often differ so profoundly in their popular judgments about which struggles are "just" arguably has more to do with political differences and universal human tendencies toward partiality than with fundamental differences between Islamic and Western thought on the subject of justifiable warfare.

Abuses notwithstanding, there is a clearly articulated preference in Islamic social ethics for nonviolence over violence, and for forgiveness *('afu)* over retribution. In addition, the Quran frequently cautions people against going to excess in pursuing rights or correcting injustice. The Quran discourages unnecessary conflict, and heaps utter condemnation on those who, by selfishly pursuing their own limited goals, bring destruction, oppression, and violence *(fitna)* down upon the rest of their fellows, "committing excesses on earth" (5:33). Many Muslims find it quite natural to consider Islam a path of peace and reconciliation that directs the believer toward a condition of wholeness, well-being, and safety from harm.

In traditional Islamic societies, the ideal of a harmonious social order was closely associated with the prescriptions of *sharia* (Islamic normative and legal teachings). While there are many debates regarding the most fitting and proper manner to interpret and apply *sharia* in the modern world, the objectives of *sharia* are closely related to those of religious law in the biblical tradition. These objectives include the maintenance of proper, just relationships between the individual and God, within the family and community, among Muslims, between religious groups, and ultimately between humanity and other created things. Law is expected to support and promote societal well-being by encouraging the fulfillment of lasting, deeply rooted human needs and discouraging or deterring the pursuit of false satisfiers.

As Muslim jurists sought consensus about the rules of jurisprudence *(fiqh)* during the first several Islamic centuries, they responded not only to the religious sources and to a desire for authoritative guidance in all spheres of social and political life, but also to misuses of power by political authorities. Many *sharia* provisions, including strict rules of evidence and limits to those areas of civilian life over which the sovereign had direct personal and legal authority, were understood to have a distinctly protective function.[26] However, insofar as it is a religious law with prescriptions for recommended and discouraged as well as required, neutral, and prohibited actions, the scope of Islamic law exceeds the domain of modern Western law, in ways that reflect differing social and cultural understandings of what is required for peace.

Muslim Responses to Western Understandings of Peace

From an Islamic perspective, peace signifies an ideal state—a state of inward as well as outward equilibrium and harmony. The natural order of existence expresses this harmony, communicating signs *(ayat)* of its own dependence on a higher order from which moral injunctions are received. Through acting on religious precepts, peace is achievable. However, failure to embrace moral virtues and wisdom of divine provenance leads to disorder *(fitna)* and corruption *(fasad)*. Peace is the reward and intent of moral striving against egotism, materialism, and social injustice.

This basic understanding of peace and how it is attained differs significantly from modern secular understandings in which peace is viewed simply as an absence of violence and war, secured through rational problem solving or deterrence. It should come as no surprise, then, that Muslim thinkers have often found it more difficult to affirm common ground with Western secularist understandings of peace than with understandings of peace that claim a religious foundation, particularly from within the Abrahamic tradition.

When defining their perspective on peace and situating it within the context of contemporary intellectual debates, Muslim intellectuals often use what they perceive as the dominant Western approach as a foil for Islamic teachings. For many, the Western approach puts too much faith in institutional formulas and the power of economic and political competition to "bring out the best" in human societies. Where the Western approach celebrates human self-determination and rational self-interest, the Islamic perspective underscores divine purpose and human exertion as well as communal cooperation in the conscious pursuit of values. While the Western approach points to political pluralism, individual rights, and perhaps even consumer society as the substance of peace, the Islamic perspective affirms communal solidarity, social justice, and faith as the way of peace, and provides scope for embracing an international order based on cultural and religious pluralism in which different communities of faith "compete in good works."

Although it is arguable that such Muslim critiques of Western culture and politics are often directed more to the defense of Islamic communal identity than to the development of an alternative practice, critics are correct in claiming that the currently prevailing (but by no means only) Western approach to peace is underpinned by a competitive and often nationalistic logic, and that the policies pursued by Western great powers in modern times have demonstrated greater concern for security and expediency than for social justice.

Since the Cold War era, the dominant paradigm in the field of international relations has been "political realism" (also known as "power politics"). According to this paradigm, peace is considered separately from justice; peace is understood principally as an absence of war, and issues of distributive justice are deemed to lie beyond the purview of practical international politics. Within each state, peace is maintained through institutionalized regulations and decision-making procedures, backed by coercive rule enforcement when necessary. Where institutions are weak, as in politics among nation-states, threats to use military power become a primary rather than a secondary basis for maintaining order and dealing with intractable disputes.[27]

It is unfortunate that Muslim critiques—and to some extent Christian, Jewish, and other religious critiques—of modern political theory and practice are often dismissed as mere apologetic stances. As discussed in subsequent chapters, Muslims (like members of other religious communities) have often been guilty of the same types of faults they describe in modern Western thinking; yet viewing the West through Muslim eyes provides valuable insight into cultural differences and into Muslim definitions of current world problems. The predominant tendency in the modern West, for example, is to think about peace and conflict resolution in terms of rational order or problem solving. Following the example of such early Greek thinkers as Plato and Euripides, it is not an exaggeration to state that modern Western thinking regards reason as sacred. Passion has been posited as an opponent rather than a complement of reason—as an unruly and potentially destructive force that can easily lead to fantasy as well as fanaticism and violence. This view of passion has echoes in Christian theology and in concepts such as original sin, but its present manifestations appear more closely linked to the rationalism of the Enlightenment and of such thinkers as Immanuel Kant (1723–1804), who understood history as progress toward rationality,[28] and Georg Hegel (1770–1831), who famously proclaimed that "the real is rational and the rational real."[29] While modern advocates of political realism in the domain of international affairs have disregarded the optimism of Enlightenment rationalism for strategically calculated choices based on national interest, they have not rejected the underlying assumption that peace depends first and foremost on the subordination of emotion to reason. Security, realist logic proposes, depends on scaling back ideal aspirations in the face of immediate constraints and opportunities. Pursuing idealistic goals of justice or harmony can easily lead to destruction.

In contrast, Islamic thought has framed the distinction between reason and passion in somewhat different terms. While Islamic philosophical thought and indeed the Quran hold the human capacity for reflection in high regard,[30] Islamic tradition regards passion as a force with both positive and negative manifestations. From an Islamic point of view, the prevalence of individualistic rationality and self-interest in practical Western social thought is unconscionable and cannot possibly lead to peace. Where contemporary Western thinkers place a premium on the skillful management of competition and conflict through an international system based on a balance of power and institutions for joint economic gain,[31] Islamic thought argues in normative terms for a world order that cannot be constructed without passionate commitment to religious values and to linkages between security and justice. The assumption that peace might emerge spontaneously from the individualistic pursuit of self-interest strikes most Islamic thinkers as fanciful, particularly in the absence of consensus on higher values that might discipline self-seeking behaviors. For most Islamic thinkers, the absence of warfare among industrialized, liberal democracies is not adequate evidence for the peacefulness of the prevailing Western paradigm. After all, the performance of modern capitalist and competitive state systems can appear highly ambivalent when its record in relation to non-Western cultures, the countries of the global South,[32] and the planetary biosphere is taken into account.

For Western scholars and commentators, these Muslim criticisms are often difficult to hear—not only because of the manner in which Muslim scholars frame their arguments (in relation to religious sources and normative appeals rather than to empiricism and explanatory models), but also because Islamic ideals have been so imperfectly realized in Muslim-majority lands. Moreover, Islamic critiques often neglect to acknowledge the diversity of views that are to be found within the West. Too frequently, these critiques give only superficial attention to sophisticated self-critiques within Western thought and culture, and appear to be driven at least in part by frustration with US policies toward the Middle East and by exaggerated (and ultimately self-defeating) perceptions of the Western capacity to control internal Muslim political dynamics.

That said, it is unwise for Westerners to ignore the voices of contemporary Muslim thinkers, or to commit the same error of failing to recognize potential allies and dialogue partners. Neither the West nor Islam is monolithic with respect to peace and other humane values, and both of these cultural systems face noticeable tensions between professed and actualized commitments. Becoming familiar with struggles within Islam to realize internally defined understandings of a more just and peaceful world is now incumbent on those in the West who aspire to enlightened global citizenship. Listening to Islamic voices is essential both for the West to know itself and for coexistence in an ever-shrinking world.

The key sources of Islam, including both the Quran and the *hadith* (reports concerning the words and deeds of the Prophet), provide Muslims with a rich vocabulary of faith that has a direct bearing on issues of peace and conflict. This vocabulary gives expression to the ideals of Islam, which, like the ideals of other religions, are not static but emergent. Multiple paradigms of interpretation exist side by side, offering different—and at times divergent—solutions to the complex existential dilemmas faced by the faith community in various historical contexts and circumstances. Each historical period has provided Muslims with a different overall synthesis of Islamic precepts; each generation lives out experiences of those who have gone before, while seeking to derive new meanings directly from sacred texts as well as from immediate challenges and experiences. Much is at stake, both for Muslims and for Westerners, as current generations of Muslims sift through the legacies of the past to seek guidance for dealing with contemporary conflicts.

Unity and Diversity: Islamic Peace Paradigms

While Islam is singular with respect to its origins and primary sources, its historical manifestations are many. The struggle to realize precepts and values in social life is never easy, and differences of opinion inevitably emerge within any living and vital community. At the level of linkages between precept and practice, we may speak of multiple Islamic approaches to peace, many of which resemble traditions within other cultures and civilizations. Muslims, like Christians, Jews, and followers of other world religions, have translated their beliefs into different forms and practices in different historical eras and in diverse social and political milieus. Muslim behavior has in many times and places appeared less than perfectly Islamic, yet the diversity of historical interpretations and practices infuses the Islamic tradition with an internal pluralism that can yield unexpected resources for peacemaking.

When particular Muslim groups claim to act in the name of Islam, sophisticated and thoughtful observers should neither categorically reject nor uncritically accept the assertion that Islamic interpretation has been a principal determinant of their actions. In the process of seeking answers, they should consider various contexts of the actions, and ask themselves *which* Islam is being invoked, by whom, and for what purposes. What Islamic paradigm is being referenced, in relation to what concrete social, political, and economic conditions? If Islam is being invoked in the midst of violence, we can investigate whether specific cultural discourses emerge within a context of chronic political problems that beget a collective sense of grievance, victimization, or disempowerment. What we behold when we watch the evening news is not Islam in an abstract, essential sense, but rather a particular *understanding* of Islam that reflects both Islamic sources and the circumstances in which a specific group of Muslims are reading them.

Because inquiry into the precepts and practices of peace in Islam is a relatively new departure for scholarship, the full range and depth of Islamic approaches to peacemaking has not been represented in most contemporary studies. While Muslims often complain of media misrepresentations and academic biases favoring the study of militance, most religious writings about Islam and peace focus far more attention on religious ideals than on the struggle to implement or approximate these ideals in specific historical and modern contexts. The rich diversity of Muslim experiences with respect to peace and conflict is worthy of far more research than has been attempted to date.

Knowledge of Islamic peace paradigms, and of the historical and recent experiences that inform them, is crucial for responding to peacemaking opportunities in the Middle East and can also strengthen efforts to transform relations between the Islamic Middle East and the West. An exploration of the paradigms presented in Part 2 of this volume can enrich frameworks for cross-cultural and political conflict resolution, and suggest new approaches to Muslim, intercultural, and interfaith peacemaking.

Notes

Some material in this chapter has been adapted from Said and Funk, "The Role of Faith in Cross-Cultural Conflict Resolution," 2002.

1. Fukuyama, *The End of History and the Last Man,* 1992.

2. Huntington, "The Clash of Civilizations?" 1993; Huntington, *The Clash of Civilizations and the Remaking of World Order,* 1996.

3. Enayat, *Modern Islamic Political Thought,* 1982, p. 1.

4. It is a truism that, in precept, Islam embraces both the spiritual and the material, and is therefore immediately concerned with social and political affairs. Observers of Islamic societies should nonetheless take care to differentiate this practical dimension of Islamic concern—an ethical imperative that has genuine political significance and demands engagement in public life—from the *politicization* of Islam and its symbols, which becomes evident when regimes and their challengers use Islam instrumentally as a means of legitimizing established power or reduce Islam to a rigid political ideology. For further discussion of this distinction, see Chapter 4.

5. Abu-Nimer, *Nonviolence and Peacebuilding in Islam,* 2003.

6. Johnston and Sampson, *Religion,* 1994; Johnston, *Faith-Based Diplomacy,* 2003.

7. Panikkar, *Cultural Disarmament,* 1995, p. 63.

8. Sponsel and Gregor, *The Anthropology of Peace and Nonviolence,* 1994.

9. For further discussion of cultural frames in conflict resolution, see Avruch, *Culture and Conflict Resolution,* 1998, pp. 57–72.

10. Appleby, *The Ambivalence of the Sacred,* 2000, pp. 8–9.

11. Said, Lerche, and Lerche, *Concepts of International Politics in Global Perspective,* 1995, pp. 290–292. For another discussion of the relationship between religion and spirituality, see Arinze, *Meeting Other Believers,* 1998, pp. 101–103.

12. Galtung, *Peace by Peaceful Means,* 1996, p. 211.

13. Thomas, *The Global Resurgence of Religion and the Reconstruction of International Relations,* 2005.

14. See James, *The Varieties of Religious Experience,* 1929; Otto, *The Idea of the Holy,* 1929; Eliade, *The Sacred and the Profane,* 1959.

15. Ambler, *Global Theology,* 1990.

16. The importance of listening carefully to voices from non-Western cultures has been strongly affirmed by Fred Dallmayr in works such as *Border Crossings* (1999) and *Dialogue Among Civilizations* (2002).

17. For example, Christians who share the same doctrinal convictions have differed markedly over the proper means of engaging in politics. Despite modern pressures to shift the criteria for evaluating political action from religious norms to national interest considerations, vigorous debates over "just war." "perpetual peace," and pacifism continue among Christian ethical thinkers.

18. It is worth noting that prescriptions for responding to conflict are shaped by culture as well as theology. In modern Western Christianity, for example, the individualistic dimensions of Christian precepts are accentuated more than in non-Western or Middle Eastern Christianity; similarly, Western Jewish and Muslim practices often reflect the cultural environment in which they are situated.

19. The term *Allah* is used by Arab Christians as well as by Muslims, and has common Semitic roots with the Aramaic *Alaha* and the Hebrew *Elohim.*

20. Quran 10:10, 14:23, 19:61–63, 36:58.

21. Quran 10:25.

22. Meacham and Quinn, "The Many Meanings of Jihad to 2 Prominent Muslims," 2007, p. B9.

23. Ibid.

24. The root meanings of self-sacrifice and righteous struggle can be applied in many contexts. For example, a Western observer should not be surprised to hear Afghans characterize their daily efforts to remove antipersonnel land mines as "a kind of jihad" (Moore, "Working to Rid Afghanistan of Land Mines a 'Kind of Jihad,'" 2008).

25. Meacham and Quinn, "The Many Meanings of Jihad to 2 Prominent Muslims," p. B9.

26. Weiss, *The Spirit of Islamic Law,* 1998, pp. 182–183.

27. Robert Gilpin speaks for many in the realist tradition when he describes "the fundamental nature of international relations" as "a recurring struggle for wealth and power among independent actors in a state of anarchy" (*War and Change in World Politics,* 1981, p. 7).

28. Reiss, *Kant,* 1991.

29. Hegel saw history as a grand unfolding of reason. See Hegel, *Hegel's Philosophy of Right,* 1967.

30. Numerous Quranic verses characterize the orderly workings of the natural world as "signs for those who reflect" or "signs for those who are wise" (see, for example, 30:20–24). Many Muslim thinkers have found in these verses an affirmation of the human intellect, and of complementarity between reason and faith.

31. Metaphors from classical political economy and modern economics thrive in the modern discipline of international relations. The greatest concern with such metaphors is manifest among theorists who represent the need for security, a putatively private good of individual nation-states, as more pressing and more attainable than concerns for such global public goods as disarmament, ecological balance, and sustainable development. Neorealists often liken states to firms, maximizing their own profits within a competitive global market system. See Gilpin, *War and Change in World Politics,* 1981, pp. 87–88.

32. Payne, *The Clash with Distant Cultures,* 1995. Richard Payne argues that the United States has been more likely to rely on force in its relations with "culturally distant" countries than in its relations with countries that are perceived to be more similar in their cultural characteristics.

Part 2

Islamic Peace Paradigms

4

Peace Through Coercion: The Problem of Force in Islamic Politics

> Time and age are witness: Humanity is certainly in loss, except those who believe and do good, and enjoin truth on one another, and call upon one another to bear trials with fortitude.
>
> —Quran 103:1–3

The political histories of the world's major faith traditions are full of tensions and contradictions. Often the ideals of religions have stood in stark contrast to the public deeds of leaders who have proclaimed themselves to be religious. While strategic uses and abuses of religion seldom lead insiders to question their first principles, religious outsiders often find the gap between ideals and reality jarring. If we are to appreciate both the potentialities and the problems of religiously based peacemaking, however, we cannot preoccupy ourselves exclusively either with ideals or with the sometimes unsettling realities of actual practice. We need to analyze past uses that have been made of religion by imperfect human beings in order to better understand the heritage of current practices, and to comprehend the context within which more creative options might be explored.

Like every major religious and cultural system in the world, Islam has a political dimension. From an Islamic perspective, the ideal function of politics is to create a just public order within which the members of a community are free to live a good life in accordance with religious values. The creation of a public order that is widely regarded as just, however, is no easy task, and proclamation of religious aspirations is by no means a guarantee of their fulfillment. Virtually all Muslim princes, presidents, and aspirants to power have claimed to obey Islamic commands, and no doubt every Muslim leader has at one point or another been criticized for failing to observe precepts of justice and piety. Every Muslim leader has been a focus of both praise and blame for their conduct, and for the extent to which their behavior has appeared consistent with the Quran, the prophetic example, and standards identified by subsequent generations of Muslim thinkers.

In the present chapter we engage in a sweeping survey of Islamic history, in a search for better understanding of an "Islamic peace paradigm" that has a long history in Muslim political thought: "peace through coercion." According to this paradigm, peace in this world is more often under threat than secure; collective unity in delegating authority and coercive powers to a leader is vitally necessary to prevent the anarchy and destruction that might accompany civil discord or invasion by outsiders. More ambitious goals such as the achievement of social justice through adherence to religious norms remain at least nominally important, yet peace is preeminently to be experienced as an absence of war and achieved through firm administration of public order. Because dangers of dissension and insecurity are constant, leaders are entitled to expect deference from their subjects, rather than questions about their wisdom and virtue.

When discussing the "peace through coercion" paradigm, we are dealing not so much with "pure" Islamic principles as with a system of thought and practice that has been used to legitimize political authority, mobilize subjects, advance basic standards of public well-being, and justify the use of force against threatening adversaries—especially against adversaries portrayed as threats to religious faith. This system in no way exhausts Islamic ethics, and in the next chapter we explore reasons why many Muslims believe that advancing essential Islamic values requires calling key aspects of this paradigm into question. Nonetheless, this paradigm is implicated in many of the current dilemmas facing Muslim societies. Many contemporary Muslim governments implicitly utilize this paradigm when they invoke Islam to reinforce their political authority, and protagonists of Islamic revolutions draw selectively upon aspects of its intellectual heritage while rejecting traditional calls for political obedience.

Who Speaks for Islam?

On August 2, 1990, Iraqi president Saddam Hussein took much of the world by surprise when, at the first light of day, his troops crossed the border separating the Arab Republic of Iraq from the State of Kuwait and quickly defeated Kuwaiti defense forces. Soon, however, firm opposition began to develop, both among Arab leaders who feared Iraqi disruption of the regional state system and among foreign powers such as the United States, which were gravely concerned about threats to allied countries and to regional oil production. The initial reaction from the League of Arab States was swift; a resolution condemning the Iraqi invasion and calling for a full withdrawal of troops was issued on August 3.

This unusual condemnation of a member state by the Arab League did little to change the situation. Rather than withdraw from Kuwait, Saddam Hussein began to shift the focus of his rhetoric from the wrongdoings of the Kuwaiti monarchy to the faults of the House of Saud in Saudi Arabia. As the United Nations Security Council deliberated over the text of resolutions condemning the invasion and enjoining a resolute response, Hussein proceeded to challenge the legitimacy of the Saudi monarchy's custodianship over the two holiest cities of Islam, Mecca and Medina.

Working together, Western powers and key Arab regimes began to form a broad coalition against this new threat to the Middle Eastern status quo. US president George H. W. Bush underscored the importance of using US power to secure the Gulf, and soon hundreds of thousands of troops were deployed to the deserts of Saudi Arabia and to the airfields of neighboring Gulf monarchies. The rulers of Saudi Arabia and Egypt, who now felt vulnerable in the face of Saddam Hussein's new claims of Islamic leadership, wasted no time in organizing a religious response to Iraq's act of aggression. By August 10, Jad al-Haqq, shaykh of Egypt's renowned Al-Azhar University, had prepared a *fatwa* (Islamic legal ruling) outlining an authoritative Islamic response to Saddam Hussein's ambitions:

> The Qur'an calls for aiding the oppressed, and preventing oppression even until the point of fighting it. For this reason, the Azhar Al-Sharif today expresses its grave concern for the future of the Arab and Islamic Nation in light of the insistence of this sinful aggression and its excesses. Al-Azhar has called on, and repeats its call to President Saddam Hussein and his government to be true to their membership of the Arab and Islamic Nation, and to desist from this action that has aborted the Arab Nation's abilities to progress and to grow, and trapped it in a cycle of killing that will come from whence they know not.[1]

Despite the high prestige of Al-Azhar in the world of Sunni Islam, the *fatwa* was far from decisive. Alarmed at the growing presence of non-Muslim troops in Saudi Arabia—a state whose royal family claimed legitimacy through custodianship of Islam's two holiest shrines, in Mecca and Medina—many Muslims began to contest the idea of forming an alliance with Western powers against a predominantly Muslim country, regardless of its misdeeds. Others went further, arguing that Gulf monarchies such as Kuwait and Saudi Arabia represented conservatism, inequitable concentration of wealth, and subservience to foreign interests; Saddam Hussein's Arab nationalist regime, in contrast, offered the possibility of genuine anti-imperialist rebellion against an unjust regional order.

Threatened by his foes' invocation of Islamic authority and encouraged by manifestations of popular support for his bold challenges to imperialism, monarchy, and the state of Israel, President Hussein sought to expand the conflict by reframing it as a struggle between Islamic and anti-Islamic forces. While raising the possibility of linkage between Iraqi withdrawal from Kuwait and Israeli withdrawal from the occupied Palestinian territories, Hussein also began to appeal for action on the part of Islamic movements: "Until the voice of right rises up in the Arab world, hit their interests wherever they are and rescue holy Mecca and rescue the grave of the Prophet Muhammad in Medina."[2] On September 5, Iraqi television broadcast the following presidential message:

> O great Iraqi people, O faithful Arabs wherever you may be, O Muslims in our Islamic world, wherever you recall your obligations to God as partners in the confrontation of right against the falsehood and faith against evil. O sincere Islamists, for whatever path of faith in God and in human rights you have chosen and wherever you perform your duties before God, the great confrontation began on 2 August. Standing at one side of this confrontation are peoples and sincere leaders and rulers, and on the other side are those who stole the rights of God and the tyrants who were renounced by God after they renounced all that was right, honorable, decent and solemn and strayed from the path of God until they eventually opposed it. . . . It is the great confrontation of the age taking place in this part of the world, where the material has overwhelmed the spiritual and all moral and ethical values.[3]

In the end, nine Arab and fourteen predominantly Muslim states contributed soldiers to the US-led coalition that ousted Iraqi forces from Kuwait. Yemen and Sudan expressed solidarity with Iraq, while Morocco and Jordan remained neutral. Saudi Arabia's political leadership was by no means passive in the struggle for Islamic legitimacy, and obtained *fatwas* endorsing the multinational coalition against Iraq and declaring the struggle against Saddam Hussein a jihad.[4] The air war commenced on January 17, 1991, with a ground war following on February 24. Iraq suffered immense military and civilian casualties, yet Saddam Hussein's government survived punishing sanctions and sporadic regime change efforts for more than a decade, until US president George W. Bush launched Operation Iraqi Freedom in March 2003—this time without official authorization from the United Nations or enthusiastic support from predominantly Arab or Muslim states. As of mid-2008, a US-backed Iraqi government continues to battle insurgent forces as well as diverse factions and militias, with multiple sides claiming the banner of Islamic authenticity.

As a turning point in modern Arab history, the Gulf War was a decisive and transformative event. In many respects it marked a significant downturn in the prestige of Arab nationalism and the larger cause of Arab unity, and the beginning of a new era in which politically disillusioned young men would increasingly turn to Islamic movements and underground militias rather than to charismatic governmental leaders in their search for change and political redemption. But the case also illuminates broader patterns in Middle Eastern politics.

Among the many truths revealed by this case, two stand out. First, Islamic symbolism plays an important role not only at the "street" level of Middle Eastern societies, but also in elite politics and diplomatic discourse. Although the political prominence of Islam declined in the immediate postcolonial era, recent decades have seen a revival of Islam both at the grassroots and in the political posturing of leaders. Second, Islam has the potential to provide governments with legitimacy, but it can also take legitimacy away. Islam's practical meaning for politics is contested, just as it has always been since the passing of the Prophet Muhammad in the year C.E. 632. In the Middle East, even putatively secular regimes frequently rely on forms of Islamic legitimacy to maintain the loyalty of citizens and win favor among Muslims beyond their borders, yet the existence of substantial disagreement about who is "on the side of Islam" raises profound questions about the extent to which uses of Islamic symbolism are substantive, coherent, and genuine. How is it that both Iraq and its Arab-Islamic adversaries were able to obtain support for their policies from Sunni Muslim religious leaders or activists? Are such manifestly politicized uses of Islam a new phenomenon, or do they have deeper roots in Middle Eastern and Islamic history? And how can a thoughtful observer differentiate a sincere invocation of Islamic values and norms from mere political opportunism?

As we ask such questions, it is important to bear in mind that religious politics are by no means unique to the Islamic world or to the Middle East. Religion continues to play a significant role in North American politics, particularly in the United States. On the eve of US-Iraqi hostilities in January 1991, President George H. W. Bush hosted Reverend Billy Graham at the White House. "God bless you" is a common benediction in the speeches of US presidents and presidential candidates from both major parties, and George W. Bush sought to evoke religious themes when he closed his nomination acceptance speech at the September 2004 Republican National Convention by stating that Americans "have a calling from beyond the stars to stand for freedom."[5]

Uses of religion by political leaders tell us not only about the personal philosophies of individuals, but also about the cultural contexts within which they operate. Whether the context is Middle Eastern or North American, actual uses of religion sometimes reveal less about theological principles than about historical ways in which religious symbols have been invoked for rhetorical purposes—to convince an audience that a cause is just and that leaders are on the side of righteousness, together with those who support them.

Because there is no uniformity of views about how to implement Islamic values in political affairs, Muslims disagree just as often as Christians and Jews when seeking to discern the moral consequences of their belief in the God of Abraham. Views about the "most Islamic" course of action differ profoundly, despite the certainty proclaimed by those who speak in God's name.[6] Contrary to protestations that "Islam is really very simple," the authoritative sources of Islamic morality can be read in multiple ways that vary with the lived experience, cultural context, disposition, practical concerns, and learning of the interpreter. There is general agreement about sources—first the Quran, then the sayings and reported deeds of the Prophet (the *hadith*),[7] and then the practices of such eminent early Muslims as the first four caliphs (referred to in Sunni Islam as *al-rashidun*) and the rulings of eminent jurists. However, unanimity on interpretation and application is far more elusive, particularly on issues of major political concern. Yet if consensus about the divine intention is so hard to obtain, why have modern Middle Eastern leaders and political activists so often invoked Islam to legitimize rule or justify political behavior? And to what extent are modern uses of Islam in contexts of war, civil strife, and the exercise of sovereign authority consistent or inconsistent with past usages?

Islamic political discourse has deep historical roots in the Middle East. To make sense of the "Islamic factor" in the Middle East and to develop a critical capacity to weigh the claims of those who act in the name of Islam—and, indeed, to discover limits to the "peace through coercion" paradigm—it is vitally important to understand the historical origins of contemporary debates and practices.

Struggling for God: The Birth of a Public Faith

Given the intense focus in contemporary public affairs on "political Islam," "radical Islam," and "Islamic terrorism" (for the vast majority of Muslims, a contradiction in terms), it is easy to forget that the religious vocation of the Prophet Muhammad began in the mountain cave to which he often retreated for silent meditation, far away from the commercial activity and social tensions of his home city, Mecca. Islam would not have become a force in world history, of course, if it had remained only a contemplative practice pursued in seclusion. Indeed, the verses of the Quran that, according to Muslim tradition, inaugurated Muhammad's prophetic dispensation in the year C.E. 610 commanded him to "recite in the name of the Lord"[8]—that is, to bear witness to a divine message before his people. Islam would not be Islam if it were only concerned with private, otherworldly, or eschatological matters. It is a truism that Islam is concerned with all aspects of life, and is an eminently public faith.

After a period of soul-searching that lasted for two years, during which he shared his religious experience only with his family, Muhammad testified to his faith in Allah (literally, "the God") among the people of Mecca, and then endured ten years of hardship during which his call to restore Abrahamic monotheism and establish social justice was met by a mix of fear, derision, and political repression. By the year 622, when the continued survival of the Muslim faith community appeared uncertain, a dramatic new development opened a door through which Islam thenceforth emerged onto the stage of world history: the fractious tribes of Yathrib, having heard of Muhammad's reputation for honesty and fair play (and perhaps recognizing his suitability as an outsider to both the ruling elites of Mecca and the contending factions of their own settlement), invited him to migrate to their city and arbitrate their many conflicts. With this migration to Yathrib, henceforth known as Medina ("the City"), Islam became a basis for the constitution of a new state. In what has become known as the "Constitution of Medina" (Al-Sahifa al-Madina), the people of Medina accepted Muhammad as their principal leader and arbiter, who would preside over a community of long-standing and new converts to Islam as well as Jewish tribes.

Significantly, this act of migration (known as Al-Hijra), which preceded state formation in the city of Medina, is the date from which the Islamic calendar begins. Muslims date their history not from the time of the first revelation or from the birth date of the Prophet, but rather from the time when the earliest Muslims turned decisively away from the oppressive ignorance *(al-jahiliyya)* of Mecca to found the first Islamic state as exiles from their homeland.

It was at this time that the struggle of the early Muslim community to survive took on a military dimension. Few words evoke more fear and anxiety for a Western audience than *jihad.* As noted in Chapter 3, *jihad* is an Arabic word that is most appropriately and generically defined as "holy struggle" or "sacred striving," but that has often been equated with "holy war." Though the variety of meanings encompassed by the term *jihad* is no less extensive than the semantic range of the term *crusade,* it remains true that in Muslim practice the word has often been used to call for what the Augustinian tradition of Christian thought would construe as a "just war." While nonviolent forms of jihad also have a basis in Islamic texts and practices (see Chapter 7), violent interpretations of jihad as a religiously justified war are an indisputable element of historical Muslim practice.

In the Quran, references to jihad tend toward generalized exhortation of Muslims "striving in the way of God" *(jihad fi sabil Allah).*[9] Though the original context in which these exhortations emerged was often one of intense conflict between the Muslim community in Medina and the pagan community in Mecca, Quranic usage of the word *jihad* has been understood to suggest a wide range of activities intended to foster the comprehensive security and well-being of the Muslim community. It is important to note that at no point does the Quran enjoin total or unconditional warfare; verses calling for combat with oppressive unbelievers are consistently juxtaposed with warnings against the "transgression of bounds"[10] and stipulations concerning the conditions for peace.[11] Quranic exhortations concerning armed conflict are framed in defensive terms: "To those against whom war is made, permission is given [to fight], because they are wronged. [They are] those who have been expelled from their homes in defiance of right" (22:39–40).

Whereas the Quran provides an Islamic standard for *jus ad bellum* (the Latin term for "justice *of* war"—i.e., defining when fighting is justifiable),[12] the *hadith* literature provides a more detailed basis for an Islamic conception of *jus in bello* (the Latin term for "justice *in* war"), with instructions barring the use of force against noncombatants (including women, children, and the elderly as well as monks and priests) and an injunction to avoid wanton destruction of the natural environment, which is also shared by the Jewish and Christian traditions.[13] As noted previously, prophetic traditions also give more specific content to jihad as an Islamic concept, providing a clear distinction between the "greater" jihad to purify the soul and the "lesser" jihad to fight on behalf of Muslim interests and defend against forces of aggression.[14]

In addition to the Quran and *hadith,* traditional accounts of early Islamic history have also had a formative impact on Muslim beliefs about matters of war and peace. Victories in engagements such as the Battle of Badr (C.E. 624), in which the Muslims were badly outnumbered by pagan forces aligned with the commercial city of Mecca, have long been interpreted as signs of God's favor and active assistance to a community of faith with a dispensation to renew Abrahamic monotheism. In addition to their obvious literal significance, stories of early battles against numerically superior forces intent on the elimination of the Muslim community have instilled in generations of Muslims a strong sense that, to fulfill one's religious mission, both inner and outer struggle are often necessary.

Classical Islamic Political Thought

From the Hijra to the present, Islam has provided much of the vocabulary through which political actions have been conducted and morally evaluated. Given this long-standing association of Islam with public affairs—indeed, with matters ranging from prayer and family life to alms-giving and communal survival—calls to separate Islam from politics ring hollow in the ears of many if not most contemporary Muslims. How can Islam *not* be political? How could Islam *not* have something to say about matters of justice and injustice, war and peace, rule and misrule? Many principles of Islamic law deal with precisely these issues.

At the very least, the early Muslim community's struggle for survival in the face of determined opposition provides what a majority of Muslims perceive as a clear precedent for defensive warfare in the Islamic tradition. The meaning of this precedent, however, has been disputed throughout Islamic history. Whereas some Islamic thinkers sought to give jihad a purely defensive meaning, others aspired to a characterization of jihad as obligatory warfare against states that forbade the preaching of Islam and refused to pay tribute to the (presumably unitary) Islamic state. In this latter case, jihad to expand the frontiers of the abode of Islam *(dar al-Islam)* into the abode of war *(dar al-harb)* was viewed by many medieval jurists as a moral imperative—that is, as a form of "humanitarian intervention," "civilizing mission," or "preventive defense."[15]

Despite the tendency of many Western and even some Muslim thinkers to characterize "permanent jihad" against non-Muslim or insufficiently Islamic states as the most authentic juridical prescription for Muslim statecraft, the Quranic roots of this view are questionable at best. Terminology such as "abode of Islam" and "abode of war" is not present in the Quran, which also asserts that "God does not like aggressors" (2:190). That seemingly contrary outlooks were deemed useful by rulers and appropriate by jurists cannot and should not be denied, especially considering the manner in which medieval legal categories have been appropriated by insurgent Islamic movements. Making sense of early Islamic politics, however, requires careful attention to historical context.

Shortly after the death of the Prophet Muhammad in 632, the Muslim community found itself in a remarkable position. In moves that were later justified through references to reported sayings and deeds of Muhammad indicating desire that his message be heard in Byzantium and Persia,[16] the first political successors of the Prophet sought to channel the fractious energy of newly converted Arab tribesmen into preemptive strikes on the two greatest powers of the day—two empires whose proxy wars and imperial designs had led to considerable political intrigue and turmoil in the Arab lands of their shared southern periphery. A series of remarkably swift campaigns produced a stunning outcome: Arab-Islamic ascendancy over the lands of the Fertile Crescent, Persia, Egypt, and beyond.

Upon acquiring sway over most of the known world and founding new capital cities in Damascus and later Baghdad, Muslim leaders found themselves in need of new doctrines for administering a religiously, linguistically, and ethnically pluralistic empire. This need of Muslim rulers for a doctrinal basis of political legitimacy overlapped with the need of the larger Muslim community for a code that might limit the caprice of rulers through religious standards, creating conditions that were conducive to the formalization and institutionalization of Islamic legal thought. Though the early leaders of the Damascus-based Umayyad Empire sought to maximize their freedom to interpret Islam in accordance with their own political judgments, their status as caliphs allowed them to act as successors to Muhammad (the Arabic term *khalifa* literally means "successor") only in a political sense. They had the right to lead Muslims in prayer, but were not endowed with authority to innovate on religious matters. Moreover, Islam's insistence on bringing all aspects of human relations within the purview of a religious system of norms reinforced the demand for a communally accepted and nonarbitrary code that would provide guidance for all matters related to the integrity and welfare of the Muslim community.

While early Muslim religious authorities—the forebears of what was to become an institutionalized yet decentralized network of religious professionals known as the ulama—found extensive guidance for Islamic ritual and family life in the Quran and in the *sunna* (example) of the Prophet, they were unquestionably harder-pressed to reach consensus on a system of laws appropriate for the administration of an empire. Though the experience of the community while under Muhammad's guidance provided many precedents for matters of war and peace and for relations with non-Muslim states, the new scenario in which Muslims found themselves was strikingly different from any arrangement that had prevailed in the time of the Prophet. Almost overnight, the Muslim community had been transformed from a coalition of Arab tribes into a multiethnic, multireligious empire with a new center of gravity in the Fertile Crescent.

To solve problems presented by this new situation, Muslims were forced to interpret the Quran and *hadith* in light of immediate circumstances for which sacred texts provided no explicit guidance. To a considerable extent, they were able to do this by using the original Quranic vocabulary and analogies to prior experiences. For example, Muslim authorities applied the Quranic designation of *ahl al-kitab* ("people of the book") to Jewish and Christian subjects, and offered secure status along with freedom of worship in exchange for payment of a collective poll tax *(jizya)* or the formalization of a treaty arrangement. Rather than force conversions to Islam and risk turmoil—as well as direct contradiction of the Quranic verse forbidding religious coercion (2:256)—early Islamic rulers found it more advantageous to coexist with non-Muslim peoples and collect the additional revenue afforded by the poll tax.

By the time the Umayyad dynasty became firmly established in Damascus in the latter half of the seventh century, the Muslim nation, or *umma,* had effectively created a territorial "pax Islamica." To conceptualize this reality, Muslim jurists eventually settled upon the *dar al-Islam* versus *dar al-harb* distinction to demarcate a boundary between lands that were securely under Muslim rule and lands that, in the absence of such administration, they deemed hostile.[17] In the context of world history, Muslim use of such terminology was far from unique. Greco-Roman distinctions between civilized peoples and barbarians and the comparable Chinese conception of a "middle kingdom" are but two examples.

Although a basic dichotomy between *dar al-Islam* and *dar al-harb* helped to reinforce Muslim communal consciousness and provided a plausible map of the world in the early days of the Islamic empire, further historical developments required the addition of considerable complexity to this template. On the one hand, jurists found it necessary to add further territorial categories, such as *dar al-ahd* and *dar al-sulh.* Both of these terms signify the existence of an "abode of treaty"—that is, of predominantly non-Muslim lands whose leaders have signed truce arrangements with Muslims. On the other hand, Muslim caliphs of the Umayyad dynasty (661–750) and then the Abbasid dynasty (750–1258) found it increasingly difficult to maintain a semblance of political unity in the vast lands professing allegiance to them. During the latter days of the Abbasid caliphate, the idea that the principal distinction in international affairs was between *dar al-Islam* and *dar al-harb* became more difficult to sustain in the face of internal political fragmentation and usurpation of the caliph's authority by provincial leaders known as sultans (the Arabic word *sultan* literally means "holder of power" or "authority").

Unlike the first four caliphs to follow the Prophet Muhammad, known in Sunni Islam as the "rightly guided" caliphs *(al-rashidun),* the leaders of Islam's subsequent empires relied not only on Islamic norms for political legitimacy, but also upon dynastic principles, effectively enshrining monarchy as a basis of governance. Over time, the authority of the caliphate began to wane in the face of centrifugal forces, leading jurists to grant legitimacy to the concept of *saltana* (sultanate), and to argue that the role of the caliph in maintaining Islamic unity was to a considerable degree symbolic. Autonomous local rulers could legitimately claim power on the condition that they faithfully implemented divine law *(sharia)* as codified by the legal schools *(madhhabs)* of Muslim scholars. Thus did Islamic political theory begin to reconcile itself to an emergent, pluralistic state system, in which Muslim unity was absent in politics yet manifest at the cultural and social levels.

By the time the Mongols sacked Baghdad in 1258, the caliphate had become a largely symbolic reality, and rivalry among competing claimants to Islamic legitimacy had become the norm. Though the ability to seize political power by force was now more important than endorsement *(bay'a)* by traditional leaders, Islamic political thought nonetheless retained significant contractual elements, with the ruler deriving authority over the ruled primarily through claims of consultation with the ulama and support for *sharia* norms of Islamic morality. With important exceptions such as Ahmad Ibn Taymiyya (1263–1328), however, Muslim scholars discouraged rebellion against established leaders. Leaders were encouraged to become paragons of morality and virtue, with the idea of the "just ruler" receiving particular attention. Subjects, in turn, received the counsel that obedience to authority—even unjust authority—was a necessary bulwark against the threat of anarchy.[18]

Muslim scholars were well aware that the conduct of Muslim leaders often contradicted important Islamic norms, such as Quranic injunctions to manage communal affairs through consultation *(shura).*[19] Many rulers found the Islamic criminal code—particularly its rules of evidence for establishing guilt—too restrictive to maintain control over restive populations, and justified harsher policies on the grounds of *maslaha* (the general interest or common good). Muslim rulers also drew considerable inspiration from non-Islamic sources, including literature influenced by an "advice to kings" genre that had been popular with leaders of the Sassanian (Persian) Empire.[20] Administrative structures were based largely on Byzantine and Sassanian models, and in the early days of the Umayyad Empire most civil servants were non-Muslim. These non-Islamic influences were integrated within the larger vision of a moral order in which God was the ultimate sovereign, who showed favor to kings and princes insofar as they ruled with righteous intent and supported public adherence to divine law, creating conditions for prosperity in this life and felicity in the afterlife.

Greek philosophy also influenced Islamic political thought through the writings of thinkers such as the Muslim Platonist Abu Nasr al-Farabi (870–950). Al-Farabi devoted considerable effort to further development of Platonic ideas about the "excellent city" whose philosopher king aims to bring about the ultimate happiness of his subjects while confronting more warlike, corrupt, and wicked city-states ruled in accordance with less noble principles. Whereas the ulama sought to explain war and rebellion *(fitna)* in relation to more explicitly Quranic concepts such as corruption *(fasad)*, tyranny *(tugyan)*, and caprice *(hawa)*, al-Farabi theorized that, while the desire for peace is natural among human beings, it is also inevitable that some groups will deviate from what is natural and desirable.[21]

Perhaps the most original Islamic political thinker was 'Abd al-Rahman Ibn Khaldun (1332–1406), whose broad learning in *fiqh* (Islamic jurisprudence) as well as in philosophy and history enabled him to work effectively in the courts of rulers in Muslim Spain and North Africa while also producing a remarkable and voluminous *Introduction to History* (Al-Muqaddima), which foreshadowed themes that would later be articulated by the English political philosopher Thomas Hobbes. In addition to his theory about cycles of dynastic ascension and decline driven by a politics of tribal solidarity, Ibn Khaldun argued strongly in favor of the instrumental use of religion to bolster the authority of the political leader—thus making explicit in theory a long-established practice through which leaders of questionable piety sought legitimacy through efforts to demonstrate religious fidelity. With respect to warfare, Ibn Khaldun differentiated between illegitimate wars driven by petty disagreements or the savage desire for plunder, and legitimate wars waged against unbelievers (the expansive notion of jihad as articulated by such classical jurists as al-Shafi'i) or rebels. He is best known, however, for his frank analysis of the use of ethnic solidarity—be it Arab, Turkic, Berber, or Persian—to further political enterprises carried out in the name of a religion that denounces ethnic partisanship.

For Ibn Khaldun, the principal problem of politics was the problem of order, which required mutual accommodation and collaboration between the worldly domain of power politics and the religious sphere of Islamic knowledge and belief. On the basis of his study of history, he concluded that the rise and fall of empires was determined as much by the strength of ethnic and tribal solidarity as by strict adherence to more universalistic principles of faith. Where other Islamic thinkers presented their conclusions about Islamic norms in a format of deductive analogical reasoning from the Quran and *hadith*, Ibn Khaldun gave equal weight in prescriptions for worldly affairs to induction based upon observation.

Ibn Khaldun recognized that the state itself was not an inherently religious construct, but rather a conglomeration of tribal loyalties and diverse alliances. At best, it could achieve temporary stability and conditional security for its subjects, within a mixed agrarian and tribal socioeconomic context that provided strong incentives for plunder and conquest to appropriate surplus resources. Religion was therefore absolutely necessary for the maintenance of the state, and could be used to reinforce social solidarity and political authority. Without religion, the state was unlikely to persist, and without the state, religion was likely to deteriorate. Political authority, however, could not be fully bound by religious scruples, as the pragmatic norms of politics were more permissive than those of religion.

The implication of Ibn Khaldun's theorizing was a de facto separation of complementary religious and political spheres. His conclusions largely served to confirm what was already accepted implicitly in Muslim practice: de facto collaboration between prominent members of the ulama and leaders of varying moral quality, in which the latter received religious legitimation in exchange for patronage of religious institutions and support for the *sharia.* At the core of political power, however, was "group feeling" *('asabiyya)* linked to tribe and ethnicity; this power was augmented (but not generated) through efforts to secure religious legitimacy and demonstrate commitment to communal solidarity against external foes. This judgment did little to win Ibn Khaldun's ideas popularity among other ulama, yet his thought remains an important point of reference for understanding the interface between theory and practice in the traditional politics of the Muslim world, particularly in the Middle East and North Africa.

The Last Caliphate

Although it is arguable that internal struggles among Muslims rendered the *dar al-harb* versus *dar al-Islam* political cartography of jurists unrealistic even at the height of Islamic political achievements during the Umayyad and Abbasid periods (seventh to thirteenth centuries), the ideal of Muslim political unity has exerted considerable influence on collective memory and imagination. Even as the *umma* became politically fragmented and beset by creedal differences such as the Sunni-Shia divide, the vision of a united and religiously upright Muslim community struggling to preserve and extend its message in a hostile world provided a basis for communal solidarity that was not only functional for rulers, but also meaningful to ordinary believers.

Recognizing the potency of this firm sense of Muslim identity and purpose is in no way equivalent to endorsing caricatures of Islamic political history, such as the notion that Muslims were constantly working to spread Islam "by the sword." In believing themselves to be "the best community sent forth for humanity" (Quran 3:110), Muslims adhered to a notion of chosenness that is comparable to Christian and Jewish conceptions of a special historical mission. The fact that strong Christian and Jewish minorities persisted under Muslim rule for well over a millennium would seem to contradict popular Western misconceptions about a unique Islamic aversion to religious diversity. Moreover, the perception of existential threat emanating from the *dar al-harb* was not without basis in reality, as the searing experiences of invasions by the Crusaders (eleventh to thirteenth centuries) and the Mongols (thirteenth to early fifteenth centuries) illustrate quite clearly. Insofar as Muslim dynasties experienced success in warfare and conquest, they demonstrated themselves to be no less—and at times considerably more—humane than other conquering peoples.

While there may well be validity to the argument that religion-politics linkages are more intimate in Islam than in many other world religions, actual usages of religious thought to provide legitimacy for political practices and institutions reveal as much about historical circumstances as they do about the religion itself. Reflecting on the historical role of Islamic discourse in power politics as well as in more cooperative political behaviors can provide insight into continuities and discontinuities in Muslim experiences, and into dynamics of intergroup relations in an era that is no longer defined by the traditional Islamic institutions of caliphate and sultanate.

World War I and the Ottoman Jihad Fatwa

It has become commonplace for Western commentators on modern Islamic history to remark that everything changed in 1798, when Napoleon invaded the Ottoman province of Egypt during a brief but highly ambitious campaign to dominate the Mediterranean and impede British access to India. Attributing the radical regional transformation that began in the following century primarily to Napoleon's short-lived ambitions would undoubtedly be an overstatement, yet the blows suffered by Ottoman forces at the hands of Napoleon were undoubtedly part of a series of events, including setbacks in the Balkans, the Black Sea, and the Caucasus, that forced dramatic changes in the empire.

Throughout the nineteenth century, the empire that had once dominated Asia Minor, southeastern Europe, northern Africa, the Fertile Crescent, and the margins of the Arabian Peninsula experienced persistent territorial losses and growing internal strife along the lines of religion and ethnicity. Rebellions in Ottoman-occupied Serbia (1804 and 1815) and Greece (1822–1830) disrupted centuries of Ottoman preeminence in the Balkans, even as Russian advances culminating in the Crimean War (1853–1856) threatened the empire from the north and French encroachments into northern Africa brought additional lands under European sway. Not satisfied with efforts to annex Ottoman territory outright, the Western imperial powers also sought concessions in trade along with special status as protectors of Christian communities under Ottoman suzerainty. Ottoman leaders responded with a series of military, administrative, and educational reforms, but were unable to effectively withstand mounting external pressures and growing internal fractiousness, most dramatically exemplified by Muhammad Ali Pasha's direct challenge to the Ottoman throne from Egypt after undertaking his own series of reforms and infrastructure projects. A former Ottoman officer of Albanian origin, Muhammad Ali grasped power after the French invasion of Egypt, and eventually mounted an armed challenge to Ottoman power by invading Syria (1831–1841). Though he failed to create his own empire and once again swore fealty to Istanbul, Muhammad Ali succeeded in undermining the sovereignty of Ottoman rulers in Arabic-speaking lands, in a manner that foreshadowed future events.

At the beginning of World War I, after tentative experiments with constitutionalism and Turkish nationalism as means of consolidating power within an increasingly fractious empire, Ottoman leaders turned once more to Islam in a bid for political support at home and abroad. Following the initiative of Enver Pasha, an ambitious and decidedly pro-German military leader, the Ottoman Empire entered a war that would ultimately transform not only Europe but also the Middle East. Motivated by fear of Russian designs on the straits of the Bosporus and the Dardanelles as well as by desire to recover control over the Russian-occupied Caucasus and British-occupied Egypt, the Ottoman government began its war effort with an appeal to Islamic solidarity. Sultan Mehmet V emulated his brother, the recently deposed Sultan Abdulhamid II, by asserting Ottoman claims to the caliphate and to universal Muslim leadership—claims that had been emphasized far less emphatically by Ottoman rulers than by early Muslim dynasties, particularly the Umayyads and the Abbasids. To bolster the legitimacy of the new war effort, the sultan formally declared a military jihad against Russia, Britain, and France.

By seeking to rally Muslims to the cause of holy struggle with the help of a *fatwa* issued by the Shaykh al-Islam (the empire's highest religious official) in November 1914, the imperial government proclaimed its authority to lead an *umma* that extended well beyond Ottoman lands and included large populations under British, Russian, and French occupation. Ottoman authorities no doubt hoped to gain enhanced political as well as financial support, and if possible to undermine their adversaries' grip on Muslim colonies. The precarious strategic situation of the time enhanced the attractiveness of a formal jihad declaration, as did the Ottoman Empire's stature as the worldly power that could most plausibly claim to represent the political interests of Muslims. The Persian Empire, after all, was largely Shia in composition, and Mughal India had long been subjected to British rule.

The message of the Ottoman jihad *fatwa* was simple: the Ottoman Empire's war in alliance with Germany and the Austro-Hungarian Empire was part of a larger defensive campaign through which the world's Muslims were resisting foreign domination. Among the European imperial powers, Russia,

England, and France were guilty of the particularly egregious crime of seeking to bring about the downfall of the Islamic caliphate—and thereby attempting to extinguish the "light of Islam" itself. All Muslims throughout the world therefore faced an individual responsibility to join in a jihad to protect the Ottoman Empire through force of arms or provision of material support. Failure to join in this effort would result in divine punishment. Military support for adversaries of the Ottoman Empire, even if provided grudgingly as a result of threats to exterminate family members, would make Muslims accomplices to murder; hostility against Germany or Austria would similarly put the souls of Muslims at grave risk in the afterlife.[22]

Although this *fatwa* may well have helped to mobilize Ottoman subjects who were already predisposed to support the regime, there is little evidence to support the conclusion that it had a significant impact upon foreign Muslim populations. The *fatwa* did, however, arouse grave concern in Allied capitals, where politicians feared uprisings among their Muslims subjects. Together with a southern Ottoman campaign against British forces ensconced near the Suez Canal, the *fatwa* provided impetus for English efforts to forge an alliance with Sharif Hussein of the Hijaz, a regional leader who claimed descent from the Prophet Muhammad, and whose status as amir (i.e., governor) of Mecca put him in position to organize an Arab challenge to Ottoman claims of religious authority over Muslim subjects. Sharif Hussein declared the Arabs independent in June 1916, and initiated a guerrilla campaign that has become known as the Arab Revolt. Although this campaign did not catalyze a broader rebellion, it has been interpreted by Arab and Turkish historians alike as a decisive blow to the premise of pan-Islamic solidarity upon which the Ottoman Empire was based. As Sharif Hussein's forces collaborated with "Lawrence of Arabia" and Britain's Egyptian Expeditionary Force by sabotaging railroads and capturing the cities of Aqaba and Amman, they attacked not only Ottoman supply lines but also the idea of Turkish ascendancy within a pan-Islamic empire to which Muslims of all ethnic and linguistic backgrounds might theoretically owe allegiance.

Significance of the Fatwa

In retrospect, the extent to which the Ottoman jihad *fatwa* expedited the imperial war effort is questionable. Muslims in Egypt and India did not rebel against the British, and Arab tribesmen from the Hijaz actively collaborated with a non-Muslim state that, in signing the secret Sikes-Picot Agreement of May 1916, had already colluded with France to divide Syria, Palestine, Transjordan, and Iraq into areas of direct and indirect imperial rule. Despite these apparent failures, it remains arguable that the Ottoman Empire's war-mobilization efforts were indeed facilitated by the 1914 jihad *fatwa*.

Even as modernization programs moved forward during the nineteenth century, the Ottoman Empire was, in the final analysis, a political construct founded not only through force of arms and shifting alliances of ethnic and tribal groups, but also through an appeal to the common binding culture of Sunni Islam. Over the centuries, its integrity was preserved both through shrewd political maneuvering and through an explicit social contract that conferred legitimacy upon the Ottoman sultan in exchange for fealty to religious causes and patronage of institutions responsible for maintaining Sunni orthodoxy. Even the *millet* system, through which Christians and Jews were allowed to live by their own codes alongside Muslims in exchange for paying tribute to the Ottoman state, was based upon the classical juristic understanding of *jizya,* the Islamic poll tax on *ahl al-dhimma,* "the people of the covenant." In other words, Islam provided the Ottoman Empire with an integrating identity and ideology. Without determining specific policies—which were defined as much by contingent political or economic calculations as by any other factor—Islam played a constitutive role in the language and normative content of Ottoman politics. The very fact that the state was based on ideas of Islamic communal solidarity encouraged leaders to define interests in ways that not only advanced their personal ambitions, but also bolstered their political legitimacy through exertion on behalf of putatively religious causes. Although the pronouncement of the World War I jihad *fatwa* may appear somewhat cynical given the political predominance of the secularizing Young Turk movement at the time, the resort to Islam as a tool for political mobilization was consistent with Ottoman tradition (which had framed wars with Persian Shias as well as with European Christians in religious terms) and served to advance an understanding of Islam that was consistent with imperial objectives. Islam as such did not predetermine Ottoman policies, yet the persistence of the Ottoman imperial structure depended upon appeals to Islam.

As political philosophers such as Ibn Khaldun had theorized, Ottoman rulers and administrators recognized quite clearly that physical power alone cannot generate political authority—the perception among subjects that any given leader has a *right,* and not simply an *ability,* to command allegiance. In any viable political system, authority presupposes *legitimacy,* the correspondence of leadership claims and actions with expectations established within a particular political culture. Even narrowly based and oppressive regimes must fulfill the key normative expectations of some of their constituents, through a complex fit between official ideology, social structure, cultural norms, and political performance. In the Ottoman Empire the official ideology as well as dominant cultural norms were derived (some would say extracted) from a multifaceted Islamic tradition, and the social structure was understood by a majority of subjects to be constituted in accordance with Islamic customs. To maintain legitimate authority, Ottoman leaders had to be able to construe their political actions in ways that demonstrated fidelity to the prevailing paradigm of Islamic orthodoxy.

The traditional foundation of Ottoman religious legitimacy was enforcement of *sharia* law, as prescribed by classical jurists. This commitment to *sharia* further presupposed an alliance with the ulama and patronage for religious education—one of the more notable routes of upward mobility in traditional Islamic culture since the formal establishment of *madrasas* (religious schools) in the eleventh century. The authority of Ottoman rulers as guardians of Islam was further enhanced by the establishment of control over the holy cities of Mecca and Medina in the sixteenth century, and by the legendary conferral of caliphal authority upon Sultan Selim I by the last surviving descendant of the Abbasid caliphs after the conquest of Egypt in 1517. The Ottomans placed particular emphasis on their responsibilities as protectors of the holy cities, which significantly enhanced their ability to project an image as defenders of the faith. Western scholars have referred to this emphasis on custodianship of the two holy cities *(al-haramayn)* as the Ottoman Empire's "Hammadian policy."

One traditional framework for thinking about the relationship between political authority and religion has been referred to as the "Ottoman circle of equity." This series of eight interconnected maxims provided Ottoman officials with a direct way of articulating the dependence of Islam upon the state and vice versa:

1. There can be no royal authority without the military.
2. There can be no military without wealth.
3. The *reaya* (the peasantry, literally "cattle") produce the wealth.
4. The sultan keeps the *reaya* by making justice reign.
5. Justice requires harmony in the world.
6. The world is a garden; its walls are the state.
7. The state's prop is the religious law.
8. There is no support for the religious law without the royal authority.[23]

Significantly, these eight statements begin and end with royal authority. Hence the purpose of this formulation is clearly to justify the institution of the Ottoman sultanate, conceptualize its political and social functions, and underscore the linkages between military capacity and the defense of religious norms. Royal authority is the indispensable means of implementing the religious law from which order, harmony, justice, productivity, and military puissance emanate, and it is also the end toward which both productive and military activities are directed. Royal authority naturally fosters the well-being of society, which in turn generates the resources needed for strong royal authority. Religious legitimacy and military power are fused in the person of the sultan, who as caliph commands the loyalty of all Muslim believers.

In practice, this infusion of political leadership with religious purpose was vitally important for maintaining the loyalty of the diverse yet predominantly Sunni ethnic groups (Turkish, Kurdish, Arab, and Albanian) that constituted the primary basis of Ottoman power. For orthodox Sunnis, the sultan's professed obligation to apply divine law and defend the interests of all Muslims (and not exclusively the interests of Muslims under his direct control) provided a context within which leaders among subject peoples could offer an oath of allegiance *(bay'a)*. The sultan's claims as a defender of the faith were considerably less persuasive to subjects aligned with Shia Islam and other non-Sunni movements (including Alawis in Anatolia and Syria as well as Druze and Ismailis in the Levant), a reality that reinforced the tendency of many sultans to bolster their credentials for orthodoxy with efforts to drive heterodox Muslim religious movements underground. Although Ottoman treatment of non-Muslim subjects has at times been sensationalized, Ottoman leaders nonetheless appear to have found communal politics politically expedient, as rhetoric concerning jihad to extend the boundaries of the domain of Islam suggests.[24]

Abolition of the Caliphate

Whatever self-interested political calculations may have influenced the Ottoman jihad *fatwa* of 1914, it remains clear that, despite increasing tendencies toward ethnic nationalism, many Muslims within as well as beyond the territorial boundaries of the empire regarded the Ottoman sultanate as a symbol of Islamic solidarity and power. Paradoxically, when reforms known as the Tanzimat were initiated in 1839 to enhance the empire's ability to compete with Europe, the introduction of secular educational institutions and the systematization of administrative procedures helped erode the traditional ideological foundations upon which the empire was based, and did little to arrest a process of fragmentation based on ethnic and linguistic nationalisms. After an uneasy experiment with constitutionalism and the onset of a devastating war, centrifugal pressures proved irresistible. From the ashes of an empire that had united peoples from three continents through pan-Islamic solidarity, new states struggled to arise.

By the close of World War I, the end had come. In the face of European intervention, Mustafa Kemal Ataturk waged a hard-fought campaign to establish the modern state of Turkey in the Anatolian heartland of the Ottoman Empire, and went on to abolish the caliphate in 1924. In lands just to the south of this new Turkish state, a series of lines drawn on a map by British and French officials in 1916 predetermined the boundaries that would for decades plague Arab nationalists searching for independence and unity. Henceforth political authority and the claim to keep or struggle for peace would be grounded in new ideological systems—yet the eclipse of Islam was to prove temporary in nature.

Islam and Nationalism

From Pan-Islam to Modern Nationalism

The decade following World War I brought dramatic changes to the Middle East. Rather than inaugurate a new era of independence, the collapse of the Ottoman Empire led to a broadening and deepening of French, British, and Italian imperial control over Arab lands, with League of Nations mandates providing cover for British control of Palestine, Transjordan, and Iraq, and for French control of Syria and Lebanon. As the leaders of the Arab Revolt were driven from Damascus by French forces, the British sought to co-opt rising Arab national feeling by installing Sharif Hussein's sons Feisal and Abdallah as the monarchs of Iraq and Jordan respectively.

In the decades that followed, anticolonial discourse in Arab countries reflected both secular Arab nationalist and Islamic themes. To a considerable extent, political trends mirrored ideological developments in Europe, with some nationalist leaders expressing admiration for liberal ideas, and others taking interest in socialist and even fascist concepts. Islamic revivalist countermovements such as Egypt's Muslim Brotherhood also developed at this time, expressing desires for cultural and political self-determination, as well as profound concern about untoward events such as the Turkish abolition of the caliphate.

For most Middle Eastern states, independence from European colonial powers did not arrive until after World War II (see Table 4.1). Though the departure of colonial powers often left a window of opportunity for experimentation with democratic politics, liberal political ideologies faced almost immediate challenges to their legitimacy as frameworks for "normal politics." The Islamic revivalist and pan-Arab movements of the time differed on many points, but shared deep dissatisfaction with territorial boundaries inherited from European mapmakers. Where Islamic revivalists viewed European political norms as inappropriate for Muslim practice, more secular Arab nationalists often felt attracted to visions of accelerated social transformation (especially socialism) through the activism of a vanguard party and the actions of a powerful, centralized state. The founding of Israel in 1948 accelerated these tendencies; the humiliating defeat of Arab armies, despite a significant numerical advantage, undermined popular respect for postcolonial social and political elites. Military coups in Egypt, Syria, and Iraq produced more politically radical regimes dedicated to both nationalism and socialism; anti-French struggles for liberation in Algeria and Tunisia likewise yielded secularist regimes proclaiming allegiance to socialist principles. A remarkable ideological gap emerged between states competing to position themselves at the forefront of Arab nationalism, and conservative Arab monarchies such as Saudi Arabia, Jordan, and Morocco.

Table 4.1 Impact of European Powers on State Formation in the Muslim Middle East

Middle Eastern State	Colonizing European State—Year of Intervention	Date of Independence
Algeria	France—1830	July 5, 1962
Bahrain	British protectorate—late 1700s	August 15, 1971
Djibouti	France—between 1843 and 1886	June 27, 1977
Egypt	Britain—1882	Partial independence on February 28, 1922; full sovereignty after World War II
Iran	Russian and British spheres of influence, but never colonized	—
Iraq	British mandate—1920	October 3, 1932
Jordan	British mandate—1920	May 25, 1946
Kuwait	British protectorate—1899, formalized 1914	June 19, 1961
Lebanon	French mandate—1916	November 22, 1943
Libya	Italy—1911	December 24, 1951
Mauritania	France—1903–1904	November 28, 1960
Morocco	French protectorate—1912; Spanish protectorate—1912	March 2, 1956
Oman	Portugal—1508; British protectorate—1891	Expulsion of the Portuguese in 1650; independence from the British in 1971
Qatar	British protectorate—1916	September 3, 1971
Saudi Arabia	British sphere of influence, but never colonized	Unification completed on September 23, 1932
Somalia	British protectorate—1886; Italy—1889	July 1, 1960
Sudan	Britain (with Egypt)—1882	January 1, 1956
Syria	French mandate—1920	April 17, 1946
Tunisia	France—1881	March 20, 1956
Turkey	Never colonized	Established as successor state to the Ottoman Empire on October 29, 1923
United Arab Emirates	British protectorate—1853	December 2, 1971
Yemen	British in South Yemen (Aden)—1839	North Yemen established November 1918; South Yemen established November 30, 1967; Republic of Yemen established May 22, 1990, through merger of North Yemen and South Yemen

Note: This table covers "core," Muslim-majority Middle Eastern states, as well as states of North Africa that are members of the Arab League.

In many respects, the revolutionary nationalism that swept through those Arab lands with the longest traditions of settled agriculture and the most dynamic histories in international trade marked a dramatic shift away from traditional politics. Many pioneers of Arab nationalism, especially in Syria, Egypt, and Iraq, regarded it as a progressive vehicle for transforming relations between landlords and peasants, ensuring equality for Christian populations, advancing a new secular ethos, enhancing national power, and establishing solidarity with other anti-imperialist movements throughout the third world.

Nonetheless, Arab nationalism did not altogether break with Islamic culture, seeking instead to reframe Islam as a noble "national heritage." Religious legitimacy remained important for Middle Eastern regimes, and the state sought to alternately co-opt or repress religious movements. As Hisham Sharabi has noted, the language of Arab leaders continued to utilize religious symbolism and metaphor. This would in any case have been difficult to avoid, as modern standard Arabic remains remarkably loyal to the language of the Quran and of classical poetic expression; "it retains quasi-religious undertones and is full of the imagery of medieval Islamic society."[25] Evoking this Islamic heritage reminds Arabs of past glories, when their culture was at a zenith—and projects an idea of renaissance or "reawakening" in the present.

The Resurgence of Islam

For the past several decades, religious and ethnolinguistic aspects of Middle Eastern identity have coexisted uneasily. On the one hand, nationalist leaders have often succeeded in their efforts to reinforce the legitimacy of their regimes through religious symbolism, effectively implementing the theory of Ibn Khaldun. Examples are numerous. Libya's autocratic Muammar Qaddafi expounded bold and idiosyncratic doctrines, yet alluded to Islamic heritage and identity by calling a compendium of his writings the "Green Book" (green being the symbolic color of Islam). Otherwise secular Arab states have constitutional provisions stipulating that Islamic law is a primary source of legislation or that the president must be Muslim. Iran's modernist Shah Muhammad Reza Pahlavi (1941–1979) sometimes spoke of his personal relationship with God, and even secularist Turkey's flag is distinguished by Islamic symbolism: a star and a crescent moon.

On the other hand, Islam has frequently posed a challenge to nationalist regimes—most dramatically in Iran, where the Shah's elevation of classical Persian culture in matters of state gave way to an Islamic Republic in 1979. Particularly after the defeat of Arab nationalist regimes in the Arab-Israeli Six Day War of 1967, pressure for more "authentic" Islamic alternatives to the new nationalism became acute throughout the region. In recent years this conflict has become salient once again in Turkey, where Islam remains a potent source of Turkish identity and political discourse, despite the secularizing campaign of Ataturk and his successors. Since the 1990s, Islamic-oriented parties such as the Welfare Party and the Justice and Development Party have exerted a strong influence on national politics, generating two ruling coalitions in the Grand National Assembly. Just as Islam undermined exclusive tribal and ethnic loyalties during the classical era, so too has it provided a loyalty that alternately challenges and reinforces that most modern of tribes, the nation-state.

The social program of modern Islamists (i.e., of those who seek to reassert an ideological reformulation of traditional Islamic principles through modern approaches to political mobilization) differs markedly from that of secular Arab, Turkish, and Persian nationalisms, particularly with respect to issues such as private morality and the public deportment of women. Historical narratives also differ, with nationalists weaving together pre-Islamic and Islamic cultural heritages while constructing a political identity in which ethnolinguistic distinctiveness is paramount, and Islamic movements seeking identity as well as moral discipline primarily from an Islamic tradition that transcends nation-states and contains within itself a code for organizing society. In principle Islamic identity challenges the use of ethnic and linguistic distinctions as a basis for political action, and objects to secular nationalist discourse. In practice, however, there is greater ambiguity, with many Arab Islamists taking pride in the central role of Arab peoples in delivering the message of Islam, Turkish Islamists finding special significance in the decisive role played by Turks in Islamic history, and Persian Islamists embracing their own distinctive cultural and religious heritage.

Despite their basic differences, ethnolinguistic nationalisms and Islamicism exhibit similarities in several important ways. First, nationalisms in the Middle East are often similar to Islamism insofar as they seek to base political legitimacy for regimes on identities that cannot be contained by modern state boundaries. Many Arab nationalists and Islamists, for example, view current state boundaries as impositions that have sewn division, conflict, and corruption. Nationalists in Turkey feel an affinity with Turkish-speaking peoples in Central Asia, and a similar dynamic is evident in Persian communities within and beyond Iran.

Second, both nationalists and Islamists invoke the idea of a "golden age." For Arab nationalists, the model of greatness can be found in the progressive character of Arab-Islamic Spain (Andalusia) and also in the cultural and scientific dynamism of the Umayyad and Abbasid empires. For Turkish and Persian nationalists, past periods of glory may be found in both pre-Islamic and Islamic times.[26] Islamists, in contrast, tend to focus on the righteousness of the first four "rightly guided" caliphs *(al-rashidun)* to succeed Muhammad (Abu Bakr, Umar, Uthman, and Ali) and of the "pious forebears" *(al-salaf al-salih)*, who were Muhammad's companions. Though neither nationalist nor Islamic movements seek to exactly copy the conditions of their privileged eras, both desire to recapture an "essential spirit" of the past.

Third, both nationalist and Islamic movements seek to enhance the political and worldly status of their peoples vis-à-vis the West, albeit by varying means. Arab nationalists find special symbolic potency in the issue of Palestine and have often defined broad modernization campaigns as pragmatically necessary responses to neocolonialism, while Islamist movements tend to connect the Palestinian situation to a number of other conflicts within and outside the Middle East (e.g., Iraq, Afghanistan, Chechnya, Kashmir, Bosnia), and conclude that Islam and Muslims are under attack and must be defended on an Islamic basis. While some Turkish and Persian nationalists make common cause with Islamic movements (underlining, for example, historical associations of Shia Islam with Persian dynasties or of Turkish tribes with the defense of their faith), others object to the idea that Islam should play a role in the public sphere.

Uses and Abuses of Islam

In the decades following World War II, most foreign commentators on Middle Eastern affairs agreed that the rise of outwardly secular nationalisms presaged the decline of Islam as a factor in politics. Predictions that nationalism would replace Islam as a source of legitimacy for Middle Eastern states, however, proved premature. Beneath the surface, Islam remained a resilient social and cultural force, and has provided a basis for contesting the authority of sometimes autocratic regimes. The failures of most Middle Eastern states to maintain legitimacy through political and economic performance have only reinforced what many observers characterize as a broad-based "return to Islam."

One of the gravest problems of the Middle Eastern state system is a marked lack of correspondence between the boundaries of states and the identities of their inhabitants. These identities are at once narrower and broader than the identities that might be optimal for the smooth functioning of a modern state. Identities have been too narrow insofar as the collective identity projected by the state has not been strongly felt by tribal groups, religious sects, and ethnic minorities. Simultaneously, identities have also been too broad, presenting leaders with vexing challenges. How much weight should be given to the national interests of a country like Lebanon or Egypt when they appear to conflict with pan-Arab interests? When are national policies in harmony with precepts of Islam, and who has the authority to interpret Islamic political ethics for the current era? When such large questions remain unanswered, divisiveness within and among states becomes more pronounced.

A key result of this situation is the manipulation (some might call it "deployment") of religious and national symbols to reinforce the legitimacy of the state. The pattern that was evident in the case of the Ottoman jihad *fatwa* has often repeated itself in Middle Eastern politics, with dominant as well as insurgent groups seeking to strengthen themselves through strategic appeals to Islam or to the aims of revisionist national movements. Rivals for power compete to define collective identity and claim legitimate authority.

As noted previously, most modern Middle Eastern states claim in one way or another to be based on Islamic values. The state claims Islamic legitimacy in its founding documents,[27] and seeks to co-opt Islam through public discourse, symbolic politics, and patronage to religious leaders and institutions. Implicit bargains are negotiated, through which religious leaders retain authority over particular issue areas, such as family law and the censoring of publications that offend religious sensibilities, in return for cooperation with the overall domestic and foreign policy priorities of governing regimes. Islam plays an especially decisive role in the politics of countries whose leaders have sought to base their legitimacy almost exclusively on religious norms, such as the Islamic Republic of Iran and the Kingdom of Saudi Arabia.

The Iran-Iraq War

Wars in the Gulf region offer especially clear examples of how Islamic categories of meaning have often been used by modern states to justify policies that are not obviously consistent with Islamic values. Three major wars have occurred in this oil-rich subregion of the Middle East in the space of less than twenty-five years: the Iran-Iraq War of 1980 to 1988, the Gulf War of 1991, following Iraq's 1990 invasion of Kuwait, and the Iraq War, which resulted from the US-led invasion of Iraq in 2003.

These wars have had tragic consequences for the peoples of Iraq, Iran, and Kuwait. Not one of them can be simplistically categorized as a "religious war," yet all three involved efforts by political leaders to justify military strategies through religious discourse and to mobilize populations through appeals to religious identity. In all three wars, Islam was used to legitimize conflicts that at least initially followed a secular logic. Although the immediate causes of the wars can be captured through utilization of standard international relations concepts for strategic analysis, Islam must nonetheless be recognized as a factor that leaders felt obliged to deal with as they sought to justify various courses of action.

Bases for rivalry between Iraq and Iran date back decades, if not centuries, before the outbreak of war in September 1980. The immediate causes of the conflict, though, were more political than religious. The primary stakes were territorial control of the oil-rich Iranian province of Khuzestan and the Shatt al-Arab waterway (known as the Arvand river in Iran), through which the combined waters of the Tigris and Euphrates rivers—together with oil exports from both countries—reach the Persian Gulf. During the 1970s, Iran and Iraq had almost come to blows over this problem of boundary demarcation, and competing territorial claims led to active Iranian support for secessionist Iraqi Kurds. In initiating warfare in 1980, the Iraqi government hoped to sabotage Iran's Islamic Revolution, while exploiting a moment of Iranian weakness to gain increased access to the Gulf and acquire additional oil resources. As it fought back in a multiyear struggle, the revolutionary government of Iran sought not only to prevent territorial losses, but also to reassert its traditional regional predominance.

While the role of Islam in Iranian identity after the 1978–1979 Islamic Revolution was self-evident, the place of Islam in Ba'thist Iraq was more ambivalent. Saddam Hussein's ruling Ba'th Party, after all, represented itself as the vanguard party of a nationalist and socialist revolution that would eventually unite all Arabic-speaking peoples in one state. The role of Islam in this ideology was historically abstract and aestheticized, treated more as an exemplary achievement of the Arab people than as a source of concrete inspiration, let alone detailed legislation. Few Arab states were in a worse position to claim Islamic legitimacy than Saddam Hussein's Iraq when it initiated hostilities against Iran.

Still, Saddam Hussein's Iraq was a predominantly Muslim country. Despite divisions between Sunni and Shia Muslims, a common sense of Arab-Islamic identity was shared by a majority of the state's people, and it was this largely *Arab* Muslim character of the Iraqi people that Saddam Hussein sought to mobilize during the Iran-Iraq War, at the expense of both Iranians and the Sunni Kurds of northern Iraq. This Arab Muslim status of Iraq, and the specifically *Sunni* character of its ruling regime, were vitally important in Iraqi efforts to rally support from neighboring countries. Conservative Gulf monarchies such as Kuwait and Saudi Arabia played essential roles in helping to bankroll Iraqi war efforts, hoping that Iraqi success on the battlefield would undercut the Iranian Revolution and reduce its appeal as a model for their own Shia minority populations.

The Iranian Revolution had presented Saddam Hussein's Iraq with both a threat and an apparent opportunity. On the one hand, Saddam Hussein's power ultimately rested on a narrow Sunni Arab base, the majority ethnic group in Iraq being Shia Arab. Iran's Shia revolution presented Hussein with new and dangerous scenarios, which began to appear all the more troublesome when Iran's leadership called for export of the revolution and supported subversive activities in Iraq. On the other hand, revolutionary disorder within Iran created an appearance of vulnerability to a preemptive war that might settle territorial claims in Iraq's favor and perhaps even bring about the downfall of the new Iranian regime.

As it turned out, the Iraqi decision to invade Iran was a grave miscalculation: the new Iranian government was able to muster considerable popular support and mount much stiffer resistance than Saddam Hussein had anticipated. Despite initial territorial gains, the invasion soon bogged down and Iraq was forced into a defensive posture. Although Iran proved unable to defeat Iraq's qualitatively superior and better-funded forces, Iraq was unable to fulfill its primary objectives. As the United States played both sides with the hope of producing a stalemate, Arab countries provided Hussein's Iraq with billions of dollars in loans and grants to stem the tide of Iran's revolutionary forces and thereby reduce the likelihood that Iranian hegemony over the Gulf would adversely affect oil exports or radicalize Shia populations of Saudi Arabia and Bahrain.

How was it, then, that Islamic identity—and competition for Islamic *authority*—came to play a significant role in a war motivated largely by the prospect of strategic gain? First, Iran's Islamic Revolution created genuine fears among Iraq's Ba'thist establishment. Iraq's secular and predominantly Sunni regime felt threatened by the Shia Muslim revolution next door. This perceived threat to the Iraqi regime only became more intense as the war proceeded and Iran sought to appeal to Iraq's large Shia community. Second, religious identity was explicitly manipulated in both countries' propaganda, with Saddam Hussein's Iraq cynically invoking the successful seventh-century Arab campaign against the *Persian* and *non-Islamic* Sassanian Empire and the Iranian government calling upon its youth to sacrifice themselves for truth by emulating the Prophet's grandson Hussein, who was martyred near the Iraqi city of Karbala in C.E. 680—a city in which the spiritual descendants of Hussein were once again being persecuted by a ruthless and oppressive government.[28]

While the immediate causes of the war were thoroughly geopolitical, the conflict contained built-in ethnic, sectarian, and ideological dimensions that leaders on both sides amplified to strengthen domestic support and appeal for external assistance. The costs of war were horrendous for both sides, with an estimated total loss of 1–2 million lives. Faced with the grave human, environmental, and financial consequences of this dramatic foreign policy error, Iraqi president Saddam Hussein sought political and economic redemption by turning his sights to the south. When his invasion of Kuwait provoked an unanticipated response from the United States as well as from the larger international community, Saddam Hussein sought to reframe the conflict not only by capitalizing on resentment of external domination, but also by exploiting symbols of Islamic identity and piety. He called for liberation of the Israeli-occupied Al-Aqsa Mosque in Jerusalem as well as the holy cities in Saudi Arabia (now sullied by the presence of US troops in the country), and inscribed the traditional Muslim invocation and rallying cry *Allahu akbar* ("God is greater") on a national flag that had originally been intended to convey secular, pan-Arab nationalist aspirations.

From the Gulf War to the Iraq War

As noted previously, official manipulation of Islam during the Gulf War was as pronounced as during the Iran-Iraq War. As in the Iran-Iraq War, the immediate causes of conflict for the Gulf War were more worldly than theological. Of Saddam Hussein's many reasons for attacking Kuwait—desires to avoid repaying billions of dollars in war debt, to put an end to illegal "sideways" drilling under the Iraq-Kuwait border, to implement a long-standing irredentist claim, to acquire new pillaged wealth, to avenge a perceived slight from the Kuwaiti amir, and to stake a stronger claim to pan-Arab leadership—none were remotely religious in character. Only after his invasion of Kuwait in August 1990 aroused

Western as well as Arab opposition did Hussein seek to rally Islamic support and pronounce his war effort as an Islamic struggle. Hussein's Saudi adversaries, threatened by Iraqi encroachment, similarly sought to underscore the Islamically correct nature of their countermeasures.[28]

Though it is difficult to calculate war damages with certainty, the price paid by the Iraqi people for defeat in the Gulf War was comparable in magnitude to the Iran-Iraq War's impact.[29] Tens of thousands of Iraqis perished from coalition bombing efforts and tens of thousands more (some claim hundreds of thousands) perished in succeeding months and years from remarkably high infant mortality rates, which increased as a result of infrastructure destruction (including the bombing of electricity plants and the disablement of water purification facilities) and stringent sanctions. Thousands more lost their lives when the Ba'thist regime sought to repress Shia and Kurdish uprisings following the cease-fire that ended hostilities between the Iraqi government and the US-led coalition.

Yet Saddam Hussein managed to cling to power. He claimed a moral victory for withstanding a devastating assault from the United States and its allies, and took advantage of conditions produced by sanctions to reinforce the importance of patronage networks. He also redoubled his efforts to pose as a pious Muslim, erecting the grand "Mother of All Battles Mosque" as a monument to the valiance and faith of his people. This mosque was distinguished by four minarets designed to resemble Russian Kalashnikov assault rifles, four minarets molded in the image of Scud missiles, and a 650-page Quran inscribed with an ink solution containing three pints of President Hussein's blood. The mosque was but one of many constructed after the Gulf War as part of Hussein's faith campaign, which also included increased religious education in schools and greater support for religious scholars and institutions.

By the time of the Iraq War in March 2003, the formerly socialist and nationalist leader of Iraq was relying upon Islamic symbolism to a greater extent than ever before, and in a manner that arguably mocked traditional forms of integration between religion and state even as it emulated them. While the George W. Bush administration moved aggressively, without the cover of enthusiastic Muslim allies, supporting *fatwas,* or a United Nations resolution, Saddam Hussein sought to rally Muslims to the defense of Iraq as an Islamic country. In an effort to highlight his Arab nationalist and pro-Palestinian credentials, he organized irregular warfare squads under the banner, *fida'yin Saddam*—literally, "those who sacrifice themselves for Saddam," but figuratively an allusion to an earlier generation of Palestinian guerrillas who had also called themselves *fida'yin,* out of willingness to sacrifice themselves for their homeland. Compared to the Iran-Iraq War and the Gulf War, generalized Arab support for Hussein had decreased, yet outrage at what was seen as US persecution of an Arab and Islamic country convinced some Muslim religious leaders to endorse the idea of defensive military jihad on behalf of a fellow Muslim state.

Islam and Political Realism

When seeking to extrapolate from the experiences of the earliest Muslim communities and create a framework for the politics of an emergent Islamic empire, most exponents of classical Muslim jurisprudence and philosophy refused to endorse a secular realpolitik based on expediency. However, there is evidence to suggest that their interpretive efforts were colored by realistic political considerations and pressures to work with, rather than against, the grain of their times. They formulated their understandings of Islamic norms within a context of acute conflict, in which political authority was believed to be fragile and the threat of anarchy very immediate. Quite often they faced new and complex situations for which there was no exact precedent in past Islamic rulings, and were confronted with the challenge of reaching conclusions that might enable as many people as possible to live in peace and security.

Many contemporary Muslims believe that classical Islamic thinkers largely succeeded in their efforts to apply the principles of the Quran and *sunna.* Despite damaging civil wars and devastating foreign incursions, Muslims presided over the world's most dynamic civilization for centuries. Muslim leaders engaged with non-Muslim monarchs not only through warfare, but also through treaties and trade. Muslim practices did not provide non-Muslim minorities with fully equal status, but their place within the Muslim polity was well-defined and generally secure. Despite the emergence of significant gaps between theory and practice, the ideal of unity through a largely symbolic caliphate provided an enduring focal point for communal solidarity in the face of internal divisions and external threats, and proved flexible enough to accommodate multiple power centers. Classical Islamic jurisprudence and philosophy offered coherent moral aspirations, while also granting leaders scope to pursue the collective interest *(maslaha)* of the Muslim community as they perceived it.

Others take a more critical view of the classical legacy, placing emphasis either on the inapplicability of past thinking to the present era or on failure of past thinkers to give full expression to Islamic political values. Some, for example, would liken the classical era to the Christian Middle Ages, and suggest that religious thinking took place too close to the seat of power, and therefore tended to serve the interests of particular rulers more than substantive religious values. Reformist and revivalist thinkers, for example, have argued that past Muslim thinkers were too quick to accommodate themselves to non-Islamic institutions and concepts, such as monarchy and empire, and too willing to abandon the more egalitarian possibilities inherent in the Quran and in the Arab tribal ethos. From this point of view, Islamic political theory borrowed too heavily from the Sassanian and Byzantine traditions. The Ottoman "circle of equity," for example, was inspired by a pre-Islamic Persian concept.[30]

Critics of classical political thought argue that it was often in the interest of a Muslim ruler to represent himself as the sole legitimate leader of the *umma,* to label rival leaders as "rebels," and to distract attention from local injustices through preoccupation with the politics of Muslim communalism. By prioritizing form and symbolism over substance, Muslim leaders could acquire political legitimacy and even a reputation for justice while practicing dynastic politics in a manner that differed very little from precedents set by pre-Islamic empires. Thus could Islamic symbolism be used as a veil for policies that were more worldly than Islamic, in which justice was deferred in favor of order and the pursuit of a stable political status quo—an absence of subversion or civil discord.

Clearly, it would be misleading to oversimplify the classical Islamic literature on war and peace, and unfair to typecast jurists and philosophers as agents of their rulers. A careful reading of classical Islamic political thought reveals important and unresolved debates about the bases of political order and the question of whether it is righteous for Muslims to submit to unjust leaders. For better and for worse, Muslim intellectuals have been reluctant to embrace the thinking of modern writers in the European tradition of realpolitik, with their open endorsement of nationalistic rivalry and attempts to theorize competition among states within an international balance of power system. The Muslim tradition of political thought has been hesitant to part with the ideal of unity, as well as with the notion that peace—even a security-focused, "absence of war" peace—depends in no small part on the virtue of top leaders. If many thinkers eventually endorsed a rather minimalist set of expectations, as exemplified by famous juristic statements that Muslims must accept unjust leadership rather than risk anarchy, fair-minded analysts must acknowledge mitigating circumstances—including the inherent volatility of agrarian social orders—that led them to seek stability and social cohesion rather than more ambitious objectives.

Classical Islamic political thought was highly complex and has by no means been transmitted to the contemporary context of Middle Eastern politics as a coherent package. Insofar as Islamic ideas continue to influence political outcomes, they are heterogeneous and contested in nature. Nonetheless, a number of important themes in Middle Eastern political discourse exhibit continuity with classical ideas, and are consistent with what we have described as a "peace through coercion" paradigm within Islam. These themes may be summarized as follows: (1) reliance on Islam as a key foundation for political legitimacy, (2) a pessimistic reading of history, (3) a concern for dangers posed by political change, (4) a focus on struggle against hostile external forces, and (5) a minimalist conception of peace as an absence of war.

Islam as a Foundation for Political Legitimacy

Islam plays a central role in Middle Eastern political culture, providing a set of symbols and values that leaders frequently invoke to endow their regimes with an aura of religious legitimacy. As the admittedly extreme case of Saddam Hussein suggests, it is often more important to *appear* deferential to Islam (i.e., to construct mosques, support religious education, express solidarity with oppressed Muslims in other regions, and be seen praying on television) than to behave in a manner that is substantively Islamic, insofar as Islamic values assert the importance of egalitarianism, social justice, due process, and accountability. When contemporary Muslim leaders engage in symbolic public behaviors while vigorously undermining any and all challenges to their political authority, their conduct falls short of ideal standards even as it perpetuates practices that have a historical basis.

Religious symbolism is at the center of politics throughout the Middle East. Even in Turkey, where Ataturk's cultural revolution left a decisively secular imprint upon the state and military, popular attitudes toward Islam as a source of public integrity have guaranteed substantial public support for religiously oriented political organizations such as the Welfare Party, the Virtue Party, and the Justice and Development Party. The recent electoral victories of "soft" Islamic politicians in Turkey present a major challenge to assumptions concerning secularization. Elsewhere, Ba'thist Syria's constitution requires that its president be a Muslim, while the monarchs of Jordan and Morocco claim direct descent from the Prophet Muhammad. Some states, like the Kingdom of Saudi Arabia and the Islamic Republic of Iran, rely upon Islam for political legitimacy every bit as much as the Ottoman Empire and other premodern Muslim polities.

Although recourse to Islamic political symbolism became more indirect and allusive when Arab nationalism was at its post–World War II apogee, the resurgence of Islam in recent decades has led many states to place increasing emphasis on their Islamic credentials. The results of this reliance upon Islam for political legitimacy and authority vary, including, at a minimum, direct state sponsorship of religious professionals. In Saudi Arabia and Iran, the state is actively involved in efforts to propagate a particular Islamic creed beyond national boundaries. Involvement of the state in patronage of religious activities is by no means a one-way street; the state gains a measure of control over the pronouncements of religious authorities in return for its support.

If Islam plays a well-established role in the Middle Eastern public sphere, it is a role that a majority of the region's Muslims do not contest. In Iran, for example, there is greater support for redefining the role played by public Islam than for secularism as such. Elsewhere in the Middle East, monarchs and presidents alike make public displays of their respect for Islamic values. This identification of a fallible ruler with transcendental authority can create problems in any state, but for most Muslims, a role for Islam in politics means hope for stability, order, public integrity, unity, and social justice, and an accessible language they can invoke to challenge corruption and abuses of power.[31]

In practice, Islam can either empower or disempower a state. By invoking (and arguably misusing) Quranic passages concerning obedience to "those charged with authority among you" (4:59) and the dangers of civil disorder *(fitna),* leaders can reinforce their claims to rule over their subjects and attempt to silence opposition. Citizens nonetheless have recourse to scriptural themes that are equally salient, particularly admonitions against injustice and oppression. Though active support for state policies can sometimes discredit Muslim clerics in the eyes of dissidents, alliances with Middle Eastern regimes have allowed many religious leaders to reinforce their status in society and challenge what they see as deviations from authentic Islamic norms and beliefs. Thus do they participate in a long-standing tradition of Islamic politics, through which the state embraces religious institutions and these institutions, in turn, buttress the state.

A Pessimistic Reading of History

A key premise of classical Islamic thought—a premise that has been shared by all the world's major religious traditions—is that human beings can achieve their full status as moral agents only through adherence to sacred teachings. As understood within the context of Islamic tradition, this has meant that an individual's capacity for moral action is contingent on adherence to divinely revealed ethical standards, especially those of Islam and the "people of the book" (particularly, Judaism and Christianity). By adhering to revealed standards, a human being can reach profound heights of spiritual elevation and virtue. Deviating from the divinely revealed path, however, creates space for ignorance *(jahl),* corruption *(fasad),* civil disorder *(fitna),* and injustice *(zulm).*

Though Islamic teachings reject the concept of original sin and propose that humans are born with a sound nature *(fitra),* historical as well as contemporary exponents of Islamic orthodoxy have typically argued against conceptions of human potential such as those upon which much of modern Western thought is based, particularly the notion of a morally self-defining, rational agent who uses his or her own intellect to differentiate between right and wrong. Though conservative religious understandings of the human condition have been challenged throughout the Middle East by those who have affirmed optimistic notions of progress and by those who have favored material explanations (e.g., Marxism) for human shortcomings, strong support remains for traditional views according to which human freedom (construed as freedom from adversity as well as from sin) is attained only through the constraint of divine law. Such traditional views have been reinforced by perceptions of a gap between precept and practice in the modern Western tradition—for example, discrepancies between ideals of universal human rights and realities of differential treatment according to racial identity, or between stated aspirations toward universal peace and the traumatic recurrence of major wars. Many have taken this as a vindication not only of the traditional Islamic anthropology, but also of more puritanical outlooks predicated on a strongly felt need to reverse moral and political decline.

The latter outlook is especially evident among exponents of the modern *salafi* movement. The *salafi* movement, which has come to be associated with the teachings of austere Muslim preachers such as Muhammad Ibn 'Abdul Wahhab (1703–1792), proposes that Muslims have endured centuries of decline because they have deviated from the standards of the first generations of Muslims, who were companions of the Prophet. By projecting the "pious forebears" *(al-salaf al-salih)* and the first four "rightly guided" caliphs *(al-rashidun)* as the models of Islamic orthopraxis, *salafis* have developed a revivalist perspective that seeks to correct for the perceived errors of past generations by challenging much of traditional Islamic thought, from mysticism and philosophy to classical jurisprudence.[32]

In contrast, mainstream Islamic thought manifests its precautionary view of the human condition in a less revisionist manner, seeking continuity with the legacy of past thinkers. Following the lead of Plato, many early Muslim philosophers believed the mental as well as moral capacities of diverse human beings to be unequal in nature, and posited a strong human need for obedience to authority. Jurists, for their part, have more consistently underscored Quranic passages highlighting the exalted transcendence of God than passages that affirm God's nearness, forgiveness, and love for those who do His will.[33] Historically, such tendencies in the Islamic intellectual tradition provided considerable scope for a hierarchically arranged social order within which prerogatives of leaders received more consideration than the rights of subjects.

Dangers of Political Change

In the twenty-first century no less than in the past, a key concern of those Middle Eastern Muslims who adhere to "peace through coercion" assumptions is that political change could bring anarchy in its wake. This fear tends to be rooted first and foremost in the volatility of present social, economic, and political realities, but also draws upon historical memories and the aforementioned assumptions about human nature. Much more than North America or even Europe, the Middle East remains a region in which historical consciousness is greatly valued among learned individuals, and in which the overall patterns of history are not understood to involve continual progress or constant improvement.

The perception that the present era is not markedly different from the past—and may in some important respects be worse—has a number of important political consequences. First, it correlates with a firm belief in the human propensity for conflict, and in a corresponding conviction about the value of order and stability in social and political relationships. This latter conviction is asserted in social affairs as well as in religious formulations that place a stronger emphasis on behavioral submission than on development of personal capacity for moral reflection. Second, this distrust of progressive notions reinforces cultural collectivism and weakens tendencies toward individual expression. Security for the individual, after all, is not necessarily to be found in the institutions and laws of the state so much as in social networks and kinship groups. Third, doubt about prospects for historical progress reinforces tendencies toward authoritarianism in the political sphere. Fear of anarchy becomes a greater concern than the abuse of power. This concern exists not only among secular elites and ruling classes, but also among traditionally oriented religious leaders who, like members of previous generations who made concessions to political expediency, regard civil discord as a profound threat to religious values.

One should not, however, overstate the role Islamic interpretation plays in the perpetuation of Middle Eastern authoritarianism. There are many factors that have predisposed contemporary Middle Eastern governments to instability, and most of these factors are not unique to the Middle Eastern historical experience. Despite modern tendencies toward secularism in the Christian West (now understood as an outgrowth of the "render unto Caesar" principle), Christianity's reconciliation with democracy is a relatively recent historical phenomenon. Islam's religiously empowered caliphate and sultanate have correlates in Christendom's "Holy Roman Empire" and "divine right of kings," just as contemporary efforts by autocratic governments to co-opt religion bear comparison with patterns of church-state symbiosis that only recently fell into disfavor in Latin America.[34] Given these parallels, analysis should not dwell exclusively on religious doctrines. Broader processes of social, economic, and political change must also be taken into account.

Nonetheless, religious and cultural ideas do have an impact on political realities. The classical political vocabulary is relatively inarticulate with respect to such notions as a "loyal opposition," and conceptions of consultation *(shura)* and consensus *(ijma')* have more often been used by leaders to project a misleading image of harmony than to provide vehicles for political dialogue, accountability, participation in decisionmaking, and the advancement of social justice.

Struggle Against Hostile External Forces

A defining characteristic of the "peace through coercion" paradigm has been an enduring preoccupation with external forces threatening not just the individual Muslim state, but also the larger community of Islam. Whereas, in practice, Muslim dynasties and states in the Middle East as well as in other regions have found themselves in conflict with other Muslim powers at least as often as with non-Muslim communities, the greater emphasis placed on threats from beyond the Islamic world would appear to reflect not only normative concern for fostering Muslim unity, but also the pragmatic interests of regimes intent on maintaining the loyalty of their subjects. By speaking of an ongoing jihad to make the message of Islam known in hostile and presumably benighted lands, past Muslim rulers engaged in a form of posturing that was not entirely different from contemporary Western deliberations about humanitarian intervention and preemptive defense. In the present era, however, the word *jihad* more readily evokes images of self-defense and personal sacrifice in the face of intrusive outsiders. While there are some Muslim thinkers who claim that there has not been a legitimate basis for jihad since the destruction of the Abbasid caliphate in 1258, the concept of vigorous struggle to defend Islamic societies from invasion, occupation, or humiliation nonetheless retains popular resonance—a resonance that figures such as Osama bin Laden have sought to exploit.

For virtually all contemporary Middle Eastern governments, jihad is more a religious category for justifying warfare than an actual framework for policy formulation.[35] While the classical theory is largely defunct—and frequently abused, especially when invoked by nonstate actors—modern formulations of nonviolent or "civic" jihad to advance Muslim societies remain embryonic, and have received little encouragement from Middle Eastern authorities. The idea of defending Muslim states and societies—like the concept of national defense in the West—remains largely military in content, as do conceptions of political power. In practice, a strong emphasis on matters related to security (preventing rebellion, deterring invasion, or, in times past, extending the Islamic "zone of peace") has often reduced the preoccupation of Muslim rulers with social justice and development priorities. In addition to consuming valuable resources, warfare creates conditions during which any ruler—Muslim or non-Muslim—can silence or at least muffle opposition, particularly if the cause is understood to be just.

Peace as Temporary Absence of War

Taken together, these preoccupations and expectations suggest a worldview in which war is "the normal state of things,"[36] and in which peace must be construed minimalistically as a temporary absence of wars and of gross violations of Muslim human rights. Since the classical era, Islamic interpretations that are consistent with this view have construed the Quranic vision of peace as a condition that cannot be fully realized in this world. The result has been an Islamic paradigm that sharply differentiates between religious or spiritual peace *(salam),* a condition of the soul and of paradise, and political peace, the fragile peace or "cease-fire" that can be attained in this world.

In this paradigm, as in the Western paradigm of political realism, prospects for eliminating injustices that fuel conflict are unfavorable. Peace can only be attained through vigilant preparation for war. Like the Roman general who once said, "If you want peace, prepare for war," Muslim statesmen have sometimes invoked a reported saying of the Prophet, "Paradise is under the shades of swords."[37] In other words, the continued existence of goodness and righteousness in the world—indeed, the preservation of Islam and of other revealed religious teachings—can only be maintained through military preparedness. "Did not God check one set of people by means of another," states the Quran, "there would surely have been pulled down monasteries, churches, synagogues, and mosques, in which the name of God is commemorated in abundant measure."[38]

Insofar as it focuses minds on the superior character of the peace that can accompany the afterlife, this view of the world as incorrigibly conflictual and prone to corruption has often been acceptable to religious thinkers. It extrapolates in a plausible manner from Quranic narratives concerning the struggles of the prophets to make their truths known in a hostile world, to the proposition that religion can only survive when backed by political power. If the Prophet Muhammad and his companions had to struggle to survive the military onslaught of pagan Meccan tribes and there is no unequivocal evidence for historical progress, why should contemporary generations of Muslims presume they can avoid such trials?

Conclusion

When analyzing Islamic politics in the Middle East and other regions, it is extremely important to avoid falling into the trap of cultural or religious exceptionalism—the presumption that Islam is fundamentally and irreconcilably different from Christianity or the West on all meaningful indices of comparison, and that it forbids principled or pragmatic compromise with non-Muslims or with the modern world. In many respects, Islamic historical experiences appear similar to those of Western Christianity. Despite doctrinal differences concerning the relationship between religion and politics, exemplified most clearly when mainstream Islamic practices are compared with early Christian and post-Reformation understandings of the "render unto Caesar what is Caesar's and unto God what is God's" principle, both traditions are marked by historical experiences in which the use and abuse of religious symbols by political authorities has played a marked role. Both traditions have recognized the importance of connecting spiritual values with public life, and both have experienced the danger that can arise when those who wield power are free to justify contingent political decisions on the basis of absolute values and confidently assert that their own sovereignty upholds the sovereignty of God. When political and religious authority is fully delegated to a particular individual or group, the exercise of that authority can easily grow unaccountable.

Significantly, both Islamic and Christian "just war" traditions regulating the use of force have a mixed record. Although these traditions have on some occasions constrained leaders by holding them accountable to religious criteria, they have also been utilized by heads of state in a manner that is more symbolic and rhetorical than substantive and disciplined. Norms regulating the resort to war respond to needs of the religious conscience for a morally accountable framework of self-defense, yet the habits of political leaders can deprive these codes of their content. As the cases explored in this chapter suggest, just war traditions tend to be more elegant in precept than in practice. Calculations of just cause are rarely objective and disinterested, and once the furies of war are unleashed, they become quite difficult to contain. Chronic gaps between precept and practice lead to the development of competing and at least partially secularized intellectual frameworks, within which the exercise of power is understood to have "its own logic" and unavoidable demands. In the West, this outlook is reflected in a school of thought known as "political realism" or "power politics"; in the Islamic world, similar ideas have been entertained by Ibn Khaldun, authors of the "Mirrors for Princes" literatures, and—at least tacitly—by those members of the ulama who have practiced deference toward caliphs and sultans as well as modern kings and presidents.[39] Muslim radicals also embrace this logic of power when, in the pursuit of authority or their own understanding of substantive justice, they abandon Islamic moral restraints on the use of military force and become inextricably entangled in the same undisciplined struggles for preeminence that they once criticized.

Like the Bible, the Quran upholds a vision of the human condition that is both hopeful and demanding. This vision includes what Muslims have understood as a realistic assessment of human capacities for destructive behavior, and it was to control or challenge such tendencies that political thinkers developed a "peace through coercion" tradition—a state-centric framework of thought and practice that privileges military-political concerns, underscores potential for inter-Muslim and intercommunal strife, empowers leaders, and presents a view of the human condition in which use of force is often necessary to create social order and maintain security.

Historically, the "peace through coercion" paradigm has reflected central concerns of Muslim elites, and of those members of the educated classes who have worked closely with the political leadership. In its earliest formulations, it offered a framework for dealing with the rapid ascent of the Muslim community to power in the Middle East and beyond, and provided guidelines for relations with non-Muslim states and Muslim "rebels." Later, it provided a means of coping with the gradual decentralization and fragmentation of Muslim political power after the decline of the Abbasid caliphate and the rise of sultans. As an approach to peace, present manifestations of the "peace through coercion" tradition prescribe acceptance of a competitive international order, and continue to posit a central role for military force in politics, as well as a metaphorical correspondence between the divine-human and sovereign-subject authority relationships. Among those who tacitly or explicitly accept key premises of the paradigm, relations between the earthly sovereign and his subjects are characterized by strong expectations of loyalty and a tradition of patriarchal order that is understood to have a protective function. Strong authority is regarded as necessary to safeguard Islamic teachings and enforce collective discipline.

In the contemporary world, the "peace through coercion" paradigm for Islamic political culture supplies a framework of legitimacy utilized by many states. According to this paradigm, leaders proclaim a desire to provide security and advance collective Muslim interests, and in turn expect to receive support and deference from their populace and from religious leaders. Peace is understood to depend on obedience to duly constituted authority, which preserves unity and keeps enemies at home and abroad at bay. Justice is embodied in the personality of the leader and in his personal strivings more than in institutions and in equitably observed norms of public accountability. The greatest threats to order and justice are understood to derive from external rather than internal sources; these threats limit prospects for international cooperation and domestic political reform. A constant theme of the "peace through coercion" paradigm is the need for strong leadership in the defense of society; the recurrence of threats means that real and enduring peace has more to do with the afterlife than with political relationships in this world.

Whatever merits the "peace through coercion" paradigm can legitimately claim for creating order and defending collective interests, critics point out that the paradigm fails to do justice to more hopeful and life-affirming visions that can be found within Islamic sources and historical traditions. Some have argued that traditional approaches to politics have stifled social justice aspirations in the name of order, effectively elevating security above all other values.[40] The paradigm contains many admonitions against dissension and civil conflict, but provides little guidance on how the energies of civil society might be unleashed in a way that contributes to lasting social betterment and new bonds of affinity among nations.[41] Because a great deal of license is granted to leaders to protect society and religious norms as they see fit, Islamic values can be invoked by a state without actually being implemented, for the sake of augmenting state power or dynastic authority, and marginalizing political opposition through challenges to the loyalty or religious legitimacy of adversaries. In international relations as well as in domestic politics, the "peace through coercion" paradigm can encourage efforts to portray rivals—be they Muslim or non-Muslim—as opponents of Islam. Opposition forces also make ready use of this tactic, often in response to political repression.[42]

"Peace through coercion" represents only one of several paradigms for Islamic politics, and fails to gain the assent of many committed Muslims when stated in formal and explicit terms. *Practices* linked to the paradigm may generate much emotional interest, yet more formal *theories* highlighting the veiled realities of power politics rarely satisfy. The persistence of this paradigm depends to some extent on a gap between elite practices and popular perceptions. Because the paradigm is at least partially implicated with many recurrent problems of the Middle Eastern state system—including democratic deficits, maldistribution of resources, economic underperformance, competition for Arab or Islamic leadership, overmilitarization of politics, and failure to provide open channels for loyal opposition and active political participation—much would appear to depend on the strengthening of Islamic frameworks that are less disempowering of Muslim citizens, and that provide guidance for fuller realization of Islamic values that pertain to peace.

Notes

1. al-Haqq, "Fatwa Against the Iraqi Invasion of Kuwait," 2002, p. 247.
2. Quoted in Piscatori, *Islamic Fundamentalisms and the Gulf Crisis,* 1991, p. 6.
3. Hussein, "Call for Jihad," 2002, p. 239.
4. Piscatori, *Islamic Fundamentalisms and the Gulf Crisis,* 1991, p. 9.
5. Bush, "President's Remarks at the 2004 Republican National Convention."
6. See Abou El Fadl, *Speaking in God's Name,* 2001.
7. Islamic tradition makes a distinction between utterances of the Prophet Muhammad that were understood to be divinely inspired revelations and those that reflected his human efforts to impart wisdom to the community. The former provided the text of the Quran, while the latter became the basis of an extensive *hadith* literature—volumes of prophetic sayings that were collected and recorded by subsequent generations of Muslims.
8. Quran 96:1.
9. See, for example, Quran 2:218, 9:20, and 9:81. Direct and explicit Quranic references to warfare (for example, 2:190, 4:74, and 4:84) use verbs connected to the noun *qital* (literally, "fighting" or "combat") rather than to *jihad.*
10. Quran 2:190, 2:194, 4:90.
11. Quran 2:192–193, 8:61.
12. Quran 4:75 ("And why should you not fight in the cause of God and of those who, being weak, are ill-treated—men, women, and children whose cry is, 'Our Lord! Rescue us from this town, whose people are oppressors, and raise for us from You one who will help'"); 2:190 ("Fight in the cause of God those who fight you").
13. Ramadan, *In the Footsteps of the Prophet,* 2007, pp. 201–202.
14. A *hadith* that has often been used to support this distinction states, "The most excellent jihad is that for the conquest of self" (cited in Suhrawardy, *The Sayings of Muhammad,* 1990, p. 63). According to this tradition, the "greater" jihad is the struggle to subdue base passions and behave in an exemplary manner.
15. For a critique of ideas about war and peace that were developed during the Abbasid era (750–1258), see Safi, "War and Peace in Islam," 1988. See also Hashmi, "Interpreting the Islamic Ethics of War and Peace," 1996.
16. See, for example, Tariq Ramadan's commentary on the reported rejection of Muslim emissaries by Byzantine and Persian leaders in *To Be a European Muslim* (1999), p. 124.
17. For a discussion of classical usage of these terms and debates about their contemporary relevance, see Ramadan, *To Be a European Muslim,* 1999, pp. 123–131.
18. Khadduri, *War and Peace in the Law of Islam,* 1955, p. 13.
19. Quran 3:159, 42:38.
20. Black, *The History of Islamic Political Thought,* 2001, pp. 108–114; Lambton, "Islamic Mirrors for Princes," 1971, pp. 419–442.
21. Butterworth, *Alfarabi, the Political Writings,* 2001.
22. See Peters, *Islam and Colonialism,* 1979, pp. 90–91.
23. Guilmartin, "Ideology and Conflict," 1988, esp. p. 726. The Ottomans were

not the first to conceive of the Islamic polity in such terms; for earlier notions such as a "circle of power" predicated on just rule, see Black, *The History of Islamic Political Thought,* 2001, pp. 54, 111–112, 126–127.

24. Christians and Jews often (but not always) fared relatively well under Ottoman rule, despite the lack of equal civic status under the *millet* system. For example, Sephardic Jews expelled from Spain after the Reconquista sought refuge in Ottoman and other Muslim lands, and Ottoman architecture owes a great deal to contributions from the Armenian Christian community. Tragically, coexistence lost ground to ethnic conflict during the nineteenth century as imperial setbacks led many nationalists to regard minority communities as members of a fifth column. The point of total collapse was reached during World War I, when the new Young Turk government accused the Armenian people of treason and sought to bring about their expulsion and elimination. See Walker, *Armenia,* 1990.

25. Sharabi, *Nationalism and Revolution in the Arab World,* 1966, p. 93.

26. For commentary on nationalism and Islam in a Persian context, see Hunter, *Iran in the World,* 1990, pp. 11–14.

27. All Arab constitutions except the constitution of Lebanon list Islam as the national religion. The constitutions of Egypt, Yemen, Oman, and Kuwait describe Islamic law *(sharia)* as a primary source of legislation. Saudi Arabia's basic law describes the Quran and prophetic tradition as the authentic constitution of the state.

28. For a discussion of religious themes evoked during the Iran-Iraq War, see Hjarpe, "Historiography and Islamic Vocabulary in War and Peace," 1997.

29. For further discussion of how these events have affected the Iraqi people, see Ismael and Ismael, *The Iraqi Predicament,* 2004; Hooglund, "The Other Face of War," 1991.

30. Black, *The History of Islamic Political Thought,* 2001, p. 54.

31. From the beginning, Islamic rule was expected to have a *contractual* basis. The sovereign was to exercise power representing both the will of the community and the traditions of the Prophet. After experiences with political turmoil, de facto monarchy, and invasion, some Muslim thinkers began to preoccupy themselves with duties of obedience to a sovereign who fulfilled certain basic minimum requirements with respect to the *sharia.* Islamic values nonetheless retain significant potential in calls for accountability and social justice—a theme we explore in the next chapter.

32. Abou El Fadl, *Speaking in God's Name,* 2001, pp. 174–176. In many respects, contemporary *salafi* religiosity bears comparison to strains of early Protestantism explored by Michael Walzer in *The Revolution of the Saints* (1969).

33. Murata, *The Tao of Islam,* 1992, pp. 9, 70.

34. Casanova, "Civil Society and Religion," 2001.

35. In *Islam and Colonialism* (1979), Rudolph Peters argues that "today the jihad call has become a slogan based on national (political) considerations" (p. 158).

36. Safi, "War and Peace in Islam," 1988, p. 31.

37. *Sahih Bukhari,* vol. 4, bk. 52, no. 73.

38. Quran 22:40.

39. For an account of past Muslim debates on the tension between ideal Islamic norms and pragmatic political ethics *(siyasa),* see Khalidi, *Arabic Historical Thought in the Classical Period,* 1994, pp. 191–200, 222–231.

40. Enayat, *Modern Islamic Political Thought,* 1982, p. 12.

41. These challenges are central themes in Fergani et al., *The Arab Human Development Report 2002.*

42. Hafez, *Why Muslims Rebel,* 2003.

5

Peace Through Equity: Islamic Perspectives on a Just and Cooperative World Order

> O you who believe: Be steadfast in your devotion to God and bear witness impartially: do not let hatred of others lead you away from justice, but adhere to justice, for that is closer to awareness of God.
>
> —Quran 5:8

In its formal, institutional characteristics, the contemporary state system in the Middle East differs profoundly from the order that prevailed prior to the advent of Western colonial rule. Between Napoleon's invasion of Egypt in 1798 and the end of World War II in 1945, the region's Muslim polities were absorbed by the European state system and economy through imperialism and colonialism. Only Iran and the Anatolian heartland of the Ottoman Empire were not subjected to direct rule from the West. As a result, the region was changed forever, and though pan-Islamic as well as pan-Arab themes were prominent in anti-imperialist struggles, actual campaigns for freedom were fought locally. When European powers withdrew, they left behind state institutions derived from their own historical experiences.

The modern Middle Eastern state system may be described, without much exaggeration, as the illegitimate progeny of the Peace of Westphalia. The Peace of Westphalia, enacted in 1648 to put an end to thirty years of religious and geopolitical warfare in northern Europe, created a sharp disjuncture in the history of the European state system. In substance, it amounted to an effort to secularize international politics by nationalizing religion and more firmly institutionalizing the sovereign territorial state. By recognizing the sovereign statehood of principalities that had long been subject to the Holy Roman Empire and affirming the right of rulers to determine the Catholic or Protestant religious orientation of their polity, the Peace of Westphalia struck a direct blow to the medieval notion of a united Christian Europe secured through allegiance to a particular dynasty.

After the Peace of Westphalia, political legitimacy was increasingly based on local nationalism, and the logic of international relations became increasingly secular. This reduced the power of the Catholic Church and eased some of the religious tensions brought on by the Protestant Reformation, yet it also cleared the way for a competitive, "balance of power" system that resulted in increasingly destructive wars among sovereign states that unabashedly placed their own immediate interests above common interests and values.

The peoples of the Middle East entered the Westphalian state system as objects of European competition for overseas colonies. The institutions they inherited from colonizing powers reflected the norms of a different political culture than that to which they had long been accustomed. Although many former subjects of the Ottoman Empire welcomed its dissolution after World War I, the process through which this breakup occurred was beyond the control of the vast majority of Middle Eastern peoples. European modernity was imposed, leaving Middle Eastern peoples with the challenge of adapting to changes that were not of their own devising. At a time when Britain and France were establishing administrative control over Palestine, Jordan, Iraq, Syria, and Lebanon, Turkish modernizer Kemal Ataturk's abolition of the caliphate was experienced by many of the region's Muslims as a direct challenge not merely to the endangered ideal of Muslim unity, but also to Islam itself.

Middle Eastern states were born with an identity crisis. Their illegitimate Westphalian parentage created problems that the secular idioms of Turkish, Arab, and Persian nationalism have not yet solved. Setbacks related to the Arab-Israeli conflict, inequitable development, and misgovernance have further undermined the legitimacy of nationalism and augmented interest in Islam as an alternative basis for national and international politics.

Viewed through Westphalian lenses, the increasing prominence of Islam in Middle Eastern politics is a theoretical anomaly. However, imposing expectations derived from the European experience distracts attention from the cultural and historical realities of the Middle East. Because there is no equivalent of a centralized Catholic Church in Islam, religious reform or modernization is unlikely to result in the kind of fragmentation that accompanied the Reformation and Counter-Reformation in Europe. The most significant religious divide, between Sunni and Shia Muslims, has existed for centuries without undermining the appeal of Islamic unity as an ideal objective. Bonds of religious solidarity remain strong throughout the region, and among Arabs the language through which political relations are contracted is also the language of religious scripture—another significant difference from the European experience, in which Latin's status as the international language of educated discourse was rapidly declining by the time of the Peace of Westphalia. When these factors are considered in relation to the traditional Islamic affirmation of communal unity and a corresponding devaluation of interest- or ethnicity-based politics, it appears far more appropriate to ask *what kind of role* Islam will play in regional politics than to ask how soon Middle Eastern politics will resemble those of Europe.

In the contemporary Middle East, Islam remains a primary language through which Muslims project their political identities and concerns. In addition to its social functions, Islam serves a practical role in politics by offering recourse to a transcendental order to which the leaders can be held accountable. Islam offers a vocabulary of resistance to corruption and repression, and a vocabulary of hope for a cultural future in which religious standards of justice can find expression. In contrast to the West, where secularism is typically associated with an expansion of individual freedom, prosperity, and the cultivation of a religiously neutral public sphere, many peoples in the Middle East have come to associate secularism with increases in state repression and constriction of civil society.[1] State-led modernization efforts, even when sincerely intended to catalyze national progress, have heightened centralized control over social and economic life while failing to generate genuine participation in decisionmaking processes. Aspirations for justice and social change are often expressed in an Islamic vocabulary.

As a system of values and ideal norms, Islam provides encouragement for cooperation among Muslim-majority states and enjoins mutual support in cases of adversity. Yet as an ethical system infused with notions such as the unity of humankind, the Islamic heritage can also be mobilized in ways that support the emergence of a more equitable world community. Among Muslims as well as among Westerners, it is not difficult to find a profound sense of weariness with "power politics" paradigms, and a desire for forms of interaction predicated on common standards, appreciation of diversity, and respect for human dignity. The American Muslim imam Feisal Abdul Rauf relates this sentiment to a strong desire among many of the world's Muslims to "be included as a full, welcome member in the family of humankind, meriting equal treatment."[2] By choosing to retain Islam as a frame of reference, Muslims are not necessarily rejecting the appeal of broader forms of human belonging. They are, however, seeking to meet the world on their own terms, by retrieving a clear sense of collective identity and solidarity as they face challenges such as managing political insecurity and reconciling tradition with modernity.

While it is true that some revisionist Muslim thinkers desire a world order in which the current distribution of power between Islam and the West is reversed rather than merely balanced, many Muslims have directed their intellectual as well as practical energies toward ideals of a more genuinely equitable world order within which their values can be accommodated. Though responsive to popular perceptions and grievances, the Islamic discourse articulated by diplomats in multilateral forums tends to mirror this latter conception of Islam, as a moral framework that calls for a just and cooperative world order to which religious pluralism is integral. Such an understanding of Islam is also prevalent among contemporary Islamic reformists, who are seeking to direct the communalistic energies associated with popular Islamic revivalism toward mature forms of expression that facilitate Islamic-Western understanding and cooperation.

Islam in Contemporary Multilateralism

The continuing prominence of Islam in the public life of predominantly Muslim countries is reflected not only in debates about domestic policies but also in deliberations over international affairs. Since the collapse of the Ottoman Empire, Muslim civic and political leaders have sought new ways of manifesting Islamic identity on the global stage, and have formulated multiple approaches to multilateral cooperation—especially but not exclusively among Muslim states. While some voices have indeed appealed for a resurrection of past institutions such as the caliphate, others have aspired to forge a new Islamic "subsystem" within the broader international system, in which Islamic values and solidarities can play a heightened role and find expression at such forums as the United Nations. These activities merit attention as part of a larger dialogue among Muslims concerning the nature of the present world order and the bases for international cooperation.

When Kemal Ataturk abolished the Ottoman caliphate on March 3, 1924, and officially transferred its powers to the Turkish Grand National Assembly, an era of Islamic history came to a close. For centuries, Muslims had accommodated themselves to a largely symbolic caliphate, as a consequence of the political decentralization of the Abbasid Empire and its eventual collapse in 1258. After the Mongol conquest, the caliphate's political significance faded dramatically; descendants of the Abbasid caliphs sought refuge in Cairo and claimed the title until the Ottoman conquest of 1517, but were able to do little more than provide religious legitimacy to the Mamluk dynasty, which was ruling Egypt and the Levant at the time. The Ottomans claimed the caliphate only intermittently, after first inducing the Abbasid descendant Al-Mutawakkil III to renounce all claims of Muslim leadership.

Since the dissolution of the Ottoman caliphate, efforts to reestablish this classical Islamic institution have been ineffectual. Sharif Hussein, a former governor of Mecca, claimed the title *amir al-mu'minin* ("prince" or "commander" of the faithful) two days after the Ottoman caliphate's abolition, but few rallied to his cause. The man who had led the Arab Revolt during World War I was soon driven from his lands by King Abdul Aziz Ibn Sa'ud, founder of modern Saudi Arabia. Transnational conferences intended to reestablish the caliphate were met with failure, and for many years the idea of reviving the institution as a vehicle for Muslim unity was overshadowed by the rise of non-Islamic political ideologies.

The eclipse of pan-Islamic frameworks for collective action corresponded with a tremendous upsurge in the dynamism of ethnic nationalisms. Modern Turkey was reborn from the ashes of the multiethnic Ottoman Empire, while Arab nationalism became a primary vehicle for rallying against European colonialism in North Africa and the Levant. As a primarily Shia country, Iran was not deeply affected by the demise of the Sunni caliphate, yet the rise of nationalism in other lands only reinforced the Persian nation-building efforts of Reza Shah Pahlavi, a Russian-trained general in Iran's army who took power in 1925.

Given the widespread diffusion of Arab peoples throughout North Africa, the Levant, and the Arabian Peninsula, Arab nationalism was an inherently transnational enterprise. As European colonialism receded, newly sovereign Arab states were quick to found the League of Arab States in March 1945 as a vehicle for international solidarity as well as for the coordination of policies pertaining to economic and social integration, communications, cultural affairs, and health. However, ideals of Arab unity spread more rapidly than the political will for compromise among Arab leaders, and cooperation to advance common social and educational goals has often proved far easier than collaboration on issues that are more closely linked to national interest or security. Even potent symbolic issues such as the status of Palestine have aroused dissension as well as agreement.

Doctrines of Arab nationalism, like those of Turkish and Persian nationalism, were influenced by secular thinkers who perceived Islam as a heritage and source of national pride, but not as a primary source of political identity.[3] Protagonists of Middle Eastern ethnic nationalisms sought to create modern nation-states in the region by introducing new institutions and principles of social mobilization. Arab nationalism, however, differed from Persian and Turkish nationalism insofar as the linguistically based community it projected was extremely difficult to reconcile with emerging state boundaries, and posed a direct challenge to the territorial status quo.

While Arab nationalism remains a potent source of political identity throughout the Middle East, recent decades have witnessed a strengthening of local, state-based identities (for example, Jordanian, Kuwaiti, or Moroccan identity) and of state-transcending Islamic identities. To some extent, Islamic identity negates state- and ethnicity-based identities, for example when Islamic activists seek to forge transnational alliances or challenge the ideological bases of secular states such as Algeria, Egypt, or Syria. At the same time, Islamic loyalties have often proved compatible with a sense of pride in ethnic and national history. Arab leaders deliberating over policy toward the Arab-Israeli conflict, for example, have focused a great deal of attention on the status of Muslim holy places, particularly Al-Aqsa Mosque and the Dome on the Rock. These latter structures, which rest atop the area Jews and Christians refer to as Temple Mount, are believed by Muslims to mark places visited by the Prophet Muhammad during a visionary night journey in the month of Ramadan.

Though original Arab League declarations responding to the question of Palestine were couched in the secular language of national rights,[4] the historical and religious significance of Jerusalem (Al-Quds) among Muslims was an extremely important factor in determining regional responses to conflict between the Palestinian and Zionist national movements. This response became more explicitly religious after the June 1967 Arab-Israeli War, which resulted in Israeli occupation of East Jerusalem and the West Bank as well as the Gaza Strip and the Golan Heights. The shocking defeat of three Arab states—Egypt, Syria, and Jordan—by Israeli forces was a tremendous setback to secular Arab nationalism, and provided impetus for a popular turn toward more conservative and religious bases of collective identity. When the Al-Aqsa Mosque was damaged in an arson attack on August 21, 1969, Muslim political leaders in the Middle East and beyond responded by convening an international "Islamic summit conference" in Rabat, Morocco, that would lead to the founding of a new international organization, the Organization of the Islamic Conference (OIC). Widespread Muslim perceptions of incapacity in the face of the Israeli-Palestinian impasse and concerns for the integrity of Islamic shrines became the basis for the modern world's first faith-based intergovernmental organization.

The officially stated purpose of the OIC was to safeguard Muslim interests and advance the well-being of Muslim peoples. The charter of the OIC, formulated in 1972, defines the organization's primary goals in the following terms:

1. To promote Islamic solidarity among member-states.
2. To consolidate cooperation among member-states in the economic, social, cultural, scientific and other vital fields of activities, and facilitate consultation among member-states in international organizations.
3. To endeavour to eliminate racial segregation and discrimination and to eradicate colonialism in all its forms.
4. To take necessary measures to support international peace and security founded on justice.
5. To coordinate efforts for the safeguard[ing] of the Holy Places and support of the people of Palestine, and help them regain their rights and liberate their land.
6. To strengthen the struggle of all Muslim peoples with a view to safeguarding their dignity, independence, and national rights.
7. To create a suitable atmosphere for the promotion of cooperation and understanding among member-states and other countries.[5]

This brief statement of goals was intended to provide a basis for institutionalized cooperation among the world's predominantly Muslim states. Two dozen states were represented at the September 1969 summit in Morocco, and by 2001 fifty-seven states had become members, representing approximately 1.3 billion Muslims. The officially stated goals of the organization reflect both "world order" concerns that were at the center of international political discussions ("to endeavor to eliminate racial segregation and discrimination and to eradicate colonialism"; "to take necessary measures to support international peace and security founded on justice") and concerns that are more specifically Islamic or Middle Eastern ("safeguard the Holy Places and support of the people of Palestine"; "to strengthen the struggle of all Muslim peoples").

Operationally, the OIC functions much like regional international organizations that are not religiously based. The organization has a permanent secretariat located in Jeddah, Saudi Arabia, and a number of standing committees and subsidiary organizations that carry out programs to advance cooperation in a variety of fields, from economics, trade, development, and exchange of technical knowledge, to the advancement of education and transmission of Islamic culture. Every three years the OIC sponsors the Islamic Summit Conference of Kings and Heads of State and Government; the Islamic Conference of Foreign Ministers occurs on an annual basis. The OIC is represented at the United Nations by a permanent delegation, and its own meetings are regularly attended by observers from the United Nations, the Non-Aligned Movement, the League of Arab States, and the Organization of African Unity.

As an intergovernmental organization based on religious identity, the OIC plays a rather unique role in the international system. On the one hand, it is engaged with efforts to bolster religious solidarity, strengthen Islamic cultural identity, advance the collective interests of Muslim peoples, and draw attention to specific Muslim causes. On the other hand, the OIC seeks to participate within the larger international order, in a manner consistent with the advancement of Islamic interests and values.[6]

The particularistic aspect of the OIC is most readily apparent in the considerable attention it gives to such powerful symbolic issues as the future of holy places in East Jerusalem and the status of the Palestinian people. On such issues, the OIC seeks to develop shared positions and amplify the influence of Muslim states in international forums. In some respects the OIC can even be regarded as a modern substitute for the traditional caliphate, in which authority is shared jointly by leaders of predominantly Muslim states.

At the same time, the OIC seeks to articulate Islamic values and norms in a way that is responsive to broader, ecumenical conversations about international relations and human rights. The OIC charter and other major announcements have articulated a conception of peace predicated on justice that invites dialogue with non-Islamic value systems and discussion of ways in which contemporary international law might be applied to settle long-standing disputes.

The OIC has sought to intervene in many international conflicts, from the Iran-Iraq War and turmoil-stricken Afghanistan to the standoff following Saddam Hussein's invasion of Kuwait. The organization has also pushed for international action on issues affecting disadvantaged Muslim groups such as the Palestinians and Bosnian Muslims. To date, OIC conciliation efforts in conflicts among Muslims have generated only mixed results, although the organization did play a significant role in shaping international consensus concerning the Soviet invasion of Afghanistan in 1979.[7]

No conflict has drawn more consistent OIC attention than the Israeli-Palestinian conflict. Though political rhetoric at OIC meetings is rarely conciliatory toward the state of Israel, official positions have tended to cleave closely to United Nations Security Council resolutions and a "land for peace" formula that would involve Israeli withdrawal from lands occupied during the 1967 war, the establishment of a Palestinian capital in East Jerusalem, and recognition of a "right of return" for Palestinian refugees. An April 2004 "Declaration on Palestine" issued by the OIC's Al-Quds (Jerusalem) committee officially endorsed the peace plan articulated by Arab League members at a 2002 Beirut meeting, as well as other frameworks such as the "Road Map" sponsored by the United States, the European Union, Russia, and the United Nations.[8]

Critics of the OIC have argued that its functions are more symbolic than practical. On the issue of terrorism, for example, member states have been unable to arrive at a consensus position that would be regarded as "satisfactory" in Western contexts, without clauses implying exceptions for "movements of national liberation." With respect to conflicts among Muslim countries within and beyond the Middle East, the OIC has seldom received adequate empowerment from member states to make a significant difference. In recent decades Middle Eastern diplomats have demonstrated greater confidence in the International Court of Justice at The Hague than the good offices of regional organizations such as the OIC. Like the Arab League, the OIC lacks legal mechanisms for institutionalized dispute settlement processes; distrust among leaders ensures greater candor in bilateral negotiations between Middle Eastern states than in multilateral forums.[9] Arab-Israeli conflict and contests for national leadership have often overshadowed other issues, including substantive, proactive technical cooperation among member states. Furthermore, the OIC represents states rather than citizens, a fact that raises legitimate questions about the extent to which positions taken by the organization manifest both Islamic precepts and the preferences of diverse Muslim populations.

Shortcomings notwithstanding, supporters can legitimately claim that, as a multilateral organization dedicated to furthering the interests and values of Muslim states, the OIC remains relevant. The OIC's Islamic Solidarity Fund and Islamic Development Bank have become major international actors in their respective fields of relief and development finance,[10] and the organization appears to be providing an outlet for a genuine desire among Muslims in the Middle East and other regions to see state leaders acting in ways that reaffirm commitments to Islamic solidarity. The constituencies served by the OIC arguably share a more "real" sense of community than those served by many regional intergovernmental organizations such as the Association of Southeast Asian Nations or the Organization of American States. There would appear to be a strong desire among a large proportion of the world's Muslims to have Muslim governments engaged in cooperative activities in the cultural, technical, and political domains, and working to amplify "Islamic voices" in international forums.

Whatever its level of practical efficacy, the OIC provides an example of how contemporary Islam is being articulated as an integrated cultural, religious, and political framework—as a "particular universalism" that contrasts with other modern cultural and ideological systems such as Western liberalism and socialism. A prime example of this can be seen in the Cairo Declaration on Human Rights in Islam (CDHRI), adopted at the nineteenth Islamic Conference of Foreign Ministers of the OIC on August 5, 1990. Although it does not explicitly negate the Universal Declaration of Human Rights (UDHR), and in many respects can be read as a Muslim response to this charter document in the international human rights movement, the CDHRI asserts that, for Muslims, final authority on issues of human rights derives from *sharia* law. Like the UDHR, the CDHRI affirms universal human dignity, forbids discrimination based on race, sex, belief, and political affiliation, and prohibits torture as well as slavery. Unlike the UDHR, the CDHRI seeks to ground human rights discourse in a context of revelation and divine sovereignty; provisions concerning traditional gender roles (with a specifically stated male responsibility to support the family) and the nature of religious freedom have generated controversy in the international human rights field. With respect to religion, the CDHRI guarantees freedom of practice but does not cover freedom to change religions or express unorthodox beliefs—a consequential distinction that is highly problematic from the standpoint of the UDHR.[11]

Documents such as the CDHRI indicate that consensus on universality in the field of human rights is likely to prove elusive for some time to come. While the CDHRI arguably provides enhanced leverage for Muslim human rights advocacy in a number of key areas, its areas of divergence with the UDHR point to the need not just for Islamic-Western dialogue, but also for attentiveness to contemporary debates over Islamic interpretation.

The Ethos of a "Middle People"

Among "mainstream" Middle Eastern Muslims, Islam is typically understood as a message of universal moral accountability that seeks to unite humanity rather than divide it. This message includes not only specific ritual and legal prescriptions for those who follow the way of the Prophet Muhammad, but also a broader ethical and theological appeal. Interpreters of the Quran who highlight its inclusivity point to passages stating that a messenger was sent to every people, and stipulating that salvation is possible for all who believe in God, do good works, and believe in a day of reckoning—in other words, for all those who comply with the universal existential imperative of religious teaching: surrender to a divine reality that transcends the human ego.[12]

One of the more important Quranic concepts for understanding Muslim identity is that of a "middle people" *(umma wasata).*[13] This idea is illustrative of a well-established tradition of Islamic thought on matters of world order and religious pluralism. According to this tradition, the task of Muslims is not to replace all other communities, but rather to act as witnesses within the world who enjoin justice and renounce idolatry not only in matters of religious worship, but also in their values and actions. As a "middle people," Muslims occupy a position that may be regarded as midway between "East" and "West," and are also expected to act with moderation and balance in all affairs, including politics. They have a vital and dynamic role to play, upholding an inclusive rather than particularistic standard of justice. From a cosmopolitan Islamic standpoint, peace is not an exclusively eschatological affair pertaining to the afterlife, nor is it a mere absence of war or turmoil. Peace is a state of balance and equilibrium attainable through justice and adherence to religious principles.

The triumph of Islam in seventh-century Arabia has long been understood by Muslims as the advent of a just world order. This advent involved (1) the delivery of a clear, final divine message with practical instructions for integrating spirituality with all aspects of human life; (2) transformation of a fractious reality of competing Arab tribes into a coherent and ethical political entity; (3) the replacement of an exploitative economic system characterized by hoarding and callousness toward the weak with an economic order defined by concern for the needs of society's weakest members; and (4) the decline of an unjust international system dominated by the feuding Byzantine and Sassanian empires and the rise of a new Islamic polity that promised to bring order and security. While many Muslims are quick to concede that this "just world order" was short-lived—a problematic system of dynastic rule began with the fifth caliph—the idea that Islam seeks peace through equity and justice has often been championed by Muslim intellectuals and indeed by ordinary believers.

Western and Islamic views of the early Arab conquests are likely always to differ—one side's "preemptive defense," after all, is another's aggression—but it is important for outsiders to recognize that, in Muslim historical narratives, Islam is understood to have been a progressive, tolerant, and civilizing force with binding rules constraining injustice and wanton violence. Such understandings of Islam as a "religion of peace" are based on the premise that Islam challenges root causes of human violence such as egotism, tribalism, racism, and nationalism as well as economic exploitation, and brings security and well-being to humankind through the establishment of justice. Even a cursory reading of the Quran reveals numerous injunctions concerning the importance of social justice in society, together with passages such as the following, which stipulates that the requirements of just conduct are binding in all situations, even when self-interest might appear to dictate otherwise: "O you who believe: Stand out firmly for justice, as witnesses to God, even if it is against yourselves, your parents, or your kin."[14]

Such conceptions of Islam are evident both in popular Muslim discourse and in political and diplomatic pronouncements such as the Cairo Declaration on Human Rights in Islam. Although not always dominant in practice (domestic practices are often less progressive than pronouncements issued in diplomatic contexts), these understandings reflect more than mere politeness in the presence of "others"; they say much about how Muslim communities see themselves, and about a pattern in Islamic belief in which peace is more than an absence of war. They are reflective of a worldview in which Islamic revelation holds a privileged position without negating the possibility of "divinely inspired" sources of morality in other cultures.

In an Islamic context, affirmation of human rights evokes a tradition of egalitarianism in which human equality before law is combined with a strong communitarian exhortation to group solidarity. *Hadiths* of the Prophet Muhammad support an ethos of human equality in the face of the Creator, without regard for external criteria such as race or social status.[15] Though there are also Islamic traditions that exist in tension with this egalitarianism, the idea of equality before God is strongly felt among Muslims. Equality of believers, in turn, becomes a basis for solidarity, binding the community together for the benefit of both the individual and the collective.

A central theme in Islamic thought has long been the imperative of social justice. Muslim egalitarianism and communitarianism are understood to include redistributive mechanisms through which the prosperous provide for the basic needs of the poor in a manner that ensures their ability to live with dignity *(karama)*. Religious teachings condemn conspicuous displays of accumulated wealth, and call for efforts to safeguard the well-being of the needy, orphans, and wayfarers. Providing for the needy is a religious obligation, fulfilled through mandatory taxation as well as through voluntary donations; failure of Muslim states to fulfill the demands of social justice is a major theme raised by contemporary Islamic movements, as Larbi Sadiki notes in a discussion of beliefs behind Islamic activism in a number of Middle Eastern countries. These movements base their challenges to governmental authority on claims about the ideal structure of Muslim social and political life:

> The [first] caliphs . . . made it their job to inquire about the welfare of their people, ensuring that all were reasonably fed and clad. Their example . . . is worth following because they had the wisdom to realize that living below poverty disturbs religiosity, civility, and stability. Accordingly . . . anything that impinges on the believers' *karama* [dignity] and upsets the moral and social fabric of society . . . must be opposed.[16]

It has become commonplace among specialists on Islamic politics to note that the traditional Muslim understanding of community *(umma)* cannot easily be reconciled with the modern nation-state system. As noted in the previous chapter, appeals to pan-Islamic solidarity may at times serve the interest of narrowly based regimes. Nonetheless, a sense of communal belonging is sincerely felt by ordinary Muslims, and is encouraged by the Quran and the *hadith.* Communal solidarity—beyond ethnicity, kinship, and race—is one of the most widely celebrated Islamic virtues, from the time of the Prophet to the present day. Muslims are commanded to treat one another with justice and respect, as a prerequisite for fulfilling their community's dispensation in the world. Quranic verses, together with the tremendous political success experienced by the early Muslim community, have guaranteed an enduring consciousness of communal responsibility as a sacred norm. According to conventional narratives, Muslims were triumphant against great odds when they maintained unity—first against their Meccan oppressors and then against the reigning superpowers of the seventh century—and experienced setbacks at times of internal division. During times of unity, justice prevailed, and during times of division, Muslims followed self-seeking leaders rather than the values that had been bequeathed to them.[17]

Although some of the most articulate expositions of the "peace through equity" perspective are the work of modern reformist thinkers,[18] the idea that religious norms and ethical values take precedence over mere expediency in political action is deeply rooted in the Quranic ethos, in the memory of righteous political orders established by Sunni Islam's four "rightly guided" caliphs (Abu Bakr, Umar, Uthman, and 'Ali), and in the efforts of traditional Islamic jurists to identify moral limitations on the conduct of war. While early Islamic jurisprudence generated a system of norms for the conduct of international relations in which conflict between the Muslim state and non-Muslim states was regarded as normal, historical practices of peacemaking and alliance formation with non-Muslim states resulted in the creation of legal categories designating lands with which the Muslim state was at peace: *dar al-sulh* or *dar al-ahd* (both of which can be translated as "the land of treaty/truce"), and *dar al-aman* ("the land of security"). One Muslim jurist, Fakhr al-Din al-Razi, proposed that the original distinction between *dar al-Islam* and *dar al-harb* ("land of Islam" and "land of war") was less appropriate than an alternative formulation, *dar al-ijaba* (the "land of Islamic practice") and *dar al-dawa* (the "land of invitation"). This latter set of concepts maintained a clear Islamic sense of mission—at a minimum, educating non-Muslims about Islam—without the more strongly militarized connotations of the *dar al-Islam* versus *dar al-harb* binary.

As modern historians have observed, the most culturally productive and dynamic periods of Islamic history were periods that permitted open intellectual exchange between Muslim and non-Muslim scholars. Muslims in medieval Spain and Baghdad engaged in active intellectual collaboration with Jews and

Christians, by working to translate, preserve, and enrich the heritage of ancient Greece and Rome. Such instances of Muslim coexistence with Jews and Christians can be attributed not only to opportunities for mutual gain (Jews and Christians contributed a great deal to the development of Islamic science, philosophy, and medicine), but also to the intrinsic openness of the Quran to affirmations of human diversity. The following verses are illustrative:

> To every people [was sent] a messenger: when their messenger comes [before them], the matter will be judged between them with justice, and they will not be wronged. (10:47)
>
> O mankind! We created you from a single [pair] of a male and a female, and made you into nations and tribes, that you may come to know one another. Verily the most honored among you in the sight of God is the most righteous of you. (49:13)

During the classical era of Islamic ascendancy, worldly success imbued Muslims with a sense of self-confidence and security in their relations with non-Muslims. Such verses provided rulers with a clear basis for sponsoring collaborations that, in their judgment, greatly benefited the Muslim community.

Like all other major world religions, Islam was not without those who interpreted promises of salvation in exclusivist terms. There is indeed an exclusivist strain of Islamic thinking, exemplified by Arabian Wahhabism and by the South Asian Deobandi school of thought, which maintains that only strictly observant Muslims may earn God's favor. If God indeed sent messengers to every people, then the heedlessness of these pre-Islamic cultures must have led to distortion and alteration of divinely revealed truth. Islam as revealed to the Prophet Muhammad, therefore, must be the only reliable, viable, and straight religious path.

As commonplace as these assumptions may be in some quarters of the contemporary Muslim world, the persistence of strong Christian and Jewish minority communities in the Middle East until modern times demonstrates that rigid exclusivism and triumphalism were not the norm in historical interactions. Traditional arrangements provided "protected" *(dhimmi)* status to Jews, Christians, and "Sabians" (a category of monotheists mentioned in Quranic verse 5:69, and sometimes associated with the Mandaeans of present-day Iraq and Iran), reflecting the dominant orthodox perspective, according to which the legitimacy of some non-Muslim beliefs was acknowledged even as Islamic teachings were regarded as purer and more complete. Though categories such as *kafir* ("unbeliever" or, literally, "one who covers the truth") were obviously useful in times of conflict with foreign adversaries, pluralistic passages in the Quran provided a religiously grounded paradigm for governing religiously diverse Middle Eastern societies. Restrictions that were typically applied to non-Muslims, including the poll tax and a prohibition against occupying high state offices, conflict with contemporary human rights standards and yet appear moderate in their historical context.[19]

To date, Western commentators have been slow to recognize Islamic theology's capacity to prescribe amicable interfaith relations, and the events of recent decades have at times seemed to confirm flagging Muslim commitment to inclusiveness and to the protection of minority communities. While it is true that situations of war often prove damaging to minority communities (the Crusades, for example, were disastrous for European Jews), it remains deeply tragic that current Islamic-Western tensions have rendered minority religious communities in the Middle East increasingly insecure, and that radicalized Muslims have chosen to regard non-Muslim minority groups as members of a disloyal "fifth column." This can be seen in present-day Iraq, where war has exacted a toll not only on Christians and members of opposing Muslim sects, but also on Yazidis and Mandaeans.

From Identity Politics to Interpretation of Islamic Values

In our present era, much may well depend on the extent to which the full potential of an Islamic "peace through equity" paradigm is realized. At its best, Islamic political culture has manifested concern not just for the sanctity of its own teachings, but also for a more ecumenical and magnanimous conception of divine guidance within which Muslims could not claim exclusive privilege. There would seem, then, to be a rich basis for a Muslim worldview in which Islamic commitment is valued not just for the benefits it confers upon believers, but also for the role that Islamic teachings prescribe for Muslims in a pluralistic world order and emergent global community.

A key barrier to the deepening of Muslim commitment to a "peace through equity" paradigm is that a large proportion of contemporary Muslims feel they have been placed on the defensive by the West as well as by their own repressive states, which are perceived to depend on Western support. The belief that the West is actively or tacitly coordinating efforts to subdue Islamic movements and defeat national liberation struggles has encouraged many Muslim activists to revive adversarial intellectual frameworks that appear to describe current dynamics, such as the classical notions *dar al-Islam* and *dar al-harb*. The resultant sense of siege makes it difficult for Muslims to feel that they have a stake in the contemporary world order, and revives interest in populist formulations of the "peace through coercion" paradigm.

The perception that Islam itself is under attack reduces commitment to an impartial standard of justice, and makes it difficult for many movements to accept the "soft" unity of transnational solidarity and reliance on new international organizations such as the OIC. As an alternative, some of the more radical organizations hold out the ideal of restoring Muslim unity at the level of political organization—a form of unity that has proved elusive for well over a thousand years. Others argue strongly for the reform of particular Muslim states, but remain highly skeptical of visions in which Muslims must rely on cooperation from non-Muslims to achieve dignity and social justice.

The struggle to define a dynamic Islamic ethos for the twenty-first century (or, in the Islamic calendar, the fifteenth century) is taking place at a time in which religious authority is highly contested. Recent decades have brought tremendous upheavals to Middle Eastern societies. In addition to promoting economic transformation and rural-urban migration, modernization programs have produced sweeping changes in the educational realm. Modern curricula, intended to prepare citizens for productive activity in a changing economy, have dramatically increased literacy and generated new classes of professionals that did not exist in previous eras of Islamic history. These changes in education, combined with other trends such as the rise of egalitarianism and populism in political discourse, have placed new pressures on both the state and custodians of traditional Islamic thought. Increasingly, traditional centers of authoritative Islamic learning such as Al-Azhar University in Egypt have found themselves competing with self-trained authorities who claim that the upper tiers of the ulama have been co-opted by the state, and have thereby been led away from true Islamic teachings. As more doctors, engineers, and teachers have assumed leading roles in Islamic movements, a de facto "democratization" of the interpretation process has occurred.

One of the most widely debated topics in modern Islamic thought is the proper basis for *ijtihad,* the exercise of independent reasoning in the interpretation of authoritative Islamic values. Derived from the same Arabic root as *jihad (j-h-d), ijtihad* connotes personal striving in the pursuit of legal and ethical knowledge. Whereas historical jurisprudence gave precedence to group consensus *(ijma')* and imitation of prior generations *(taqlid)* at the expense of *ijtihad,* contemporary Muslim thinkers—faced with momentous changes and past syntheses that are no longer experienced as vitalizing—have sought to create greater scope to the latter principle. The ongoing debate is still quite fractious, as Muslims associated with classical institutions of religious learning compete for religious legitimacy with rivals who rely on nontraditional credentials and their own readings of religious texts. Where the traditionalists at established institutions tend to apply *ijtihad* cautiously, modernist reformers and antimodernist fundamentalists adopt a more permissive stance toward this concept, albeit to advance quite different social and political programs.[20]

Preoccupation with *ijtihad* dates particularly to the late nineteenth century, when imperial encroachment on the Middle East increased concern that Muslims needed to absorb certain forms of Western expertise—especially in the physical and military sciences—to maintain independence while achieving greater communal strength and dynamism. This first wave of reformist thought was oriented toward assimilating key Western insights and adapting Islamic teachings to the demands of the modern era. Subsequent disappointments with the modernization experience and with continuing Western influence on politics as well as social mores led to a second wave of thought about *ijtihad,* this time oriented toward the creation of well-organized "Islamist" movements that could challenge and ultimately capture the increasingly intrusive modern state. Through a populist appeal, the leaders of these revivalist movements have often emulated European mass political movements of the 1920s and 1930s, and have defensively sought to reformulate Islam as a political ideology that might compete with Western liberalism and communism.

The sense of urgency that drove twentieth-century revivalist movements has led to critical evaluations of much historical Muslim practice, along with the conclusions reached by traditional Muslim intellectuals—especially philosophers and mystics, but also jurists of an insufficiently activist orientation. As a substitute, many revivalist leaders have aspired toward the ideal of a pristine "Islamic state" modeled on the early caliphate, to implement *sharia,* promote social justice, and defend Muslim interests in the face of external threats. In the view of such revivalists, the Muslim *umma* faces threats comparable to the era of Crusaders and Mongol invaders from the east. The principal source of threat is external, yet Muslim societies have become weak and inequitable in large part due to their laxity in practicing the purest forms of Islam, and the compromises of corrupt leaders.

The activism of many contemporary Islamists evokes a historical Muslim practice known as *tajdid* (renewal). This practice, through which small groups of Muslims act decisively to defend the purity of basic Islamic precepts from cultural accretions and doctrinal deviations, is based on an oft-cited prophetic *hadith* stipulating that God will "send to His community at the head of each century one who will renew its faith for it."[21] Orthodox Sunnis have traditionally recognized a number of historical figures as providentially sent (but not prophetic—Muhammad was the last of the law-giving prophets) "renewers" *(mujaddid),* notably Ahmad Ibn Hanbal (780–855), Abu Hamid al-Ghazali (1058–1111), Abdul Qadir Jilani (1078–1166), Ahmad Ibn Taymiyya (1263–1328), and Ahmad Sirhindi (1564–1624). Though precise teachings of *mujaddid* have varied considerably and there is no universally accepted list of authentic renewers, *tajdid* movements have shared a strong reaffirmation of divine transcendence (the orthodox formulation of *tawhid,* divine unity) and concern for maintaining the integrity of *sharia* vis-à-vis non-Islamic cultural influences, through adherence to the prophetic *sunna.* Contemporary Islamists share these core objectives, while adding a much greater emphasis than most historical figures on challenging corrupt political authorities.[22] Although some Islamic movements, such as the Egyptian Muslim Brotherhood, have come to speak against political violence and argue that a more authentically Islamic social order can be achieved by democratic means, others have responded to state repression by becoming more combative and uncompromising. Osama bin Laden's call for a renewed Islamic caliphate, to enforce *sharia* rule and unite all Muslims in a struggle with non-Muslim adversaries, represents the extremist end of current Islamic activism.

As vital as it is to recognize the interpretive nature of Islam—the practical implications of religious values are contested, not settled—sensitivity to the social and political contexts in which claims are made can help observers recognize significant departures from the "spirit" of the tradition. There are many, for example, who argue that bin Laden's system of beliefs is more "anti-Western" than Islamic in substance, and that his appropriation of jihad discourse is both opportunistic and contrary to established precedents.[23] In calling for attacks on individuals without regard for combatant and noncombatant status, bin Laden's public pronouncements directly contravene the norms of the Islamic just war tradition.[24] Moreover, as an architect rather than a jurist by training and as an individual who has held no public office, bin Laden lacks both the authority to issue religious pronouncements[25] and the entitlement to call for jihad—traditionally the prerogative of the Muslim caliph. His political grievances are widely shared, but his methods and grandiose claims to religious leadership have little basis in the mainstream Islamic tradition.

The extent to which Al-Qaida stands outside the Islamic mainstream becomes quite evident when one considers reactions to the events of September 11, 2001, by Muslims in positions of religious leadership. Despite occasional expressions of skepticism about US accounts of these events—including ironically revealing comments expressing doubt that Arabs or Muslims could marshal the skill and expertise necessary for such a sophisticated operation—religious leaders almost uniformly condemned the September 11 attacks as violations of Islamic and humanitarian standards.[26] Sadly, much of the sympathy for the United States evoked by the terrorist attacks evaporated with the onset of the Iraq War in 2003; some of the same religious leaders who had roundly condemned the perpetrators of terrorism in 2001, including popular Qatar-based scholar Yusuf al-Qaradawi (who had signed a *fatwa* authorizing American Muslims in the US military to fight in the Afghanistan campaign),[27] now expressed support for Iraqi resistance to US occupation.[28]

Muslim support for the United States after September 11 and opposition following the invasion of Iraq indicate that there is no fixed and invariable Islamic position on the United States or, more generally, the West. Western choices matter a great deal, and can reinforce either communalistic appeals for confrontation or inclusive calls for collaboration in pursuit of shared values. The mobilization of non-Iraqi Arab volunteers to fight in Iraq and the further radicalization of some Western Muslims following the invasion were eminently foreseeable outcomes.

The heightened tensions that followed the outset of the Iraq War also raise legitimate concerns about the present intellectual climate in the Muslim Middle East. When a particular Muslim country is attacked by a non-Muslim power, without the sanction of international law or an unambiguous threat posed by the former to the latter, the spirit of Muslim solidarity inevitably demands a response. Many responses to the tragic situation of Iraq, however, have displayed little awareness of injustices perpetrated by Iraq's previous Ba'thist government, and have only deepened the sufferings of the Iraqi people. Bombings in Europe have further tarnished the image of Islam in the West. The question naturally arises, then, as to whether emotion, symbolism, and a viscerally felt need to reverse political humiliation have been substituted for thoughtful reflection about how Muslims can transform their call for communal and universal justice into appeals that (1) can be understood and appreciated by non-Muslims, and (2) can inspire cross-cultural and interreligious alliances for the creation of a more just world order.[29]

Insofar as Muslims feel that they are "under siege," authoritarian and deeply revisionist understandings of Islam maintain considerable vitality. Yet, as reformist thinkers have argued, there would appear to be a strong basis in core Islamic value commitments for a richer and more compelling Islamic understanding of peace and conflict that transcends the medieval legal synthesis and that encourages Muslims to project their commitment to justice in an equitable, democratic, and cosmopolitan manner. Narrow preoccupation with Western injustices and with threats to Islamic solidarity prevents Muslims from addressing local causes of Middle Eastern conflicts, and from taking advantage of increasingly democratic trends in the *process* of Islamic interpretation to generate traction for substantively democratic *interpretations* that unleash the energies of national and global citizens. Fortunately, such interpretations are readily available among Islamic reformist thinkers, whose readings of Islamic sources and of the Muslim historical experience hold great promise for the future strengthening of an Islamic "peace through equity" paradigm.[30]

One of the more salient correlates of contemporary Islamic revivalism is a renewal of interest in Islamic political theory, drawing upon resources from both the classical and the colonial periods. Although radical fundamentalist leaders such as Osama bin Laden are often content with a superficial appropriation of symbols from classical jurisprudence (*dar al-harb, dar al-Islam,* military jihad) and various ideological formulas for an Islamic state or renewed caliphate, moderate revivalist thinkers have placed increasing emphasis on the need for new ways of thinking about problems of domestic as well as global governance. These moderate thinkers have placed particular emphasis on democratic principles within Islamic precepts. An increasingly cohesive transnational movement of Muslim activists now advocates precisely such readings of Islam—readings that temper Islamic communalism to provide greater scope for the flowering of the individual, while explicitly affirming the merits of representative government.

An Islamic "Peace Through Equity" Paradigm

Historically, Islamic civilization has maintained a remarkable degree of cultural unity, despite the tremendous geographical distances that separated Muslims in one part of the world from Muslims in another. The central precepts of Islam—the five pillars: *shahada* (testimony to the unity of God and the prophethood of Muhammad), *salah* (prayer), *zakat* (alms), *sawm* (fasting), and *hajj* (pilgrimage)—created a compact creedal formulation that greatly assisted in the maintenance of communal cohesion, as did the development of such institutions as the ulama (learned men), the *madrasa* (Islamic school), the *madhhab* (school of law), and the *waqf* (religious endowment). These institutions, often in combination with spiritual brotherhoods known as *tariqas,* guaranteed the vitality and resilience of Islamic culture even at times when centralized political authority failed. Islam endured for centuries not through the will or piety of caliphs, but rather through the fidelity of Muslim peoples to Islamic ideals and forms of social practice.

This recognition that the vitality of Islam derives from the faith of the people rather than from the strength or virtue of a particular leader is a fundamental premise of mainstream Islamic reformist and revivalist thought. This conviction differs from the vision of radical groups such as Al-Qaida (called by some "rogue Islamists"),[31] who propose that Islam can only survive the modern age if it is purified of foreign influences and reintroduced to Muslims by an armed vanguard movement. In contrast, mainstream Islamic revivalism and reformism seek not to create a new caliphate, but rather to discover new forms for the expression of Islamic unity in the modern age. Like former Iranian president Muhammad Khatami's initiative for dialogue among civilizations, this approach seeks not to conquer the world for Islam or repel all foreign influences, but rather to guarantee cultural space for Islam, redress injustices, and advance Islamic values in a manner that need not negate broader, multilateral frameworks for world order. From this standpoint, the common denominator of transnational Islamic activism today is not a desire to aggrieve non-Muslims, but rather a deeply felt need to forge a cultural future that gives expression to Islamic identity and empowers Muslims to achieve greater dignity in their own lands. For transnational Islamic revivalists, peace is an objective to be realized through the institutionalization of just order.

Though seldom articulated systematically, much contemporary Islamic thought about issues of peace and conflict falls within the parameters of a "peace through equity" paradigm that seeks a just world order and challenges the Middle Eastern status quo. Islamic internationalism and transnationalism call not only for greater cooperation among Muslim states and societies, but also for genuine political participation, an end to official corruption, reliance upon Islamic guidelines in matters of politics and economics, and the righting of historical wrongs in Western relations with the peoples of the Middle East. Among the many distinguishing features of this paradigm are the following: (1) a vision of Islam as a religion of justice, (2) an emphasis on updating Islamic approaches to economic and political development, (3) a qualified affirmation of cultural and religious diversity, and (4) an optimistic conception of human responsibility and potential.

Islam as a Religion of Justice

Perhaps the preeminent theme emphasized in contemporary Islamic internationalism and transnationalism is that Islam as a religion calls for justice, and provides a basis for critiquing "idolatrous" ideological systems that lack a transcendent dimension, such as nationalism, tribalism, and conscience-free forms of capitalism. Although based on a strong sense of communal identity and purpose, such thinking eschews the identity politics that are frequently associated with the "peace through coercion" paradigm, and seeks to promote both a defined set of norms to guide the conduct of Muslims and also a more general set of principles that can be shared with all persons. Where power politics utilizes double standards as a basis for polarizing relations between in-group and out-group and strengthening the authority of the ruler, the "peace through equity" paradigm evokes common ethical standards and universal aspirations. All peoples—Muslims and non-Muslims alike—are capable of both justice and injustice. Because the purpose of politics is to advance the cause of justice rather than merely preserve the status quo or derive worldly benefits for a particular state, nation, or subnational group, political action must necessarily be circumscribed by strong ethical injunctions.[32]

As a rule, Islamic explanations of injustice and disorder in the world place strong emphasis on Quranic indictments of individual and collective egotism. Egocentrism leads to greed, moral blindness, and heedlessness, and the worst forms of human oppression are derived from tyranny of the human ego, referred to in the Quran as *tagut.* This is the principal source of moral transgression, and it is ultimately based on idolatry *(shirk),* the tendency to absolutize that which is relative. For many Islamic ethical thinkers, idolatry manifests not merely in the theological error of polytheism (attributing "partners" to God), but also in existential attitudes revealed by actions. Excessive devotion to personal wealth or to the interest of a particular ethnic or tribal group is a form of idolatry because it reveals lack of faith in God, ingratitude in the face of adequate means to secure a livelihood, and forgetfulness of revealed guidance.[33]

In contrast to the "peace through coercion" paradigm, in which peace is understood in conceptually "negative" and minimalist terms as a simple absence of war, the "peace through equity" paradigm conceives of peace as a presence of justice, communal self-determination, and human solidarity. Peace cannot truly be said to exist so long as major injustices persist; efforts to promote justice, then, are themselves means of peacemaking. To this end, Islam provides a comprehensive ethical system that may be understood as complementary to other cultural and religious systems, and whose normative principles can help to establish a more just and humane world. The Muslim *umma* can play a significant and active role in peacemaking by "enjoining the good and forbidding the wrong."[34]

With respect to armed conflict, the "peace through equity" paradigm is largely consistent with Western world-order thinking about the "justice of war" *(jus ad bellum)*, and attempts to restrict warfare to strictly defensive and humanitarian purposes. Although there is debate within the paradigm as to what constitutes unacceptable political violence, particularly in national liberation struggles, in principle terrorism and other actions that victimize noncombatants are categorically rejected. A special emphasis is placed on the obligations of the powerful to act justly in ways that prevent violent civil conflict—a theme that contrasts with the "peace through coercion" paradigm's focus on the prerogatives of leaders.

Economic justice is a vital theme of Islamic "peace through equity" thinking. The existence of large gaps between affluence and poverty is regarded as a major source of tension, both within Muslim states and in the larger context of global relations. Islamic thought regards the existence of economic deprivation as a social wrong caused by hoarding and failure to protect the weak from exploitation. Insofar as economic exploitation leads to social turmoil, economic justice and security are intimately connected.

Justice also implies safeguards for dissenters and an absence of political oppression—in other words, defense of human rights. As noted previously, some areas of international human rights discourse remain controversial among Muslims, particularly issues that infringe on traditional understandings of the family unit, such as gender equality and the rights of the child. These issues are receiving increased consideration from progressive Muslim thinkers, but remain contentious despite broad trends in Islamic cultures that have placed far greater numbers of women in public life than in previous historical eras. Greater agreement exists on the need for Middle Eastern governments to provide scope for more robust political participation, and to demonstrate greater responsiveness to societal voices.[35]

As an Abrahamic faith that highlights human ecological responsibility within a context of stewardship *(khilafa)* toward the natural order, there is substantial potential for the development of themes surrounding ecological accountability in the Islamic "peace through equity" paradigm. Because problems of environmental degradation and resource depletion are as significant in the Muslim Middle East as in any other world region, Muslim ecologists are finding many precedents in Islamic sources for upholding a conception of justice in which relations with the natural world are integral.[36]

Preoccupation with self-determination within the "peace through equity" paradigm's conception of justice reflects the impact of the North-South divide on modern Muslim thought, and relatively recent experiences of imperialism and exploitation as well as cultural humiliation. Obstruction of political and cultural self-determination for colonized or formerly colonized peoples is regarded as a major source of international conflict.

Updating Islamic Approaches to Economic and Political Development

The failure of secular nationalism to deliver human dignity, human development, and human rights has encouraged Muslims throughout the Middle East to pursue cultural self-determination within Islamic frameworks. Many modern Muslim thinkers have articulated critiques of Western development thinking, with its notion of a culturally uniform, linear process of social evolutionary progress. Muslim critics have contested the dominant model's conflation of modernization and Westernization, its assumptions regarding secularization, and its elevation of economic rationality and consumerism over other competing values. Where Muslim thinkers have perceived excessive individualism and insufficient communitarian concern in free market capitalist models for development, they have appreciated socialism's collectivist stance while rejecting its materialist excesses, particularly as expressed in communist experiments that have sought to uproot religion and abolish private property. Among the many institutions of the modern world economy, multinational corporations, banking practices, and volatile financial markets have attracted much criticism from Muslims attempting to redress poverty and inequality by adapting traditional Islamic teachings. These criticisms have argued against merely hanging an Islamic garb on Western socialist or liberal concepts, and have proposed that, in the long run, democracy must express a community's needs for identity, security, and growth. A genuinely Islamic economic and political order would stress the need for a strong sense of community, the need for solidarity, the need for social justice.

From a progressive Islamic perspective, egalitarianism is the basis for a collaborative conception of human freedom that may be characterized as solidaristic pluralism. Unity is based not on uniformity, but rather on the idea that both the individual and the community have rights. The result is a creative tension through which the collective is obliged to respect the dignity and conscience of the individual, in exchange for corresponding respect for majority opinion.

Islamic prescriptions concerning human solidarity and "freedom in community" equip Muslim advocates of the "peace through equity" perspective with a critique of Western liberal assumptions concerning individualism and material progress that is similar in many respects to internal Western religious critiques. Societies have so often been repressive that a strong Western liberal tradition has emerged that sees the elimination of repression and want as the chief goal of society. From an Islamic perspective, this creates a false dichotomy between the individual and the community, with the individual seen as serving the individual alone. In effect, such individualism ignores the cultural community within which human development must take place. The result is a "lowest common denominator" approach to development that seeks to maximize material satisfactions while foreshortening deliberations about how society might nurture higher values that can only be realized collaboratively.

Islamic critiques of prevailing Western norms do not necessarily presuppose indifference to the fact that cultural systems, like political, economic, and social ones, have usually contained much to impede human development, especially forces such as prejudice, chauvinism, competitiveness, racism, and sexism. From an Islamic reformist perspective, however, acknowledging and contesting such cultural norms can be achieved without the propagation of an individualistic ethos of disassociation from community, in which the right to pursue individual happiness sometimes becomes little more than a veneer concealing human isolation and even genuine unhappiness. The underlying presumption of the Islamic perspective, then, is that the cultural community is the primary center of coherence and value in human life, a repository of shared will and wisdom. Fragmenting the cultural community through individualism often fails to solve the problems it is meant to address, resulting in human subservience to political, economic, and social systems that fail to produce both human fulfillment and social justice.

In this respect it is important to note that Islamic approaches to cultural change on matters of religion, politics, and social organization are likely to remain distinct from current Western practices. Though historically the maxim "render unto Caesar what is Caesar's and unto God what is God's" was not interpreted as a justification for separation of church and state, European Christian culture did in fact maintain a more pronounced duality of religious and secular institutions and norms than Islamic culture. The notion of a "divine right of kings" ensured a major political role for religion, yet the absence of clear scriptural mandate for a religiously sanctioned legal code such as the Islamic *sharia* or Jewish *halakha* provided European leaders with more room to maneuver than in the Middle East. The world-renouncing spirituality of traditional Christianity infused European culture with a somewhat different political ideal than Islam, and also provided a basis for invidious comparison of Christian precept with church practice. By the time of the Reformation and the Enlightenment, the argument for separating church from state had become defensible for many on religious—and not simply secular—grounds. In other words, decoupling church and state was construed as a Christian solution to a genuine social problem. Many Christians, especially Protestants, came to the conclusion that excessive church involvement in the governance of society had a distorting influence on religious institutions and values.

While it is conceivable that Middle Eastern Muslim societies may yet find relevance in aspects of the European Christian experience, movement toward more dynamic practices of political participation and economic development is likely to depend in no small part on new interpretations of *sharia* principles. Solutions that appear to abruptly sever public life from moorings in religious values are more likely to deepen social conflict than engender genuine progress. Except in the Islamic Republic of Iran, there is little popular support for the notion that Muslim political and economic problems stem at least partially from excessive clerical authority and influence on the process of governance; the more decentralized nature of religious life in predominantly Sunni countries, combined with perceptions of undue Western influence on political outcomes in the Middle East region, suggest a continuing popularity of Islamic revival movements as pathways for culturally rooted modernization efforts.

Qualified Affirmation of Cultural and Religious Diversity

Whereas power-political uses of Islam are most often predicated on an outlook of communal chauvinism, mainstream Islamic reformism and revivalism—currents of thought that are reflected in internationalist proclamations formulated in multilateral Muslim forums—are explicitly open to the possibility of religious virtue among followers of other religious traditions. In this respect, moderate Islamic revivalism and most official religious discourse may claim for Islam a unique and privileged role in providing the overarching vision and values for a just world order, while taking care to avoid a theologically exclusivist stance.[37] Advocates of Islam as a source of principles for establishing a more just world order recognize a distinction between Islam in the formal, communal sense and Islam as a spiritual principle of submission to divine reality. Similarly, they recognize in Quranic references to humanity as "one nation" a basis for loyalty both to the Muslim *umma* and to the larger *umma* of humankind.[38]

For Muslim world-order thinkers, a quintessential human freedom to which all other freedoms are linked is freedom of worship. Although there are indeed Muslim countries in which this principle has been applied restrictively as freedom to practice Islam, there is a general recognition among thinkers in the "peace through equity" paradigm that religious freedom—that is, freedom from religious coercion and persecution—must be granted to all, in accordance with an Islamic ethic of tolerance and cultural coexistence.[39]

What differentiates "peace through equity" Islamic discourse from the politicized communalism of radical Islamic thought is the emphasis that the former gives to Quranic passages affirming religious diversity. Politicized communalism prefers to interpret a passage stating that God accepts no other religion but Islam[40] in a manner that minimizes the significance of a literal reading of other verses promising salvation to righteous Christians, Jews, and Sabians. Muslims who favor a power-political reading of the Quran focus particularly on passages that announce to Jews and Christians that they are deviating from the letter and spirit of revealed guidance. Where the Muslim exclusivist propounds a worldview in which Islam has superseded rather than merely fulfilled other religious traditions, the Muslim internationalist focuses first on the common ground shared by "divine religions" and, more particularly, within the Judeo-Christian-Islamic tradition of Abrahamic monotheism.

The "peace through equity" approach to pluralism may be understood as a call for shared human effort to promote cooperation in the pursuit of a dynamic ethical vision through which just and peaceful coexistence among ethnic, racial, and religious groups might be established.[41] Without negating aspirations to protect shared Muslim interests and cultural traditions, this recognition of unity beyond uniformity contradicts the notion that Islam must somehow replace or subordinate other religions for there to be peace in the world. Unlike radical campaigns to recreate a Muslim caliphate through a revolutionary rejection of the Westphalian nation-state system, inclusive Islamic thought seeks unity amid diversity. The perspective of the "peace through equity" paradigm then, is evolutionary, and seeks to restore the integrity of Islamic ideals within a present-day context.

According to this understanding, pluralism and coexistence are recognized as values in themselves and not simply as conditions that impose limitations on the realization of Islamic norms. In practice, however, there is an ongoing tension between pluralism and collective empowerment, as Muslims in the Middle East and other regions seek to counteract political marginalization and respond to a world order that is perceived to be problematic. There is a widely shared sense of having been "shut out of history" and, through colonial imposition of the present nation-state system's boundaries, denied opportunities to give political expression to Islamic identity. Such sentiments have been actively exploited by militant leaders such as Osama bin Laden, who has used the strong emotions of Muslim disaffection and humiliation to pursue a revisionist agenda based on a strict Wahhabi interpretation of the Islamic past—an interpretation that does not valorize Islam's historical capacity to produce a dynamic religious culture that accommodated religious pluralism and flourished even in the absence of political unity.

In the minds of Islamic reformists and revivalists, the idea of a "right to a cultural future" is closely linked with conceptions of "freedom in community" and international justice. With the exception of those Muslim modernists who perceive a direct correspondence between Western and Islamic ideals, most advocates of Islamic "peace through equity" visions question the universality of current international norms. They do this, however, without discounting the ideal of universality as such; rather they posit an *alternative universalism* or, in some cases, a *process-oriented universalism* in which authentic universality is a goal to be approached gradually, through respectful dialogue among civilizations and cultures (see Chapter 8). Usually, such positions are articulated through reference to Islam's built-in allowances for particularistic variation in efforts to approximate universal ideas, as exemplified by such concepts as "peoples of the book" and "protected peoples" *(ahl al-dhimma),*[42] as well as by the short Quranic *surah* (chapter) that states, "to me my religion and to you yours."[43]

In the view of Islamic world-order thinkers, the West is less tolerant of cultural diversity than is often assumed. Some have accused the West of "cultural triumphalism," an uncritical self-confidence in the applicability of one society's models for political, economic, and cultural affairs to the entire world. Though perceiving themselves as targets of culturally based discrimination and double standards, they tend to be wary of the "clash of civilizations" thesis, which devotes very little attention to the possibility that interaction among cultures might become a source of mutual learning and not merely a new source of security threats.

From an Islamic perspective, the Western pluralistic tradition sees diversity in terms of the coexistence of political systems and ideas but not of cultures. In contrast, the moderate Islamic approach to cultural and ethnic diversity seeks to accommodate differences within an overarching religious framework. While critics of limitations inherent in traditional Islamic pluralism point to the unequal status of religious minorities and a perceived elevation of Arab culture over other Islamic cultures, those who seek to broaden and adapt the traditional paradigm argue that it has allowed autonomous non-Muslim cultures to flourish within Islam to this day, while historical Western abuses relative to native cultures and minority religions indicate a need for greater humility.[44] Progressive Muslims, however, are quick to acknowledge that practice has often fallen short of Quranic principles,[45] and that the advent of the nation-state has created new tensions between national and subnational identities. A strong comparative record vis-à-vis the West during previous eras, they point out, offers little comfort in the troubled present; fresh thinking is required to address shortcomings and strengthen global aspirations toward practical reciprocity among cultural and religious groups.[46]

An Optimistic Conception of Human Responsibility and Potential

One of the distinguishing characteristics of moderate Islamic discourse is a generally positive view of human nature and potential. This view insists that the original human constitution *(fitra)* is intrinsically good and "muslim" (in the universal sense of the word), characterized as it is by innate recognition of God as Creator (Khaliq). Though Islam accepts the basic "fall from grace" narrative of the Judeo-Christian tradition, Muslim theology differs from Christian thought on the subject of "original sin." To explain human deviation from divine standards, Muslim thinkers have emphasized not only the selfish passions *(hawa)* that receive particular stress in Christian morality, but also forgetfulness *(ghafla, nisyan)* and ignorance *(jahl)*. Individual humans have the capacity to willfully disobey divine guidance, yet the more basic problem is a tendency of human groups to drift away from inspired wisdom collectively, leading to a coarsening of social as well as religious life.

The Islamic theory of prophethood arises from this vision of human existence; the role of the prophet is to make human beings aware of their socially learned as well as personal heedlessness, and to challenge them to return to a pure understanding of perennial religious precepts. There is no people on Earth that has not at some point in history received divine guidance—the Quran stipulates that "to every people has been sent a messenger" (10:47)—yet forgetfulness has caused human cultures to neglect the original sense of the teachings they have received. The purpose of Islam is to remind the world of this "original sense" inherent in divine messages brought to humanity by named and unnamed prophets, either by drawing individuals to the path set forth clearly by the Prophet Muhammad or by challenging other religious communities to reform practices and doctrines to give renewed emphasis to *tawhid* (divine unity) and *taqwah* (mindfulness of God in all aspects of daily life).

For those who focus on the *inclusive* potential within Islamic theology, the Quran provides a narrative of human origins and purpose that can be engaged by people of diverse religions and nationalities. Being a good Muslim requires serious regard for the worldly interests of the Muslim *umma,* but Islamic principles and teachings are too important to be subordinated to the vicissitudes of intercommunal politics.[47] According to Islamic moral teaching, the challenge of each individual human being—male or female—is to act as the steward or vicegerent *(khalifa)* of God on Earth, and thereby fulfill a primordial covenant *(mithaq)* between the human soul and the Creator of the universe. Actions born of forgetfulness and ignorance violate this covenant by implicitly conferring upon the human ego the status of the absolute, and thereby creating scope for arrogance, heedlessness, and greed. The unrivaled potential of the human being can only be fulfilled through human recognition of the divine origins and purposes of human creativity.

One of the many important challenges for contemporary Islamic thinking is reconciling reason and revelation. Traditional Islamic thinking resolved this tension in favor of revelation, as exemplified by Abū Ḥamid al-Ghazali's influential twelfth-century work, *Incoherence of the Philosophers (Tahafut al-Falsafa).*[48] In contrast, contemporary thinkers are finding new meaning in Quranic passages that emphasize people's use of their innate intelligence in comprehending God's signs *(ayat)* and moral guidance.[49] They place particular emphasis on the importance of an oft-cited verse eschewing the use of coercion in matters of religion: "Let there be no compulsion in religion. Truth stands out clear from error: whoever rejects evil and believes in God has grasped the most trustworthy handhold, that never breaks" (Quran 2:256). In the minds of reformist thinkers, this verse is significant not only because it rules out forced conversions and blind obedience to authority, but also because it suggests that the underlying order of the cosmos is accessible to the human intellect. The case for faith is not to be made through intimidation, but rather through force of logic, and appeals to shared human needs and experiences.

The "peace through equity" paradigm recognizes that people cannot be dissuaded from pursuing the wrong course in life through coercion or violence. Achieving positive ends both in the Middle East and in the broader world requires skillful persuasion and a search for shared moral standards. Only values that are deeply rooted in the "authentic cultures" and deep experiences of people can provide a basis for sustainable progress and creative action; in efforts to advance these ends in the Middle East and other regions, Islam provides a language of affirmation and moral aspiration.

In contrast to the "peace through coercion" paradigm's emphasis on the external, military aspect of jihad, the "peace through equity" approach to Islamic interpretation construes jihad more broadly in relation to actions that uphold ethical bases of a just peace. Although defensive military struggle is not excluded as a possible recourse in the face of oppression, the predominant emphasis is on struggle for justice through political and social channels. The goal is to delegitimize social orders founded narrowly on elite privilege, and to restore moral and ethical values to their proper place. Actions born of despair, hatred, or misguided zeal undermine these objectives.

Conclusion

As a paradigm, the Islamic "peace through equity" approach points beyond power politics, and affirms the need for cooperative and participatory political processes that can secure the well-being of the Islamic *umma* as well as the larger community of humankind. It offers a means for Muslims to find hope for a more just and life-affirming future, as well as new meaning through active participation in an emergent global community. Building on core Islamic values and commitments, the paradigm endeavors to provide an updated map to peace through justice, as well as a template for integrating such qualities as "modern," "democratic," and "Muslim."

At its best, the "peace through equity" paradigm carefully distinguishes between "Islam" and "Muslims," and differentiates between the perennial values of the Quran and the past efforts of Muslims to interpret and apply these values. In the process, the paradigm provides a basis for critical thinking about the relationship between Islam and politics, and for recognizing ways in which misappropriated Islamic communal sentiments (like Western nationalist sentiments and politically manipulated religion in any context) have provided symbolic cover for power politics. By seeking moral common ground with non-Muslims, the paradigm suggests that deeds are to be judged by their content and not by the doer; justice is not simply a matter of what is good for a particular group of Muslims or for their leaders.

Simultaneously, the "peace through equity" paradigm underscores the continuing relevance of Islam. It perceives that if Muslims do not develop through their own Islamic traditions, they will continue to suffer contradictions between traditionalism and secularism as well as between fundamentalism and Westernization. Past efforts to seek progress through grafted Western ideological frameworks have increased the fragmentation of Middle Eastern cultures and sharpened divides between the elite and the masses; dynamic attempts to re-encounter Islamic values may well enable Muslim societies to bridge divides and engender lasting progress.

In the Middle Eastern context, institutions designed for the peaceful, democratic management of domestic conflicts are not well grounded in traditionally practiced social values. Economic maldistribution is pervasive, and political repression is deeply entrenched. Although local social institutions are imperfect, they do allow for the discussion of issues affecting people's lives. It is at this level that the language and values of Islam are most significant and authentic, and at which the gap between the formal institutions of state and the networks and realities of everyday life is most evident. Rediscovering Islamic values pertaining to social justice, peace, and pluralism would therefore appear vital to any significant effort to achieve lasting changes and reform poorly transplanted institutions such as Potemkin parliaments and dynastic presidential systems.

To become a genuine force for peace in the Middle East as well as in the larger context of Islamic-Western relations, protagonists of the Islamic "peace through equity" paradigm will need to overcome a number of challenges. These challenges include (1) integrating theory and practice, (2) making Muslims' aspirations for justice, peace, and dignity more readily comprehensible among non-Muslims, and (3) "mainstreaming" forms of progressive Islamic thought and action that promise to help Muslims bridge Islamic versus Western, traditional versus modern, and religious versus secular divides.

One of the first questions that comes to mind for Western observers of Middle Eastern societies concerns the relationship between professed Islamic values and the actual behavior of Muslims. Clearly, there is much to admire in Islamic precepts about justice and human diversity, yet the behavior of radical Muslims creates doubts in the minds of outsiders. There is a gap between publicly professed ideals and actual practices.

Among Muslims, common responses to observations of this nature include defensiveness (is not the gap occurring because Muslims are under attack?) and more emphatic articulations of Islamic ideals. With respect to the latter response, the tendency is to presume that the problem is largely a matter of perception and misinformation. If Westerners cannot recognize or place trust in the life-affirming values of Islam, then surely this must be attributable to misrepresentations of these values by those whose perspective on Islamic culture is either superficial or biased.

While it would be unfair to deny that biases exist and that media coverage of Islam (like news coverage more generally) gives disproportionate attention to sensational acts of violence, there is also a need for critical reflection among Muslims. Simply put, the West has contributed to many Muslim problems, but cannot accept responsibility for all of them. Moreover, one should not be surprised if Westerners derive their initial preconceptions of Islam from observed practices of Muslims rather than from fair-minded textual studies of the relevant sources.

Middle Eastern Muslims are no more and no less prone to act on double standards than people in any other world region. Just as Americans are more likely to adhere to the norms of liberal democracy and human rights in their internal politics than in relations with adversaries, Muslims are often more zealous in the defense of their own communal rights than in the defense of the rights that their ethical system can grant to others. Muslim perceptions of disempowerment can lead to discourses that are every bit as biased as Western commentaries on terrorism that ignore injustices and indignities that contribute to political violence.[50] Westerners reveal double standards when they speak of democracy while ignoring Muslim voices; Muslims undermine Western confidence when they condemn terrorism while insisting that national liberation movements in Iraq or Palestine cannot commit terrorism. Both Muslims and Westerners have much work to do to reassure each other that talk of peace, human rights, and religious freedom is sincere rather than disingenuous.[51]

This problem of integrating precept and practice relates to a second major challenge, which is making Muslims' aspirations for justice, peace, and dignity more readily comprehensible among non-Muslim audiences. As a general rule, Westerners experience much difficulty understanding the motivations of Middle Eastern Muslims, and have little knowledge of the historical narratives within which Muslim convictions about international justice are embedded.

The Iranian Revolution is an excellent case in point. From a Middle Eastern perspective, the revolution was a *reaction* to long-standing foreign manipulation and unrepresentative leadership. From a Western and especially US perspective, the revolution was a surprising and profoundly unsettling episode during which the most powerful country in the world was humiliated by its powerlessness to effect the release of hostages held at the US embassy in Tehran. For Middle Eastern Muslims, the calls of Iranian revolutionaries for international justice needed no translation. For Western observers, these same calls seemed far more dissonant and threatening than educative. Communication was rendered even more difficult by major cultural differences concerning the role of directly religious appeals in political discourse.

Finally, sustained Muslim commitment to peacemaking is likely to require a "mainstreaming" of reformist Islamic thought and action within Middle Eastern educational systems. At present, forms of Islamic thought that promise to help Muslims bridge Islamic versus Western, traditional versus modern, and religious versus secular divides are present in many Muslim-majority countries, but the competition between religious revivalism and secular nationalism has not yet led to a new "progressive Islamic synthesis."[52] Such a development is not likely to occur overnight and cannot be orchestrated by foreign powers and interests. Yet the rise of a more coherent and compelling framework of forward-looking Islamic thought would bode well for the "peace through equity" paradigm.

Notes

1. Safi, *Tensions and Transition in the Muslim World,* 2003, p. x. These experiences, combined with memories of the colonial era, have led many Muslim thinkers to highlight what they see as inherent deficiencies in Western models for state and society, emphasizing phenomena such as empty consumerism and unbridled political and economic competition. Though one-sided, these views are not entirely inconsistent with some genres of internal Western self-critique.

2. Abdul Rauf, *What's Right with Islam,* 2004, p. 8.

3. Barnett, *Dialogues in Arab Politics,* 1998, p. 60.

4. MacDonald, *The League of Arab States,* 1965, pp. 85–88, 317–318, 325–326.

5. al-Ahsan, *OIC,* 1988, pp. 23–24.

6. Ibid.

7. Eickelman and Piscatori, *Muslim Politics,* 1996, p. 140.

8. Malaysian National News Agency, "Declaration on Palestine," 2004.

9. Author interview with Mokhtar Lamani, former ambassador of the OIC to the United Nations, Waterloo, Ontario, July 25, 2007.

10. Eickelman and Piscatori, *Muslim Politics,* 1996, p. 141.

11. Kazemi, "Perspectives on Islam and Civil Society," 2002, p. 50.

12. For universalistic Muslims, the principles underlying Muslim practices are more fundamental than the forms, and though Islam may be a specially favored path to truth and human well-being, it is not the only possible path. See Chapter 8.

13. Quran 2:143.

14. Quran 4:135.

15. Ramadan, *In the Footsteps of the Prophet,* 2007, pp. 196–197, 212–213.

16. Sadiki, "Popular Uprisings and Arab Democratization," 2000, p. 77.

17. Historically Muslim communities have experienced many political as well as religious schisms, yet despite these conflicts the ideal of Islamic solidarity has remained strong. For centuries, Muslims throughout the world maintained remarkably similar views with respect to ritual practice and the basic principles of Islamic law *(maqasid al-sharia);* this shared platform of religious norms facilitated interaction and

exchange among Muslims from diverse cultural and religious backgrounds. For more on patterns of unity and diversity in Islamic civilization, see Said and Sharify-Funk, *Cultural Diversity and Islam,* 2003.

18. See, for example, Abu Zahra, "International Relations in Islam," 1968; and al-Ghunaimi, *The Muslim Conception of International Law and the Western Approach,* 1968.

19. Though not without tension, relations with Persian Zoroastrians and, later, with Hindus and Buddhists typically followed the pattern established with Middle Eastern Jews and Christians. In his *Concise Encyclopedia of Islam* (1989), Cyril Glassé summarizes the historical implications of *dhimmi* status in the following terms: "This was usually accompanied by a number of social restrictions which could range from the remarkably oppressive to the remarkably liberal depending upon the place and the epoch" (p. 98). In *The Great Theft* (2005), Khaled Abou El Fadl seeks to differentiate historical abuses (e.g., requiring non-Muslims to wear clothing that distinguishes them from Muslims) from what he understands as authentic Islamic values, and argues that oppressive practices were derivative from "apocryphal traditions" and "pure fabrications that are inconsistent with the historical practices of the Prophet" (p. 205).

20. For a modernist perspective on *ijtihad,* see Fazlur Rahman's *Islam and Modernity* (1982) and *Revival and Reform in Islam* (2000). Rahman was a pioneering figure in contemporary liberal Islamic thought who concerned himself with articulating hermeneutic principles through which the Quranic ethos could be grasped as a dynamic whole, to provide a compass for the application of Islamic values to contemporary problems.

21. *Sunan Abu Dawud, Kitab al-Malahim,* chap. 1.

22. Historically, this ideal of a return to pure Islamic faith has often included a strong mystical appeal; Abu Hamid al-Ghazali and Abdul Qadir Jilani, for example, did much to reconcile *sharia*-oriented Islamic communitarianism with the Sufi ethos of seeking inward purification of the soul *(nafs)* and direct, personal knowledge of the divine presence. This mystical tendency can still be found among contemporary Muslims, but it is not a defining feature of modern revivalist movements.

23. Abou el Fadl, for example, applies the classical juristic category of *hiraba* ("waging war against society") to the conduct of contemporary groups that practice violence without discrimination and seek to terrorize their adversaries (*The Great Theft,* 2005, pp. 242–249).

24. For translations of bin Laden's statements, see Lawrence, *Messages to the World,* 2005.

25. The criteria for issuing a *fatwa,* or legal opinion, have traditionally been quite demanding. *Fatwas* are offered by learned jurists in response to a question posed by an individual or court of law. Generally advisory and informative rather than binding and enforceable in nature, a *fatwa* differs from a *qada',* or court judgment. *Fatwas* are nonetheless based on authoritative precedents and can range in length from single-word responses to major treatises. They typically focus on specific matters or right or wrong conduct, but can also deal with more general religious issues, including theology, philosophy, or the nature of religious obligation. There are many criteria for issuing a credible *fatwa.* First and foremost, a *fatwa* must be issued by a *mufti.* A *mufti* must be a person of good standing and moral character, with thorough training in Islamic law and skill in legal reasoning. Furthermore, a *mufti* is expected to refrain from producing opinions when angry, ill, or fatigued, and must be careful to avoid a case in which there is a conflict of interest. For further details, see Esposito, *The Oxford Dictionary of*

Islam, 2003; Martin, *Encyclopedia of Islam and the Modern World,* 2004; Newby, *A Concise Encyclopedia of Islam,* 2002.

26. See Gregorian, *Islam,* 2003, pp. 104–105; Kurzman, "Islamic Statements Against Terrorism," 2008.

27. Abdul Rauf, *What's Right with Islam,* 2004, pp. 287–291.

28. Gerges, *Journey of the Jihadist,* 2006, p. 242.

29. For commentary on tensions between communalism and universalism in Islamic thought, see Senturk, "Sociology of Rights," 2006. See also Boase, *Islam and Global Dialogue,* 2005.

30. See, for example, Khan, *Islamic Democratic Discourse,* 2006.

31. Khan, "Radical Islam, Liberal Islam," 2003.

32. AbuSulayman, *The Islamic Theory of International Relations,* 1987, p. 20. See also Nyang, "Scriptural Faith and Ethnicity," 1997.

33. In the foreword of AbuSulayman's *The Islamic Theory of International Relations* (1987), Ismail al-Faruqi writes, "The reasoning of Islam is founded on the repudiation of tribalism and nationalism; for it regards ethnocentrism, whether based on racial, real estate, linguistic or cultural particularism, as evil and unbecoming of humans" (p. xxv).

34. Quran 3:110.

35. For a survey of Muslim attitudes on these topics, see Fattah, *Democratic Values in the Muslim World,* 2006.

36. Foltz, Denny, and Baharuddin, *Islam and Ecology,* 2003.

37. Abul-Fadl, "Contrasting Epistemics," 1990.

38. Sachedina, *The Islamic Roots of Democratic Pluralism,* 2001.

39. Boase, *Islam and Global Dialogue,* 2005; Eickelman, "Islam and Ethical Pluralism," 2002, pp. 127–131; Hashmi, "Islamic Ethics in International Society," 2002, pp. 166–169.

40. Quran 3:85.

41. Khan, "Islam as an Ethical Tradition of International Relations," 1997.

42. The following Quranic passage (5:68–69) on the "people of the book" exemplifies this attitude toward diversity: "Say: 'O People of the Book! You have no ground to stand upon unless you stand fast by the Torah, the Gospel, and all the revelation that has come to you from your Lord.' . . . Those who believe [in the Quran], those who follow the Jewish [scriptures], and the Sabians and the Christians—any who believe in God and the Last Day, and work righteousness—on them shall be no fear, nor shall they grieve."

43. Quran 109:6.

44. Mazrui, "Islamic and Western Values," 1997.

45. Sadly, Quranic passages affirming diversity and forbidding coercion (for example, 2:256, 5:48,10:47, 49:13, 109:6) have often been neglected.

46. Said and Sharify-Funk, *Cultural Diversity and Islam.*

47. These are major themes in Farid Esack's works, *On Being a Muslim* (1999) and *Qur'an, Liberation, and Pluralism* (1997).

48. al-Ghazali, *The Incoherence of the Philosophers,* 2002.

49. See, for example, Kurzman, *Liberal Islam,* 1998; Arkoun, *Rethinking Islam,* 1994.

50. Lindner, *Making Enemies,* 2006.

51. With respect to religious freedom, it is worth noting that even many Muslim world-order thinkers are highly sensitive about the issue of non-Muslims proselytizing within the boundaries of majority Muslim states. The reasons for this relate not only to

traditional Islam's attitude toward apostasy (which is not altogether unlike traditional Christianity's attitude toward heresy), but also to a historical experience in which missionary activity was experienced as an integral part of colonialism. Though the persistence of traditional attitudes cannot be attributed solely to external influences and geopolitics (for a critical view, see Saeed and Saeed, *Freedom of Religion, Apostasy, and Islam,* 2004), the growing militarization of Islamic-Western relations arguably creates an unfavorable environment for the advancement of new thinking on this issue.

52. Said, Abu-Nimer, and Sharify-Funk, *Contemporary Islam,* 2006.

6

Peace Through Conciliation: Forms of Islamic Conflict Resolution

> But if the enemy inclines towards peace, do thou also incline towards peace—and trust in God, for He hears and knows all things.
>
> —Quran 8:61

At the root of contemporary Western practices of conflict resolution is an attitude of pragmatism that, at first glance, would appear somewhat contrary to an Islamic social ethos. Western pragmatism, after all, gives greater priority to practical results than to moral theory, and adopts a flexible attitude toward means in the pursuit of achievable ends. In the context of conflict resolution, fixed understandings of what might be good or just receive less consideration than interests that can be served through mutual adjustment between parties.

In contrast, Islam would appear to project a different ordering of priorities, giving more weight to moral injunctions than to calculation of costs and benefits. Instead of an open-ended process of mutual adjustment aimed toward the satisfaction of competing interests, Islam prescribes adherence to explicit standards. How can a conflict be truly resolved, Islamic thinkers suggest, if there is more pressure to find a compromise than to formulate a substantively just settlement? Should not the top priority be working to bring conflict outcomes into line with moral norms and historical precedents?

At an abstract level, such differences appear difficult to bridge. A closer investigation of historical Muslim practices, however, reveals a surprising amount of principled flexibility in the application of Islamic precepts. Pragmatism as a moral theory may well conflict with Islamic sensibilities, yet Islam is not without practical peacemaking methods. Some of these methods are directly rooted in religious texts, while others reflect creative interplay between Islamic texts and cultural contexts of interpretation and application.

Amid the many conflicts that afflict the contemporary Middle East, some analysts have noted the "tentative emergence of local methods of conflict [resolution] such as religious- or tribal-based conciliation processes."[1] Although these local methods have yet to prove their effectiveness for overcoming various forms of nationalistic, intercommunal, economic, and political tension, increased interest among Middle Eastern Muslims in recapturing elements of Islamic identity and cultural heritage has produced a corresponding desire to bring traditional values and processes to bear on divisive conflicts that have thus far resisted appeals for unity or for foreign intervention. The result is a heightened curiosity not only about ideal outcomes, such as social justice, Muslim solidarity, or intercommunal harmony, but also a concern for improving the effectiveness of processes through which peace might be obtained through conciliation and moral suasion. This attentiveness to both process and optimal outcomes distinguishes a "peace through conciliation" paradigm based on indigenously rooted approaches to conflict resolution, through which adversaries can be encouraged to "incline towards peace."

The Prophet as a Model for Peacemakers

Muslim narratives about the Prophet Muhammad portray him not only as an inspired religious and political leader, but also as a peacemaker and as a bringer of unity to feuding Arab tribes. Traditional stories about Muhammad's early life emphasize his trustworthiness both as a merchant and as an arbitrator of disputes. According to traditional narratives, Muhammad once arbitrated a dispute among tribes over who had the right to complete repairs to the Ka'ba, the black stone building in Mecca that is the focal point for Muslim daily prayers. Because the local Arab tribes believed the Ka'ba to have been built by Abraham and his son Ishmael (Isma'il), the party to place the final, chiseled stone in the structure would acquire special honor and prestige. Still a young man when invited to settle the dispute, Muhammad counseled the tribes to appoint representatives who would share the honor by hoisting the stone into position together using a large sheet of cloth. Once the sheet and stone were at the proper elevation, Muhammad joined the effort by helping to slide the stone off the sheet and into place.[2]

During his prophetic career, assuming political leadership put Muhammad in a position that required him to deal with countless disputes among his followers as well as between his own faith community and its adversaries. As recounted in Chapter 4, Muhammad's arrival in the city of Medina was associated with taking up the position of chief arbitrator of conflicts in a city of feuding tribes. As he formalized this role in consultation with the people of the city, he negotiated what has become known as the "Constitution of Medina" (Al-Sahifa al-Madina), by means of which Muslims entered into a social and political contract with the tribal groups of the city.[3]

Arguably the most significant of Muhammad's negotiations occurred in the year 628, when he and a large contingent of followers approached the city of Mecca to perform a rite of pilgrimage at the Ka'ba. When a heavily armed, mounted Meccan force attempted to intercept this lightly armed group of pilgrims, Muhammad sought shelter on sacred ground where fighting was forbidden, at a place known as Hudaybiyya. There he agreed to a ten-year truce with his adversaries. Though many Muslims felt that this truce *(hudna)* was actually a capitulation, the "Treaty of Hudaybiyya" soon generated quite favorable results. Many more tribes entered into alliances with the Muslims, and when allies of Muhammad's opponents breached the treaty by attacking members of a group that was under his protection, the Muslim community had become formidable enough to force the city of Mecca to surrender without a battle.

Muhammad's conflict with the Meccan oligarchy was ultimately resolved by a decisive political victory on the part of the Muslims. A striking theme of this victory, however, was magnanimity toward former enemies. Rather than persecute his former enemies, Muhammad pardoned them, offering amnesty in exchange for an oath of allegiance.[4] The Muslims reconciled with Mecca's powerful Quraysh tribe, whose leaders soon became prominent members of the expanding Islamic community. A son of Abu Sufyan—the Meccan who is often portrayed as Muhammad's greatest nemesis—demonstrated the extent of this transformation when he became the first leader of the Umayyad dynasty, based in Damascus.

Negotiation, mediation, and arbitration were not exclusive strategies for the early Muslim community. Yet the role of conflict resolution in the Muslim community's early struggles cannot be ignored, and its significance has received recognition throughout Islamic history. In conflict resolution as in other fields, Muslims have drawn guiding precedents and principles from the example of the Prophet and the words of the Quran. Popular piety is informed by stories of Islam's founding figures, which highlight their ability to model virtues such as wisdom, forbearance, and forgiveness.[5]

Conflict, Community, and Forgiveness

According to a classical Islamic perspective, conflict occurs when individuals or groups are unable to discipline or sublimate passion *(hawa)* or egotism through adherence to ethical and legal standards. Subservience to internal cravings and external fixations alienates human beings from their true purpose, leading to antagonism, conflict, and oppression.[6] Wherever there is competitive pursuit of wealth or glory, and the granting of greater priority to tribalism *('asabiyya)* and selfish desires than to revealed values and norms, humans have failed to grasp their proper status and role within the scheme of reality.[7] They have committed the existential equivalent of idolatry: deification of that which is not authentically divine.

Muslims vary widely in the degree to which they frame these arguments in apologetic terms. Most agree, however, that there is a principled resistance within Islam to economic and political ideas that accentuate self-interested competition at the expense of higher moral goods.[8] If the ultimate purpose of life is for human beings to follow inspired guidance, then processes for resolving differences cannot be value-neutral or utilitarian. They must be directed by imperatives of justice and moral transformation.

From an Islamic theological perspective, then, Islam itself is a force for resolving conflicts in the world on a principled basis, first through a preventative program of moral education, and second through the articulation of a system of values for distinguishing between just and unjust claims. As noted in the previous chapter, this system of values has sometimes been understood to provide a normative basis for an intrinsically pluralistic world order—a world order in which Muslims are able to cooperate with non-Muslims on an equal basis, "competing in good works"[9] but not seeking material power or wealth for its own sake. For many contemporary Muslims, Islamic reformist and revivalist programs dedicated to "enjoining what is right and forbidding what is wrong"[10] provide a vital set of principles for preventing, managing, and settling destructive conflicts. If current-day Muslim societies suffer too much from ethnic conflict, corruption, inequality, and repression, this is because authentic Islamic teachings have been neglected.

Non-Muslims, of course, are inclined to regard this approach to conflict as overly moralistic and insufficiently dedicated to pragmatic analysis of causes, effects, and institutional remedies. This response is rooted in the Western tendency to accept conflicts of interest as natural, and to value effective management or regulation of conflict as a more realistic priority than the inculcation of public virtue.

The moral aspect of Islamic approaches to conflict, however, is not limited to the promulgation of rules and standards. One aspect of Muslim cultural reality that is often missed by Westerners is the persistence of a strong Islamic tradition affirming forgiveness of human shortcomings as an essential basis for social existence. The need of the human soul for forgiveness *(maghfira)* from God is a constant theme of Islamic spirituality, and this motif of forgiveness also carries over to Islamic social teaching. Precisely because human beings often fall short of ideal standards, bringing hardship and suffering to themselves and to others, they are in need of patience, forgiveness, and toleration. Estrangement among people is itself a moral wrong, and reconciliation can bring a greater moral good than retribution when responding to clear injustice or crime.

Islam's perspective on forgiveness or pardon *('afu)* is evident even in teachings pertaining to crimes resulting in injury or death. Because such affairs generate grief and rancor that challenge the very stability and cohesiveness of society, they are not merely matters taken up by a state or supreme authority against offending individuals; they are matters that must be addressed by the larger community. The Quran consistently holds out forgiveness as the preferred option, as the following paradigmatic passage suggests: "The recompense of an injury is an injury the like thereof; but whoever forgives and makes reconciliation, his reward is due from God; and God loves not those who do wrong" (42:40).[11]

Islamic sources provide a regulating framework for retributive justice of the type practiced by most societies since the time of Hammurabi (an eye for an eye), and Islamic jurisprudence offers specific guidelines intended to limit the scope of retaliation. To prevent unending blood feuds between families and tribes, Islamic law prescribes a principle of proportionality in retribution or reprisal *(qisas)*. At the same time, Islamic norms strongly enjoin forgiveness as a divinely favored moral good, and as a social good encouraged through *diya* (material compensation for the relatives of a killed or injured person, sometimes referred to as "blood money"). Rather than mandate either mechanical retribution or a cost-free pardon, Islamic teachings have often been understood to promote forgiveness and restoration of harmonious relations as ideal goals. To forgive in the face of a grave offense, even to the extent of refusing to accept material compensation, is a source of honor and moral courage: "And he who is patient and forgives—that, surely, is a matter of high resolve."[12] A person who forgives gains social esteem for an act that is understood to reveal magnanimity, generosity, and faith.

Injunctions for forgiveness and reconciliation are closely linked to Islam's strong emphasis on the importance of communal unity. The following traditions are exemplary:

> The believers are but a single brotherhood: So make peace and reconciliation between your two [contending] brothers; and fear God, that you may receive mercy. (Quran 49:10)
>
> In most of their secret talks there is no good: but if one exhorts to a deed of charity or goodness or conciliation between people [secrecy is permissible]: To him who does this, seeking the good pleasure of God, We shall soon give a reward of the highest [value]. (Quran 4:114)
>
> Shall I not inform you of a better act than fasting, alms and prayers? Making peace between one another: enmity and malice tear up heavenly rewards by the roots. (from the *hadith*)[13]

Such prescriptions from the Quran and prophetic *hadith* underscore not only the many challenges that the early community of Muslims faced while seeking to maintain unity, but also the positive value that Islamic tradition places on peacemaking, particularly within the context of an *umma* with a strong sense of historical mission. There are many other sayings affirming similar themes, such as the importance of avoiding suspicion and hostility, and the significance of symbolic gestures in rituals of reconciliation:

> Abu Huraira reported Allah's Messenger (may peace be upon him) as saying: "Avoid suspicion, for suspicion is the gravest lie in talk and do not be inquisitive about one another and do not spy upon one another and do not feel envy with the other, and nurse no malice, and nurse no aversion and hostility against one another. And be fellow-brothers and servants of Allah."[14]

> Shake hands and rancor will disappear. Give presents to each other and love each other and enmity will disappear.[15]

Though Islam places a particularly high value on maintaining peace and harmony among believers, it would be a mischaracterization of core Islamic precepts to claim that they only apply to internal relations among Muslims. A close reading of the Quran and the *hadith* literature reveals many generic injunctions favoring forgiveness and reconciliation, and some that clearly address relations with non-Muslims and former oppressors: "It may be that God will grant love [and friendship] between you and those whom ye [now] hold as enemies. For God is Oft-Forgiving, Most Merciful" (Quran 60:7). Such passages challenge Muslims to remain open to the possibility of future reconciliation even in the midst of intense conflict. Situations that demand moral humility and forgiveness provide human beings with the opportunity to embody the integral and oft-repeated divine attributes of compassion and mercy, which are invoked at the beginning of each Quranic *surah* (*Bismillah al-Rahman al-Rahim,* "In the name of God, the Merciful and Compassionate") as well as by the divine name *Al-Ghafur,* "the Oft-Forgiving."

The Quran and the *hadith* contain many passages detailing the consequences of heedlessness and unrighteous action, but also provide statements stipulating the preeminence of grace and forgiveness. In the *hadith,* for example, there are sayings affirming that God's mercy exceeds his wrath.[16] Such scriptural citations provide an overview of principles invoked in Islamic conflict resolution practices—practices in which adherence to understandings of revealed truth is a paramount concern, together with (and not in opposition to) an overarching interest in achieving or restoring harmony among peoples who may or may not share the same fundamental beliefs and commitments.

Traditional Arab-Islamic Arbitration

For Muslim practitioners of conflict resolution, Islamic sources offer concepts and norms pertaining to third-party intervention. The core concepts are present in the Quran and the prophetic tradition, but have deeper historical roots in traditional Arab practices of dispute resolution. Among the more significant of these concepts is *tahkim,* a form of authoritative mediation or arbitration in which one or more persons of high social status seek to bring the shared wisdom of a community to bear on a social or political conflict.

Traditional practices of arbitration reflect the tribal social structure of pre-Islamic Arabia. To cope effectively with conflicts within as well as between social and political groups seeking subsistence in an environment characterized by scarcity and insecurity, the Arab peoples required a flexible mode of dispute resolution that was compatible with decentralized authority, strong family and tribal loyalties, and a largely oral code of customary law. Such realities were inhospitable to adjudication, yet well suited to a mediation-arbitration system in which prominent men with reputations for honor and integrity could be appointed at the behest of disputing parties to resolve conflicts in accordance with historical norms and values. Arbitration could be used to settle minor disputes before they escalated (for example, disagreements over grazing rights or business dealings), or to arrive at authoritative settlements to major quarrels and even blood feuds or wars between tribes.[17]

Considerable insight into the nature of traditional Arab and Islamic arbitration can be gained through analysis of terms that are closely related to the word *tahkim,* lexically as well as practically. Whereas *tahkim* refers to the act or practice of arbitrating, the practitioner of arbitration—the arbitrator—is referred to as a *hakam* or *hakim.* The latter term, *hakim,* possesses broader connotations, suggesting a person who rules, governs, or otherwise holds authority over others. To hold authority in a pre-Islamic or early Arab-Islamic context was to be in position to arbitrate disputes within the community. A person who demonstrated excellent judgment or discernment, either in the settlement of disputes or in other matters, was known as *hakīm,* wise.

In many respects, Muhammad's social and political role among his followers was like that of a traditional arbitrator, albeit with his authority amplified by his prophetic status. The Quran itself makes references to Muhammad's role as an arbitrator who passes judgments in light of revealed standards and values, and outlines a broader view of human history in which divine guidance has been extended through prophetic figures as a means of settling differences in light of enduring truths.[18] Though Islam is credited with providing a final statement of these truths, previous revelations are not negated. Instead, the Quran calls upon each divinely guided community to apply the guidance it has received: "To each of you we have given a law and a way and a pattern of life."[19]

Muhammad arbitrated conflicts before his rise to the leadership of the first Muslim political community in 622, but it was only after the Hijra (the Muslim flight from oppression in Mecca to refuge in Medina) that this political role became prominent. Upon his arrival in Medina, he was appointed the chief arbitrator of this fractious oasis community, which had been plagued by divisive conflicts among rival tribes. In the Constitution of Medina he is cited as the authority before whom lasting disputes must be brought.

Medina at that time was a settlement consisting of multiple tribal groups, several of which were Jewish. Although many of the people of the city accepted Islam, a large proportion continued to adhere to Judaism. The Constitution of

Medina spelled out in specific terms a new political order for the city, in which religious differences were accommodated and consultation was enshrined as a central principle of decisionmaking. Contemporary Muslim democrats see special significance in the fact that the world's first predominantly Muslim state was founded upon both negotiation and the granting of explicit rights to non-Muslim minorities.[20]

Because political order in the Muslim Middle East has long entailed substantial decentralization of authority, *tahkim* has remained a viable practice even to the present day. The forms that *tahkim* takes have changed over time, particularly with respect to mundane commercial arbitration, which has become highly institutionalized and formalized. However, traditional uses of *tahkim* with religious overtones persist, and the Prophet Muhammad is still viewed as a model of the virtues required to be an effective arbitrator. Other early Muslim leaders, such as the first four caliphs, are also regarded as worthy of emulation in this regard. Despite the advance of modern legal systems, traditional forms of arbitration persist in Middle Eastern practices for settling disputes in accordance with *sharia* principles or, particularly in rural settings, for achieving a settlement that reflects both Islamic principles and tribal customary law.[21]

From an Islamic perspective, the key criterion for sound arbitration practice is that it be conducted in accordance with legitimate standards by individuals who have the trust of their communities. In addition to positive cases of arbitration such as those conducted by the Prophet Muhammad to settle differences among tribes and followers, there are also cases of failed arbitration, the most infamous of which is an arbitration between the caliph 'Ali (the Prophet's cousin and son-in-law) and his Muslim adversaries in 657.

Faced with an increasingly disunited empire and major rebellions against his rule as the fourth caliph of Islam, 'Ali agreed to settle differences with his rival, Mu'awiyya, the governor of Damascus and a relative of the previous caliph, after an indecisive battle at Siffin in present-day Syria. Each side appointed one of the two arbitrators, who deliberated between themselves over a solution to the crisis of authority. Mu'awiyya's representative, 'Amr Ibn al-'As, is said to have tricked 'Ali's representative, Abu Musa al-Asha'ri, into betraying 'Ali and calling for the appointment of a new Muslim leader; 'Amr Ibn al-'As, in turn, betrayed Abu Musa by calling for the appointment of Mu'awiyya as the new caliph of all Muslims. Both Shia and Sunni Muslims regard this as a case of arbitration in which an unjust ruling was derived through the deceptiveness of one arbitrator and the gullibility of the other. Buoyed by this blow to his adversary's legitimacy, Mu'awiyya later seized the caliphate, ending the era of "rightly guided" Muslim leaders and deepening the alienation of those Muslims who had come to define themselves as "partisans of 'Ali" *(shi'at 'Ali)*.[22]

For Muslims as well as for Christians, the challenge of maintaining unity in the face of competing claims to political leadership has been one of the greatest trials of the faith community. Early divisions such as those between 'Ali and

Mu'awiyya have led to the enduring schism between Sunni Muslims (who accepted Mu'awiyya's political authority for the sake of political unity, despite their doubts about his personal integrity) and Shia Muslims (who insisted that true religious and political leadership could only be found among descendants of the Prophet). In relation to arbitration and other forms of conflict resolution, however, most Muslims agree that legitimate outcomes depend on the moral rectitude of the third party and the soundness of the principles guiding his or her intervention—hence the emphasis that is placed on *sharia* and on the Quran in deriving a framework of principles for resolving conflicts.

Processes of Peacemaking and Reconciliation

Though historical efforts to arbitrate major political disputes were often unsuccessful, Middle Eastern Islamic societies developed elaborate practices for resolving intense conflicts among individuals, tribes, and members of rival kinship groups. When conflicts became violent, it was the responsibility of the larger community to initiate a peacemaking process known as *sulh,* and to thereby work toward reconciliation *(musalaha)* if possible. Traditional practices have been displaced to a considerable extent by the legal systems of modern states, yet *sulh* remains a vital concept in Arab-Islamic thought about peacemaking, and is still practiced in many rural areas of the contemporary Middle East. The goals of *sulh* include limiting destructive conflict, reinforcing social solidarity, and promoting a restorative rather than retributive conception of justice.

As a concept, *sulh* is linked to Middle Eastern practices of conflict resolution that predate the advent of Islam, and that have been used extensively by Muslim as well as non-Muslim communities. Like *tahkim,* it is a form of third-party intervention used to restore harmony to relations between families or tribes. Where *tahkim* pertains first and foremost to the settlement of competing moral and material claims, *sulh* relates primarily to righting wrongs and settling violent conflicts—conflicts that pose a direct and immediate threat to the security and honor of family groups, and that could potentially instigate a cycle of retaliation, or blood feud.

Sulh mixes elements of arbitration or strong persuasion with an active process of mediation by respected leaders of a community. The process attempts to achieve the following aims: to prevent acts of revenge once a crime has been committed, to restore the honor of victimized persons and their relatives, and to rehabilitate offending persons and their relatives in a way that upholds collective morality and the prospect of communal harmony. As a practice with origins in a tribal society, it is based on different assumptions than those of the modern Western legal system. Though crimes may be committed by individuals, victimhood and responsibility are assigned at the collective level. In other words, if a man from one extended family group attacks a man from another group, the family of the attacker is held responsible for the offending behavior, and the family of the attacked man has been offended as a collective. Where *sulh* was traditionally practiced, crimes such as murder were not considered to be crimes against a state; rather they were crimes that violated the dignity and integrity of the victim's kinsfolk.

Together with the moral principles of the Quran, dignity and honor *(sharaf)* play a powerful role in Islamic conflict resolution practices such as *sulh*.[23] In tribal societies, the security of a group is a function of its reputation for honorable conduct and collective strength. An honorable tribe, then, deals with other groups on a fair and magnanimous basis, but vigorously acts to defend its own members when they are threatened by outsiders. In traditional intertribal relations, as in modern international relations, the capacity to retaliate for a perceived offense is indispensable for collective security. Retaliation is understood to foster deterrence by counteracting the appearance of exploitable weakness, and by restoring dignity or "face" to those who have been harmed or offended. Capacity to uphold the honor and physical integrity of each group member—and to "even the score" when these principles are violated—is the basis for maintaining collective prestige and well-being.

Fortunately, highly tribal societies have a strong social fabric, and develop institutions to create order and prevent destruction. In Arab-Islamic contexts, *sulh* was traditionally used to foster a sense of moral accountability that transcends tribal loyalty, and to make peacemaking itself an honorable, dignity-granting activity. According to the moral code upon which *sulh* is based, crimes are deeply dishonorable for those who are affiliated with the perpetrator, and threaten the public good by aggrieving and humiliating those associated with the victim. To prevent bloodshed and destruction, the larger community must therefore take responsibility to ensure that perpetrators cannot act with impunity, and to provide victims with options for restoring their dignity that do not require retaliation or foster an appearance of weakness and vulnerability. Insofar as possible, positive social relations must be regenerated and justice must be reestablished.

The profound tensions created by a willfully injurious act in a communalistic context create a necessity for strong third-party intervention, to provide an opportunity for members of victimized as well as offending groups to save face and settle accounts, without further harm or bloodshed. In Arab-Islamic contexts this was often accomplished through the formation of a mediation committee, or *jaha*. As a group of respected religious and tribal leaders, the *jaha* lends its own prestige to the cause of social harmony. Its task is to persuade disputants to make peace with one another for the sake of the larger community and its religious and social values.

The basic logic of the *sulh* process is that, for reconciliation to occur, offending parties must agree to acts of atonement that are in some sense humbling, and those who have been offended must receive material or at least symbolic and emotional compensation for the harm done.[24] The task of the *jaha* is to provide a legitimate framework within which wrongdoers can acknowledge responsibility without undue humiliation, and within which victims can be rewarded for acts of magnanimity.

Though at times prominent members of a community seek to intervene before requested to do so by the family of the perpetrator, it is traditional for *sulh* to begin when relatives of a person who has transgressed (usually by committing an act of violence, such as assault or murder) seek assistance from local notables. Asking for help in securing a truce, or *hudna,*[25] implies implicit acceptance of responsibility for a breach and a desire to limit further bloodshed. The first task of leaders who have been asked to serve in a *jaha* (a delegation that can include up to twenty persons) is to exert moral and social pressure on the offended family to forgo retaliation and begin a *sulha* (*sulh* refers to peacemaking in a generic sense; particular peace and reconciliation processes between family or tribal groups are referred to as *sulhas*).

The need for a *hudna* is critical, for without a truce the aggrieved party is entitled to pursue retribution. The following Quranic citation conveys the context of this principle:

> If two parties among the faithful fight, make reconciliation *[aslihu]* between them. But if one of them transgresses all bounds against the other, then fight the aggressor until they comply by the command of God. But if [the aggressor] complies, then make peace between them with justice, and be fair: For God loves those who are fair and just. The believers are brothers, so make peace and reconciliation between your two brothers; and fear God, that you may receive mercy. (49:9–10)

Collective action against a putative aggressor is by no means a given, and often cases reveal themselves to be more complicated than they first appear. However, unwillingness to accept collective accountability for a violent crime provides the offended party with grounds for retributive action. Only an admission of responsibility and a declaration of willingness to make amends can create space for a new dynamic characterized by collective responsibility to "make peace and reconciliation."

Once it has been assembled, the first task of a *jaha* is to visit the family of the victim. *Jaha* members inform this family that the offender's kin have accepted responsibility and requested a truce period during which the conflict can be settled. For the victimized family, accepting a *hudna* means renouncing the right to retaliate for a clearly specified period of time, during which the *jaha* will work to achieve reconciliation. Acceptance of a truce is never guaranteed, yet *jaha* members devote the full weight of their prestige to the task of persuasion. They listen to family members as they express their pain and loss, and request that the aggrieved persons agree to a truce for the sake of the community and its sacred values, and to thereby honor those who have been entrusted with the task of peacemaking. Like other aspects of the *sulha* process, these encounters have a number of highly ritualized—yet still meaningful and emotionally intense—aspects.

Like the truce embraced by the Prophet Muhammad at Hudaybiyya or like the cease-fires that were once used to suspend a war between rival Bedouin tribes, the *hudna* is a temporary measure. By pushing for a *hudna,* the *jaha* seeks to prevent a blood feud and buy time for the *sulha* effort. The *hudna* provides breathing space for negotiation and caucusing; the *jaha* begins a process of shuttle diplomacy, seeking agreement on the amount of damages (*diya* or, in Western discourse, "blood money") that the family of the offender must pay to the family of the victim. As in the initial persuasive effort, when prestigious *jaha* members humble themselves by pleading with the victimized family, this negotiation process also requires efforts to overcome powerful emotions and to work toward a settlement that symbolizes the gravity of the offense committed, but that will not be beyond the means of the offender's kin group.

If agreement on reparations can be reached, the next stage of the *sulha* process is an actual meeting between the families. The offender must be readmitted to the community after first demonstrating shame and remorse to the family of the victim. On some occasions, reconciliation *(musalaha)* is sealed when a member of each side ties a knot in a white flag. The most suspenseful moments occur, however, when the offender approaches the blood relations of his victim with an escort of kinsmen and *jaha* members, walking humbly with his gaze to the ground. The offender and his relations then shake hands with members of the aggrieved family, and offer the agreed compensation to the family of the victim. At times, the victim's family may refuse payment of the *diya,* as an act of magnanimity that accords with Quranic statements concerning the spiritual virtues and heavenly rewards that inhere in acts of forgiveness. Such a refusal to accept payment underscores the nobility and forbearance of the victim's family, and places the offender's family in a relationship of social indebtedness and gratitude.

After the *diya* has been exchanged, the process of restoring social relationships continues. The family of the offender visits the home of the victim's relatives, who serve bitter coffee to their guests. The *sulha* process concludes with a banquet for the victim's extended family and the larger community, hosted by the offender's family. The public meal completes the reconciliation effort with dramatic symbolism. By breaking bread together, the estranged families resume normal, trust-based social relations.

Through the offending family's contrition and demonstrated will to reconcile (as expressed through the *diya* and the communal feast as well as through verbal declarations and humble behavior), the honor and dignity of the victim's family has been restored. If it has responded to the entreaties of the offenders with great magnanimity, this family may even find that its social status and reputation have been enhanced. Though humbled by the misdeed of their kinsman, relatives of the offender have also recovered their dignity through the honor of holding a public banquet. The kissing and embracing that sometimes accompany the final ceremony may at times involve forced repression of powerful emotions, but the choreography of the reconciliation event is intended to provide an opportunity for genuine forgiveness and new beginnings.[26]

The basic form of the *sulha* ritual is adaptable. In many cases, the distinction between victim and victimizer may be far from clear-cut. If both sides have transgressed or if a blood feud has already taken place, then the losses and crimes of both sides must be accounted for. Efforts to deal with such ambiguous situations have often involved calculation of the losses incurred by each side, followed by calculation of damages and simultaneous exchanges of "blood money."

The *sulha* process provides insight into key values of traditional Arab-Islamic culture.[27] On the one hand, great emphasis is placed on collective solidarity, and on the dignity of the kinship group. Family members and relatives are closely bound to one another, and obliged to respond to offenses against one person as if they were attacks on the group. As US soldiers have learned since the beginning of their occupation of Iraq in 2003, even inadvertent violations of the dignity and honor of an individual and his or her social group (through injury or violating the sanctity and integrity of a home) can inspire great indignation and resistance, including willingness to accept suffering so long as a grave offense goes unavenged. On the other hand, remarkable weight is also placed on values of communal harmony, collective discipline, social justice, and forgiveness; there is a strong expectation that efforts to right a wrong through acknowledgment and compensation should be accepted by the aggrieved party. If properly respectful and remorseful gestures have been made, including willingness to pay symbolic compensation, choosing to pursue a vendetta can damage a family's reputation and social standing.

The *sulha* process also reveals the high prestige associated with the role of peacemaker in Arab-Islamic culture. In a traditional context, peacemaking was an activity reserved particularly for those of high social status, with reputations for justice, wisdom, and fair play. Though grassroots peacebuilding activities organized by younger members of society have begun to emerge in recent decades in milieus such as post–civil war Lebanon,[28] traditional peacemaking delegations have most typically consisted of elders, and have often included tribal shaykhs, village headmen, and religious leaders.[29]

In the modern context, the principles of *sulh* and *sulha* only override those of modern civil and criminal law in highly traditional (and usually rural) contexts, or in situations where the official legal system lacks legitimacy or power. Israeli occupation of the West Bank and Gaza Strip, for example, reinforced usage of traditional conflict resolution,[30] as did the civil war in Lebanon. Nonetheless, even among more settled population groups in stable political environments, reconciliation rituals are sometimes used to supplement official legal processes. The symbolism of *sulh* retains considerable vitality, and has inspired efforts to expedite transitional justice after violent conflict.

The Israeli-Palestinian Conflict: Give *Hudna* a Chance?

Of the twentieth century's many tragic conflicts, few attracted greater interest or involved more indirect stakeholders than the struggle between Arabs and Jews for control of the land of Palestine. In its early stages between the first and second world wars, this struggle pitted two rapidly growing nationalist movements against each other, each seeking to found a modern state in British-occupied Palestine. One movement, organized by European Jews who had recently immigrated to the biblical homeland of their ancestors, believed that founding a Jewish state was necessary to escape the prejudices and persecution Jews faced in scattered diaspora communities. The other movement, within the well-established Arab Muslim and Christian communities living in Palestine at the time of renewed Jewish immigration, perceived the new developments as colonialist in nature and regarded Palestine as an integral part of a larger Arab nation—a nation that had until recently been ruled by the Ottoman Empire.

By the time the Israeli government and the Palestine Liberation Organization recognized each other through the Oslo Accords in 1993, Arab-Israeli confrontation had led to five major wars (1948, 1956, 1967, 1973, 1982). The existential nature of the rivalry, linked to a zero-sum struggle in which each side sought identity and security through control of scarce territory, had also contributed to gradual erosion of secular nationalist platforms that had once played a powerful role. Though the conflict has often been characterized as an inherently religious struggle, founding organizations on both sides of the Israeli-Palestinian divide, including the Israeli Labor Party and the Palestine Liberation Organization, placed far more emphasis on ethnic nationalism and worldly struggles to establish secure, modern nation-states than on explicitly religious ideals and objectives.[31]

It is a cruel irony of history that post–World War II (and post-Holocaust) national redemption for Israeli Jews—the founding of the Israeli state—meant national humiliation and dispossession for Palestinians. Military victories that restored Israeli faith in divine providence after the devastation of the Holocaust gradually deprived Palestinians of their faith in secular nationalism. Thus did both societies respond to the traumatic vicissitudes of the twentieth century by enlisting religion in the search for national empowerment. Among Israelis, the religious nationalist impulse became most powerfully evident in the settler movement that sought to reclaim large swaths of the predominantly Palestinian West Bank as national patrimony in the years following the Six

Day War of 1967; among Palestinians, religious nationalism led to the rise of Hamas during the 1990s, and to a broad-based reassertion of Islamic cultural identity.

Among Israelis and Palestinians alike, religious nationalism finds both maximalist and moderate expressions. While some Israeli settlers are willing to offer land for peace, others refuse to countenance a peace agreement with Palestinians that deprives them of their ancient religious heartland. Some Palestinians assert that any recognition of an Israeli state is tantamount to a rejection of Islam, while other observant Palestinian Muslims merely propose that peacemaking must be conducted in a principled manner that is consistent with Islamic values.

Explanations for the failure of the Oslo process to bring lasting peace to Israelis and Palestinians during the 1990s vary widely; political commentators as well as scholars have pointed to the unwillingness or inability of both sides to restrain political violence, as well as to profound power imbalances, insufficient popular commitment, ineffective mediation, failures of leadership, religious extremism, and cultural miscommunication. Some have focused primarily on the difficulty of the outstanding issues: withdrawal of Israelis from Arab lands occupied during the 1967 war, the development of reliable security cooperation between once-bitter adversaries, the sharing of Jerusalem, and the return or compensation of several million Palestinian refugees. The resurgence of fighting in 2001, however, prompted those seeking a way forward to explore novel approaches that might correct for the perception that the US-led peace process lacked legitimacy among the peoples of the region.

The advent of the Oslo Accords in 1993 sparked debate among members of the Palestinian Islamic movement: Should they follow the lead of their more secular counterparts in the Palestine Liberation Organization by embracing negotiations to establish a small Palestinian state that would exist alongside Israel, or should they remain steadfast in their commitment to forming an Islamic state on all lands west of the Jordan river? Was there a way for committed Islamic activists to negotiate a better future for Palestinians without abandoning their convictions about Palestine's rightful borders?[32] Were maximalist demands the only way for Palestinians to recover their lost dignity, or was the path of moderation and gradualism truer to Islamic values? Should Muslim activists participate in a "peace process" that privileged pragmatism over religious values, or reject it?

For years after the signing of the Oslo Accords, Palestinian Islamic leaders such as Shaykh Yassin of Hamas sought to triangulate between alternate pathways. They asserted their commitment to realizing maximalist goals (with a single, Islamic state of Palestine replacing the state of Israel) over the long term, while also professing willingness to enter temporary, renewable truces in exchange for territorial compromise. Such proposals were unacceptable to Israeli leaders, and the development of a low-grade state of armed conflict between

Israel and militant Palestinian organizations soon dampened hopes for the Oslo process. Israeli efforts to assassinate Palestinian militants from Hamas and Islamic Jihad alternated with Palestinian suicide bombings targeting buses as well as restaurants and markets. Israeli leaders characterized their campaign as a war against terrorism; Palestinian militants represented their indiscriminate attacks on Israeli civilians as justifiable resistance to occupation and as retaliation for harm to civilians caused by Israeli operations.

The destructive and escalatory nature of this conflict cycle became strikingly clear when negotiations gave way to open warfare in early 2001. The subsequent Israeli-Palestinian conflict soon became known as the "Second Intifada" or "Al-Aqsa Intifada." Whereas the First Intifada (see Chapter 7) had been led by Palestinian nationalists, the Second Intifada invoked religious identity more directly and sought legitimacy through a declared intent to liberate the Al-Aqsa Mosque in Jerusalem's Al-Haram al-Sharif (for Israelis, Temple Mount).

The increasing ferocity of Israeli-Palestinian hostilities and the central role of Islamic identity in the Palestinian struggle prompted many Israeli as well as international commentators to reconsider the potential value of the call for a temporary peace that Hamas leaders had issued during the 1990s. Having witnessed the effectiveness of a Jordanian *hudna* in the context of a family feud, Israeli businessman Eyal Erlich floated the idea that an Israeli-Palestinian *hudna* could become the first step toward a renewal of peace efforts.[33] The Israeli government rejected this proposal, but Palestinian leaders such as Yasser Arafat and Mahmoud Abbas embraced it. With Egyptian backing, Abbas actively sought to persuade leaders of Hamas and Islamic Jihad to agree to a truce.

Late in June 2003 these attempts were successful; Hamas and Islamic Jihad, the two leading Palestinian Islamic resistance organizations, proclaimed a unilateral, forty-five-day *hudna* in their relations with Israel. Ariel Sharon and other Israeli leaders, however, were not persuaded that the initiative was sincere. Highlighting the temporary nature of the truce, they refused to accept the declaration as a promising development, and instead argued that it was a diversionary tactic intended to buy time. Israeli forces continued to target leaders of the two Palestinian militant organizations, which formally abandoned the truce in August and resumed hostilities.

In early 2004, Hamas leaders renewed their advocacy of the *hudna* option, this time for longer periods. Hamas political leader Abdul Aziz al-Rantissi proposed a ten-year truce modeled on the example of the Prophet; in exchange he demanded a provisional Palestinian state on the West Bank and Gaza Strip. This proposed arrangement did not, however, involve recognition of Israel's legitimacy as a state. Shaykh Ahmed Yassin, Hamas's founding spiritual leader, offered a 100-year cease-fire, contingent on the return to Palestinians of all territories captured during the Six Day War of 1967 (i.e., the West Bank, Gaza, and East Jerusalem). Israeli officials again dismissed these proposals as duplicitous; when Hamas resumed its former tactics, Israeli forces killed Yassin in March 2004 and Rantissi in April.

From an Israeli perspective, the idea of an Islamic-style truce with Palestinian militant organizations was difficult to embrace. For many Israelis, the repeated involvement of Hamas and Islamic Jihad in terrorist activities such as bus bombings made the concept of a temporary cease-fire unacceptable. How, Israelis asked, could they negotiate with such organizations? And even if they accepted Islamic resistance groups as negotiating partners, how could they accept anything less than an unconditional and final peace agreement in exchange for uprooting Jewish settlements and returning the West Bank and the Gaza Strip? Might not the proposal for a *hudna* be a ploy intended to create space for Palestinian rearmament? Would not a conditional cease-fire provide Palestinians with a loophole for exploiting any perceived Israeli infraction? And if the Islamic past was the precedent, had not the Prophet Muhammad reopened his conflict with the Meccans after they violated the truce? For a wary Israeli public, the *hudna* had brought a reprieve from the struggle with the Palestinians, but no guarantees.

Palestinians, however, viewed the cease-fire through different lenses. Many regarded *hudna* as an Islamically legitimate option that not only afforded a respite from endless struggle, but also allowed a face-saving basis for stepping back from maximalist demands, such as "liberation" of all of historical Palestine. From this perspective, the concept of *hudna* provided a legitimate, Islamic basis for negotiations and treaties with the far more powerful Israeli state. Because it was conditional, the *hudna* did not entail a final surrender or renunciation of rights. If accepted by the Israelis, the *hudna* would postpone hard, final choices, but would also enable Palestinians to begin working for a more livable present and future, without sacrificing national honor.

As of mid-2008, the prospect of a long-term Israeli-Palestinian *hudna* appears highly uncertain. Because Hamas's victory in the 2006 Palestinian elections was followed by an international boycott and a subsequent split between Hamas and the Palestinian Liberation Organization, with the former taking power in Gaza and the latter retaining control of the West Bank, the prospect of an integrated Palestinian negotiating position has become increasingly problematic. In any event, the cultural specificity of the *hudna* concept would appear to limit its appeal to those who do not partake of an Islamic identity.

As a peacebuilding tool, *hudna* has both strengths and weaknesses. Strengths of *hudna* include its low-risk, conditional nature and usefulness as a face-saving means of buying time for more serious peacemaking initiatives. As a traditional Islamic practice rooted in Arab history as well as in the example of the Prophet Muhammad, strong religious arguments can be made for adversaries to "give peacemaking a chance" by accepting a cease-fire. Though perhaps most useful in a uniformly Islamic context—and most readily applied in relations between tribes and family groups when state institutions are weak or hold questionable authority (as in the occupied Palestinian territories and contemporary Iraq)—the practice of *hudna* has symbolic resonance and can potentially be invoked in conflicts between Muslims and non-Muslims, as was the case during the age of early Islamic caliphates. In that classical era, *hudnas* were regarded as temporary truces between the Islamic state and non-Muslim adversaries; in the view of most jurists, these truces were to be of up to ten years in duration (like the Prophet's "Peace of Hudaybiyya"), and potentially renewable. Though temporary and conditional in nature, upholding a *hudna* has long been considered a binding obligation and matter of honor. There may well be conditions under which non-Muslim parties might consider it advantageous to explore possibilities for a *hudna* with Muslim counterparts; conversance in the vocabulary and terms of *hudna* might well open doors for peacemaking and provide weaker Muslim interlocutors in asymmetrical conflict situations with a sense of cultural empowerment and affirmation.

The strengths of *hudna,* however, can also be construed as weaknesses. As a conditional and temporary peace, *hudna* offers no guarantees of a comprehensive and lasting settlement to conflict. Moreover, the meaning of *hudna* is contested even within an Islamic context; classical jurists disagreed as to whether peace agreements between a Muslim state and a non-Muslim state could be renewed indefinitely. While many jurists believed that a truce could indeed be extended so long as both sides were willing to uphold it, the Shafi'i school of Islamic law ruled that only a ten-year truce with enemies of the Islamic state was permissible.[34] In contemporary discussions, the existence of ambiguity on this issue can undermine the confidence of non-Muslim parties to a *hudna.* At best, *hudna* offers a partial peace—peace as an absence of fighting—and only the hope that a full, "positive" peace might be negotiated through further trust-building and conflict resolution measures.

As incomplete as the *hudna* model for peacemaking may be, there are many conflicts in which a cease-fire is no small achievement. In such cases, *hudna* provides a vocabulary and a set of precedents that provide leverage for further conflict resolution efforts. To date, such efforts have not borne fruit in the Israeli-Palestinian conflict. As part of a larger peacemaking initiative stabilized by external powers acting as guarantors, results might conceivably differ.

One of the more important challenges in the Israeli-Palestinian conflict—and indeed in several other Middle Eastern conflicts—is transforming the role that religious identity plays in daily encounters among disputants. Experiments with *hudna* have attempted to respond to this challenge, by drawing upon practices and symbols that, when invoked in a compelling manner, can help to lend legitimacy and substance to peacemaking efforts. Knowledge of traditional peacemaking practices employed by Muslims as well as by Middle Eastern Jews and Christians can help reduce perceptions of threatened religious and cultural identity.

In addition to *hudna,* some Israeli-Palestinian peacemaking efforts have also sought to draw upon the symbolism of *sulh,* particularly in grassroots peacebuilding activities involving cultural exchange and dialogue. One such effort to adapt this traditional Middle Eastern framework to contemporary needs is the Sulha Peace Project, a nongovernmental interfaith initiative that attempts to build trust among Abrahamic religious communities in Israel-Palestine, restore dignity and respect, and prepare people on opposing sides of the conflict for peace. At annual gatherings, the Sulha Peace Project brings together thousands of Jewish and Arab participants to discuss wounds inflicted by the conflict, to share hopes for a more peaceful future, to educate each other about their respective cultures, and to experience interfaith prayers rooted in the Abrahamic religions. Through diverse activities, organizers of the gatherings aspire to dispel mutual ignorance, generate awareness of the conflict's emotional and human toll, and foster spiritual openness to the possibility of reconciliation. Though they operate under no illusions that their grassroots coexistence programs can substitute for political commitment and concrete changes "on the ground," leaders of the Sulha Peace Project hope their actions can complement official diplomacy and point the way to a broader rapprochement among the children of Abraham.[35]

Life After Civil War: Dilemmas of Transitional Justice

In recent decades, increasing numbers of scholars and international affairs practitioners have dedicated themselves to the creation of comprehensive frameworks for analyzing the many political and social challenges associated with achieving reconciliation after civil war or repressive governance. By addressing a multitude of problems that must somehow be mitigated if there is to be a return to "normal life," they have attempted to formulate practical guidance for "transitional justice"—that is, for responding to the wrongs of the past in a manner that provides closure and accountability while also cultivating reconciliation and genuine respect for human rights norms. While South Africa's transition from apartheid to racially inclusive democracy is among the most famous cases in the transitional justice literature, modern political history is replete with a wide range of other examples of societies that have wrestled with issues of justice and reconciliation after dictatorship or collective violence.

Approaches to transitional justice have varied widely, in ways that reflect differing political circumstances as well as cultural contexts. In South Africa, the principal goal of transitional justice was atoning for the sins of the apartheid era by means of the now-famous Truth and Reconciliation Commission, through which those who had committed acts of political violence provided full disclosure in exchange for a hope of amnesty. A "restorative" rather than "retributive" model of justice was adopted, emphasizing repentance and reparation rather than revenge; this approach was motivated not only by political calculations—no white South African leader would have willingly negotiated away a system that guaranteed white privilege without assurances that vengeance would be limited—but also by explicit efforts to draw upon a Christian moral vocabulary that was widely shared across racial lines. In Latin America, approaches to transitional justice have similarly attempted to come to terms with the wrongs of the past, combining human rights documentation with a range of different prescriptions to restore accountability, including institutional reform, amnesty programs, and attempts to prosecute leading human rights offenders. In postgenocide Rwanda and postwar Sierra Leone, United Nations–sponsored tribunals prosecuted prominent offenders. By also utilizing a localized system of grassroots *gacaca* courts to address crimes against humanity that had been perpetrated on a massive scale, Rwandans drew upon traditional community justice practices to accelerate the trials of thousands of alleged offenders and—whenever possible—reintegrate minor offenders into social life. The people of Sierra Leone complemented their United Nations tribunal proceedings with a full-scale truth and reconciliation commission and "district support committees" intended to facilitate the reconciliation process by engaging civil society.

A survey of major political transitions reveals that there is no "one size fits all" model, and that efforts to reestablish social consensus about "right" and "wrong" necessarily require appeals to deep-rooted cultural values. Given the prominent role played by Islamic culture in Middle Eastern societies, it stands to reason that effective regional approaches to transitional justice would require attentiveness to Islamic values and precedents. Though the precise criteria for legitimacy are disputed, Islamic principles for conflict resolution, with their emphasis on forbearance and their provisions for restorative justice, would appear to offer guidance for navigating a number of difficult political transitions.

The Problem of Silence

A common dilemma faced in many post–civil war societies around the world pertains to the difficulty of "speaking the truth" about the scope and intensity of past offenses. The parties involved in negotiating a settlement often have a vested interest in discouraging efforts to document instances of torture and "disappearance" as well as other forms of political violence. Moreover, fears that revisiting the past will open old wounds and renew violent struggle can result in pressure to silence dissonant voices. Yet when there is social and political pressure not to discuss violations of basic human rights principles, factions are free to develop their own self-serving narratives about the conflict, without public debate to broaden their perspective and correct biases. A culture of impunity can emerge, in which the rights abusers of the past remain in positions of authority, and needed reforms of legal and security institutions are neglected.

Lebanon's effort to transcend the bitter legacy of civil war (1975–1990) is a case in point. For a decade and a half, a country whose capital had once been hailed "the Paris of the Middle East" became a field of bitter strife after the state collapsed on account of multiple pressures, including rivalries within and among Muslim, Christian, and Druze communities, large-scale activities by Palestinian resistance groups, left-right political cleavages, and intervention by neighboring powers such as Israel and Syria. Amid shifting, kaleidoscope-like patterns of conflict among militias and occupying armies, this small Middle Eastern nation suffered more than 100,000 deaths, a comparable number of injuries, and large-scale displacement of civilian populations.

After a number of external efforts to bring peace to Lebanon, a successful formula was finally achieved in 1989 through negotiations of Lebanese parliamentarians (elected before the outbreak of civil war) at Ta'if, Saudi Arabia. These negotiations, sponsored by the Arab League and encouraged by Lebanese notables, brought about an agreement to end the civil war and effect changes in the confessional system by which Lebanon was governed. According to the Ta'if Accord, the Sunni prime minister and the multiconfessional parliament would receive greater power relative to the traditionally Maronite Christian president. Syrian forces within Lebanon were granted a mandate to act as peacekeepers, within a larger framework containing provisions for a staged withdrawal from the country.

For many Lebanese citizens, the Ta'if Accord was a mixed blessing. It had ended a brutal civil war, creating space for reconstruction and a "return to normal" in many areas of life. Virtually no family had been untouched by the suffering of the civil war, and many welcomed the opportunity to move forward. Yet the ghosts of the past did not disappear. Many former militia leaders achieved a seamless transition from military leadership to political office, becoming "respectable" members of the Lebanese parliament. Although the Ta'if Accord contained a pledge to abolish political sectarianism and return displaced persons to their homes, the document did not include provisions for documenting the devastating human rights legacy of the civil war, or for holding those responsible for abuses and atrocities accountable. Only one civil war–era leader, Samir Geagea, head of the powerful and anti-Syrian Lebanese Forces militia, was prosecuted for war crimes.

While it may have been both impossible and undesirable to pursue civil war leaders and those who had been most directly responsible for human rights violations, a number of Lebanese civic leaders came to believe that the country had paid a price for attempting to simply "bury" the past. The insistence of many political leaders on silencing discussion of the civil war period came with a price: missed opportunities to accurately record human rights abuses for the public record, inadequate efforts to address the mistrust that had developed among members of different factions and religious groups, and failure to devote adequate resources to facilitate the rehabilitation of those affected by trauma and dislocation. Activists proposed major initiatives such as an indigenous truth and reconciliation commission based on an adapted *sulh* model, or a campaign of domestic peacebuilding with a strong educational component, but were disappointed when Prime Minister Rafik Hariri—the architect of postwar reconstruction—famously described the years of violence as a "war of others [i.e., Israelis, Palestinians, Syrians, Americans, and various other Western and Middle Eastern peoples] on our land." If the voices of those who had suffered were suppressed, many wondered, how could Lebanon's many rival groups overcome self-referential storytelling, and recognize that virtually every community had endured and inflicted scars? How could reconciliation be achieved without a measure of honesty, reparation, or accountability? Had the lessons of the war truly been learned?

These questions remain unanswered. Since adoption of the Ta'if Accord, international pressures and internal cleavages have continued to plague the country, leading to protracted confrontation between rival political factions. Though leaders appear to have been sufficiently chastened by the civil war experience to place a priority on restraining vigilantism and reckless militia violence (see Chapter 7), national unity and reconciliation remain elusive.

Amnesty and Accountability: Challenges of Truth, Reparation, and Reform

From independence until 1992, Algeria's government had been dominated by a single party, the revolutionary National Liberation Front. When socioeconomic conditions in Algeria began to deteriorate during the 1980s for reasons attributed to stagnant oil prices as well as to an inefficient state apparatus afflicted by corruption, a rise in political dissent followed. Citizen protests in the late 1980s gave impetus to reforms, including a referendum on a new constitution and national elections. When the Islamic Salvation Front won a decisive victory during the first round of elections, the secular Algerian military establishment panicked, staging a coup that set off a decade-long civil war in which an estimated 150,000 to 200,000 people died, and thousands more went missing.

After the cancellation of the elections and an ensuing rebellion by the Islamic Salvation Front, the political environment in Algeria became increasingly chaotic. In the midst of guerrilla fighting and counterinsurgency, atrocities against civilians (including abduction, torture, extrajudicial execution, rape, and bombing) were committed by both sides, often in a mysterious and brutal manner that left both responsibility and strategic purpose in question. The Islamic Salvation Front splintered into a number of different Islamic opposition groups, some of which drew strength as well as radical ideological conviction from fighters who had only recently returned from war against the Soviet occupation of Afghanistan.

Because the consequences of the conflict were so deeply damaging to Algerian society, public pressure began to build for the military-backed government to seek a settlement. Many Algerians saw themselves as victims trapped between relentless adversaries who had spread a climate of fear, poverty, and insecurity throughout the country. In 1999, the government offered clemency to armed insurgents who were willing to renounce violence, and a presidential decree in January 2000 granted amnesty to several hundred resistance members who had been adhering to cease-fires since 1997. In November 2004, President Abdelaziz Bouteflika proposed a general amnesty. This proposal, called the Charter for Peace and Reconciliation, extended amnesty to all who disavowed further armed struggle, on the condition that they had not "killed, raped or placed bombs in public places."[36] In addition, the charter provided a blanket amnesty for all state officials, providing no legal recourse to relatives of victims killed or abducted by the government forces. Numerous international human rights organizations, including Amnesty International, Human Rights Watch, the International Center for Transitional Justice, the International Commission of Jurists, and the International Federation for Human Rights, sharply criticized this initiative for evading the demands of justice, accountability, and institutional reform, and for its seeming indifference to victims of violence. How, critics asked, could Algeria overcome the legacy of the past without exposing painful truths through public inquiry and recourse to the court system to redress human rights abuses? Should not victims be allowed a voice in the transition process?

Despite these criticisms and significant protests from opposition groups, the charter passed a referendum after a hasty government effort to secure parliamentary endorsement. Supporters of the charter argued that the civil war had become unsustainable, and that the only way to end the fighting was to grant immunity from prosecution—a proposition that was not without appeal to Algerians who hoped merely for security and an end to bloodshed. Overall, the charter succeeded in solidifying cease-fires and stabilizing the country, but the actual process through which amnesty was granted to insurgents was far from transparent.

When viewed through the lenses of an Islamic "peace through conciliation" paradigm emphasizing both justice and forgiveness, the Algerian reconciliation charter grants insufficient attention to procedural and substantive demands for justice, and therefore fails to provide an adequate foundation for genuine forgiveness. In Algeria as in Lebanon, concerns remain that, because the transitional justice process was largely devoid of restorative measures and consideration for the needs and rights of victims, the extension of amnesty lacks legitimacy. While the need for an alternative to violent retribution is broadly acknowledged, the moral and emotional consequences of the war have not been satisfactorily addressed. Writing in Lebanon's *Daily Star,* one critic of the process remarked that, in contrast to the transition process in South Africa, which achieved a measure of restorative justice, the Algerian amnesty effort falls short: "[The government] denies Algerians the right to truth and justice, which are essential keys to lasting peace and national reconciliation. The South African Truth and Reconciliation Commission, established after the end of apartheid, provided a forum for victims of abuse to be heard, and for the perpetrators of violence to testify in exchange for amnesty from prosecution."[37]

Without question, Algeria's return from the most chaotic days of the civil war is a welcome development. What remains to be seen, however, is the extent to which the Charter for Peace and Reconciliation can provide a measure of healing after an exceptionally wounding period in Algerian history. A fuller realization of Islamic principles for reconciliation would appear to call for additional measures that might amplify the voices of victims, record their stories, and secure concrete gestures of remorse and reparation from prominent government officials as well as opposition leaders.

Algeria is by no means the only Middle Eastern country to struggle with issues of amnesty and accountability within a context of political transition. Similar issues have also emerged in such disparate contexts as Morocco and Iraq.

At first glance, Morocco's attempts to come to terms with the past appear quite different from those in Algeria, and much more manageable. Morocco achieved independence from French colonial rule in 1956, and since that time has been ruled by a series of monarchs: Muhammad V, Hassan II, and Muhammad VI. Under Hassan II, who ruled from 1961 to 1999, Morocco became deeply divided between supporters and critics of the monarchy. To maintain the political status quo, Moroccan security forces took frequent recourse to a range of repressive measures, including the imprisonment, torture, exile, and assassination of dissidents. Though the scope and intensity of these activities decreased during the latter years of Hassan II's reign, memories of abuse persisted, casting a shadow over King Muhammd VI's succession to the throne in 1999.

From the beginning, Muhammad VI sent signals that he intended to foster a more open and democratic political order than had his father and grandfather, with a more genuinely empowered parliament and a vibrant civil society. To symbolize his professed intent to deal with past excesses, he established the Equity and Reconciliation Commission. Like truth commissions in South Africa and in various Latin American countries, this commission was charged with documenting past human rights abuses in order to provide a clear historical record and create a baseline for restorative justice.

While conducting its inquiry, the Equity and Reconciliation Commission privately consulted with thousands of Moroccans who had experienced human rights abuses, while also investigating formerly secret prisons and interviewing security personnel. To create a sense of popular participation and involvement in the proceedings, several victims of human rights abuses were allowed to share their experiences with a national audience in televised hearings.

After documenting human rights violations and shedding light on the governmental apparatus that made them possible, the commission concluded that the crimes it had uncovered were not merely the acts of wayward individuals. Rather, they reflected a pattern of events for which the state itself was responsible. The commission's final report therefore called for serious reforms to the Moroccan constitution. Official recommendations placed particular emphasis on the need for an independent judiciary and effective oversight of national security institutions. To make amends with victims, the commission also offered monetary reparations and medical care.

In the regional context of the Middle East and North Africa, Morocco's Equity and Reconciliation Commission was unprecedented. Its proceedings generated a great deal of public debate about previously taboo issues, and resulted in an impressively transparent treatment of past human rights issues. By including reparations for many victims, the commission came closer to Islamic norms for reconciliation, according to which admission of wrongdoing and willingness to provide compensation create conditions favorable for forgiveness. The commission was not, however, without its detractors.

Critics of the Equity and Reconciliation Commission point out that, despite its success in opening discussion of past events, its mandate to achieve change and genuine reconciliation remains unfulfilled. Few of its recommendations regarding judicial reform and security sector oversight have been implemented, and new reports of torture are not uncommon. The monarchy itself remains largely beyond the scope of public criticism, and new anti-terror laws adopted after the 2003 Casablanca bombings have granted the security services broad powers to detain suspected dissidents. Though the surprising candor of the commission's efforts to deal with the past offers a promising precedent for the region, the fact that the commission was initiated by the monarchy to facilitate a political transition rather than negotiated with an opposition movement (as in South Africa) would appear to limit the likelihood of sweeping systemic changes.

Superficially, Iraq's current attempts to achieve transitional justice bear a much closer resemblance to those in Algeria. The scenario differs, however, insofar as transition efforts have also included strong retributive measures against Saddam Hussein and his key lieutenants, and have occurred within the context of a partially internationalized insurgency that views the country's US-sponsored, Shia-dominated government as doubly illegitimate, despite claims to an electoral mandate.

In Iraq as in Algeria, an amnesty has been offered to rebel forces by the government, on the condition that they put down their arms and return to civilian life. In 2006, Iraqi prime minister Nouri al-Maliki linked his amnesty invitation to provisions for prisoner release and integration of militias with national security forces. Although the effort is not without successes, Iraq's progress toward national reconciliation appears quite limited. Critics of governmental priorities have pointed out that, by making the trial of Saddam Hussein the public centerpiece of transitional justice efforts, focusing specifically on atrocities committed in the predominantly Shia town of Dujail following an assassination attempt in 1982, opportunities for public education and restoration of national unity have been missed. By managing Hussein's trial with the intent of securing a death penalty for the former dictator, Iraq's new government arguably failed to create a credible public inquiry into the widespread abuses of previous decades. Had televised, systematic hearings investigating crimes against Kurds and Shia Arabs as well as Sunnis taken precedence over sweeping de-Ba'thification and the drive toward retributive measures against elites, Iraq's transitional justice process might have achieved broader legitimacy and greater restorative impact.

While pressures for speedy vengeance would no doubt have been difficult to transcend, the fact that many Sunnis have come to regard Saddam Hussein as a national and sectarian martyr should give pause. Speculatively dwelling upon missed opportunities, of course, should not distract from present challenges and future needs. The current persistence of sectarian and militia-driven violence suggests that any future negotiations between government and opposition will necessarily have to include efforts to grapple with issues of truth, restoration, and reconciliation.

An Islamic Paradigm for Reconciliation

> And hold fast, all together, by the rope which God [stretches out for you], and be not divided among yourselves; and remember with gratitude God's favor on you; for you were enemies and He joined your hearts in love, so that by His grace, you became brethren.
>
> —Quran 3:103

In comparison to Western approaches to conflict resolution, Islamic tradition offers frameworks that are decidedly communitarian. Solidarity and harmony are regarded as key values, together with a conception of justice that provides scope for retribution while enjoining restoration and forgiveness as a greater good. Although upholding shared norms that stabilize social relations is viewed as an essential priority, actual processes of mediation and reconciliation depend quite heavily on religiously based moral suasion, appeals to magnanimity, and affirmation of spiritual rewards that accompany forbearance and forgiveness.

The differences between Western and Islamic approaches to conflict resolution mirror some of the differences between Western and Islamic perspectives on conflict. In Middle Eastern Islamic culture, conflict is typically regarded as a negative phenomenon that threatens cohesion and harmony in the family, community, or nation. It follows, then, that conflicts are a matter of concern for the entire social group and not just the immediate stakeholders. Individuals are generally hesitant to openly, directly, and explicitly assert their interests, unless rules of respect and propriety have already been broken and the conflict has escalated to a high level of confrontation.

The modern Western tradition views conflict as natural and, in comparison to Middle Eastern Islamic culture, is less averse to forms of communication that address or express conflict directly. A common assumption of economic as well as social and political thinking is that open confrontation among conflicting interest groups is not only permissible, but often valuable. While professionals and scholars who specialize in conflict resolution do not necessarily disagree with this assessment, they tend to regard positive conflict outcomes as the product of deliberate effort and intentionality, and therefore seek to channel conflict toward "win-win" outcomes and durable, mutually beneficial solutions.[38]

While conflict resolution specialists have begun to develop newer approaches designed to prioritize human needs and nonadversarial processes,[39] mainstream Western conflict resolution most typically reflects a cultural outlook of pragmatic individualism and a style of instrumental problem solving. Critics have suggested that overemphasis on expediency and technique can result in an engineering approach that neglects broader relational and social goals.[40] Others have argued that, however suitable modern Western techniques may be in their original cultural milieu, their applications in more traditional or non-Western contexts are limited.

John Paul Lederach, a leading scholar and practitioner of cross-cultural approaches to peacebuilding, has observed substantial differences between contemporary Western conflict resolution approaches and traditional Latin American methods that are derived from indigenous culture and embedded in communal values. On the basis of his work in the region, Lederach concludes that "insider partial" mediators—who are by definition well versed in local cultural meanings and expectations, and often have vested interests in conflict outcomes—have better chances of making important contributions than mediators who play the North American role of the disinterested, impartial outsider.[41] Other scholars have also recognized the role that culture plays in conflict and peacemaking, and have affirmed the need for approaches to conflict resolution that are sensitive to non-Western realities and value systems.[42]

Distinctively Islamic approaches to conflict resolution resemble other non-Western approaches insofar as they frame conflicts as matters of communal and not just individual concern and underscore the importance of repairing and maintaining long-term social relationships. Islamic approaches to conflict resolution draw on religious values, social networks, rituals of reconciliation,[43] and historical practices of communal and intercommunal coexistence. Strong emphasis is placed on linkages between personal and group identity, between individual and collective responsibility for wrongdoings, and between attentiveness to "face"-related issues (public status, shame, reputation for generosity) and the achievement of restorative justice within a context of continuing relationship. Conflict resolution efforts are directed toward the discernment of right or wrong conduct, the recognition of mutual rights and obligations, and the need for public apology, compensation for losses, and if possible, forgiveness.[44] Conflict resolution mechanisms are legitimized and guaranteed by communal leaders and (traditionally) elders who facilitate a process of reconciliation in which the principal disputants must sometimes defer to the preferences of influential relatives who share the consequences of their actions. History and custom are regarded as sources of stability and guidance that provide lessons for shaping a common future.

Outcomes of Islamic "peace through conciliation" practices can vary considerably, depending not only on the judgments of individuals guiding mediation-arbitration processes, but also on the quality of historical relations between estranged collectives and on the manner in which victimized groups choose to claim their rights. Because Islam places a strong emphasis on establishing social justice and equity through the application of religious norms and laws, individuals who are deemed to have been wronged are placed in a position in which they may pursue their rights competitively or—in exchange for the "higher" satisfactions of community approval and spiritual atonement—choose to grant forgiveness. In cases where multiple wrongs exist and no party is a clear victim or offender, effort must still be made to assess the scope of the harm inflicted by and suffered by each party, so as to establish a clear basis for compensation and forgiveness transactions. Settlements are regarded to be far more binding if witnessed before an entire community, and if members of entangled groups recognize a vested interest in holding their brethren accountable. Because violation of an agreement is regarded as an affront to the mediating party or parties, traditional Islamic conflict resolution practices favor mediators of high social status, whose appeals for peace can be difficult to dismiss.

Challenges for Islamic Conflict Resolution

As a paradigm, "peace through conciliation" translates Islamic precepts into practices that can be used to bridge gaps between individuals and social groups, while restoring a sense of justice and goodwill to relationships. In contrast to the "peace through equity" paradigm it places greater emphasis on renewing positive relations through a communicative process, and in comparison to the "peace through coercion" paradigm it depends far more on moral suasion than compulsion. The "peace through equity" paradigm, in turn, assigns higher priority to distributive justice and structural causes of conflict.

Many of the practices associated with the "peace through conciliation" paradigm have very deep roots. This is an asset insofar as the practices have enduring cultural resonance and relate directly to a firm sense of religious identity. However, it can also be a liability insofar as the Muslim world in general and the Middle East in particular are becoming increasingly urbanized and distant from the small-scale communities and tribal settings in which traditional practices originated. Though functional in their original contexts, the classical forms of these practices are not operable for many potential practitioners, and tend to place women into informal, "backchannel" roles—roles that may have a dramatic effect on outcomes, but that many contemporary women may find restrictive.

There are a number of challenges facing practitioners of "peace through conciliation," among the most important of which is keeping practice up-to-date and responsive to modern milieus and social environments. As traditional elders lose some of their sway in Middle Eastern culture, younger individuals have begun to take a more active interest in conflict resolution and peacebuilding activities, and have sought to adapt and update customary concepts and procedures, often through integration with aspects of Western practices. New generations of trainers will no doubt bring added dynamism and updated forms to such centuries-old ways of managing conflict as *tahkim* and *sulh.*

Applying Islamic conflict resolution principles to macro-level social and political conflict also remains a challenge for the "peace through conciliation" paradigm. Many questions remain unanswered. How, for example, might Muslim scholars, politicians, and conflict resolution practitioners work together to develop appropriate Islamic models for modern problems of transitional justice? Are the experiences of Western Christian nongovernmental organizations that concern themselves with peacebuilding, such as the Mennonite Central Committee and Catholic Relief Services, relevant to Islamic efforts to develop and refine religiously rooted peacebuilding practices? How can principles of "peace through conciliation" find greater scope for application in contemporary Middle Eastern conflicts—international, intercommunal, sectarian, and civil? Can conflict resolution principles be applied to expedite democratic governance and enrich Islamic models for government by consultation *(shura)*? And what might Western diplomats learn by engaging Middle Eastern Muslims to identify ways in which Islamic principles of conflict resolution might be brought to bear amid intense or protracted rivalries such as those in Israel-Palestine, Iraq, US-Iranian relations, or the Western Sahara?

Although much remains unknown about possible applications of Islamic conflict resolution models, creative experiments are under way. Children in Gaza, for example, have been trained for peer mediation using the example of Arab-Islamic village headmen *(mukhtars)*, and regionally adapted forms of conflict resolution training have been undertaken by nongovernmental organizations such as Bethlehem's Wi'am, the Palestinian Center for Resolving Social Disputes, and the Lebanon Conflict Resolution Network.

In addition to grassroots and social applications of traditional Islamic and Middle Eastern conflict resolution principles, consideration should also be given to ways in which these conciliation practices might be used as models and metaphors at the international level. Informal and highly personalistic mediation practices have been used in the past to resolve disputes among Arab leaders; at the very least, the development of an updated and refined vocabulary for discussing Middle Eastern and Islamic approaches to conflict resolution might shed light on principles that have already been applied to ease personal rivalries or settle boundary disputes. There may also be possibilities for multilateral organizations such as the Arab League and the Organization of the Islamic Conference to devote resources to the development of greater institutional mediation capacity, for utilization in a manner that is both focused and sensitive to regional politics and culture. Traditional Islamic approaches to conciliation cannot offer a panacea for Middle Eastern conflicts, yet history has transmitted a rich legacy of experiences and models that await utilization by those who are willing to reclaim and adapt them.

Notes

1. Milton-Edwards and Hinchcliffe, *Conflicts in the Middle East Since 1945,* 2001, p. 109.
2. Iqbal, *Diplomacy in Early Islam,* 1992, pp. 27–28.
3. Moussalli, "An Islamic Model for Political Conflict Resolution," 1997, p. 51.
4. Armstrong, *Muhammad,* 1992, pp. 243–245; Aslan, *No God but God,* 2005, p. 106.
5. Abdalla, "Principles of Islamic Interpersonal Conflict Intervention," 2000–2001; Abu-Nimer, "A Framework for Nonviolence and Peacebuilding in Islam," 2000–2001.
6. Crow, "Nonviolence, Ethics, and Character Development in Islam," 2001.
7. The following Quranic passage (21:92–93) illustrates these principles: "Your community is but one community, and I am Your only Lord. Therefore serve Me. People have divided themselves into factions, but to Us they shall all return."
8. This understanding attributes factionalism and severe conflict to ignorance and stubbornness in the face of moral and spiritual truth. As we noted in Chapter 5, it has led many modern Muslim thinkers to portray individualism and nationalism as threats to Islamic values.
9. Quran 5:48.
10. Quran 3:104.
11. See also 2:178 and 5:45.
12. Quran 42:44.
13. Cited in Perry, *A Treasury of Traditional Wisdom,* 1971, p. 699.
14. *Sahih Muslim,* bk. 32, no. 6214.
15. *Malik's Muwatta,* bk. 47, no. 47.4.16.

16. *Sahih Muslim,* bk. 37, nos. 6626–6627.

17. Moussalli, "An Islamic Model for Political Conflict Resolution," 1997, pp. 49–50.

18. "Humanity was a single community, and God sent prophets to give them glad tidings and warnings, and sent the Scripture with them containing the truth to judge between them in matters of dispute" (Quran 2:213). For further elaboration and commentary, see Moussalli, "An Islamic Model for Political Conflict Resolution," 1997.

19. Quran 5:48.

20. As a delineation of fundamental political principles, the Constitution of Medina did not last forever or prevent the emergence of serious conflicts. The onset of war between Mecca and Medina—in which the Muslims were most often outnumbered and faced with better-equipped forces—sharpened communal cleavages between the Muslim and Jewish communities, which eventually resulted in accusations that leading tribes of indigenous Jews had betrayed the Muslims at a moment of great peril during the Battle of the Trench in 627. The Constitution of Medina did, however, establish precedents that have been invoked in later periods of Islamic history.

21. Abu-Nimer, *Nonviolence and Peace Building in Islam,* 2003, pp. 92–94.

22. For a more detailed account of this arbitration, see Moussalli, "An Islamic Model for Political Conflict Resolution," 1997, pp. 60–64.

23. Lang, *Sharaf Politics,* 2005.

24. Irani and Funk, "Rituals of Reconciliation," 1998, p. 66.

25. The Arabic term *'atwa* is sometimes used to refer to this truce or "cease-fire," which may require a preliminary payment to the family of the victim in exchange for agreement to proceed with the peacemaking process. See Lang, *Sharaf Politics,* 2005, p. 136.

26. Lang, *Sharaf Politics,* 2005, pp. 90–97.

27. Ibid., pp. 89–90.

28. Mathews, *War Prevention Works,* 2002, pp. 104–105.

29. Abu-Nimer, "Conflict Resolution Approaches," 1996.

30. Palestinians living under Israeli rule, whether as citizens of the state of Israel or as subjects of Israeli military administration in the West Bank and (formerly) in the Gaza Strip, have often preferred the framework of traditional practices to other available options. *Sulha* remains an integral component in community peacemaking. See Smith, "The Rewards of Allah," 1989; Jabbour, *Sulha,* 1996; Lang, *Sharaf Politics,* 2005, pp. 81–82.

31. Smith, *Palestine and the Arab-Israeli Conflict,* 1996, pp. 77–78, 300–301.

32. Israeli settlers wrestled with similar questions: Is giving up land tantamount to rejecting the will of God? Or is preventing avoidable loss of life a higher principle? See Appleby, *The Ambivalence of the Sacred,* 2000, pp. 81–85.

33. Israeli journalist Hanna Kim wrote about Erlich's *hudna* proposal in *Ha'aretz* on January 2, 2002. See Gold, "The Diaspora and the Intifada," 2002.

34. AbuSulayman, *The Islamic Theory of International Relations,* 1987, pp. 17–18.

35. Sulha Peace Project, "Our Vision," 2008.

36. Human Rights Watch, "Algeria," 2005.

37. Labidi, "Amnesia Is the Price of Algerian Peace and Reconciliation," 2006.

38. Fisher, Ury, and Patton, *Getting to Yes,* 1991.

39. Burton, *Conflict,* 1990; Laue, "Contributions of the Emerging Field of Conflict Resolution," 1988.

40. Scimecca, "Conflict Resolution in the United States," 1991.

41. Lederach, "The Mediator's Cultural Assumptions," 1995, pp. 80–82; Wehr and Lederach, "Mediating Conflict in Central America," 1991.

42. Augsburger, *Conflict Mediation Across Cultures,* 1992; Avruch, *Culture and Conflict Resolution,* 1998.

43. Irani and Funk, "Rituals of Reconciliation," 1998, pp. 59–61.

44. Ibid., p. 67; Satha-Anand, "The Politics of Forgiveness," 1996.

7

Peace Through Nonviolence: A Paradigm of Peaceful Striving

> Let there be no compulsion in religion: Truth stands out clear from error. . . . God is the protector of those who have faith: From the depths of darkness he leads them forth into light.
>
> —Quran 2:256–257

It is a truism that Westerners tend to view the Middle East through the twin lenses of political violence and religious fanaticism. Perceptions are formed and conditioned by a daily barrage of images from the Israeli-Palestinian conflict, Iraq, and other regional hotspots. The resultant impressions have become so deeply ingrained that it is often difficult to perceive nonviolent aspects of Middle Eastern social and political reality, or to conceive of ways in which nonviolent change might become viable.

Middle Eastern Muslims, of course, take offense at Western stereotypes. After all, did not the most destructive conflicts of the twentieth century take place largely in Europe? And why dwell upon centuries-old images of Islamic imperialism when Western imperialism is a more recent phenomenon? Are not contemporary Muslims who advocate violence often themselves victims of injustice and oppression?

Such questions challenge us to examine patterns of violent and nonviolent political activity in a circumspect manner. The peoples of the Middle East have paid a heavy price for the deadly conflicts and geopolitical stalemates of the past century, and though the Middle East lags behind many other regions in the implementation of democratic forms of governance, it may be less of an "exception" to global trends than most Western commentary suggests. While some political actors have indeed been unable to conceive of ways to reach their objectives without resorting to violence, there are nonetheless many nontrivial Middle Eastern examples of nonviolent steadfastness in the face of foreign occupation or exploitation by domestic elites. In many but not all cases of Middle Eastern nonviolent resistance, protagonists of change have made active use of Islamic principles that condemn wanton acts of destruction and support unarmed struggle against oppression.

Like many other religious and cultural traditions, Islam contains within itself textual resources and historical precedents for nonviolent activism. Virtually unknown outside the Islamic world and frequently misrepresented by those who have encouraged political violence, the "peace through nonviolence" paradigm provides a compelling counterargument to many simplistic assumptions about Islam and those who follow it. To better understand this paradigm and its potential relevance in coming decades, we now turn to Islamic teachings that condemn the use of violence to effect political change and to examples of unarmed struggle in the Middle East region.

Quranic Perspectives on Violence and Nonviolence

A survey of the Quran reveals not only passages that grant legitimacy to armed resistance to oppression, but also strong admonitions against wanton bloodshed and the use of force to achieve selfish ends. Like the Torah and the Christian Bible, the Quran identifies Cain's offense against Abel as the first instance of violence in human history, and clearly marks this episode as a great wrong, through which Cain became responsible not only for his own sins but also for those of his brother. In the Quranic narrative, Abel confronts Cain before the latter's fateful action, and issues a remarkable proclamation: "Even if you stretch out your hand against me to kill me, I shall not stretch out my hand against you to kill you. I fear God, the Lord of the worlds" (5:28). From this event, the Quran asserts a moral imperative to protect life that is reminiscent of a teaching in the Jewish Talmud: "On that account, We decreed for the Children of Israel that if anyone slew a person—unless it be for murder or for spreading mischief upon the earth—it would be as if he slew all humanity; and whoever saves a life, saves the whole of humanity" (5:32).

This story of human origins and of the earliest act of violence establishes the sanctity of human life, while also foreshadowing the difficulties inherent in protecting innocent lives from those who pursue political and private interests without moral restraint. Reflective followers of other traditions will detect a familiar tension that follows from condemning violence while allowing scope for the use of force as a defensive measure or basis for combating oppression.

As noted in previous chapters, the Quran does not enjoin a categorically nonviolent or quietist ethos. A large number of passages create a clear basis for Islamic just war thinking. Yet the text's condemnation of aggression and strong call for limits on violent, acquisitive, and exploitative behavior is hard to miss. From a Quranic standpoint, the ends clearly do not justify the means. Unregulated violence is a source of disorder and moral corruption; restraining oneself and meeting indignities with composure is a great moral virtue.

One of the more common refrains of the Quran is that fear and remembrance of God—hallmarks of personal piety—impose discipline and awareness of accountability on human action. A person who remembers God renounces violent aggression, and embraces patience *(sabr)* in the face of provocation. The following verses exemplify this theme:

> Peace unto you for that ye persevered in patience! Now how excellent is the final Home. (13:24)
>
> But turn away from them, and say "Peace!" (43:89)
>
> Fear God, and know that God is with those who restrain themselves. (2:194)

A number of passages in the Quran accentuate the priority that must be given to persuasion in matters of faith and belief, and discourage efforts to achieve uniformity or consensus through coercion. The preaching of religion must be conducted in a civil manner, and ultimate responsibility for human affairs belongs to God. As the Quran states, "Thou art not one to overawe them by force *[bi-jabbar]*" (50:45). This passage and others like it oblige Muslims to avoid violating the basic Quranic teaching of "no compulsion in religion" (2:256)—even while steadfastly advocating the Islamic message.[1]

As noted in previous chapters, the Islamic conception of jihad is multidimensional. While the "lesser" jihad *(jihad al-asghar)* may involve use of force to meet with actual or potential threats to the Islamic community, the "greater" jihad *(jihad al-akbar)* is an intensely personal struggle to live an upright and spiritual life. Because jihad is essentially a striving to protect and advance Islamic values, there is considerable scope in Islamic sources for enjoining nonviolent resistance to injustice, as an alternative to *fitna*—violent insurrection or civil discord—and to the humiliation of passively accepting injustice.

Chaiwat Satha-Anand is one of many contemporary Muslim thinkers who are reappraising the role of nonviolent action in Islamic political ethics. These thinkers are drawing attention to patterns of action that, though fully consistent with Quranic ethics, have often been overlooked both by classical jurists (whose first preoccupation was often the well-being of existing Islamic states) and by present-day Muslims who refuse to tolerate repressive regimes. Starting with the premise that "aggression is prohibited in Islam and the fighting that is permitted has its limits,"[2] Satha-Anand seeks to rethink jihad in a manner that takes into account both the increasingly destructive nature of modern warfare and the demonstrable capacity of nonviolent social struggle techniques to effect political change without bloodshed.

Satha-Anand's basic premises about jihad and justifiable warfare are drawn directly from the classical tradition of Islamic jurisprudence, yet his application of these principles to the modern age is innovative, reflecting both a sober critique of contemporary violence and a reevaluation of the potential inherent in nonviolent methods of action. Following classical ideas about the multidimensional nature of jihad, he defines this essential concept as "an effort, a striving for justice and truth that need not be violent."[3] Highlighting the Quranic injunction to oppose oppression and injustice, Satha-Anand uses modern terminology to describe the ultimate purpose of jihad: ending "structural violence" (that is, conditions that are characterized by deep inequality, preventable human suffering, and an inequitable distribution of life chances).[4] To remain true to their calling, Satha-Anand argues, Muslims have no choice but to oppose injustice—combating "tumult and oppression" with determination, yet without "transgressing limits" that define the Islamic just war tradition. More specifically, Muslims must ensure that their efforts to defeat unjust rulers and institutions do not exceed moral bounds by harming civilians and noncombatants. In an age of automatic weapons, plastic explosives, nuclear weapons, and terrorism, he suggests, violent campaigns against injustice have become increasingly at odds with the Islamic moral tradition. Yet nonviolent methods of action offer a compelling alternative to passivity that is deeply resonant with core Islamic values.[5]

According to Satha-Anand, Islam's incompatibility with passivity in the face of injustice is an asset for those seeking to promote an ethos of active nonviolence: "Complete submission to the will of Allah means that if Muslims are oppressed and too weak to fight back, they nevertheless must refuse to obey an unjust ruler. . . . Whether Muslims are weak or strong, they must do something, and it is this tendency toward action that enables them to engage easily in nonviolent struggle."[6] The collective as well as personal disciplines of Islam, Satha-Anand suggests, can empower Muslims to oppose repression and injustice with determination—without resorting to forms of violence that can easily escalate into violations of Islamic morality.

Precedents for Nonviolent Action

Those who advocate Islamic approaches to nonviolent action are by no means without examples from the formative period of Islamic faith and practice. As is well known, the first half of Muhammad's prophetic career was carried out in a manner that was eminently compatible with principles of nonviolence. The Meccan oligarchy challenged the Prophet's message of religious and social reform not only through propaganda, but also through a program of active persecution that included torture and assassination attempts. For thirteen years (C.E. 610–623), Muhammad consistently enjoined patience and steadfastness; Quranic revelations from the period reinforce themes of spiritual discipline and assertiveness rather than military struggle.[7]

With the flight of the Muslims to Medina, the content of Quranic messages began to change. After a relatively short time in Medina, the Prophet—who had himself narrowly escaped death at the time of his forced departure from

Mecca—permitted Muslims to participate in sorties against Meccan caravans. These expeditions evoked the Arab tradition of limited intertribal raids, for sport or reprisal as well as for subsistence. Traditional narratives suggest that many Muslims had strongly pushed for this decision, and that it may well have reflected the dire economic circumstances endured by Muslim refugees from Mecca. Moreover, the Meccans had confiscated all remaining property that departing Muslims had left in their native city. Muslim raids, however, represented a significant disruption of Meccan trade, and soon escalated to open warfare. With the onset of circumstances in which the physical survival of the Muslim community was directly threatened, Quranic exhortations began to call for a vigorous—but not irreversibly hostile—Muslim response: "O you who believe! Violate not the sanctity of the symbols of God. . . . And let not the hatred of some people in [once] shutting you out of the Sacred Mosque [the Ka'ba in Mecca] lead you to transgression [and hostility on your part]. Help one another in righteousness and piety, but help not one another in sin and aggression" (5:2). Quranic verses from the Medina period call for fighting, but never for unmitigated hostility and destruction.

As discussed in previous chapters, the habit of mainstream Muslim thinkers was to interpret changing Quranic instructions on matters related to violence in a manner that gave priority to the verses that were understood to have been revealed last. As a result, traditional thinking framed the nonviolence of the Meccan period as circumstantial, while regarding the "just war" paradigm of the Medina period to be normatively binding. It should come as no surprise that such an approach to interpretation was favored by political elites during the formative Umayyad and Abbasid periods, insofar as it focused attention on foreign military threats and ruled out the possibility that Muslims might draw upon the Mecca paradigm to resist the worldly excesses of their own leaders.

For Muslim advocates of nonviolence, any reading of the Quran that negates the Mecca paradigm cannot provide a complete account of Islamic ethics, and is likely to dramatically reduce the ability of Muslims to learn from their full range of past experiences. In the mind of Abdul Ghaffar Khan, a great Muslim leader in the struggle for Indian independence from the British Empire, the fact that nonviolence "was followed by the Prophet all the time he was in Mecca" was far from trivial.[8] Relying on this precedent was for him an act of Islamic faith, and it enabled him to enlist approximately 100,000 Pashtuns as members of the world's first uniformed nonviolent army—"the army of God," as he called it. Members of this movement referred to themselves as Khudai Khidmatgars ("servants of God"), and swore an oath to serve humanity in the name of God, refrain from violence and acts of revenge, forgive cruel oppressors, devote two hours per day to social work, and prepare themselves for fearless sacrifice.[9]

Although the case of the Pashtuns has few parallels in the Middle East and indeed in most other world regions, additional cases can indeed be found that demonstrate the potential for Muslim nonviolence. Taken together, these cases support Muslim efforts to find new meaning in the Quranic injunction to cooperate in acts of righteousness, and to refuse cooperation with acts of injustice—whether injustice takes the form of unjust governance, occupation, or intercommunal rivalry.

Nonviolence and Civil Disobedience in Middle Eastern History

According to Khalid Kishtainy, a contrarian Iraqi thinker and essayist, Westerners are not entirely alone in their ideas about the Islamic Middle East as a place in which coercion and violence form the currency of politics. Centuries-old European stereotypes, he suggests, have a Middle Eastern counterpart. Among Arabs, for example, there is a strong tendency to take pride in military heritage and to celebrate military virtues. This tendency may well feed on present-day political humiliations and on a strongly felt need to confront intrusive outside forces, yet it also appears overstated and misplaced when considered in light of other bases for cultural pride in past achievements.

In Kishtainy's view, militarism and military accomplishment have never been the strong suit of Middle Eastern Arabs. Despite famous conquests of the seventh century, Arab Muslims never accumulated detailed and exact knowledge of military training, techniques, or organization. Compared to Greece's Spartans, the Prussians, the Japanese Samurai, and even the Ottoman Turks, dedication to military training and crafts among the Arabs was not exceptional.[10] According to Kishtainy, Arabs found commerce to be a far more compelling activity than warfare, which was rarely more than a part-time occupation. Before the modern era, there was no such thing as mass conscription in the Middle East, though many rulers did find it advantageous to recruit—through the granting of special privileges or through compulsion—soldiers from borderland regions. Military duties were the province of elite minorities committed to the service of kings and sultans.[11]

Kishtainy's commentary concerning the lack of a strong military tradition among the Arab peoples should not be taken as a denial of Arab competence in military enterprises. The pages of Middle Eastern history are as thick with references to military campaigns and feudal vendettas as tomes on European history; Arabs as well as Turks, Persians, Circassians, and members of other groups were involved in military affairs. Kishtainy's argument does, however, suggest a possible "reframing" of Middle Eastern (and especially Arab) political history, in which nonviolent traditions can be more explicitly recognized and valorized, creating space for new practices and experiments. Such was the case when Gandhi reread sacred texts as well as tracts on Western political philosophy, in an effort to chart a dynamic course toward Indian independence and internal reform. Let us therefore examine instances of nonviolent political action in Middle Eastern and Islamic history, and then assess the relevance of known cases to a potentially revived nonviolent ethic in regional politics.

A Word of Truth in the Face of a Tyrant

There is evidence of civil disobedience in the Islamic era as early as 644, when Arab tribesmen based in Egypt refused to obey the orders of the newly appointed Caliph Uthman and his governor. Unfortunately, what began as peaceful protest ended in political discord and the assassination of Uthman in 656. Uthman's murder, in turn, inaugurated an episode of civil conflict among Muslims that did not end until the establishment of the Umayyad Empire in 661.

Experiences of civil discord *(fitna)* had a tremendous impact on Muslim scholars, with the result that far greater intellectual effort was exerted to establish bases for maintaining Muslim unity than to clarify the grounds on which believers could challenge established political authorities. Yet the scholars of Islam's first centuries did record a number of prophetic sayings that legitimize opposition to arbitrary leaders. Among the most famous of these is a *hadith* that states, "The most excellent jihad is uttering a word of truth in the face of a tyrant."[12] Other sayings have been used by Muslim scholars to identify a number of different categories for jihad ("striving") to protect or project Islamic values: jihad by the tongue *(lisan),* jihad by the pen *(qalam),* jihad by one's money *(mal),* jihad by the sword *(sayf),* and jihad against one's own willful desires *(nafs).*[13] While jihad by the sword clearly refers to military struggles such as those between a Muslim state and its adversaries, the other varieties of striving have traditionally been understood to include preaching, truthful speech, provision for the needy, and moral uprightness. Taken together, they suggest possibilities for active nonviolent struggle to establish a just and humane social order.

Some of the most compelling historical examples of nonviolence on the part of Middle Eastern Muslims can be found in cases of invasion by ruthless armies that were—at least nominally—composed of Muslim soldiers. Moroccans, for example, have long recited narratives of Lala Aziza, a courageous and deeply spiritual Muslim woman of the fourteenth century who reconciled conflicting tribal groups and on one occasion persuaded the governor of Marrakesh to desist from his acts of military aggression against the people of her region. According to traditional narratives, she approached the general and his army as they approached the region of Seksawa, where she lived. Her face-to-face debate with the general was couched entirely in Islamic discourse, emphasizing the injustice of harming God's creation and the superior virtue inherent in obeying the demand of the Creator to act with justice. Unsettled by the woman's fearlessness, personal charisma, and apparent ability to anticipate his own arguments, the general gave up on his ambition to subjugate her people.[14]

In another intriguing case, famous Muslim scholar 'Ali Ibn Muhammad al-Jurjani (1339–1414), a writer of encyclopedic works, confronted the marauding armies of Tamerlane (known in the Islamic world as Timur) when they marched on the city of Shiraz in 1387. Like Lala Aziza, he is reported to have approached the invaders without protection, seeking a personal audience with the leader of the military forces. Tamerlane, who had previously pillaged and razed a number of important Persian cities, was so impressed by al-Jurjani's learning and unflappability that he spared the city of Shiraz. Though al-Jurjani was obliged to reside with Tamerlane in Samarkand until the latter's death in 1405, his moral courage in the face of a formidable adversary had spared Shiraz from violence.

Quietism and Parallel Governance Structures

In response to what they perceived as excessive worldliness and abuse of power by Muslim leaders, some early Muslim communities withdrew from active cooperation with their political leaders. Such tendencies were particularly pronounced among the Shia and Sufi movements. During the Abbasid era, many Shia leaders refused to sanction calls to military jihad by rulers whom they deemed unjust.[15] Sufi personalities often expressed similar reservations about established political and religious authorities, and in many but by no means all cases prescribed quietism and active avoidance of sultans and their courts.

For centuries, the Ottoman Empire faced considerable opposition to its efforts to govern Shia communities in Iraq. Over time, the Iraqi Shias developed parallel governance structures, including their own court systems, methods of taxation, schools, and social welfare services. Though noncooperation at times gave way to armed resistance, they effectively resisted conscription into the Ottoman army.[16]

National Movements

Modern times have produced many well-documented episodes of nonviolent opposition to oppression. In most cases, the resort to nonviolent strategies and tactics has been understood in pragmatic terms rather than as a philosophically or theologically motivated choice. During the period of anticolonial struggles, campaigns of citizen mobilization tended to rely on the language of secular nationalism as much as the symbols of Islam. Yet the existence of numerous examples of nonviolent or minimally violent resistance is instructive. Nonviolent action is part of the political repertoire of Middle Eastern Muslim activists, and closer scrutiny of the historical record may help to reinforce potential for peaceful change in the region.

Unarmed popular resistance to European colonialism figures prominently in the history of most Middle Eastern countries. During the 1880s, when the

British Empire established de facto control over the Egyptian government, peasants opposed increases in taxation through rent strikes and occupation of land. Three decades later, nonviolent action became more prominent in the Egyptian national movement; utilizing strikes and boycotts, opponents of colonial rule sought to make Egypt ungovernable. The decade preceding independence in 1922 saw successive campaigns that defied specific colonial policies and gave voice to a generalized sense of humiliation that accompanied subordination to a foreign government. Students and lawyers as well as railway, tram, telegraph, and postal workers organized strikes; government officials committed themselves to work stoppages after the introduction of martial law in 1914. The importance of these methods in securing Egyptian independence from England was not lost on Gandhi, who integrated many Egyptian practices into his *satyagraha* campaigns in India.[17]

In most of North Africa as well as in Syria and Iraq, resistance to European colonialism involved a more complex mixture of violent and nonviolent measures. Popular historical narratives give pride of place to armed resistance, but noncooperation with colonial edicts played a powerful role in galvanizing national movements and generating social solidarity.

The end of the colonial era turned out to be a mixed blessing. New forms of misgovernance and corruption became commonplace, as centralizing states consolidated power and eroded the traditional autonomy of nonstate entities. The decline of tribalism relative to the centralizing state brought both potential for social progress and dangers of abuse, for the tribal system had previously mediated relations between the people and authoritarian rulers, placing a check on the power of autocratic sultans who generally maintained distance from society and governed in a minimalist manner. To assert authority and gain deference from subjects, the centralizing state promised new social services in the domains of education, healthcare, employment, and welfare.[18] These social goods, however, were also accompanied by increased repressive capacity.

The Iranian Revolution

Together with political and economic underperformance, the oppressive habits of nationalist governments strongly reinforced Islamic movements in Middle Eastern societies. The most dramatically successful Islamic movement came to the forefront of world politics by surprise, through the Iranian Revolution of 1978–1979. Frequently caricatured in Western analysis as a quintessentially violent upheaval, the seismic shift in Iranian politics that brought about the downfall of Muhammad Reza Shah was predominantly nonviolent.[19] Popular resistance to the Shah took many forms, including strikes and boycotts as well as demonstrations that grew increasingly massive in response to applications of repressive force. The actual downfall of the Shah was brought about by a complex coalition of actors from across the Iranian political spectrum, including socialists and nationalists as well as Islamic activists. Clerics played a major role in encouraging and coordinating resistance, and the covert distribution of audio cassettes containing sermons by Ayatollah Khomeini heightened the motivation to resist oppression.

By the time of the revolution, Iranian security agencies had a well-earned reputation for ruthlessness in dealing with dissenters. Protagonists of revolution, however, succeeded in transforming this reputation into a political liability; when a sit-in by theology students in Qom was forcibly dispersed in January 1978, dissidents decided to commemorate the dead every forty days, in accordance with the traditional Islamic mourning period.[20] These subsequent protests were also met with brutal force—resulting in the deaths of hundreds of unarmed civilians—and the Iranian government gradually deprived itself of religious as well as popular legitimacy. Increasingly, Iranian society refused to cooperate with governmental authorities. Strikes by oil workers and a general strike in late 1978 threatened to paralyze the country. Demonstrations sometimes gave way to riots when met by state violence, with opposition forces targeting symbols of the Western-aligned government such as large banks, department stores, and cinemas for destructive action. Yet opponents of the Shah largely avoided efforts to challenge police or military forces through force of arms. On January 16, 1979, the Shah of Iran fled his country, and two weeks later Ayatollah Khomeini returned from abroad.

Despite highly combative, anti-Western revolutionary slogans, the defeat of the Shah was accomplished with remarkably little organized violence on the part of opposition forces. The postrevolutionary regime-consolidation period, however, pitted divergent revolutionary factions against one another, and the restraints used during the overthrow of the previous government were abandoned during the struggle to institutionalize a radically new system of rule. Campaigns against opponents of the Islamic Republic, combined with a war against Iraq that began when Saddam Hussein organized an invasion in 1980, left deep scars on the Iranian people. By the 1990s, a new generation of students had arisen to question the role that authoritarianism played in the early years of the revolution, and once again raise the challenge of nonviolent evolution toward a political system in which Islamic and democratic values could reinforce one another.[21] Increasing confrontation with the United States following the election of Mahmoud Ahmadinejad as president of Iran in 2005 has sharpened Iran's internal divides between conservative and reformist factions.

Bread Protests

Most political unrest in Middle Eastern countries falls far short of the radical change associated with Iran's Islamic Revolution. Popular protest is often infused with Islamic social justice themes, and has acquired the greatest legitimacy when centered around the most basic issues, such as the price of bread and other basic staples. Bread protests—and at times riots—in countries such as Egypt, Jordan, Morocco, Sudan, and Tunisia have provided a vehicle for dissent that has in some cases led to significant government reforms. Though often spurred by a decline in subsidies and dissatisfaction with changes in economic policy that adversely affect the poor, these protests have opened space for greater political pluralism in Sudan, Algeria, and Jordan.[22]

As a relatively new phenomenon, Middle Eastern bread protests reflect popular dissatisfaction with policies of a seemingly unaccountable state—a state that is simultaneously repressive, inequitable, and failing to support the weakest members of society as it adapts to the global economy. Because Islamic values place a strong priority on providing for one's family as a basis for the dignity *(karama)* of believers, and because Middle Eastern rulers have long sought to maintain political support through the granting of benefits in the areas of education, healthcare, housing, public sector employment, and food, sharp fluctuations in the prices of basic commodities have a profound impact on the legitimacy of a government.[23] In a context of generalized economic hardship and rising unemployment, cuts to subsidies on such essential foodstuffs as bread can activate vigorous social protests. A recurrent theme of these protests is linkage between Islamic social justice norms and the right to subsistence. The scope of protests often goes beyond economic policy, however, as efforts are made to achieve broader reforms such as an expansion of political participation and a reduction in nepotism and corruption.[24] Bread protests in Sudan during 1985 played an important role in sparking a general strike that ended the autocratic government of Ja'far Numayri,[25] leading to a short-lived democratic experiment from 1986 to 1989.

Palestine and the Arab-Israeli Conflict

Middle Eastern governments are most vulnerable to popular protests when their rule appears not only corrupt, repressive, or inefficient, but also excessively vulnerable to outside influences. When Middle Eastern peoples feel that they have little control over their economic and foreign policies, and when these policies appear to be inspired by foreign experts or determined in the capitals of distant nations, grassroots disaffection quickly follows—particularly in the presence of stark economic inequalities and a generalized sense of stagnation or malaise. Political turbulence in the Middle East today is heightened by a pervasive perception that the peoples of the region have not recovered the dignity they lost during the colonial era, and have little power to control their own destiny.[26]

Undeniably, one of the most potent symbolic issues in Middle Eastern politics has long been the Israeli-Palestinian conflict. This conflict has occupied center stage in the region since the Arab-Jewish hostilities of 1947–1949 yielded both a new Israeli state and several hundred thousand Palestinian refugees. Viewed as a godsend by Jews fleeing extermination at the hands of the Nazis during World War II,[27] the Arab peoples experienced the creation of a new Middle Eastern state by European Jews as an assault on their own national aspirations. Most Arabs and a strong majority of Middle Eastern Muslims regard the Israeli occupation of Palestine—especially occupation of Palestinian territories acquired during the 1967 Arab-Israeli War—as humiliating. Though Arab leaders have expressed willingness to recognize an Israeli state within its original postindependence boundaries, protagonists of more radical visions have regarded the suffering and displacement of the Palestinians as a justification for ongoing violent struggle.

Skeptics have often discounted the capacity of nonviolence to prevail in a conflict as intense as the Arab-Israeli confrontation, yet concerted nonviolent action campaigns have led to significant gains for the Palestinian cause. Nonviolent action played a noteworthy role in the early Palestinian national movement, when Palestinians used civil disobedience to oppose Turkish as well as British policies.[28] During the 1980s, civil disobedience combined with boycotts of Israeli goods and direct nonviolent interventions dramatically increased the political and economic costs associated with Israeli occupation of the Palestinian territories conquered during the 1967 Arab-Israeli War. As an opposition campaign that mixed highly disciplined nonviolent tactics with acts of limited or symbolic violence—most notably through hurling stones at Israeli soldiers in the Gaza Strip and West Bank—the First Intifada (1987–1993) reduced the power imbalance that had hitherto prevented meaningful negotiations about Palestinian independence.[29] It created pressure for the post–Gulf War Madrid Conference of 1991 and for subsequent Israeli negotiations with the Palestine Liberation Organization. Although the movement itself pursued Palestinian nationalist goals and included a religiously mixed leadership, activists encouraging noncooperation with the Israeli occupation of Palestinian lands made deliberate efforts to strengthen their campaigns through the invocation of Islamic values such as solidarity, justice, discipline, and steadfastness *(sumud)*.[30]

In comparison to the Second (Al-Aqsa) Intifada, which began in September 2000, the First Intifada incurred fewer material as well as human costs for Palestinians and generated greater diplomatic and political gains. Whereas the First Intifada sent a clear message that Palestinians demanded self-determination and an end to the construction of settlements on occupied lands, the Second Intifada's use of asymmetrical warfare and suicide bombings sent a different message about the nature of Palestinian national aspirations. Where the First Intifada sparked a hitherto absent resolve among many Israeli citizens and international leaders to push for equitable peace negotiations, the Second Intifada reflected the increasing alienation between Israelis and Palestinians, and ultimately contributed to a deepening conflict spiral. Ariel Sharon, whose visit to Temple

Mount (Al-Haram al-Sharif, a holy site claimed by both Jews and Muslims) had helped to spark the Second Intifada, responded by building a security wall that cut deeply into West Bank territory, rendering the prospect of a territorially and economically viable Palestinian state more tenuous.

In contrast to the First Intifada, which generated hopes for a political solution to the tragic Israeli-Palestinian conflict, the Second Intifada both reflected and contributed to a mounting sense of despair at the failure of negotiations initiated during the 1990s. The resultant impasse had left Israelis feeling deprived of security and Palestinians frustrated at their lack of power, dignity, and hope for the future. The Second Intifada did not, however, lead to a cessation of nonviolent action campaigns or of calls for a just and sustainable Israeli-Palestinian peace addressing the full range of issues that divide the two peoples, from ending occupation and defining territorial boundaries to sharing Jerusalem and arriving at compromises over the status of Israeli settlers and Palestinian refugee populations. Significant majorities of Israelis as well as Palestinians continue to support—at least passively—the concept of a comprehensive negotiated settlement,[31] and the conclusion of this painful chapter of Middle Eastern history has yet to be written.[32]

Iraq

Since the US invasion of 2003, the word *Iraq* has become virtually synonymous with violent, internecine conflict. Nonetheless, even in the midst of anti-occupation and intercommunal warfare, there have been notable cases of nonviolent action. One of the more significant of these occurred in August 2004, when US forces were engaged in a tense standoff with members of Muqtada al-Sadr's Mahdi Army after days of fighting in the city of Najaf, Iraq. A contingent of the Mahdi Army had taken refuge in a mosque dedicated to Imam 'Ali, the son-in-law of the Prophet Muhammad. This mosque has long been one of the most venerated shrines in Shia Islam.

In the midst of this confrontation, Ayatollah 'Ali al-Sistani, the most senior and widely respected Shia cleric in Iraq, returned to his country after an absence for heart treatment in London. Sensing an opportunity to reassert his leadership in relation to a rebellious junior cleric and also to save the sacred shrine from the desecration that would result from an armed attack on the Mahdi Army, Ayatollah Sistani led a march on the Imam 'Ali Mosque. Masses of unarmed Muslims converged on the site with the declared intention of protecting the holy shrine. Their presence provided an invaluable face-saving opportunity for al-Sadr's forces as well as for the US forces, who had reportedly been preparing for a final assault. Al-Sadr's forces withdrew from the shrine out of deference to Sistani, and the US forces accepted this move as a de facto retreat that obviated the need for further fighting. Though the march did not catalyze a broader peace movement to address Iraq's widespread violence and disorder, the initiative did succeed in preventing further bloodshed and destruction at one of the most revered sites in Shia Islam.

Lebanon: The Cedar Revolution

Another recent case of nonviolent action in the Middle East occurred in early 2005, when massive popular protests combined with international pressure compelled the Syrian army to withdraw its occupation forces from Lebanon. Though the Syrian military presence in Lebanon had been legitimized for peacekeeping purposes by the 1990 Ta'if Accord, which ended Lebanon's long civil war (1975–1990), Syria's presence in the country had become unpopular as a result of a deepening perception that Syria was dominating Lebanese domestic politics and placing its own interests ahead of Lebanon's, particularly with respect to trade and use of Lebanese proxies such as Hezbollah to confront Israel.

Yet the Syrian presence was not entirely unwelcome in Lebanon. For years a significant proportion of Lebanese citizens—including a majority of the nation's Shia population—have embraced Syria as a major player in their country's politics and as an ally in the conflict with Israel. Israel had invaded Lebanon in 1982 to combat cross-border raids from the Palestine Liberation Organization, and had occupied a significant swath of southern Lebanese territory from 1982 through 2000. Over time, however, the Lebanese population grew less sympathetic to the coercive behavior of Syrian policymakers, who have used pressure on Israel from the Lebanese front as a bargaining chip in efforts to reclaim their own lost territory: the Golan Heights, occupied by Israel in 1967.

When Israel withdrew from all Lebanese territory except for a small area that had once been claimed by Syria (the Sheba Farms, adjacent to the Golan Heights) in May 2000, friction between Lebanese factions and the Syrian government increased. Many Lebanese politicians began to grow impatient with the continued Syrian military presence as well as with Syrian support for Hezbollah, an organization that most Lebanese accepted as a legitimate opposition force so long as their territory was occupied, despite its designation as a terrorist group by the Israeli and US governments. The call for major changes in the asymmetrical relationship between Syria and Lebanon grew louder, but went unanswered. The final straw came in 2004, when the Syrian government exerted pressure on Lebanese politicians to change their own constitution, and thereby allow pro-Syrian president Emile Lahoud to extend his term in office. Lebanese politicians, led by former prime minister Rafik al-Hariri, decided to form a coalition against the continued Syrian military presence, and encouraged foreign efforts to push for Syrian withdrawal through a United Nations Security Council resolution.

On September 2, 2004, the United Nations Security Council approved Resolution 1559, calling for withdrawal of all "foreign forces" from Lebanese soil and for a cessation of intervention in Lebanese politics. One month later a cycle of assassinations began, directed against prominent Lebanese members of an emergent anti-Syrian coalition. The deaths of numerous journalists, politicians, and media personalities climaxed on February 14, 2005, with the killing of Hariri in a high-tech car bomb attack.

Because Rafik al-Hariri was not only a prominent politician but also a billionaire businessman who had invested heavily in the post–civil war reconstruction efforts he helped orchestrate as prime minister, a majority of Lebanon's people interpreted his murder as a direct attack on the integrity of their society. The event catalyzed unprecedented opposition to Syria's continuing military and intelligence presence, and to pro-Syrian leadership in the Lebanese government. Widespread popular disaffection found expression in a massive vigil on Beirut's Martyrs Square, and in a public funeral that was attended by approximately 250,000 of the country's 4 million people. In this gathering as well as at subsequent demonstrations, protesters gave pride of place to the country's cedar tree flag as well as to banners with slogans calling for truth, freedom, independence, and unity.

In a relatively short time, strong grassroots leadership had emerged to promote continued opposition to the Syrian military presence, as well as to Lebanese subservience to the government in Damascus. As rallies, marches, and vigils continued, official political opposition leaders openly expressed their support for the protesters. Crossing beyond previous boundaries of acceptable political speech, they called for the suspension of key figures within the Lebanese security establishment, a United Nations–led investigation of Hariri's assassination, free elections, and the full withdrawal of Syrian intelligence officers and troops. Official as well as unofficial opposition leaders held continuous organizational meetings, and attempted to draw lessons from such nonviolent popular revolutions as Georgia's Rose Revolution (2003) and Ukraine's Orange Revolution (2004). Students set up a camp in Martyrs Square, and pledged that they would not leave until the government accepted their demands. As the campaign gained momentum during several weeks of continuous activity, news of protests was spread by pamphlets as well as by phone and e-mail. Commitment to the movement was sufficiently widespread to cause masses of people drawn from all of Lebanon's communal groups to close their shops or leave their workplaces, homes, and schools; on many occasions during February and March 2005, business activity and public transportation ground to a halt. On February 28, the Syrian-backed prime minister resigned, giving added impetus to the protest movement. Western governments strongly backed the movement, and applied increasing political pressure on Damascus to comply with Security Council Resolution 1559.

Though significant counterdemonstrations were held by pro-Syrian and Hezbollah-affiliated groups—including an enormous Hezbollah-organized gathering of 500,000 in Beirut—direct confrontations were avoided and nonviolent discipline was maintained. The opposition responded to Hezbollah's rally with an even larger rally of approximately 1.2 million people on March 14, during which protesters sang and offered flowers to soldiers. International support for the Lebanese opposition became increasingly solid and consistent, impelling Syrian leaders to pledge a withdrawal. By April 26, 2005, this withdrawal had been completed and a United Nations–sponsored investigation of Hariri's assassination—an investigation that would ultimately implicate the direct involvement of Syrian leaders—had begun. In the fresh parliamentary elections that soon followed, the Lebanese opposition bloc won a majority of seats. Lebanon's Independence Intifada, as some called it, had led to the Cedar Revolution.

The events of the following year—particularly a month-long war between Israel and Hezbollah that threatened to erase the gains Lebanon had made since the end of the civil war—represented a new threat to the integrity of the country, and deepened the divide between the country's rival coalitions. In the aftermath of that summer 2006 war, Hezbollah and its allies persistently challenged the legitimacy of the Western-oriented government; the resultant gridlock between opposing camps led many commentators to worry that Lebanon's fragile, confessionally based democratic system had once again become an arena for proxy conflict between external powers, with Syria and Iran supporting one faction and the United States and France bolstering its counterpart. Nonetheless, the Independence Intifada of 2005 has provided an intriguing example of mass nonviolent struggle in a Middle Eastern context, with rival groups demonstrating impressive capacity for social mobilization and disciplined political action.[33]

Which Role for Islam?

In Lebanon's Independence Intifada, as in several other historical Middle Eastern cases of nonviolent action, campaigns against unjust or abusive authority have not always relied upon Islamic values and symbols as a primary basis for rallying popular support. It is arguable, however, that insofar as Middle Eastern Muslims have been active participants in the cases described, Islamic culture has played at least an indirect role. In the Lebanese case, large numbers of Muslims—primarily but not exclusively Sunnis and members of the country's Druze community—saw no contradiction between their religious identities and their actions in solidarity with Lebanese Christians. In a similar fashion, multiple Middle Eastern national movements have experimented with a variety of nonviolent action methods, justified their appeals to resist colonial authority on both secular and religious grounds, and made active use of religious networks.[34] Islam may not have been the primary motivating factor in these movements, but in a region where religious culture runs deep, engagement with Islamic symbols and values—including the value of human dignity—was necessary. In such cases, Islam should not be regarded as the singular cause of rebellion or as the decisive factor in choosing one method over another, yet it was undeniably an element of the context in which political actions were chosen and justified.

Bread protests and Ayatollah Sistani's intervention in the US-Iraqi conflict reveal the potential of Islamic discourse and identity to be key factors in the orchestration of nonviolent action campaigns. Bread protests emerge from deep grassroots discontent, and rely heavily on religiously affiliated leaders and an Islamic social justice vocabulary. Ayatollah Sistani's efforts to protect Shia holy places could not have been initiated on any other basis than Islamic values and precedents.

In any conflict situation, Islamic vocabulary can be used for multiple purposes. There are strong warrants within Islam for moral restraint and for steadfast yet nonviolent resistance to oppression. Yet Islamic symbols and identities can also be used to reinforce an escalatory "us versus them" dynamic, as occurred in Israel-Palestine during the despair-filled months of the Second Intifada. In the First Intifada, Islamic culture was a galvanizing factor that made enduring hardship more bearable, but in the Second Intifada, Islamic vocabulary was used in much more combative ways, except during efforts to secure a cease-fire or *hudna* (see Chapter 6). Much, then, would appear to depend on leadership, interpretation, and the existential situation of disputing parties.

Another key factor that must be addressed is the relative novelty of nonviolence as an explicit hermeneutical topic in Islamic thought. Like other major religious traditions, Islam has a moral vocabulary that condemns wanton violence and encourages restraint. Efforts to think through the implications of Islamic values for modern forms of nonviolent action, however, are still at an early stage of development.

Nonviolence and Islamic Revivalism

When exploring the topic of Islam and nonviolence, important questions arise about the potential to embrace nonviolence at a deep level, as a principled strategy for social change and human betterment. In virtually every national context of modern Muslim revival movements, activism has begun nonviolently. However, because Islamic revivalism challenges narrowly based regimes, campaigns for religious and political reform almost inevitably come face-to-face with a repressive security apparatus. Confrontation and conflict escalation can easily ensue, leading to political violence and the formation of radical factions within revival movements. When this occurs, the actions of the radicalized minority or of a repressive government generate further polarization within society, decreasing the prospects for peaceful change and accommodation.

The Muslim Brotherhood provides an excellent example of this pattern. Founded in 1928 by Hassan al-Banna, a schoolteacher who was deeply disturbed both by the rising spirit of secularism among his society's elite strata and by the humiliation of Egyptians and Muslims in their relations with Western powers, the Muslim Brotherhood soon became the prototypical Islamic revival movement, with branches throughout the Arab world. At a time when the British Empire still exerted profound influence over Egypt and—along with France—maintained colonial control over broad swaths of Muslim territory throughout the region, al-Banna's call for a cultural and political reassertion of Islamic values found a ready audience. His challenge to the perceived compromises of leading politicians and clerics met widespread applause, and soon his movement had acquired as many as a million followers.

In its early years, the operating methods of the Muslim Brotherhood were almost entirely nonviolent. Al-Banna hoped to transform Egyptian culture through education and the formation of a strong, revivalist counterculture that could demonstrate authentic Islamic values to the masses. As the movement grew more powerful, however, relations with the government became increasingly tense and the movement itself became more undisciplined. Rivalry between the Brotherhood and the Egyptian monarchy grew, leading to street clashes and the formation of a secretive military wing within the larger revivalist movement. In December 1948, after negotiations between al-Banna and the government failed, Prime Minister Mahmud Fahmi al-Nuqrashi ordered the dissolution of the Brotherhood. Amid the ensuing confrontation, the prime minister himself was assassinated by a member of the movement. In early 1949, the government sought to eliminate the Brotherhood by assassinating al-Banna, making mass arrests, and executing or imprisoning the revivalist leadership.[35]

The Muslim Brotherhood's fortunes improved for a time after Gamal Abdul Nasser and the Free Officers Movement seized power from King Farouk in 1952, but frictions between Nasser's Arab socialism and the Brotherhood's Islamist program soon became apparent. When co-optation efforts failed, Nasser resorted to ham-fisted and often brutal efforts to suppress the Brotherhood. This drove the movement underground, accelerating the radicalization of such famous revivalist thinkers as Sayyid Qutb. The Brotherhood experienced a more hospitable political environment again during the 1970s under Anwar Sadat, who hoped to bolster his government's legitimacy and marginalize socialists and communists by demonstrating strong Islamic credentials. By the late 1970s, the Egyptian government and the Brotherhood again moved toward confrontation, this time over Sadat's policies of openness to the West and peace with Israel. This confrontation ultimately led to Sadat's assassination by a radical splinter group from the larger Egyptian Islamic movement.

The Muslim Brotherhood was forced to endure an underground existence throughout the 1980s and 1990s, though government policies became more accommodating as unofficial leaders asserted moderate positions and consistent opposition to political violence. Starting in 2004, Brotherhood members became active in the broader Egyptian Kifaya movement, calling for an end to the authoritarian rule of President Hosni Mubarak and opposing the prospect of a "father-son" political transition such as Syria's in 2000. By 2006, Brotherhood-affiliated parliamentary candidates, running as independents, achieved a strong showing in national elections despite government pressure and the inability of the Brotherhood to act as an open political party in a one-party-dominant state. Some analysts began to speculate that the Brotherhood was nearing maturity as a political and social organization willing to compete for influence in accordance with democratic rules and principles.

Islam and Nonviolence: An Ongoing Dialogue

> Every time they kindle the fire of war, God extinguishes it.
>
> —Quran 5:64

Though it is not widely recognized, an Islamic paradigm for nonviolence does in fact exist. Some of the most notable recent applications of this paradigm have occurred in South Asia and Southeast Asia,[36] but nonviolent strategies of social change have also been used in Middle Eastern political struggles such as those described above. Although a serious history of nonviolent resistance to oppression and injustice in Islamic civilization has yet to be written, there are clear bases for conscious, deliberately nonviolent strategies of political action in Islamic precepts, which emphasize the incompatibility of tyranny, oppression, violence, and reckless subversion with religious faith.[37] Muslim advocates of nonviolent struggle emphasize that, while Islam may be incompatible with passivity in the face of manifest injustice, Islam provides a framework within which nonviolence can be embraced both as a positive value and as a method of action with demonstrated capacity to generate change, particularly when pursued in conjunction with serious training and strategic planning. In developing their case, they point to the inherent capacity of Islam to generate strong group solidarity, along with willingness to face suffering for a just cause.[38]

Commentators such as Khalid Kishtainy and Chaiwat Satha-Anand have argued that core Islamic traditions provide an excellent basis for developing the collective discipline and solidarity needed for nonviolent struggle. Kishtainy has noted that religious fasting in Ramadan is "natural training for hunger strikes," while practices associated with prayer gatherings and religious chanting can easily be adapted to give focus and vitality to demonstrations, sit-ins, and marches.[39] Satha-Anand proposes that Islam's classic five pillars (witness to God and His Messenger, daily prayer, alms, fasting, and pilgrimage) provide a framework for Muslim nonviolent action. Witnessing that there is no god other than God *(shahada)* provides grounds for disobedience toward unjust authority—toward any power that interferes with the fulfillment of God's commandments. Daily, ritual prayer *(salah)* instills both discipline and a sense of human solidarity and equality, as Muslims who assemble for collective prayer stand shoulder-to-shoulder, regardless of wealth or status. The mandatory giving of alms *(zakat)* reminds Muslims that they have a responsibility to devote attention to the needs of others and work for a more humane society. Fasting *(sawm)* provides lessons in patience and self-sacrifice as well as in empathy for the suffering of others. The Muslim rite of pilgrimage *(hajj)*, in turn, fosters a sense of unity among all Muslims, regardless of national origin, race, or class.[40]

Although recognizably Islamic in inspiration, such interpretations are not yet part of the Muslim mainstream. Like Christians who doubt the pathway taken by Martin Luther King Jr., many Muslims have equated nonviolence with passivity and humiliating subservience to authoritarianism or imperialism. In other words, they regard nonviolence as a strategy that is already applied by Muslims on a daily basis when they submit to unjust rulers, and discount it on that basis. Noticing that Western leaders have called for nonviolence on the part of Arabs and Muslims far more consistently than they have provided verbal support for genuine nonviolent resistance campaigns, some have come to associate talk of nonviolence with double standards or hidden agendas. Others, most of whom are unfamiliar with cases of successful nonviolent action and with the theoretical underpinnings of nonviolent strategy, simply question the viability of unarmed refusal to cooperate with potentially brutal adversaries.

A survey of the history of Islamic revival movements, however, reveals that Muslim political organizations have achieved greater gains through nonviolent resistance and persuasion than through violent opposition to narrowly based regimes. Violent resistance pits loose networks of activists against the full, unrestrained force of the national security state. In contrast, long-term nonviolent strategies can derive leverage by resolutely calling for a government to live up to its stated principles of democracy and social justice—and then actively working to occupy and enlarge political space. When resistance is violent, the government is able to justify its human rights violations by decrying external subversion and declaring a state of emergency. When resistance is nonviolent, human rights violations still occur, yet the nonviolent discipline of the opposition movement allows it to gain the moral high ground, undermining the legitimacy of those who have ordered or permitted abuses.

There is much that could be learned from in-depth, comparative study of violent and nonviolent Middle Eastern political movements. A great deal of experience with confronting authoritarian rule remains to be harvested. Much might also be gained if today's broad-based Islamic revival movements could commit more wholeheartedly to an Islamic paradigm of nonviolent action—of steadfast moral struggle against repression, with clearly stated democratic objectives. Active, informed commitment to nonviolence could provide contemporary Middle Eastern movements with an alternative strategy to terrorism and other forms of political violence. Whereas the consequences of violent resistance strategies have already been demonstrated, nonviolent strategy holds the possibility of achieving objectives in a less costly and more efficient manner.

Nonviolence motivates people to act justly and to demand just and ethical action, without resort to physical coercion or combat. The first premise is never to participate in anything that is immoral. Nonviolent action is based upon principle, yet undertaken in the tactical way that is best for making the moral point effectively. The key principle behind nonviolent tactics and strategy is the relation of ends to means: there is no separation. The effect of an act together with its intention determines its character. The means used, through their effect, determine what the actual ends are. Unjust means cannot bring about just ends. The means must therefore be just and appropriate to their intended ends, with consideration for all likely effects and side effects. This correspondence of means and ends is the heart of nonviolence.

Nonviolent action is always intended to have an effect. Most often, nonviolent action, when successful, is a catalyst for building the moral and political support required to change social and political policy. Historically, many Muslims have made this moral point effectively through their willingness to suffer for their principles. The late Ayatollah Muhammad Shirazi, a strong advocate of Islamic nonviolence, argued that this willingness to suffer for the sake of truth would be of greatest benefit to Muslims and to the modern Islamic movement if it could be harnessed to an ethic of nonviolent steadfastness, rooted in "a very strong and resilient character, which can withstand any assault with total tolerance, and without retaliating, even if there is the opportunity to do so."[41]

Courage, the will to act, must be balanced by moderation. To be just, one must be reasonable and act reasonably. Being reasonable involves a number of qualities, including taking the time to understand and evaluate a situation carefully before acting, so that action will take into account all of the elements of the situation and be an appropriate response to them.

As a power technique, principled nonviolence is action directed toward both justice and peace. It is a means of wielding power, a strategy that is designed to fight a violent opponent who is willing and well equipped to wield military force. It is a strategy designed for use against opponents who cannot be defeated by violence. Nonviolence does not immediately reduce the violence of the opponent, but it is designed to render the opponent's violence ineffective by dramatizing injustice and revealing the true nature of a repressive political order. This objective is undermined when advocates of social and political change meet violence with violence, but advanced when activists exercise restraint and capitalize on a dynamic known as moral or political jujitsu.[42]

The weapons of nonviolence consist of psychological, economic, and political methods, including nonviolent protest and persuasion; social, economic, and political noncooperation; and direct nonviolent intervention.[43] Like other strategies, such as conventional war or guerrilla war, nonviolence has its own requirements for effectiveness that need to be adhered to in order to produce the maximum impact of techniques. The success of nonviolence depends on a number of factors.

There must be a grand strategy with realizable objectives. There must be an incremental motion from one realizable objective to the next. The grand strategy must be adaptable to change without losing track of values. Intensive training, self-reliance, and self-discipline are necessary for the individual and the group. There is no room for improvisation.

Viewed from a global perspective, nonviolent strategy has a long history with varying degrees of success. Success sometimes has come through changing the minds and attitudes of the principal opponents, but that is rare. More often, partial success has been achieved through accommodation, with the adversary yielding to some of the nonviolent movement's demands without immediately losing power or control. Nonviolent strategy has also demonstrated its capacity to produce nonviolent coercion of the opponent, in which case a growing movement for change wins the struggle for social support and political legitimacy, forcing its adversaries to capitulate. In recent years, nonviolent means of effecting major political change have been utilized in many parts of the world, including Chile, South Africa, Poland, Serbia, Ukraine, and Georgia. Nonviolent methods also played to predominant role in Kyrgyzstan's Tulip Revolution of 2005. Historically, nonviolent strategists have wielded significant power in conflicts when their causes resonated with large numbers of people and they applied the principles of nonviolence skillfully.

Many discussions of Islam and nonviolence begin and end with the observation that pacifism—conceived as an absolute commitment to abstain from the use of force—is difficult to reconcile with Quranic narratives (a tension that may also appear when reading the Torah and Old Testament from a nonviolent perspective). Moreover, like many if not most Westerners, Muslims tend to associate nonviolence with a passive attitude of withdrawal from social conflict. Those who reject nonviolence on such grounds tend to reduce it to its negative and moralistic aspect (calls for restraint from acts of violence), while failing to engage sophisticated theoretical and empirical reflections on means-ends linkages in political action.[44] When it is reduced to a form of disengaged quietism, nonviolence has indeed been incompatible with the authoritative judgments of mainstream Muslim religious leaders. Yet there is nothing in Islam that is fundamentally incompatible with thoughtful, determined application of nonviolent strategies for social and political change.

One of the foremost challenges of nonviolence is to embody moral precepts and remain true to one's convictions in circumstances that appear unfavorable. The essential task of nonviolence, then, is not passive resignation in the face of provocation, but rather the discovery of principles of action to realize widely shared moral preferences through collaborative efforts and, when necessary, through solidarity and nonmilitarized confrontation. When framed in such practical terms, it becomes evident that nonviolence is eminently compatible with the aims of Islamic morality. Islam may not enjoin unconditional pacifism, yet it can affirm nonviolence as an active and principled political strategy for overcoming repression and achieving social justice.

Notes

1. Related passages on this topic include 16:125 ("Invite all to the way of the Lord with wisdom and beautiful preaching, and argue with them in ways that are best and most gracious, for the Lord knows best who have strayed from His path"), 18:27 ("Say the truth is from your Lord; let him who will, believe, and let him who will, reject it"), and 10:99 ("If it had been the Lord's will, they would all have believed, all who are on earth! Will you then compel humankind against their will to believe?").

2. Satha-Anand, "The Nonviolent Crescent," 1990, p. 26.

3. Ibid., p. 27.

4. Ibid., p. 28.

5. Satha-Anand, "Transforming Terrorism with Muslims' Nonviolent Alternatives?" 2006. See also Satha-Anand, "Muslim Communal Nonviolent Actions," 2003.

6. Satha-Anand, "The Nonviolent Crescent," 1990, p. 34.

7. The following passages are exemplary: "And if any strive, they do so for their own souls; for God is free of any needs from the created worlds" (29:6); "And those who strive in Our way, We will certainly guide them to Our paths; for verily God is with those who do right" (29:69).

8. Easwaran, *A Man to Match His Mountains,* 1984, p. 103. Khan was by no means the only Muslim social change advocate to underscore the importance of the Meccan period in Islamic political ethics. The vitality and contemporary relevance of the Meccan experience was also stressed by Mahmoud Mohamed Taha (1909–1985), a Sudanese activist, politician, and protagonist of Islamic reformist thinking, in *The Second Message of Islam* (1996).

9. Johansen, "Radical Islam and Nonviolence," 1997, p. 70. See also Nagler, *Is There No Other Way?* 2001, pp. 242–247.

10. Kishtainy, "Violent and Nonviolent Struggle in Arab History," 1990, p. 10.

11. The military practices of Middle Eastern Muslim polities were often quite complex. Early Islamic empires such as the Umayyad and Abbasid developed practices of recruiting soldiers from border regions, so as not to depend on the fickle loyalty of local tribal leaders. Over time, several Muslim states (including the Abbasid and Ottoman empires) sought to construct an independent military caste of "slave soldiers" captured in foreign lands. As newcomers to Islam and to predominantly Muslim territories, these foreign conscripts owed allegiance to no one but the Muslim sultan or caliph, who compensated them with social privileges and prestige for their loyalty and service. The ethnically distinctive "slave armies" that resulted often became quite

influential in their own right. From the mid-thirteenth century until 1517, a group of "slave soldiers" known as the Mamluks formed the ruling class of Egypt. See Lapidus, *A History of Islamic Societies,* 1988, pp. 127–128, 147–148, 316–317.

12. In the *hadith* collections *Sunan al-Tirmidhi* and *Sunan Ibn Majah.* See also Schleifer, "Jihad and Traditional Islamic Consciousness," 1983, p. 183.

13. This has also been formulated as jihad "by the heart," "by the tongue," "by the hands," and "by the sword." See Schleifer, "Understanding Jihad," 1983, pp. 128–129.

14. Kadayifci-Orellana, "Religion, Violence, and the Islamic Tradition of Nonviolence," 2004, pp. 59–60. See also Combs-Schilling, "Sacred Refuge," 1994.

15. For a short account of the Shia understanding of jihad, see Sachedina, *The Islamic Roots of Democratic Pluralism,* 2001, pp. 119–121.

16. Kishtainy, "Violent and Nonviolent Struggle in Arab History," 1990, p. 20.

17. Ibrahim, "Introduction," 1990, pp. 6–7.

18. Sadiki, "Popular Uprisings and Arab Democratization," 2000, pp. 79–80.

19. Bennett, "Arab-Muslim Cases of Nonviolent Struggle," 1990, pp. 48–50.

20. Keddie, *Modern Iran,* 2003, p. 226.

21. See ibid., pp. 269–284.

22. Sakidi, "Popular Uprisings and Arab Democratization," 2000, pp. 84–85.

23. Ibid., pp. 77, 79–80.

24. Ibid., p. 82.

25. Bennett, "Arab-Muslim Cases of Nonviolent Struggle," 1990, pp. 54–56.

26. Political arrangements prior to the colonial era were by no means unproblematic, with significant rivalries among Muslim empires and dynasties as well as periodic rebellions by disaffected groups. The early Arab nationalist movement was forged within a context of Ottoman domination as well as European encroachment. European colonialism, however, was experienced as an especially grave offense against the dignity of Muslims, and as a deeply unsettling challenge to traditional Islamic culture and identity. See Bogle, *The Modern Middle East,* 1996; Voll, *Islam,* 1994, pp. 84–151.

27. The vision of a modern Jewish state in the Middle East, though rooted in perennial Jewish ties to the Holy Land, began to take concrete form late in the nineteenth century in response to European nationalism and anti-Semitism. Because the Holocaust fulfilled Jewish fears of extreme European prejudice in an almost unimaginable way, contemporary Jews point to the events of World War II as the definitive justification for an independent Jewish state. In the light of these European causes of the modern conflict over Palestine, present tensions in the Middle East appear all the more tragic. Rabbi Michael Lerner has likened the painful collision of Jews and Palestinians to a man leaping from the second story of a burning building and landing on another person (*Healing Israel/Palestine,* 2003, p. xiv).

28. Kishtainy, "Violent and Nonviolent Struggle in Arab History," 1990, pp. 19–20.

29. King, *A Quiet Revolution,* 2007.

30. Abu-Nimer, *Nonviolence and Peace Building in Islam,* 2003, pp. 174–178.

31. Even among the 44 percent of Palestinian voters who backed Hamas in the 2006 parliamentary elections, approximately half support a two-state solution to the conflict. See *The Economist,* "Hamas Won't Go Away," 2008.

32. For a more in-depth exploration of Islamic perspectives on violence and nonviolence in the Israeli-Palestinian conflict, see Kadayifci-Orellana, *Standing on an Isthmus,* 2007.

33. Safa, "Lebanon Springs Forward," 2006.

34. Esposito, *Islam and Politics,* 1987, pp. 69–85.

35. Dekmejian, *Islam in Revolution,* 1995, pp. 76–77.

36. For an in-depth study of nonviolent Muslim resistance to British imperialism in South Asia, see Johansen, "Radical Islam and Nonviolence," 1997. For an introduction to Southeast Asian applications of nonviolence, see Satha-Anand, *The Nonviolent Crescent*, 1996.

37. Harris, "Nonviolence in Islam," 1998.

38. Satha-Anand, "The Nonviolent Crescent," 1990. See also Paige, Satha-Anand, and Gilliatt, *Islam and Nonviolence*, 1993.

39. Kishtainy, "Violent and Nonviolent Struggle in Arab History," 1990, p. 23.

40. Satha-Anand, "The Nonviolent Crescent," 1990, p. 37.

41. Shirazi, *War, Peace, and Non-Violence*, 2001, p. 113.

42. Sharp, *The Politics of Nonviolent Action: Part Three*, 1973, pp. 657–697

43. Sharp, *The Politics of Nonviolent Action: Part Two*, 1973; Sharp, *There Are Realistic Alternatives*, 2003, pp. 39–48.

44. See, for example, Ackerman and DuVall, *A Force More Powerful*, 2000; Ackerman and Kruegler, *Strategic Nonviolent Conflict*, 1994.

8

Peace Through Universalism: Islamic Spirituality and the Culture of Peace

> And Peace to all who follow guidance! —Quran 20:47
>
> And one of His signs is the creation of the heaven and earth and the diversity of your languages and colors; surely there are signs in this for the learned.
> —Quran 30:22

Any discussion of peace in Islam would be incomplete without reference to Islamic spirituality, and to its potential role in religious and cultural dialogue. In the Middle East as in other regions of the Islamic world, spirituality has by no means been confined to mosques and *madrasas* (religious schools), and has found expression in the literary and visual arts as well as in informal social organizations and in the solitary pursuits of individual seekers of truth. Particularly in the form of mysticism known as Sufism, Islamic spirituality has demonstrated a remarkable capacity to bridge cultural divides. This can be seen in the fact that Jalaluddin Rumi, a Sufi poet who wrote of the soul's love and longing in Persian couplets during the thirteenth century, has been among the bestselling poets in the English language for many years, with his works appearing in numerous translations.[1]

In this chapter we explore perspectives within Islam that relate peace to inner transformation and spiritual harmony. Although the instrumental relevance of these conceptions of peace to the mechanics of peacemaking in a time of war may not seem immediately apparent, we believe that awareness of the "depth dimension" of Islamic culture and of Islam's most universalistic expressions is vital both for Muslims and for those hoping to appeal to the most magnanimous and irenic aspects of Muslim history and experience. By beginning with Sufism, we seek to open a window to the inner world of Islamic spirituality, and to an Islamic "politics of the heart" that links peace in the world to processes of internal transformation within each human being—processes that develop spiritual character and a forgiving attitude toward human limitations. This overview of Sufism provides a basis for exploring universalistic understandings of the Islamic spiritual mandate—understandings that, though not necessarily dependent on a Sufi approach to spirituality, represent the Islamic tradition's capacity for fostering inclusiveness and appreciation for human differences.[2] According to this universalistic Islamic perspective, global cultural and religious diversity is a resource for humanity rather than a challenge to Islamic particularity. Islam's particularity manifests not through negating other religious paths but rather through aspiring to provide an encompassing "divine overview" of the world's religious history and an essentialization of perennial wisdom. The existence of many revelations of truth testifies both to the graciousness of God and to unity within human diversity.

Finding Peace: The Path of Sufis

At the deepest level, the search for peace in Islam relates to the personal quest for nearness to God, for direct perception of the sacred. Like Christianity, Judaism, and other world religions, Islam developed its own mystical tradition to account for the spiritual experiences of dedicated seekers, and a rich vocabulary describing the inward struggle to overcome conflict within oneself and find peace in God. Over time, those who excelled in articulating principles and methods of spiritual discipline became known as "Sufis" (or in the Shia context, specialists in *'irfan*, a discipline of inner spiritual knowing), and came to exert a powerful yet subtle influence on Islamic culture.

The peace sought by the earliest Islamic mystics, like the peace sought by other mystics within the Abrahamic traditions, was a peace that surpasses conventional understandings—a peace with, in, and through God. Though they did not consider themselves to constitute a separate sect within Islam, they were united by a more ambitious and demanding understanding of the spiritual path than was conventional among their co-religionists. They aspired not so much to attain a heavenly reward in the afterlife, as to "meet" God in life through intensification and internalization of religious practices and a deeply intentional commitment to "doing what is beautiful" *(ihsan)* in daily activities and observances.[3]

The Emergence of Sufism

Most Muslims trace the emergence of Sufism *(tasawwuf)* to the time of the Prophet and his immediate companions, but as a distinct social phenomenon, Sufism first began to make its presence felt as a countermovement to changes in the Islamic community that accompanied the rise to worldly power. Mere decades after the death of the Prophet, the creation of a new Islamic empire had brought unprecedented wealth and influence to the Arab peoples. While worldly success caused many to slacken in their commitment to spiritual practice and to key Islamic values such as social justice, some Muslims actively chose to turn their backs on the fame and fortune that had become possible in urban centers such as Damascus and Baghdad. Instead, they donned simple garments of wool *(suf)* and sought knowledge of God far from the distractions of the cities, in a manner akin to the Desert Fathers of early Christianity. Many engaged in spiritual retreats in the desert wastelands; those whose spiritual qualities established them as "religious virtuosi" (in the terminology of Max Weber) became teachers of Islam's "inward path," and attracted small and informal communities of spiritual seekers hoping to live in accordance with the highest wisdom taught by Muhammad and his companions and descendants.

By the third century of the Islamic era (early Abbasid period), Sufism had became a popular movement within Muslim culture. Though some Sufis were indeed persecuted or ostracized for real or suspected heresy, exponents of mainstream Sufism sought to underscore their acceptance of the core doctrines and practices of Sunni and Shia Islam—even as they formed distinct fellowships, or *tariqas,* with leaders who were understood to possess special knowledge of God and of the path toward spiritual realization. There was always a degree of tension between exoteric and esoteric aspects of Islam, but Sufism was rarely absent from the Islamic social fabric.

Deeply rooted in historical Islam, Sufism is typically understood as the Islamic equivalent of the contemplative disciplines present in other world religions. Though members of Sufi fellowships often met behind closed doors and took care not to offend their more exoteric brethren, the Sufi tradition was by no means merely an elite phenomenon. Sufism was often close to the center of Muslim communal life, where it inspired the development of widespread networks, became an ethos for urban craft guilds, and spurred the construction of special meeting houses known as *zawiyas* or *khanqahs.*[4] Particularly in South Asia, Southeast Asia, and sub-Saharan Africa, the spread of Islam was greatly expedited by the teachings of Sufi Muslims, many of whom earned their livelihood as traders. In intellectual circles the Sufi outlook influenced many of the best minds of Islamic civilization, including the famous jurist, moralist, and theologian Abu Hamid al-Ghazali (1058–1111), who characterized Sufism's core teachings as integral components of Islamic orthodoxy.[5] Islamic humanistic traditions, including mystical poetry in Arabic, Persian, and Urdu, are saturated with Sufi influences,[6] and though the precise impact of the Sufi outlook on contemporary Islamic societies is difficult to gauge,[7] the broad-minded ecumenical and universalistic tendencies within Sufism have endowed present generations of Muslims with a rich heritage that can be used to build bridges of cross-cultural and interreligious understanding in the modern world.

Principles of Sufism

Though not typically defined in opposition to religious orthodoxy, Sufism has long included a critique of formalism and legalism in matters of religion. From a Sufi perspective, appreciation for truth must ultimately be "caught" through association with a spiritual teacher and can never be satisfactorily taught through books and institutionalized learning. While most Sufis respected institutional frameworks and regarded them as necessary to the spiritual life of the community, their teachings radicalized Islam's rejection of idolatry, recognizing that excessive ideological attachment to beliefs about God and divine will can become a hindrance to spiritual development. Insistent in their conviction that knowledge *about* God differs from knowledge *of* God, they focused their energies on what they understood to be the most important goal of human life: attaining awareness of God's nature through "taste" *(dhawq)* and divine "unveiling" *(kashf)*.[8] Anything less than this, they suggested, was equivalent to hearing about a wonderful city but remaining in one's own small village, relying solely on the reports of others who had traveled there.

Among Sufis, the most important daily practice or litany is called *dhikr* (pronounced "zikr"), which means "remembrance." As Jalaluddin Rumi emphasizes repeatedly in his poetry, true remembrance of God only occurs when mundane ego consciousness is transcended. "Remember God," enjoins Rumi, until you forget yourself."[9] According to the Quran, God is "nearer than the jugular vein" (50:16). Forgetting the self and remembering God—indeed granting all true existence to God, and renouncing one's own insistence on a separate existence—brings about inner peace and spiritual elevation. Within this renunciation of willful individual consciousness, existential freedom is realized not as an outward escape from constraints ("freedom to do"), but rather as an inward liberation from the ego. Freedom from the dictates of the ego leads to active and inspired participation in a greater wholeness ("freedom to be").

From a Sufi perspective, knowing God and attaining inner peace is a matter of cleansing the soul of human forgetfulness and returning to a purified state that reflects the soul's original state of covenant with God. Through invoking God's unity and remembering that one's soul (like all of creation) comes from and returns to Him, God becomes available and accessible to each believer. The spiritual teacher in Sufism serves as an exemplar and guide who helps the seeker travel the spiritual path to "presence" and wakefulness within all-embracing divine unity.

The Sufi path to God, though traveled communally with others, is ultimately a process of internal transformation. Drawing upon the Quranic statements concerning various stages of the soul's development, including a "commanding" or egotistical soul, a "blaming" or self-deprecating soul, and a "contented soul" at peace with God, Sufism expounds a process through which individuals can undertake the "greater struggle" *(jihad al-akbar)* against one's own resistance to God, so as to transcend the tyranny and deception of the "commanding soul" as well as the inner conflict of the "blaming soul" to reach the contentment and peace that only spiritual enlightenment can bring.[10] According to Sufi teaching, the path to true peace involves a great jihad against forgetfulness and associated wayward tendencies. In the words of Rumi, "Internal enemies are the real enemy. After all, external enemies are nothing. . . . Now we are doing battle with thoughts so that the good thoughts may defeat the bad ones and expel them from the kingdom of the body."[11] Sufi Quran commentaries echo this theme by providing internalized readings of passages that describe outward struggle with enemies of the faith; in these commentaries, the most dangerous "unbeliever" is understood to be the lower self rather than an outer adversary.[12]

Those who affirm Sufism as a transformative approach to peace within Islam emphasize that, while Sufism focuses human attention squarely on the greater jihad of inner purification and transformation of character, it does not presuppose quietism. Generally speaking, the Sufi tradition places stronger emphasis on the presence of the individual within society than do the contemplative traditions of many other world religions.[13] Contemplation of the divine is by no means considered to be a monastic or priestly specialization, nor is it regarded as an activity that can only be pursued through withdrawal from work and the fulfillment of social duties. Authentic spirituality is found in living an "ordinary"—and ideally humble—life as a householder and engaged community member. Sufi teachings declare that the material and the spiritual are in reality one, and suggest that no one can claim to be spiritual if they are unable to make a good thing of this life. Conversely, one cannot truly make a good thing of this life without putting one's spiritual life in proper order.

Sufi spirituality affirms a comprehensive outlook predicated upon the Islamic theological principle of *tawhid,* understood holistically to mean not only the unity of God but also the presence of God within His creation and the complete dependence of creation upon its divine foundation—a condition described by some Sufi metaphysicians as the "unity of being" *(wahdat al-wujud).*[14] According to this view, only God is truly existent, whereas the created world is radically contingent and expressive of divine activity. In the words of Rumi, "He hides from our sight, and from Him all emanates; My beacon is the Hidden One, Whose works are visible."[15]

Sufism in no way negates Islamic teachings concerning the transcendence and incomparability of God. Rather, Sufi thinkers have stressed that God's continuing presence in His creation fulfills the principle of transcendence: God is too unlimited to be constrained in or contained by the heavens, and therefore cannot exist in complete separation from the world.[16] The task of the seeker, then, is to strive to efface his or her ego and personal desires in such a way as to begin harmonizing with the divine presence.

In the Sufi tradition, *tawhid* is experienced by grasping a personal relation to the absolute, and by actively partaking in the greater harmony of a universe saturated with the presence of God. In the teachings of influential thirteenth-century Sufi philosopher Muhyiddin Ibn 'Arabi, *tawhīd* refers to the overall harmony and patterning of existence.[17] It is natural law in the broadest possible sense: each individual person has a unique place and a special obligation to act in support of the divine purpose, within a world of created things that reflect diverse attributes of their creator.

A common Sufi teaching states that God created the universe as a mirror in which He might know Himself by seeing His attributes reflected. All things therefore exist for a purpose and manifest some aspect of the divine nature; nothing in the universe exists by accident. As the clearest expression of the mirror, humanity plays a role in reflecting back to God knowledge of His own attributes in the most perfect manner possible. The work of the spiritual practitioner, in turn, is an unending process of polishing the human heart—of removing rust and debris so that God's qualities can be seen reflected there. Perceived with clarity through the eyes of a cleansed heart, each of the world's created objects is likewise a mirror of the Creator's attributes, and a reminder for the seeker to cultivate these character traits of God *(takhalluq bi-akhlaq Allah)* in the self and in all relationships.[18] The natural world provides daily lessons in God's divine qualities, from majesty and beauty to creative power, generosity, subtlety, and peacefulness.[19]

Sufis have long maintained that the path of spiritual development requires integration of human consciousness's analytic and intuitive modes. Complementary functioning of the rational and the intuitive is regarded as a measure of human wholeness and creativity. To this end, Sufis have expressed their teachings not only in metaphysical, practical, and ethical terms, but also in narratives. A key purpose of these stories is to develop wisdom by recognizing oneself in others and others in oneself, and thereby overcoming blind conditioning as well as the spiritual inertia that accompanies exaggerated perceptions of one's own virtue and self-sufficiency.

In encouraging seekers to forget themselves and see the reflection of God in others, Sufi teachings propose that we are what we habitually perceive or see. Knowledge is relational, and the deepest or highest form of knowledge is immediate perception of "reality"—perceiving and being that which *is.* The purpose of real knowing, therefore, is transformation—becoming free from illusions, especially the illusion of one's own separate existence. The self and indeed all things exist in God, and are connected to one another inwardly through the all-embracing divine presence. Ibn 'Arabi used the metaphor of the divine breath to convey this perception, depicting the manifestation of created multiplicity (the divine exhalation) and its reabsorption into primordial singularity (the divine inhalation), as the "breath of the Merciful" *(nafas al-Rahman).*[20]

Sufism as a Peace Resource

By offering an "inner Islam" for those seeking a path of approach to God, Sufism left a profound mark on Islamic culture. Through expressions in literature, philosophy, music, poetry, ethics, and the visual arts, Sufism infused a culture in which love was "presented as the key to Islamic life and practice."[21]

Sufis presented the soul's search for God as a spiritual romance, a relationship of lover and Beloved. True realization of the *fullness* of life emerges from unconditional and loving surrender to the divine Beloved—in a complete *emptying* of the self. In true surrender, the lover gives up his or her own willfulness out of love rather than mere compulsion, in a desire to please the Beloved and enter the Beloved's embrace. Doing the will of the Beloved and renouncing self-importance is the path to true freedom, and to a way of being in the world that is loving, wholesome, and beautiful. Jalaluddin Rumi likened this state of being to a dance of the soul with the divine Beloved—a dance comparable to the pirouette of a dust particle on the face of the sun, or in a bright beam of sunlight:

> Shouldn't every Sufi dance like a speck of dust on the sun
> Of eternity, that he might be delivered from decay?[22]
>
> * * *
>
> And when the bosom of the motes
> is filled with the glow of the sun,
> They enter all the dance, the dance
> and do not complain in the whirling![23]

According to this ethos of love, God shines into the world through clear hearts. Love is experienced as a dynamic force rather than as a personal emotion or sentiment. Progress on the spiritual path requires that the aspirant allow divine love to penetrate the personality at all levels, infusing thoughts, words, and deeds with consciousness and purpose. The incandescent light of God's love manifests in the world as it transforms the receptive heart and purifies the soul that is willing to accept the pain of spiritual death and rebirth. By abandoning self-will, the lover of God discovers that, "We are like iron scraps—Your love: the magnet."[24]

Spiritual preoccupation with God's love produces not only intoxication ("Be drunk on Love," states Rumi, "for only Love exists")[25] but also sobriety. Spiritual maturity is reached when gross worldly thoughts and intoxications are abandoned, allowing thoughts to reflect love, words to become those of a lover, and deeds to be directed toward or offered on behalf of the Beloved. The words of Rumi are again instructive:

> Love comes on strong, consuming herself, unabashed.
> Yet in the midst of suffering
> Love proceeds like a millstone,
> Hard surfaced and straight-forward.
> Having died to self-interest,
> Love gambles away every gift God bestows.[26]

In such a state of awareness—a station of "nearness" to God and sensitivity to God's creation—peace becomes a healing quality of the soul that can be shared with others and expressed through magnanimity and constancy in friendship. The face of God becomes apparent amid acts of service directed toward the establishment of just and harmonious relations among created things.[27]

The spiritual ethic of Sufism has broad ecumenical appeal as a call to intimacy with God and fellowship with humanity. Many generations of Muslims have encountered this tradition through formal institutions and brotherhoods as well as through the medium of popular poetry. The cultural reach of Sufi-inspired poetic traditions is often underestimated by those who regard Sufism merely as an esoteric system; while there are undeniably Muslim lands in which religious puritanism has dampened public enthusiasm for mysticism and devotional poetry, Sufi traditions are regarded as an integral part of Islamic cultural heritage in regions as diverse as northern and western Africa, the Levant, and Persia, as well as central, southern, and southeastern Asia.[28]

The peacebuilding potential of Sufism is particularly evident in works by such classical Sufi poets as Muslihuddin Sa'di (thirteenth century) and Shamsuddin Hafiz (fourteenth century). Sa'di, a wandering merchant and preacher, achieved lasting renown as a composer of elegant verse as well as prose. His Persian and Arabic works combine edifying aphorisms and moralistic teachings with entertaining tales about human foibles and virtues. In Islamic contexts he has long been appreciated for the warm humanity and humor of his anecdotes as well as for the depth of his spirituality and wisdom; Western readers such as Ralph Waldo Emerson have been impressed by the expansiveness and universality of his humanistic sentiments. In one of his most famous poems—inscribed at the United Nations building in New York and often cited by modern Iranian diplomats—Sa'di likens all of humanity to a single human body. If one limb of humanity's body experiences pain, others who make up the same body must feel pain also.[29] In another poem, Sa'di expresses an even broader sense of identification with the natural world: "I am joyous in the world of nature for the world of nature is joyous through Him / I am in love with the whole cosmos for the whole cosmos comes from Him."[30]

Such life-affirming celebrations of divine immanence also characterize the poetic works of Hafiz, who has often been characterized as the most esteemed and lyrical poet in Iranian culture. Like Sa'di, Hafiz sought to communicate a profound sense of participation in human life and in the phenomena of the natural world, to which he added a sharp rebuke for forms of spirituality associated with hypocrisy and a false sense of separateness or superiority. For Hafiz, authentic spirituality was found in a full and fearless embrace of the human condition and of the soul's innate longing for completion through human relations as well as through the embrace of a divine Beloved. In his poetry, worldly images of celebration and tribulation merge with glimpses of hope and transcendence:

Though the deluge shall arrive,
And threaten everything alive,
Noah's there to be your guide,
And steer you through the typhoon's eye.
Despair not.

If desire for the Way is in your heart,
Then set yourself to depart
And plant your foot upon the sand,
Though the thorn leave its jagged brand.
Despair not.

Though our lives may be unsafe
With purposes which we can't relate,
Remember, that in any race
There always is an end.
Despair not.

We are all lovers, separated;
Under a watchful, tenacious Eye.
For God Knows All:
Our state is his design.
Despair not.[31]

Readers of Hafiz's poetry have long attested to its capacity to speak to a diverse audience in a remarkably personal manner. While detractors have rejected what they see as inappropriate themes and metaphors in Hafiz, such as wine, intoxication, and romantic entanglement, others have embraced what they experience as a remarkably inclusive account of each soul's journey from egocentric isolation to a paradisiacal state. In Hafiz's critique of religious pretentiousness and hypocrisy, such readers have nonetheless found a spiritually resonant vision of the fundamental unity of all humankind that rejects a notion of humanity rooted in exclusiveness, together with a humanization of the sacred and consecration of the human. For Hafiz, the humanization of the sacred requires a destruction of idols—a destabilization of complacent, everyday awareness—that permits new ways of experiencing the truths and realities of the human condition. The consecration of the human means the recognition that sacred activity is not apart from the immediate, the personal, and the interpersonal, and that sacred meaning is present in the deeper impulses behind seemingly mundane struggles and aspirations. Such recognition creates scope for spirituality to become a "real" rather than compartmentalized aspect of human existence, and leads to a reinvestment of the sacred in the affairs of daily life.

Iconoclastic aspects of Sufi culture, reflected in the works of authors such as Sa'di and Hafiz, have created space within Islam for a spirituality capable of transcending socially defined categories and in-group versus out-group boundaries. Although sectarian mystics were not unknown in Islamic history, many Sufis saw no reason to believe that the circle of divine providence excluded non-Muslims. Rumi, for example, stated in more than one context that knowledge of divine realities cannot be exhausted or fully contained by a single doctrinal system: "Love's path is outside of all religious sects."[32] From this perspective, religious forms have been revealed by God as means to human realization; while they serve a vital function in structuring and guiding human life, they should not be allowed to become idols. Realization of God requires cultivation of a wise capacity to recognize contexts that shape meaning, discern underlying principles, and distinguish between inner essence and outer form. Sacred forms and doctrinal slogans can be used instrumentally to advance purposes that are antithetical to authentic religious values; mundane or seemingly "profane" aspects of human existence can also become sources of deep spiritual inspiration.

Even when calling attention to hypocrisy and injustice, Sufis have often cautioned their listeners to cultivate a forgiving attitude toward humanity: "Excuse all the seventy-two nations at war," Hafiz pleads. "They did not see the truth, and took the road of fable."[33] Evoking a similar sentiment at the micro level of human relations, Sa'di counsels: "If wrong be done, thine injurers forgive. By pardoning them thyself may'st pardoned live!"[34] All the vicissitudes of life exist within a divine context; progressing from a "lower" to a "higher" (or alternatively, from a "fragmented" to an "integrated") state requires not only discernment, but also an expansive quality of the human heart that transforms human relationships and permits new beginnings.

As spiritual counselors, Sufis have called for assiduous effort to transcend all affectations of the human ego that tend toward divisiveness, and that entrap the soul by causing forgetfulness of life's true objectives. Authentic spirituality cultivates peaceful character, and renunciation of anger and pride:

> When you see the face of anger
> look behind it
> and you will see the face of pride.
> Bring anger and pride
> under your feet, turn them into a ladder
> and climb higher.
> There is no peace until you become
> their master.
> Let go of anger, it may taste sweet
> but it kills.
> Don't become its victim
> you need humility to climb to freedom.[35]

From this perspective, the path to freedom and the path of reconciliation are one.

Inclusive Islam: A Harmony of Divine Messages

One of the most famous and elliptical Quranic narratives on the human capacity for moral agency begins with God declaring to a host of angels His intention to create a "vicegerent on the earth"—that is, to create human beings and make them privileged and responsible custodians of the natural order. Rather than rejoice at this news, the angels are overcome with dismay, sensing not only a challenge to their own position of preeminence in the hierarchy of creation, but also a keen sense of foreboding and indignation: "Will you place there one who will create disorder and shed blood, while we celebrate your praises and glorify your holy name?" Rather than respond to this seeming affront directly or deny the validity of the angels' concerns, God offers a terse and enigmatic rejoinder: "I know what you know not" (2:30).

Muslim commentators on this Quranic narrative stress that the angels foresaw very real human capacities for destruction and injustice. Their doubts about humanity were not without prescience[36]—yet God perceived what the angels could not: humans, despite their "lowly" stature as creatures of clay, possess a unique capacity to uphold God's trust. It is for this reason that Muslim philosophers have held the view that humans are "unfinished beings" located somewhere between the beasts and the angels, with an inherent ability to descend *below* the level of animals or to ascend *above* the heights of the angels. The human soul goes astray when, forgetting its pre-eternal covenant with God, it becomes captivated by appetites, egotism, and false absolutes such as the pursuit of wealth or status. The human soul becomes ennobled, however, when there is remembrance of God and resistance to gross as well as subtle forms of idolatry, including arrogant attachment to one's racial or ethnic identity.[37] Even an exclusivist pride in one's own religious identity can become a form of idolatry that detracts from realization of God's unity and designs.

From the standpoint of Islamic spirituality, the ultimate purpose of religion is to make possible peace within the soul and peace with God. As noted in Chapter 5, the Quran states that all of the world's historical peoples, at one time or another, received divine messengers (10:47). Interpreters differ over the present status of pre-Islamic divine messages, with some maintaining that previous revelations have been corrupted and others drawing from the Quran a less pessimistic view. Muslim theologians agree, however, that (1) no people has been deprived of guidance, and (2) the essential message of pre-Islamic prophets is *islam*, understood as perennial human religiosity: acknowledgment of and reverent submission to God. When people followed their messengers, they received divine safety and protection; when they turned away from those who guided them, hardship followed.

Contemporary Muslim discussions about the meaning of human religious diversity are richer than many Westerners suspect. For some Muslim thinkers, particularly those who take a puritanical view of their tradition and believe that God is only willing to accept human spirituality in the exact forms taught by the Prophet Muhammad, religious diversity is problematic. A broad "mainstream" of Muslim belief accords official recognition to Judaism and Christianity as revealed religions, while hesitating to extend such recognition beyond traditions that were an integral part of the first Muslims' social and religious milieu and that are explicitly mentioned in the Quran. In contrast, authoritative voices among Muslims who embrace the esoteric or Sufi dimension of Islam have often called for respectful communication among all of the world's "divine religions," including Hinduism, Buddhism, Taoism, and Confucianism, as well as various forms of indigenous spirituality such as those found among native North Americans. Exponents of this universalistic theology of religions, such as Seyyed Hossein Nasr, are convinced that a magnanimous acknowledgment of value in other religious traditions does not threaten Islamic uniqueness or the integrity of Muslim religious practice. In Nasr's view, Islam's distinctiveness is reinforced by its potential to offer a confident but not overbearing "meta" perspective on human religious experience—a view that, especially in the modern age, can securely make common cause with other traditions in reasserting essential spiritual principles: "Islam has been there to remind its followers over the ages that there is no possibility of peace on earth without peace with Heaven, and today it is called upon to also assert that peace with Heaven requires, as never before, peace between the messages that, through Divine Wisdom, have descended from Heaven over the ages."[38]

For Nasr and for other Muslims who embrace this ecumenical spiritual orientation, Islam's status as the last of the major world religions allows it to affirm previous revelations and their accumulated wisdom about the spiritual journey.[39] Islam retains its core theological claims with respect to the uncompromisable principle of divine unity, while supporting dialogue among spiritual practitioners on a basis of appreciation and mutuality.[40]

Warrants for such a perspective may be found in a variety of Quranic passages, of which the following are exemplary:

> Those who believe [in the Quran], those who follow the Jewish [scriptures], and the Christians and the Sabians—any who believe in God and the Last Day, and work righteousness shall have their reward with their Lord; on them shall be no fear, nor shall they grieve. (Quran 2:62)

> And there are, certainly, among the People of the Book, those who believe in God, in the revelation to you, and in the revelation to them, bowing in humil-

> ity to God. . . . For them is a reward with their Lord, and God is swift in account. (Quran 3:199)[41]

Like followers of such world religions as Buddhism and Christianity, Muslims have sought to spread the message of Islam through proselytizing. Muslims regard Muhammad as the "seal of the prophets," and as the deliverer of a message that has been carefully safeguarded and that is relevant to all humankind. Yet the Quran also states that points of difference among believers in different religions will not be settled in this world (2:113). Comparative evaluation of the prophets affirmed by Judaism, Christianity, and Islam is discouraged (2:136), and Muslims are instructed not to dispute with the "people of the book"—Jews and Christians living under Islamic administration—"except in a manner that is seemlier" (29:46). On the basis of such instructions, an accessible vision has emerged within historical Islam for seeking peace through respectful dialogue that upholds core doctrinal commitments while affirming commonalities.

Advocates of a "peace through universalism" paradigm within Islam seek to engage with representatives of differing cultures and religions on the basis of what they understand as a Quranic principle of divinely sanctioned pluralism. Human diversity exists as a function of divine will and not of human caprice alone.[42] In light of this diversity, exchanges of views about the world's many pressing problems and disagreements ought to be conducted in a way that not only clarifies the relevance of Islamic values but also calls upon others to act on the guidance they have received. Pressing contemporary issues such as war, terrorism, poverty, and environmental degradation are evidence that humans have not allowed themselves to be transformed by the teachings of their respective traditions. Because people cannot be compelled to practice the teachings of Islam or of any other religion, the best possible politics is a moral politics in which Islamic teachings become the basis of an urgent appeal to all of humanity.

In affirming religious pluralism within a context of divine unity, the Islamic universalist paradigm attempts to walk a tightrope, postulating a deep harmony of purpose shared by world religions without denying the uniqueness of religious forms and practices. Deep resonance is possible across traditions—in the thirteenth century, Jalaluddin Rumi went so far as to state that, "Prayer differs according to religion, but faith does not change by religion"[43]—yet religious traditions cannot be forced to surrender their autonomy and distinctiveness. The essence of faith may have a recognizable fragrance wherever it is found, but forms are necessary vehicles for this fragrance. In its prescriptions for coexistence, the universalist paradigm therefore echoes the Quranic injunction for religious traditions to "compete in good works" (5:48). Although differences among religious traditions are inevitable and can lead to conflict, the existence of diversity is ultimately a divine blessing that can bring about mutual enrichment.

The potential for universalism, tolerance, and inclusiveness within Islamic culture is eloquently evoked in the Quran with the words: "and we have made you into nations and tribes that you may come to know one another" (49:13). At first glance, the vision contained in this simple statement may appear somewhat paradoxical: that the reality of ethnicity and cultural diversity is an expression of the divine will, while at the same time humankind is directed to embrace an underlying unity. However, from the standpoint of the "peace through universalism" paradigm, human unity cannot be achieved through uniformity.[44] Recognition of the fundamental solidarity and connectedness of all human beings is best expressed through respect for pluralism.[45] So long as diversity does not degenerate into factionalism and strife *(fitna),* each community of human spirituality can be seen as a part that reflects the whole. Applying the most essential teachings of each tradition is the surest means of preventing violent dissension, and provides a foundation for broad and inclusive involvement with the human prospect.

Appreciative Encounters: Past, Present, and Future

When sifting through the legacies of interaction among major religious traditions, it sometimes takes a discerning eye to locate instances of appreciative encounters. Insofar as most traditions have written their official histories with other priorities in mind, effort is required to uncover examples of genuine mutuality inspired by a spiritually grounded respect for others.

Nevertheless, many Muslims take pride in the ethics of coexistence they find in the Quran and the *hadith,* and in what they regard as a largely positive historical record in the domain of Abrahamic interfaith relations. Painful exceptions notwithstanding, including that of the "mad" Egyptian Fatimid caliph al-Hakim, who razed the Church of the Holy Sepulchre in 1009, classical Islamic society provided a template that, in the context of its time, permitted some remarkable forms of interreligious cooperation. Many of the "high points" of Islamic civilization were arguably made possible not so much by the unique genius of Muslim scientists, philosophers, and poets, as by the coexistence that Islamic precepts supported. Articulators of the "peace through universalism" paradigm often note that the Islamic ethic facilitated cultural and intellectual collaboration among Muslims, Jews, Christians, and members of other religious communities in ways that enabled scholars to assimilate and enrich the wisdom of previous civilizations.

Stories of interreligious mutuality within an Islamic context often begin with reports of Muhammad's early encounters with Christians, before his recognition as a prophet. Muslims have long held that it was the monk Bahirah, in the city of Bosra, near Damascus, who first recognized Muhammad's prophetic dispensation while the latter was a child accompanying a trading party.[46] A similar narrative reports that Waraqa Ibn Naufal, cousin to Muhammad's wife Khadija, helped Muhammad interpret the meaning of his first Quranic revelation.[47] While the emergence of such accounts might seem natural for a religious tradition seeking legitimacy as the fulfillment of the Abrahamic tradition, it is worth noting parallel traditions attributed to both Muhammad and his successor, the caliph Abu Bakr, specifically including monks and hermits among those people who must be left in peace as the first Muslim political communities began to take shape.[48] Although a saying of Muhammad expressly prohibits monasticism in Islam, monks and nuns have often received special consideration and respect among Muslims for the depth of their religious commitment and the rigor inherent in their individual and collective disciplines—disciplines that in many respects mirror those of Muslims, such as fasting and daily ritual prayer.[49] For centuries, the monks of St. Catherine's monastery at Mount Sinai sought to remind surrounding Bedouin tribes of their obligation to protect resident Christians by displaying a parchment, attributed to Muhammad, with explicit commands to safeguard the members of this contemplative community.

From a Western standpoint, it may come as a surprise that some narratives of mutuality between Muslim and non-Muslim communities are associated with themes of forbearance at a time of conflict. Muslim accounts of the conquest of Jerusalem in 638, for example, highlight the fact that many Christian subjects of the Byzantine Empire had already become alienated on account of imperial efforts to impose doctrinal correctness. These accounts also note the caliph Umar's role in resisting a triumphalist approach to Muslim administration of this holy city. As the second caliph of Islam (634–644), Umar reportedly sought to cultivate amicable relations with Jews and Christians as "people of the book." In his treaty with the Greek Christian patriarch Sophronius, Umar guaranteed life, property, and freedom of worship to the resident Christians, in exchange for a poll tax and support in the face of Byzantine raiders. This agreement provided one of the primary models for future Muslim relations with subjects regarded as *dhimmis*, "protected peoples." Jews, who had previously been barred from Jerusalem by the Byzantines, were invited to return.[50]

According to Muslim tradition, Umar visited with the Christian patriarch at the Church of the Holy Sepulchre. During this visit the Muslim call to prayer was sounded. The patriarch invited Umar to pray inside the church, and remarked that suitable prayer rugs were available should he desire them. The patriarch was surprised when Umar politely declined and left the church to pray outside. After completing his prayers, Umar explained to the patriarch that he had feared praying inside the church would compromise its status, providing Muslims with a pretext for converting the church into a mosque—and thereby Islamizing one of Christianity's most sacred sites. To this day, there is a mosque dedicated to Umar outside the Church of the Holy Sepulchre, and the Holy Sepulchre itself remains a Christian shrine. Intriguingly, the keys to the Holy Sepulchre have been held in safekeeping by a Palestinian Muslim family for centuries. This arrangement suits the local Christian denominations—Eastern Orthodox, Roman Catholic, and Armenian Apostolic—who have at times experienced strong disagreements while jointly managing the interior space of the church.

In Islam as in other religious cultures, past events and precedents are very much alive in the present, albeit through varied interpretations. Remembered events play a powerful role in determining the ways in which scripture is read. The fact that a party of Muslims found refuge in Christian Abyssinia during the earliest years of Islam, when the religion was still a persecuted minority faith, has contributed to a positive regard for dedicated Christians that can still be found among many Muslims, despite intervening events such as the Crusades and colonialism. Appreciation for the Jewish tradition arises from somewhat different historical sources.

Although early political competition between Arabian Jews and the Prophet Muhammad's emergent Muslim community left residues that once again became painfully evident during the modern conflict over Palestine, competition for monotheistic legitimacy and political authority in seventh-century Medina is by no means the only story that can be told. For most of Islamic history, vibrant Jewish communities significantly enriched the Middle Eastern Islamic and Mediterranean cultural environment, and elder generations of Muslims in countries such as Iraq, Syria, Egypt, and Yemen can still remember a time when they were actively engaged in business with their Jewish neighbors.[51]

During the ninth and tenth centuries, Baghdad, the Abbasid Empire's capital, became one of the most cosmopolitian cities ever known, where Muslim, Jewish, and Christian scholars collaboratively searched for knowledge. Along with Cordoba in Andalusia, Abbasid Baghdad was one of the two focal points of a remarkable research program: collection, translation, and synthesis of all known sources of human knowledge. Not only Greek, but also Indian, Iranian, and Chinese forms of knowledge were integrated into this synthesis; Syriac Christian and also Jewish scholars played a particularly vital role in an officially sponsored effort to translate Greek scientific and philosophical texts into Arabic.

Some of the more inspiring cases of Muslim coexistence with the "people of the book" can be found in Andalusia—Islamic Spain—between the eighth and fifteenth centuries. In Andalusia (Al-Andalus), cooperation among Muslim, Jewish, and Christian scholars reached unprecedented heights for the medieval world.[52]

Muslims first arrived in Spain in 711, as conquerors. Following the rise of the Spanish Umayyad dynasty at mid-century, this frontier region of Islamic civilization became a place of remarkable prosperity and cultural dynamism and began to exert an influence on European Christendom. At the seat of the empire in Cordoba, the arts and sciences—from poetry and philosophy to medicine—flourished under official patronage.

The Jewish communities of Andalusia prospered greatly during the Umayyad era of Muslim Spain (756–1031). This was a time of impressive cultural vitality, during which Jews developed what is known as Sephardic ("Spanish") culture and became significant contributors to the richness of Arab-Islamic society. Conditions were sufficiently favorable during the tenth century for Hasdai Ibn Shaprut (915–970), a Jewish scholar from a successful and learned family, to become the grand vizier to Caliph Abd al-Rahman III. In addition to serving the caliph as a diplomat and as a specialist in the medical sciences—he presided over diplomatic negotiations with Byzantium and organized the translation of a Greek medical encyclopedia—Hasdai was also active in efforts to promote a revival of Jewish learning. He encouraged Jewish scholars to settle in Andalusia, and provided patronage for literary, philosophical, and scientific endeavors; subsequent generations have regarded him as a pivotal figure in a broader renaissance of European Jewish learning—a renaissance that began in Cordoba even as the prominence of the Jewish community in Baghdad had fallen into relative decline. The depth of Jewish participation in the Andalusian Arab culture was such that Cordoba-born rabbi Moses Maimonides (1135–1204)—one of the greatest and most influential thinkers in Jewish history—wrote most of his works in the Arabic language.[53]

As the ornate palaces and luxurious gardens of cities such as Cordoba and Granada attest, it was in Andalusia that some of the more illustrious Muslim leaders aspired to build on the face of the earth a mirror image of paradise, described in the Quran as the "abode of peace" (10:25). The model of Andalusian coexistence that took shape within this context appears far from perfect when judged by modern standards. Political and theological competition continued among the faith communities, especially between Muslims and Christians. The experiment eventually came to a close, first with the rise of less tolerant Muslim dynasties in the twelfth century, and later with the completion of the Christian reconquest in 1492 and the subsequent expulsion of Muslims and Jews (many of whom fled to Muslim lands) from the Iberian peninsula. While it lasted, however, Andalusia provided a clear image of the dynamic cultural possibilities that can accompany genuine attempts at coexistence. These possibilities include not only enhanced intellectual productivity and insight but also a "rich dialogue of daily life where one learns to accommodate the customs and beliefs of another through myriad quotidian interactions while baking, laundering, buying, selling, sowing, and reaping."[54] Imperfect and incomplete as it may have been, the Andalusian experiment at its best provides an illustration of enlightened Muslim rule during Islam's golden age, and an example of Islamic theology and spirituality's more accommodating and mutualistic expressions.

For the "peace through universalism" paradigm, historical examples of positive interfaith encounters predicated on mutual respect and even appreciation are not lost to the past. They are alive in historical narratives, and provide a legacy upon which present generations can creatively build. Contemporary activists whose work can be situated within this paradigm do not attempt to reconstruct rules and structures that governed interfaith relations in the past—rules that no longer appear so progressive as they once did—but nonetheless draw upon these examples as metaphors and suggestive models. The implicit assumption is that the spirit of past encounters can be evoked in ways that suggest new and dynamic practices for cultivating understanding and respect in our present era. An illustrative example can be found in the Cordoba Initiative, founded in 2002 with the stated purpose of "building a broad multifaith coalition to help repair damage that has been done to Muslim-American relations over the last fifty years."[55]

One relatively well-known example of a Muslim-initiated effort to foster interreligious and intercultural solidarity is the "Dialogue Among Civilizations" initiative. This initiative, presented as a constructive response to the "clash of civilizations" hypothesis of Samuel Huntington, symbolized an Iranian desire to explore new, nonconfrontational approaches to relations with the West and the broader international community. Advanced by Iran's reformist president Muhammad Khatami in 1998 during an address at the United Nations, the concept simultaneously affirmed both the importance of the world's diverse heritages and the importance of seeking common values. In an action that now appears sadly ironic, the General Assembly of the United Nations declared 2001 the "Year of Dialogue Among Civilizations." Despite the increased polarization that accompanied the political events of that year, the idea of intercultural and interreligious dialogue as a vital confidence-building measure for a pluralistic world has survived in the form of the present "Alliance of Civilizations" initiative, inaugurated in 2005 at the United Nations during the tenure of Secretary-General Kofi Annan. This project seeks to develop a program for collective action to redress rising Islamic-Western tensions.

In addition to these high-level efforts, Middle Eastern governments and civil society organizations have in recent years begun dedicating increased efforts to interfaith dialogue.[56] One example of a project that reflects an Islamic "peace through universalism" paradigm is the Fez Festival of World Sacred Music. This event, held annually in Morocco since 1994, brings together sacred music artists from the Middle East and around the world for a week of concerts, lectures, exhibitions, and films. The purpose is to encourage exchange at one of the deeper levels of human cultural expression, by highlighting how music can reflect universal human spiritual sensitivities and an aspiration toward communion with the divine. In addition to the concerts and performances, the festival also provides a forum for supplementary presentations, exhibitions, and activities that highlight points of unity within the diversity of global spiritual heritages. In 2001, the United Nations designated the festival and its organizers as "unsung heroes of dialogue," along with six other award recipients, for reaching across divides to embrace the "other."

The Fez Festival, which includes participants from diverse world religions and goes beyond conservative definitions of "people of the book," bears the imprint of a Sufi principle according to which diversity is a form of divine blessing, or *baraka.* The existence of cultural and religious pluralism magnifies rather than reduces human reverence for divine creativity, and reinforces the Quranic teaching that "wheresoever you turn is the face of God" (2:115). Rather than prejudice in the face of differences, Sufi teachings such as those of Ibn 'Arabi—who was born in Andalusia but also traveled the length and breadth of North Africa and the Middle East—call for attitudes of humility and respect. In one of his more often-recited poems, Muhyiddin Ibn 'Arabi sought to express what he had come to experience as a powerfully heartfelt capacity to embrace others:

> My heart has become capable of every form:
> It is a pasture for gazelles and a convent for Christian monks,
> And a temple for idols and the pilgrim's Ka'ba,
> And the tables of the Torah and the book of the Qur'an.
> I follow the religion of Love:
> Whatever way Love's camels take, that is my religion and my faith.[57]

From such a standpoint, every religious culture and every created thing manifests divine qualities. Differences of doctrine remain, yet the ultimate measure of each system of faith is its ability to bring the believer into relationship with the whole of reality in a way that manifests divine love. For Ibn 'Arabi and those of similar disposition, an inclusive, all-embracing outlook represented the fulfillment of Islamic universalism.

Challenges and Opportunities

The "peace through universalism" paradigm, which stresses transforming human character, creating equilibrium within the soul, and developing harmony among people of diverse faiths, offers a view of peace and peacemaking distinctively different from the paradigms reviewed thus far. From this standpoint, peace is a process of being and doing that connects the inner life of the individual to his or her community and to the larger life of the world. Peace is always in the making, but never fully made. It requires justice in the world of social relations and structures, as well as a more fundamental just ordering of human life at the micro level, predicated on self-knowledge, self-transcendence, spiritual authenticity, and openness to the uniqueness of others.

The just ordering of human life ultimately leads to harmony and to a naturally unfolding desire to "do what is beautiful."

The paradigm's strengths relate directly to its universality, powerful blending of ethical and aesthetic categories, and potential to foster deep and spiritually sophisticated forms of intercultural dialogue. The ecumenical character of much Sufi thought creates natural bridges across serious and long-standing divides, and the all-encompassing understanding of divine unity associated with this tradition makes it resistant (though not impervious) to forms of thought that dehumanize outsiders. In many acute intercommunal conflicts, from Israel-Palestine to Nigeria, individuals with a deep grounding in the Sufi tradition have been among the first figures to step forward in pursuit of interreligious reconciliation, even while maintaining a strong sense of loyalty to their communities of origin. Though opinions vary, Sufis have often manifested considerable flexibility and open-mindedness on the issue of gender roles—a matter of no small importance in contemporary intercultural conflicts.

Islamic mysticism, of course, is not a dominant trend in contemporary Islamic culture. Though it can be encountered in unexpected places—many Westerners would be surprised to know that Islamic mysticism is integral to the intellectual training of many Iranian clerics—neither the Sufi tradition nor the "embracive" conception of Islamic identity outlined in this chapter receives universal assent and affirmation. Particularly in our present era, when many Muslims feel that their historical status and security in the world have been lost, there are strong pressures in many quarters to dispense with humanistic, esoteric, and universalistic understandings of Islam so as better to seek strength through uniformity and puritanical notions of reform. Today's present mood of decline, inauthenticity, and vulnerability correlates with heightened concern for maintaining boundaries, redressing worldly injustices, and reducing Islamic principles to formulas that can be easily assimilated and disseminated.

Historically, many of the most inclusive and magnanimous conceptions of Islamic mission and spirituality have prevailed at times when Muslim communities were confident of their strength and secure in their cultural and religious identity. Without a doubt, it is easier for a successful, self-confident culture to embrace diversity than it is for a culture that has begun to experience a new sense of vulnerability or decline. The emergence of new anxieties in the West about immigration and cultural diversity suggests that this tendency is universal rather than particular to Muslims, and that exclusively spiritual or ideational explanations for inclusiveness or exclusiveness are incomplete. Islamic rulers of the classical or golden age, like North Americans and Europeans in much of the twentieth century, recognized that their prosperity, prestige, and power depended on their ability to embrace newcomers and draw upon their intellectual and practical resourcefulness.

Much therefore depends on questions of leadership, vision, and creative imagination. In the past, Muslims demonstrated a capacity to embrace diversity that was generally progressive in its particular time and context. As already noted, Islam granted religious freedom—but not fully equal citizenship—to Christian and Jewish as well as Zoroastrian communities, provided that they paid their poll tax, or *jizya.* Such rights were also extended, albeit more inconsistently and ambivalently, to members of southern Asian religious communities such as Hindus and Buddhists. Little thought was given to the possibility of embracing "secular humanists"—a category of identity that simply did not exist, and that would have been inaccurately subsumed by other categories presuming a lack of self-restraint or moral concern. Resurrecting past forms of inclusive community in the modern age would not appear to be an adequate response to present forms of pluralism. Nonetheless, legacies of the past can be adapted and expanded in ways that give new life to old principles and enrich modern understandings of "peace culture."[58]

From the standpoint of the "peace through universalism" paradigm, spiritual values for the present and future are best expressed in a nonpartisan way that speaks to universal human needs for transcendence, unity, and justice. Religious and spiritual traditions may require renewal if they are to respond to the contemporary context of human life. Though most religious and ethical systems promote reciprocity and goodwill, their institutions and outlooks are too frequently identified with the very aspects of the past that contribute to current division and conflict.

Despite these challenges, Islamic visions of human life rooted in spirituality, transformative surrender, and expansive embrace retain considerable vitality and potential. Islam's universalist paradigm, whether expressed through Sufism or other forms of ecumenical Islamic thought, has by no means been rendered irrelevant by present-day forms of religious partisanship. The "peace through universalism" paradigm offers an intellectually and spiritually compelling worldview, and permits principled adaptation to cultural change without sacrificing Islam's basic critique of Western individualism and materialism (a critique that, incidentally, is shared by many Western religious communities).[59] This paradigm could provide seeds for developing creative responses to modern Muslim experiences of fragmentation and culture shock, and alternatives to visions of the world that dismiss the unmeasurable as "unreal."

With the shrinking attraction of secular ideologies and increasing pressures toward "retribalization" of the world, the "peace through universalism" paradigm has the potential to facilitate interfaith and intercultural efforts to forge a new peace culture. Exponents of Islamic universalism can easily make common cause with followers of other traditions who share their conviction that visions of humanity's place in the universe need not be limited to the horizons observed by the physical sciences. At the present historical juncture, marked both by tremendous threats to the planet's ecological balance and by daunting divisions between religious and cultural groups, it has become tremendously important for Muslims who draw upon their tradition's deeper resources to take their place beside members of other faith traditions in common efforts to foster the transformations necessary for a more peaceful, harmonious future.

Historically, the Sufi tradition has played an important role in efforts to bridge divides between Islam and non-Islamic cultural systems. As contemporary Muslims seek to restore lost dimensions of their religious culture and reach out to non-Muslim communities, this tradition retains considerable appeal. Through its affirmation of unity, Sufism can offer a powerful counterpoint to religious and political discourse rooted in fear and intercultural alienation, together with a stimulus for appreciation of Islamic spirituality among followers of other religious traditions. By providing a language that encourages human solidarity and affirms the wholeness of human life, it can nourish a universalist Islamic paradigm that seeks to overcome trends that fracture humanity on the basis of exclusive identities, closed cultural systems, and unequal classes.

Notes

Some of the material in this chapter was originally presented by Nathan Funk at the "Symposium on Mevlana Celaleddin-i Rumi and Inter-Cultural and -Civilization Dialogue," organized in Toronto by the Canadian Interfaith Dialogue Center, November 3, 2007.

1. Lewis, *Rumi,* 2000, p. 1.
2. Some authorities use the term "Sufism" comprehensively to refer to all mystically inclined Islamic spirituality; others use it more narrowly to refer to particular threads of the Islamic spiritual tradition. In this chapter, we associate Sufism with the most universalistic and transformative aspects of Islamic spirituality, while giving special attention to the broad but often subtle impact of mysticism on historical Islamic culture.
3. Murata and Chittick, *The Vision of Islam,* 1994, pp. 267–269.
4. Trimingham, *The Sufi Orders in Islam,* 1998.
5. al-Ghazali, *The Niche of Lights,* 1998; al-Ghazali, *On the Duties of Brotherhood,* 1975.
6. See, for example, the works of Sadi al-Shirazi and Jalaluddin Rumi. Annemarie Schimmel's *Mystical Dimensions of Islam* (1975) provides a useful introduction to a broad range of Sufi thought and expression.
7. Islamic reform and revival movements have sometimes sought to displace Sufism, yet Sufi traditions still remain vital. See Nasr, *Traditional Islam in the Modern World,* 1987. See also Sirriyeh, *Sufis and Anti-Sufis,* 1999.
8. Murata and Chittick, *The Vision of Islam,* 1994, p. 238.
9. Cowan, *Rumi's Divan of Shems of Tabriz,* 1997, p. 57.
10. Over the centuries, Sufi thinkers developed a psychology of the soul with many stages of transformation toward realization. The three stages referred to here are drawn from Quranic references to the "commanding soul" *(nafs al-ammara),* the "blaming soul" *(nafs al-lawwama),* and the "soul at peace" *(nafs al-mutma'inna).*
11. Thackston, *Signs of the Unseen,* 1994, pp. 60–61.

12. For Sufi commentary on the process of *mujahada*, "spiritual striving/struggle," see Sands, *Sufi Commentaries on the Qur'an in Classical Islam*, 2006, pp. 30, 91–94. See also Muhaiyaddeen, *Islam and World Peace*, 1987; Bayrak, *Divine Governance of the Human Kingdom*, 1997.

13. While there are rigorous spiritual disciplines within Islam, there is no monasticism. See Nasr, *Sufi Essays*, 1973. See also Crow, "Nonviolence, Ethics, and Character Development in Islam," 2001.

14. Corbin, *Alone with the Alone*, 1997; Izutsu, *Sufism and Taoism*, 1983.

15. Cowan, *Rumi's Divan of Shems of Tabriz*, 1997, p. 82.

16. Some authorities on mysticism relate the Sufi understanding of *tawhid* (divine unity) to "panentheism": the proposition that God's presence permeates all creation, and that all of creation exists within a divine context ("God in all, all in God"). This theological position is distinct from "pantheism," a term that associates the visible world with God in a manner that tends to negate the principle of divine transcendence. See, for example, Teasdale, *The Mystic Heart*, 2001, pp. 83, 199, 220–221.

17. For further exposition of these themes, see Coates, *Ibn 'Arabi and Modern Thought*, 2002; Izutsu, *Sufism and Taoism*, 1983.

18. Murata and Chittick, *The Vision of Islam*, 1994, p. 304.

19. As Schimmel states in *Deciphering the Signs of God* (1994), "God's attributes of majesty, *jalal*, and beauty, *jamal*, which are related to each other like man and woman, as it were, form the fabric of the created universe" (p. 226). See also Nasr, *The Heart of Islam*, 2002, p. 5.

20. Chittick, *The Sufi Path of Knowledge*, 1989, pp. 127–128; Izutsu, *Sufism and Taoism*, 1983, pp. 131–135.

21. Murata and Chittick, *The Vision of Islam*, 1994, p. 309.

22. Cowan, *Rumi's Divan of Shems of Tabriz*, 1997, p. 109.

23. Schimmel, *Look!* 1991, p. 61.

24. Ibid., p. 28.

25. Cowan, *Rumi's Divan of Shems of Tabriz*, 1997, p. 75.

26. Helminski, *The Ruins of the Heart*, 1981, p. 18.

27. In the words of Mona Abul-Fadl ("Community, Justice, and Jihad," 1987), "it is *wajh'Allah*, the Countenance of Allah, which [the sincere Muslim] seeks. . . . The serene and contented self, *al Nafs al Radiya al Mardiya*, and the self which has found its innermost sense of peace, *al Nafs al Mutma'inna*, are anchored in that infinite and unassailable source from which they draw" (p. 25).

28. Peace researcher and conflict resolution practitioner John Paul Lederach has written of his surprise when, while participating in a peacebuilding workshop in Tajikistan, a participant approached him to share a story of building trust with a "warlord" through conversations over their shared passion for Sufi poetry and philosophy (*The Moral Imagination*, 2005, pp. 16–19).

29. In Edward Rehatsek's translation of *The Rose Garden* (1990), the verses are rendered thus: "The sons of Adam are limbs of each other / Having been created of one essence / When the calamity of time afflicts one limb / The other limbs cannot remain at rest / If thou hast no sympathy for the troubles of others / Thou art unworthy to be called by the name of man" (p. 41).

30. Cited by Nasr in "Islam, the Contemporary Islamic World, and the Environmental Crisis," 2003, p. 95.

31. Boylan, *Hafiz*, 1998, p. 20.

32. Mafi and Kolin, *Rumi*, 2001, p. 16.

33. Gray, *The Green Sea of Heaven*, 1995, p. 99.

34. Cited in Arberry, *Persian Poems*, 2005, p. 136.

35. Mafi and Kolin, *Rumi,* 2001, p. 77.

36. The Quran, for example, offers an account of Adam and Eve's banishment from paradise to earth (2:35–36) that is similar to the biblical narrative, and also contains the story of Cain and Abel.

37. Nyang, "Scriptural Faith and Ethnicity," 1997, p. 240.

38. Nasr, *The Heart of Islam,* 2002, p. 221.

39. Shah-Kazemi, *Paths to Transcendence,* 2006.

40. Shah-Kazemi, *The Other in the Light of the One,* 2006.

41. See also 4:162.

42. The following passages from the Quran are quite clear on this point: "If your Lord had so desired, all the people on the earth would surely have come to believe, all of them; do you then think that you could compel people to believe" (10:99); "And had your Lord so willed, He could surely have made all human beings into one single community: but [He willed it otherwise, and so] they continue to hold divergent views (11:118).

43. Thackston, *Signs of the Unseen,* 1994, p. 33.

44. Ibid., p. 29.

45. Boase, *Islam and Global Dialogue,* 2005.

46. Guillaume. *The Life of Muhammad,* 1990, pp. 79–81.

47. Ibid., p. 107.

48. Ramadan, *In the Footsteps of the Prophet,* 2007, p. 201.

49. Kiser, *The Monks of Tibhirine,* 2002, p. 37.

50. Armstrong, *Jerusalem,* 1997, p. 233.

51. Modest Jewish communities persist in Iran and Morocco, albeit in smaller numbers than in the decades before the establishment of the modern state of Israel. Other Middle Eastern Jewish communities have been more dramatically affected by emigration to Israel and the West.

52. Menocal, *The Ornament of the World,* 2002.

53. Unfortunately, the rise of the Almohad dynasty during the twelfth century forced Maimonides and his family to flee a resurgent intolerance in Andalusia. Maimonides eventually secured a prestigious post as a physician in the court of Saladin in Egypt. See Nuland, *Maimonides,* 2005.

54. Lowney, *A Vanished World,* 2005, p. 207.

55. Abdul Rauf, *What's Right with Islam,* 2004, p. 274. This US-based organization's cofounders are Imam Feisal Abdul Rauf and John S. Bennett.

56. Nasr, *The Heart of Islam,* 2002, pp. 52–53. See also Abu-Nimer, Khoury, and Welty, *Unity in Diversity,* 2007.

57. Nicholson, *The Tarjuman al-Ashwaq,* 1978, p. 67.

58. Boulding, *Cultures of Peace,* 2000.

59. As viewed through the lenses of Islam's universalist paradigm, culture is a resource whose function is to nurture and give expression to qualities that fulfill human existence. Cultural creation is essentially a communal process in which freedom is achieved through collaboration with others, rather than through a purely liberal and individualistic doing of one's own thing. From this perspective, the communal nature of human creativity involves a certain amount of discipline, self-restraint, and self-sacrifice.

Part 3

Recommendations

9

Preparing for Peace

We began this study by suggesting that contemporary Islamic-Western relations have reached a point of crisis—a moment of danger and also of opportunity. On the one hand, the momentum of current events appears to be leading toward increasing conflict and a deepening sense of mutual alienation. Each act of violence or counterviolence appears capable of eliciting a retaliation of equal or greater severity. On the other hand, the threat of further escalation has a galvanizing effect on those who seek to avert further deterioration toward the worst prejudices of the past, and who hope instead to transform attitudes formed in mutual ignorance and to reform practices that prevent the emergence of trust.

In many respects, policy choices are mediated and constrained by interpretations of history, and by preconceptions about the "other's" character and behavioral repertoire. Those who fatalistically resign themselves to escalating conflict tend to view Islamic-Western conflict as an unalterable fact of history, an outcome of incompatible doctrines and values. From this standpoint, there are no transformative policy options: long-term management of delicate, conflicted relations and the pursuit of a decisive cultural or religious victory are the only clear choices. Those who reject these conclusions offer a different reading of history and of the "other," in which two interdependent macro-cultures or civilizations have become tragically entangled in dangerous and unnecessary conflicts that can produce no "winner." These conflicts threaten the interests and values of both sides—interests and values that are shared, as well as concerns and priorities that make each side distinctive.

Protagonists of this latter standpoint—and we count ourselves among them—argue that talk of an intractable "clash of civilizations" dramatically oversimplifies contemporary Islamic-Western conflict, and yet is conducive to self-fulfilling prophecy. Instead of appealing to dramatic images of confrontation, they express caution with respect to static generalizations about innate cultural differences, and call for the development of constructive policy initiatives.

Their approach invites prospective thinking about ways in which present tensions might gradually be transformed through a program different in content and character from the present "war on terror."

Genuine security for Western societies can be achieved only through policies that are sensitive to multiple currents within Muslim and Middle Eastern societies, and that facilitate rather than impede the expression of actively peaceful, life-affirming manifestations of Islamic identity. As we have endeavored to show, history and Islamic interpretation have equipped contemporary Muslims with many ways of thinking about peace and peacemaking; while some patterns of interpretation and practice are ethnocentric or even triumphalist, others are not. The diversity of Islamic approaches to peace mirrors variations also found within other religions and cultures, including Jewish, Christian, and Western secular traditions. Knowledge of this diversity can provide a powerful basis for intercultural bridge building and for innovative policy frameworks designed to reverse current trends toward mutual incomprehension and violence.

Islam: Source of Identity, Resource for Change

A central proposition of this study is that understanding the many roles of Islam in Middle Eastern culture and politics is essential for making sense of conflict and processes of social change. Assigning a prominent role to religious culture and identity as a factor in conflict, social change, and peacemaking need not presume the insignificance of more conventional political and economic structures and processes (see Chapter 3). In highlighting the role of Islam, we need not fall into the habits of reductionism that characterize the story of confrontation (see Chapter 2). We need only recognize that religiously defined values and symbols are highly significant factors in the politics of most Middle Eastern societies, and that efforts to bypass or repress this reality are unlikely to bear fruit.

For most committed Muslims, Islam is more than just "religion" as understood in contemporary Western contexts. It is both a creed and a cultural heritage, an enduring system of meaning and a basis for harmonious social order. It provides a template of values and norms to regulate social practices ranging from marriage and inheritance to war and peace. Though Islam often competes with other cultural codes and value systems, including nationalism and secular modernism, it has proven to be remarkably resilient in its cultural staying power. Faced with domestic developmental setbacks as well as conflict in international relations, Muslims in the Middle East and many other world regions have responded by deepening their identification with Islamic culture rather than by abandoning it.

In practice, Muslims with diverse belief systems and cultural orientations are using Islam as they so often have in the past—not only as a *constraint* on social and political change, but also a *resource* for facilitating social interactions and advancing valued goals. As an esteemed cultural and religious frame of reference within which social institutions are embedded, Islam supplies a context of meaning to family life, economic transactions, social service, and many varieties of professional and political as well as religious association. In the face of economic maldistribution and political institutions that are experienced as unresponsive, Islam does indeed provide a vocabulary for parties and movements that oppose the status quo in the name of social justice. Yet it is also defining the discourse of religious intellectuals, the practices of Islamic courts, the spirituality of popular movements, and a core identity for new generations.

The varied character of Islamic social life attests to the vitality of Middle Eastern cultures, which are proving to be remarkably resilient as Muslims engage with Western social systems. Many forms of Western culture have already been universalized, and Muslims in the Middle East as well as in the United States and Europe are proving that they can retain their identity while responding to modern challenges. If the role of religion in politics is still a matter of contention in Muslim countries, Muslims are by no means unique. Disputes within Middle Eastern Islamic societies may strike outsiders as acute, but they are similar in kind to debates under way in Israel, India, the United States, and many other countries throughout the world.

Modern revivalism has dampened the nationalist spirit of the mid-twentieth century and heightened the public role played by Islam in society, yet the ways in which Middle Eastern Muslims understand their religion and its values vary considerably. Patterns of variation in Islamic thought reflect geography—Islam in Saudi Arabia differs in significant ways from Islam in Syria or Morocco, and so on—as well as diverse "cultures of interpretation" that cut across spatial boundaries. Islamic meaning is contested in ways that have major implications for Islamic-Western relations, and for internal debates about issues like democracy and social change. Cultures of interpretation include Muslim secularists, progressive Islamic reformists, mainstream Islamic revivalists, radical Islamists, and neotraditionalists (see Table 9.1). These typological categories, of course, do not exhaust the complexity of Islamic thought, nor are they mutually exclusive and invariant intellectual positions.

Like all religious systems, Islam is internally pluralistic, with multiple schools of thought, subcultures, and ethical traditions that are bound together by a shared historical narrative, an overarching sense of identity, and a common vocabulary for speaking about the sacred. When particular Muslim groups claim to act in the name of Islam, sophisticated and thoughtful observers should neither neglect nor uncritically accept the "Islamicity" of the actors and actions. It becomes useful to ask *which* Islam is being invoked, by

Table 9.1 Cultures of Islamic Interpretation and Attitudes Toward the West

	Perspective on Islam and Present Status of Muslims	Attitude Toward the West
Muslim secularist	Varying attitudes—Islam as cultural and civilizational heritage, and as a private set of values ("religion is a personal matter"); little difference between Islamic and Western norms; perceived threat from reactionary "fundamentalists"	Western culture viewed with favor as modern and progressive; varying attitudes toward Western policies vis-à-vis Muslim immigrant populations and Muslim-majority countries (assimilationist/conformist and alienated/critical perspectives both present)
Progressive Islamic reformist	Islam as a dynamic set of principles embedded in the Quran; need to give new life to principles in changing historical contexts; need for self-critical Muslim thought and scope for fresh interpretations (liberal approach to *ijtihad*); diversity within Islam viewed as a potential resource	Western achievements taken very seriously; democracy and free inquiry seen as authentically Islamic; criticisms of Western culture and politics comparable to internal "self-critiques" offered by Western religious communities; lack of Western sensitivity to Islam partially (but not entirely) to blame for ineffective policies and Muslim radicalization
Mainstream Islamic revivalist ("moderate" Islamist or Salafi; "populist" Islam)	Islam as a pure set of forms and principles embodied in the Quran and *hadith* literature; traditional interpreters subject to critique for subservience to rulers, and for failure to apply Islamic principles vigorously to social, political, and economic problems; reformists criticized for trying to imitate the West, lacking authenticity	Technological and scientific aspects of Western culture acceptable; cultural and political aspects of the Western experience should be critically reappraised and corrected; Western policies intended to control Muslim peoples and extract their resources, but most Westerners uninformed; Western prejudices against Muslims (and ignorance of Islam) permit harmful policies
Radical Islamist or "fundamentalist"	Islam as a pure and unchangeable set of forms and principles embodied in the Quran and *hadith* literature; traditional interpreters subject to harsh critique for quietism, subservience to rulers, and failure to impose Islamic principles in all spheres of life; reformers viewed as agents of imperialism; practice of uncorrupted Islam depends on righteous leadership and "authentic" Islamic state; diversity within Islam categorically rejected (extreme sectarianism)	Technological aspects of Western culture acceptable; cultural and political aspects of the Western experience must be denounced; Western policies intended to subordinate and humiliate Muslim peoples, extract their resources, and destroy Islam; West as enemy and agent of corruption; most Muslim political leaders complicit with the enemy
Neotraditionalist	Islam as a pure set of forms and principles derived from the Quran and *hadith* literature and interpreted by qualified, authoritative scholars; proper application of Islamic values depends on knowledge of both sources and traditional syntheses; true Islam now threatened both by overly politicized Muslims without proper training and by cultural Westernization	Varying attitudes; some Western technologies and practices are compatible with Islam, while others are clearly not (sociomoral concerns); Western society suffering malaise from lack of religious knowledge and displacement of traditional religious frameworks; Western policies generally based on ignorance of Islam and historical biases

whom, and for what reasons and purposes. Frameworks that sensitize us to diverse Islamic interpretive styles such as neotraditionalism, progressive reform, secularism, and various types of revivalism help us to recognize the presence of diversity among Muslims, while also shedding light on the new challenges that the modern period has posed for religious life. Many contemporary Muslims feel at least partially cut off from their cultural past by rapid changes in society and culture, and are carefully evaluating competing frameworks for finding meaning in the past and purpose in the present.

As valuable as it is for Western policymakers to be aware of major schools of thought within Islamic interpretation, and to recognize the vital importance of progressive reformists and mainstream revivalists in influencing future directions of Islamic thought and culture, it would be a mistake to presume that a particular school of thought contains either "natural allies" or "implacable enemies" to be opposed under all conditions and at all costs. Even radical Islamists, for example, may prefer nonviolent participation in the political process to more destabilizing activities when personal safety and freedom to organize are guaranteed. Secularist Muslims who are comfortable with Western culture may nonetheless support repressive policies that transform "mainstream" Islamic revivalists into radicals. Rather than seek to polarize Muslims with respect to their understandings of Islam and Islamic values, Western leaders and civic activists would be wiser to seek opportunities to engage Muslim publics on themes related to four out of five of this volume's paradigms.

Islamic peace paradigms are nonexclusive with respect to cultures of interpretation. Key premises of the "peace through coercion" paradigm, for example, are embraced not only by some neotraditionalists who are skeptical about what they see as the utopianism of radical Islamists but also by secular Muslims who fear political instability. "Peace through equity" reflects commonsense understandings of many mainstream Islamic revivalists and progressive reformists, yet there are many neotraditionalists, secularists, and even radicals who would claim key tenets of this paradigm as their own.

With respect to politics and peacemaking, there is no denying that Middle Eastern Islamic cultures have been impacted by historical forms of competition for power—that is, by the "peace through coercion" paradigm. Many of these practices are not regarded by most Muslims as deeply Islamic, yet in the past they were accepted as normal by Muslim philosophers as well as by jurists who embraced what Hamid Enayat describes as an attitude of "conservative realism."[1] In Middle Eastern history as in Western history, the higher ideals of religion often diverge from the realities of observed human behavior, most notably in the domain of politics. Enayat states the paradox this way:

> [A] misconception about the fusion of religion and politics in Islamic culture is to think that in historical reality . . . all political attitudes and institutions among Muslims have . . . conformed to religious norms. Often the reverse

> was true: the majority of Muslims, for the greater part of their history, lived under regimes which had only the most tenuous link with those norms, and observed the *Shari'ah* only to the extent that it legitimised their power in the eyes of the faithful.[2]

Competition for authority and influence among ambitious Muslim leaders has led to practices that have arguably "bent religion out of shape," or that have utilized Islamic symbols and categories as instruments. The use of Islam—or any religion, for that matter—as a banner rather than as a compass can easily sharpen intergroup competition, justify the resort to force, and push the ideal of a "full" and lasting peace to the distant horizon. As a result, peace becomes reduced to stability and security, and to a temporary absence of war. Qualities such as justice may still be ascribed to the leader, yet there is little hope of establishing a more comprehensively just social system.

From the standpoint of the "peace through equity" paradigm, many of the problems afflicting the Muslim Middle East are due not only to dysfunctional forms of Western intervention, but also to actions permitted by the "peace through coercion" paradigm. The "peace through equity" paradigm is in many respects a more accurate reflection of Muslim idealism than the "peace through coercion" paradigm, even though the paradigm is at present internally contested between those who advocate a "cosmopolitan" perspective in which Muslim identity presupposes active world citizenship, and those who prioritize the distinctiveness of Islamic values and the special needs of Muslim nations, along with a more conservative understanding of issues such as democracy and human rights. However, despite these differences, the "peace through equity" paradigm provides a clear articulation of Islamic values that link peace to social justice, and it embodies the hopes of many Muslims for a more just world order in which they are active participants.

The "peace through conciliation" paradigm provides additional insights into Middle Eastern Islamic culture and practices associated with peacemaking. It reflects traditional forms of social organization and mediating behavior, as well as the efforts of contemporary Muslim diplomats and conflict resolution trainers to update these forms in ways that respond to current needs and realities. While this paradigm's principles and methods have been applied more often at the village and community level than in international relations, Westerners as well as Middle Eastern Muslims would do well to reflect on its premises and cultural resonance as they consider ways to augment the legitimacy and effectiveness of regional peace efforts. This paradigm also offers a potential basis for the formulation of modern Islamic approaches to restorative justice and postwar reconciliation.

The "peace through nonviolence" paradigm also contains vital insights and challenges for Middle Eastern peacemakers. While most Middle Easterners are uncomfortable with ideals of absolute pacifism, those who espouse this paradigm provide a compelling argument that Islamic values can provide fertile soil for determined nonviolent resistance. Though these arguments need further testing, the dissemination of Islamic frameworks for nonviolent resistance may yet offer hope for breaking cycles of violence in Middle Eastern countries in which opposition movements have too often vacillated between resignation and insurrection. The "peace through nonviolence" paradigm offers inspiration for carefully planned efforts to develop nonviolent change strategies, and encourages the articulation of moderate yet substantive goals that might mobilize broad coalitions of actors.

The often-overlooked capacity of many Muslims to identify with a remarkably pluralistic theology of religions is a core theme of the "peace through universalism" paradigm. Although this paradigm cannot claim to offer a comprehensive set of prescriptions for Middle Eastern conflicts, it nonetheless supplies a worldview especially well-suited to intercultural and interreligious bridge building, and to the development of coexistence based on mutuality between Muslim and non-Muslim religious cultures in the region and beyond. This paradigm also conveys a deeply rooted model for the development of peaceful character and a horizon of aspiration for those seeking to enrich Islamic "peace culture."

Taken together, these paradigms demonstrate the significant potential for peacemaking action within Islamic culture. For Muslims they offer a range of options, choices, and challenges; for non-Muslims they provide fresh stimulus for thought about how peacemaking partnerships can be constructed across religious and cultural boundaries.

These paradigms can also help to identify strategic challenges. The tragedy of current Western—and especially US—policies toward the Middle East is that they have inadvertently strengthened a small but vocal minority of Muslim radicals who have rejected what they see as the injustices of the "peace through coercion" paradigm while preserving many of its traditional thought forms[3] within a utopian and exclusivist variation on the "peace through equity" framework. It is emphatically in the interest of both Western and Middle Eastern leaders to act in ways that alleviate the despair that feeds such desperate and totalistic thinking, and to demonstrate that choosing the pathways of equity, conciliation, and nonviolence can generate more fruitful results.

The Need for New Thinking

Much of the vitality of Islamic politics in the contemporary Middle East reflects both anxiety about social change and a deeply felt need for a cultural future that provides Muslims with dignity and purpose. In the view of many Islamic activists, the erosion of traditional values is proceeding at an alarming pace, with no new life-giving values taking their place. This sense of anomie is compounded by conflicts such as those in Israel-Palestine and Iraq and by the perception that Muslims everywhere are hemmed in by numerous life-denying forces related to dependent globalization, foreign hegemony, and the failure of indigenous elites to provide viable strategies for democracy and development. To assert themselves politically and prevent a disintegration of social and cultural life, Middle Eastern Muslims have increasingly chosen a religious vocabulary to express their existential and practical concerns.

As discussed previously, many Western observers have reacted to this revitalization of Islam with alarm, focusing narrowly on historical traditions of "Islamic power politics" and on the most militant strains of Islamic revivalism. Our analysis has sought to demonstrate that such an approach misrepresents the many roles played by Middle Eastern Islam, equating public expressions of Islamic solidarity to the extreme religious ideology propagated by such figures as Osama bin Laden. Counterexamples illuminated by Islamic peace paradigms and by a more careful study of grassroots Islamic politics demonstrate the continuing relevance of Islam in the search for peaceful avenues of social development and in efforts to cushion the wrenching dislocations of modernization.[4]

Recognizing Islam as a deeply embedded and yet dynamic cultural framework and not merely as a vehicle of staunch traditionalism or anti-Western extremism holds the potential to significantly increase the effectiveness of Western security policies. An overwhelming majority of politically engaged Muslims are seeking to restore dignity to an old civilization, not to create a new empire. If supported in their efforts to be modern within the framework of their own culture, Muslims stand a much better chance of recovering their former stature. Their widespread exclusion from active participation in political life contributes greatly to tensions in Middle Eastern societies that can be overcome only through policies designed to support inclusion in a real and substantive manner.

A Choice for Americans

While entertaining options about how to engage Muslims, Americans in particular must choose how they wish to conceive of their own national identity and project it in the world. The United States has the power to select between two paths—one likely to polarize the nations of the world further, and one capable of transforming the existing transnational disorder.

The first path is that of "America the Strong." Because its actions are motivated by fear, America the Strong will continue to pursue an increasingly stark unilateral foreign policy predicated on ensuring its own security in ways that other nations regard as threatening and contrary to their interests. To reinstall order in a manner believed to be in line with its own narrowly conceived interests, the United States will continue to support its perceived friends and undermine its perceived enemies based on calculations of short-term strategic advantage, with little regard for proclaimed core values or long-term consequences. By choosing short-term security, America the Strong will use power in ways that ensure lasting strife and resentment.

The path of "America the Brave" relies on the courage to make short-term, unilateral concessions as well as bilateral compromises to ensure long-term global prosperity. This path is one of leadership instead of control. In choosing this path, the US response to mounting disorder will be a commitment to advancing a more humane global community. The priority in maintaining security will be to address the root causes of disorder instead of concentrating on strategic advantage. Rather than building ever-higher barriers around itself, America the Brave will explore options for constructing bridges to Arabs and Muslims. By recognizing that it needs the world and vice versa—and indeed that the whole world needs the whole world—America the Brave will seek to engage Arabs and Muslims as partners and in doing so set the stage for a new era of cooperative relationship.

Current US policy in the Middle East has become a significant source of Islamic-Western acrimony. Muslim opinions concerning the motivations behind US policy vary, yet the most widespread impressions are that the US government is, at best, strangely indifferent about issues that concern Muslims and, at worst, actively hostile to Islam. US professions of support for democracy lack credibility among Middle Eastern Muslim audiences, who are convinced that US policies are motivated by a desire to control the region's natural resources by backing repressive allies and undermining strategic adversaries.

The future of democracy in the region depends in no small part upon what Americans do at this critical moment in history. However, substituting pro-democracy interventions for traditional support of repressive regimes only promises further disarray; the case of Iraq indicates quite clearly that military interventions evoke the specter of the colonial past, mobilize popular resentment, and create a high-pressure political environment in which human rights abuses appear "normal." While repressive regimes can be imposed by subversion, democracy cannot be successfully implanted from the outside, and certainly not by subversive means: it is an indigenous and delicate flower that only flourishes when rooted in the dreams and hopes of the great majority of a nation.

The United States still has a chance to help catalyze a new process. To do this, Americans will need to adopt policies that seek to pinpoint and address major irritants in US–Middle Eastern relations, while attempting to lead by example. Because the United States is open for all to see, with its many problems, virtues, and strengths visible at will, the US example is extremely powerful. When US rhetoric on democracy and human rights appears to be contradicted by "with us or against us" foreign policy practices and by an instrumental attitude toward international law, confidence in the United States and in the prospect of democratic change declines. A "new tune" in US foreign policy and actions that correspond with this message might nonetheless have a significantly positive impact. The most powerful weapon in American hands for the promotion and spread of democracy in the region is not subversion, or military aid, or even development aid or diplomacy. The effectiveness of the United States in supporting change abroad depends on an empathetic capacity to comprehend the aspirations of others as they themselves define them, together with commitment to fostering an emergent transnational consciousness that trusts in the promise of substantive, participatory democracy and organic processes of change. The transnational consciousness is not molded by the Western media, nor created by elites and intellectuals. It is the cry for human dignity that finds its expression throughout the world in activism for human rights and inclusive, egalitarian social practices.

As noted in previous chapters, supporting change in the Muslim Middle East requires conversance with a religious vocabulary of cultural expression. The "Islamic phenomenon" does indeed pose a challenge to modernization theory's presumptions about secularization, but it is less incongruent with the Western historical experience than conventional wisdom allows. From the enterprising Protestant ethos examined by Max Weber to the Indian independence movement led by Gandhi, religion has often been at the forefront of social, economic, and political transformation. In a Middle Eastern context, appreciating the positive potential of changes under way in the domain of religious civic activism—and not merely extremist threats—can create opportunities for new types of engagement. Such engagement can be based on a broader appreciation of how shifts in religious understanding have affected the course of modern Western history, and exerted a major impact on the emergence of new cultural syntheses. Evidence of religious influence on social and political development can be found in European and North American labor movements, anti-slavery movements, and peace movements. Religion has been used to bring down boundaries or spur resistance to oppression in the US civil rights movement, in Eastern Europe under communism, in South Africa under apartheid, and in Latin American countries struggling with economic oligarchy and political dictatorship. Civic culture in the United States is subtly underpinned by religious institutions and volunteer energies, and voting is frequently carried out in houses of worship.

Acknowledging positive roles for religion does not mean turning a blind eye to the fact that religions have also been used to justify slavery, imperialism, and opposition to workers' rights or women's suffrage. What is necessary, however, is a balanced view that does not regard progress as the child of secularity alone, and that acknowledges the role of new religious thinking in participatory governance, public accountability, human rights, and social justice. Just as surely as figures such as Osama bin Laden can misappropriate religion in the pursuit of revenge, fresh applications of Islamic values can no doubt play an important role in mobilizing human energy to overcome barriers to change in the Middle East. No country can control the outcome of internal Islamic debates, yet US policy has a profound impact on the extent to which Islamic activism will be motivated by desperation or by hope.

A Choice for Muslims

When invoking Islam, Middle Eastern Muslims are free to choose between competing discourses—most notably between a defensive, collectivist outlook that promises deliverance from external challenges through adherence to a narrow set of precepts underscoring Muslim uniqueness (particularly as understood by the "peace through coercion" paradigm), and a more broadly inclusive framework seeking to make traditional Islamic prescriptions for social justice, human dignity, and cultural pluralism relevant to the contemporary world. Where the former uses of Islam are based on belief in an idealized, unchanging, and monolithic Islam of times past, the latter uses capitalize on the potential of the "peace through equity" paradigm and are derived from belief that the practice of Islam must be as dynamic as the historical and cultural contexts within which Muslims have lived.

Progressive and reformist Muslims view Islam in existential rather than formalistic terms: the goal of Islamic practice is not merely to recapitulate the religious syntheses of earlier generations, but rather to identify the most essential Islamic values and thoroughly integrate them with practical activity. Though some progressive Muslims have been accused of excessive rationalism and eagerness to equate Islamic and Western values, few Muslim reformists believe that their approach to Islam negates the basic principle of scrupulous compliance with divine will. Rather, they propose that their practice is itself a conscientious response to the realization that divine will can only be discerned through human acts of interpretation: no believer can rest assured that his or her personal or received understanding of "the absolute" is in fact absolute and final.

When Muslims regard Islam as a dynamic process and not only as a set of revered forms, creative possibilities emerge. Making divine will real in human life becomes a continual, open-ended effort to interpret and apply essential precepts. It becomes possible to recognize Islamic norms as compatible with many if not most core values (if not always "practiced" values) of major non-Muslim cultures, and to identify potential value complementarities when priorities appear to differ. Muslims become capable of articulating a more richly substantive, Islamic conception of peace that non-Muslims find worthy of appreciation.

This framework for conceptualizing peace is comprehensive and holistic, and conducive to nonviolent social activism. As our analyses of Islamic paradigms for equity, conciliation, nonviolence, and universalism suggest, Islam may be understood to support a definition of peace that challenges both the Muslim status quo and the orthodoxy of Western international relations theory. This definition of peace can include not only the absence of war but also the presence of social justice, ecological balance, cultural pluralism, and integrated human spirituality.

While very few interpreters of Islam rule out the use of force to prevent gross abuses of human rights or to preserve social order in the face of violent subversion, Islamic traditions offer considerable scope for practices that proactively seek to establish foundations for a peaceful society and world order. Islam's strong conception of human solidarity speaks quite strongly to contemporary themes in communitarian social theory, and offers a collaborative, egalitarian understanding of human freedom well-suited to the demands of personal responsibility in a rapidly shrinking world. Though classical Islamic political theory has sometimes elevated the prerogatives of leaders above the rights of their subjects, foundational Islamic texts place great emphasis on themes of human dignity and social justice, providing firm bases for theistically informed human rights advocacy.

With respect to the environment, the Islamic precept of stewardship *(khilafa)* in human relations to the created order provides fertile ground for ecological politics.[5] Islam's foremost mystical thinkers have articulated profoundly ecumenical and multicultural visions of Islamic spirituality, and Quranic passages on gender relations can sound decidedly progressive when compared to the patriarchal practices of past Muslim (as well as non-Muslim) communities. Traditional practices of reconciliation among estranged tribal and family groups provide a rich basis for innovative contemporary applications that are being utilized today by an emergent cohort of conflict resolution trainers.

One important prerequisite for unleashing the potential of Muslims as peacemakers is the development of new thinking about the empowerment of Muslims as active citizens in their community and in national as well as transnational contexts. There is a great need in the Muslim world to integrate deliberately the person, the citizen, and the Muslim. This involves a search for truth within Islamic traditions and contexts that begins at the level of the individual. Christianity has emerged from its own encounters with modern thought by closely linking personal behavior with citizenship and social values, while Muslims today may be on the threshold of discovering the responsibilities and deeper meaning of Muslim citizenship. Citizenship for Muslims offers similar opportunities, and can be recognized not in the carrying out of decisions handed down by political leaders, but rather in proactive and value-based engagement with one's own society.

There are many questions that Muslims may find it helpful to ask. What kind of citizens can Islamic values create? What Islamic values and social mechanisms can be applied for ameliorating the conditions of modern, urban living, or for enacting participatory social decisionmaking in the absence of authoritative guidance? How can Muslims improve upon the systems of education and develop new kinds of interactive relationships between teacher and student? How can new communications technologies be used to facilitate greater information dissemination among Middle Eastern Muslims, to present them with political alternatives and greater opportunities for participation in public life? The flowering of the individual as citizen within a more open and cosmopolitan conception of Islamic community could inspire new avenues for tapping the energies of future generations while providing richer, more vibrant expressions of Islam's enduring values.

To embrace their capacity for active citizenship and participation in proactive peacebuilding initiatives, Muslims will need courageous new forms of thought and practice, rooted in a sense of secure identity that is not defined by the temptation to either uncritically reflect or categorically reject the West. Arab and Muslim elites who adopt Western culture wholesale, without a critical or discerning eye, have only perpetuated the fear of an inappropriate and monolithic cultural onslaught among religious Muslims. Some religious Muslims, in turn, have begun to redefine Islam by granting priority to those traditions that appear most contrary to Western norms, regardless of other considerations. Many cultural divisions in the Muslim world relate to tension between "overadaptation" to Western trends and fashions (especially among members of the wealthy elite) and the culturally and politically reactive stances of marginalized groups. The space between these two points on the cultural continuum, however, may yet provide new ways of thinking about citizenship, women's empowerment, religious toleration, peacemaking, governance, individual rights and responsibilities, the resolution of conflicts within society, and nonviolent social change.

Reconciling Islam and Democracy

To create greater scope for resolving social conflicts and achieving change by nonviolent means, a reconciliation between Islam and democracy will likely prove necessary. There is a great and pressing need for a revitalization of participation in public life and decisionmaking in Islamic countries. Without appropriate cultural forms for democratic participation, the innovative thinking of reformists will be muffled or suppressed, and the dynamic energy of Islamic revival will be forced into narrower channels marked by extremism and violence. Fortunately, the subject of Islam and democracy is a vibrant area of contemporary Muslim thought.

The practice of democracy is always less tidy and more dynamic than formal definitions can suggest or prescribe. There are democratic precepts in Islam just as there are in other religions. There are also Islamic traditions that, like traditions in other religions, result in transgressions against democratic ideals. The claim of incompatibility between Islam and democracy equates Western institutional forms of democracy—particularly the notion of liberal democracy—with the substance of democracy. The *substance* of democracy is a human society that has a sense of common goals, a sense of community, wide participation in the making of decisions, and protective safeguards for dissenters. The *form* of democracy may be cast in the mold of the unique culture of a people.

Nothing in Islam precludes common goals, community participation, and protective safeguards. It is true that Western liberal forms of democracy with their provisions for political parties, interest groups, and an electoral system are alien to Islamic tradition. But democracy is not built upon specific, universally prescribed institutions; it is built upon participation. The absence of democracy in Islamic countries has much less to do with a lack of religious and cultural foundations than with a lack of awareness, opportunity, and preparation.

It is no exaggeration to state that, in most contemporary Muslim communities, a thick web of political problems and unresolved conflicts creates a deep sense of powerlessness. The popularity of conspiracy theories that deny the capability of Muslims to determine their own future attests to disempowerment born of domestic authoritarianism, unaccountable security agencies, and unpopular Western foreign policies. In addition, unemployment and underemployment are experienced as grave problems by young men in much of the Muslim world, and can have a profoundly damaging impact by reinforcing despair and hopelessness.

Presently, the door is open for new thinking about Middle Eastern democracy, among both Western and regional analysts. There is a need to factor into this new thinking on democracy a consideration of the roles of the community, the individual, the state, and religion in order to fashion a model for cooperative, participatory politics that is responsive to cultural needs. In particular, a model of Islamic civil society can be constructed—a model that could include diverse organizations that have not been founded by states and express themselves in an idiom that reflects regional culture: neighborhood associations, self-help groups, charitable and medical services, women's organizations, professional organizations, and labor unions. It would be a mistake to exclude modalities of free, independent association from a conception of civil society simply because of their possible religious overtones, especially considering the disjunction between the theory and the practice of civil society in the West, where apathy, unequal access to financial resources, and the politics of interest groups detract from the vitality of civic life and the ideals of the democratic process.

Arguing that Muslim countries are "not ready for democracy" amounts to denying the dynamism of cultural and religious traditions and the aspirations of a great many Muslims,[6] and overlooking the possibility of democratic forms evolving organically out of a context of meaning familiar to people at the grassroots. Islamic values place a strong emphasis on the nobility of the person. With respect to gender rights, Islamic law granted legal personality to women before Western women were able to achieve this status.[7] Islam also accentuates egalitarianism. Though political democracy, Western or Islamic, is rarely practiced in today's Arab world, it does not therefore follow that Islam and democracy are incompatible. In this regard there are democratic precepts in Islam, as there are in other religions, to include both the preservation and the development of the community, through concern for social justice, accountable leadership, and consultative mechanisms. Though contemporary Islamic movements are sometimes ambivalent in their commitment to securing a genuinely democratic political order, research on Middle Eastern Islamic social institutions has demonstrated that their internal practices can be at least as democratic as those used by their secular counterparts.[8]

How might Muslims encourage the development of citizens animated by Islamic values and contexts? A new vision of democracy for the Middle East and other predominantly Muslim regions could include three components: dynamic stability, indivisible rights, and inclusive justice. Such a vision would be particularly helpful in efforts to help diverse social and political actors avoid the "drift" that accompanies pursuit of short-term self-interest without regard for long-term consequences. A vision is also essential for fostering the emergence of imagination, energy, commitment, and mutual responsibility.

The three elements of this vision are closely interrelated. Dynamic stability signifies the need for a social system that is orderly but not reactionary or static. Indivisible rights denotes a widening and deepening concept of equal justice under the law that embraces not only civil and political rights but also economic well-being, efforts to advance the status of women, and the right to participate in the cultural life of one's community. Inclusive justice links the local and national to the global, underscoring the need for an expanded international law that facilitates global security for all, including ecological security. Democracy in the Middle East, like democracy in other regions, needs to be rooted in a genuinely inclusive commitment to human dignity.

Democracy cannot be installed by a military coup or by a revolution from the top, because democratic behavior is a learned behavior. Both rulers and ruled have to learn it. It is particularly self-defeating to exclude Islamists from the political decisionmaking process if they are willing to participate in democratic politics. Islamic revival is a response to the failures of national governments in Islamic countries, and the central issues raised by Islamists are legitimate. Islamists attest to the realities of cultural, economic, and political marginalization, of corruption, overcentralization, and repression.

Concerns that Islamist movements may not fully respect the rules of democratic competition are also legitimate. However, these concerns can be directed with at least as much validity to authoritarian regimes and military establishments throughout the Middle East. The much feared "one man, one vote, one time" outcome of unfettered electoral competition is unsettling, but as of mid-2008 this remains a hypothetical scenario. In contrast, cases of thwarted Islamist electoral victories in Algeria, Turkey, and Palestine have been quite concrete. Allowing Islamic parties a chance to be held accountable by those who elect them would appear far more desirable for democratic evolution in the Middle East than policies that unite regional military establishments with Western powers in opposition to broad-based aspirations for accountable government and political change.

Reframing Development

"Developed"—modern and democratic—can also mean "Muslim," yet this appears improbable if "modern and democratic" means exact imitation of models prevailing in the West. Especially today, when many people in the West are trying to rethink the meaning of development to include environmental, cultural, and social factors,[9] Muslims have an opportunity to reexamine and reconstruct an Islamic idea of modernization and development as well.

At its core, the developmental process is the way in which society and its members seek to reach their self-defined potential within the context of their environment. Development is a process with a goal, even if this goal is perceived as an ever-receding one. There is always an implied utopia by which this process is measured, ideally a "preferred future" that is extracted from the experience of people and generalized into a vision of the desired society. As experience is enlarged and new challenges arise, it is natural that the utopian ideal changes. Failure to adapt ideals in the face of feedback from society and in response to cultural or environmental change can transform the dream of development into a nightmare.

Modernization is understood by Western sociologists as the adoption of modern technologies for the uses of society. It attempts to make society more rational, efficient, and predictable, especially through the use of comprehensive planning, rational administration, and scientific evolution. Modernization also carries the connotation of a more productive society, at least in economic terms. Like development, modernization is always at least a partially conscious effort on the part of individuals who have a vision of what an ideal modern society would look like. Modernization theory, however, often underestimates the extent to which culturally transplanted models and prescriptions can disrupt traditional societies.

The tragedy of development in the Middle East and other regions of the Islamic world is that societal values have been largely excluded from the formulation of development ideals. Modernization is not a substitute for development, but in much of the Islamic world, development has too often been identified with modernization imposed from above without construction of a popular base of support. Social justice, political participation, ecology, and traditional values have been sacrificed for modernization. While it would be inappropriate to romanticize traditional Middle Eastern social orders, the modernization process has done little to spur broad-based changes that can be recognized as authentic and humanizing. The consumerist lifestyle promised by the modernization process has become accessible only to the upper strata of society, leaving those left behind alternately disgruntled at their exclusion and scandalized at elite tastes for "imported" cultural products and practices.

There is much thinking to be done about development and Islam, precisely because Muslims are forced by today's conditions to make connections between two worlds. The Islamic economic doctrine of *sharia* has been compromised by traditionalist-capitalist and secularist-socialist states alike; socialists and secularists have denied that religious law has strategic utility in a context of modern material life, while capitalists and traditionalists have missed opportunities to apply *sharia* principles in creative ways that facilitate economic empowerment. Where elite planners and strategic thinkers perceive little relevance in Islamic precepts, opposition movements blame developmental failures on abandonment of these same values.

Reconciliation between Islam and development may yet become possible if the concept of development can be distinguished from Western unilinear, rationalistic, and ultimately ethnocentric conceptions of progress that leave little room for cultural values to define conditions for quality of human life. The European Enlightenment postulated progress as the establishment of dominion over nature through reason and science. The language of progress was eventually abandoned when the concept became too obviously centered on the notion of Western superiority, but the concept of development was substituted in its place. Contemporary conditions in the Middle East would appear to call for something more—not a superficial compromise or a puritanical, "nativist" reaction, but a response based on Islamic values that reflects the historical development of Islamic cultures and responds to the challenges of contemporary life.

Opportunities for Mutual Learning

Historically, both the West and Islam have relied too much on the seemingly self-evident testimonies of their beliefs and accomplishments, without sufficient recourse to genuine interpersonal or intercultural dialogue and bridge building. A new, mutually rewarding relationship has the potential to emerge between Islam and the West, where accumulated wisdom and insights provide the basis for a valued coexistence. Such a relationship would be premised not on ideas of cultural autarky or triumphalism, but on mutual respect and a desire for reconciliation.

Much progress can be made in the pursuit of reconciliation when Muslims and Westerners approach one another with humility, in a spirit of dialogue. Past moments of intercultural and interreligious openness, such as those discussed in Chapter 8, provide a glimmer of what might become possible if common ground were to be sought more actively by policymakers, elites, and concerned citizens. There is no reason to accept the proposition that the West and Islam are predestined to remain rivals; a more positive mode of cultural encounter could involve the West offering Middle Eastern Muslims the best that it has in exchange for the best that Muslims can offer to the West.

There is much in the West's hard-won achievements in science and technology as well as social and political development that not only is compatible with Muslim values, but that can also broadly support and strengthen Muslim communities. The Western regard for individualism and political freedom, combined with a commitment to political accountability and democratic pluralism, characterize some of the best of what the West offers the world. Genuine curiosity about the Western experience and serious reflection on the sources of Western strength may be necessary for Muslims to move from their painful introspection and isolation into a new period of confident and inclusive building of a just and peaceful social order in Islamic states. Muslims have much to gain from understanding the West, particularly its accomplishments in the realm of political pluralism.

Just as the West has never developed a full, unbiased appreciation of Islam, Muslims have often failed to grasp the West's greatest strengths. There is a need for inquisitive Muslim scholars (some might humorously call them Muslim "Lawrence of Arabias") who seek to discover and deeply understand not only the Western Enlightenment experience, but also the Western Christian worldview. Although Muslims will likely feel compelled to differ on many theological and practical points, the fact that Christianity emerged at a time of profound oppression and unjust occupation and yet went on to flourish for centuries deserves notice, at the very least as a source of comparative insights that can be used to promote mutual understanding. Likewise, research on diverse Christian formulas for balancing the religious with the political—including, for example, tensions between liberation theologians and other voices, and historical variations in positions staked out within encyclicals of the Catholic Church—could enliven interreligious and intercultural dialogue. Muslim scholars might find comparisons of internal religious debates on peace, justice, and human rights particularly intriguing as they continue refining their own positions on current-day concerns, controversies, and misunderstandings.

While Muslims might benefit from the Western experience in their efforts to reconcile Islam and democracy, so too could the West benefit from coming to know and respect Islam. Because Islamic traditions provide a set of powerful precepts and practices with universal implications, Islam can contribute to an integrated world order that affirms the unique value of diverse cultural traditions. In particular, Islam prescribes a strong sense of community and solidarity of people, postulates a collaborative concept of freedom, and offers a timely rejoinder to the dominant Western idea that human progress is to be measured in primarily materialistic terms. Though Muslim practice has often fallen short of Muslim principles, and though the advent of the nation-state has created new tensions between national, religious, and ethnic identities, Islam is remarkable for its explicit precepts that favor cultural and religious pluralism.[10]

In the Western pluralistic tradition, diversity is seen in terms of the coexistence of political systems and ideas, but ideals of cultural diversity have not yet been fully assimilated. Although the Islamic practice of cultural pluralism is also imperfect, it has roots in an Islamic tradition of ethnic diversity that historically fostered a tendency toward cultural breadth and flexibility. This heritage allowed autonomous non-Muslim cultures to flourish. Despite a modern rise in deviations from what should be a proud Muslim heritage of cultural pluralism, Western advocates of multiculturalism may find that the Islamic experience enriches their understanding of pathways to human coexistence.[11]

Societies have so often been repressive that a strong Western tradition has emerged that sees the elimination of repression and want as the chief goal of society. Though Muslim societies can benefit from careful study of Western individualism, they will no doubt wish to avoid the West's dichotomy between the individual and the community, in which the individual is often seen as serving only the individual. It is true that cultural systems, like political, economic, and social ones, have usually contained much to impede human development: forces such as prejudice, chauvinism, competitiveness, racism, and sexism. This does not change the fact that the cultural community is indispensable for human growth and development. Thus the cultural community needs to be served by political, economic, and social systems, rather than the reverse.

No doubt, every community needs cultural criticism and renewal to remove those things that dehumanize society or inhibit human development. Muslim collectivism can benefit from the challenge of Western individualism as surely as Westerners can benefit by seeking to appreciate aspects of Muslim communal experience. But seeking freedom through individualism alone leads to a depletion of social capital and a deterioration in the quality of human life. If Western individualism is to bring lasting happiness to the individual, an adapted model of free community may well have the potential to bring about a deeper sense of satisfaction; if Muslim ideals of community are to reach their fulfillment, revisiting traditions that underscore the dignity of the individual could provide a path forward.

Despite rising tensions in the world since September 11, 2001, real opportunities for leadership are present. Today's challenge for the West is to live up to its liberal tradition, which requires continual openness to new revelations of truth. Today's challenge for Muslims is to arrive at an expanded understanding of the original ideas of Islam. As Muslims seek to harmonize the Islamic spirit of communalism with the changing conditions of their own societies, they can contribute to the betterment of the larger world. While small-scale cultural and religious enclaves can enrich the fabric of multicultural societies, large-scale retreat from intercultural encounter by any group, be it Muslim, Christian, Jewish, Buddhist, or Hindu, is not only a denial of the rich diversity of the modern cultural experience, but also a rejection of responsibility for future generations.

Notes

1. Enayat, *Modern Islamic Political Thought,* 1982, p. 15.
2. Ibid., p. 1.
3. For example, division of the world into *dar al-Islam* and *dar al-harb;* the institution of the caliphate; dependence on military compulsion.
4. In addition to the well-known role of many Islamic organizations and movements in providing for social needs, the contributions of Muslim thinkers such as Hassan Fathy to the appropriate technology movement are also worthy of note. See Steele, *An Architecture for People,* 1997.
5. Foltz, Denny, and Baharuddin, *Islam and Ecology,* 2003.
6. Fattah, *Democratic Values in the Muslim World,* 2006.
7. Although historical comparisons offer at best limited guidance for dealing with current disputes over gender norms, many Muslim commentators have found it meaningful to note that the rights accorded to women by early Islamic law compared quite favorably with those granted not just by pre-Islamic traditions of the Near East, but also by the more or less contemporaneous legal systems and customs of Rome, South Asia, and Africa. See, for example, Goolam, "Gender Equality in Islamic Family Law," 2006, pp. 130–132; Hanafi, "Alternative Conceptions of Civil Society," 2002, pp. 70–72. Many present-day Muslim feminists, such as Azizah al-Hibri, argue that Islam itself offers powerful correctives for the patriarchal habits of traditional Muslim societies. See al-Hibri, "Islam, Law, and Custom," 1997.
8. Clark, "Canadian Interests and Democracy Promotion in the Middle East," 2007, p. 102.
9. A growing number of Western scholars have begun to question the "growth ethic" underlying the liberal democratic paradigm. In particular, they have suggested that organizing communities and ecosystems for maximum production is a highly normative (and not merely scientific) endeavor. Other values besides net growth need to be integrated into the model of development, particularly if the integrity of human and ecological communities is to be preserved. See Daly and Cobb, *For the Common Good,* 1994; Wachtel, *The Poverty of Affluence,* 1989.
10. Quran 2:256, 5:48, 10:47, 49:13, 109:6.
11. Mazrui, "Islamic and Western Values," 1997; Said and Sharify-Funk, *Cultural Diversity and Islam,* 2003.

10

An Agenda for Islamic-Western Cooperation

Quite often, thoughtful observers of US and Western relations with the Muslim Middle East allow themselves to become demoralized by the powerful inertia behind current events, and limit themselves to retrospective critiques. While critiques serve a valuable and salutary function, there is also a need for constructive recommendations that answer the inevitable question: "If not this, then what do you propose?" In the absence of a plausible expectation that different policy choices might—through persistence and patience—lead to improved outcomes, even the most forceful critique is likely to be met with pessimism and fatalistic resignation. Without a vision of possibility backed by practical steps and a coherent logic of implementation, strategic choices narrow to defense of the status quo, crisis management, and reactive self-assertion.

In the preceding chapters, we have attempted to demonstrate that, by moving beyond a truncated "terrorism versus moderation" frame of analysis for the Muslim Middle East, it becomes possible to identify significant potential for peaceful change rooted in indigenous cultural and religious traditions. Because the current atmosphere of tension between the West and the Muslim Middle East has developed through complex interactions, it is not sufficient simply to implore Middle Eastern Muslims to embrace preferred paradigms and reject those viewed as problematic. Both sides need to accept responsibility if there is to be a chance of setting a virtuous cycle in motion. It is in this spirit that we offer the following recommendations, which are intended to prompt fresh thinking about how Western policies and initiatives might overcome a troubled historical legacy and begin to foster international and regional dynamics that favor peaceful conflict resolution. These policies and initiatives would be designed with the intention of amending strategies that have heightened conflict and polarization, while creating conditions conducive to incremental "change from within" in Middle Eastern states and societies.

Not all of our recommendations are new, and readers familiar with Middle East policy debates will recognize some familiar themes. In recent years, however, Western policies toward the Middle East have lacked a vision that is responsive to the aspirations and concerns of Muslim communities and informed by awareness of peacebuilding potential within Islamic culture. Constructive measures intended to open lines of communication have been undermined by other policy choices that have sent a less peaceable message.

Without a comprehensive vision of how Western-Islamic coexistence might be achieved, the power of existing strategic assumptions and cultural mythologies is likely to overwhelm piecemeal cooperative efforts. By working with a regionally grounded awareness of conflict dynamics and sensitivity to the need for culturally rooted solutions to Middle Eastern problems, however, peaceful coexistence may yet be achieved through a sustained process involving geopolitical restraint, commitment to consensus building, and intercultural rapprochement.

Express Desire for a New Relationship in Public Discourse

Far too often, trust between Westerners and Middle Eastern Muslims has been corroded by needlessly provocative or misinformed pronouncements by opinion leaders on both sides. In the current tense atmosphere, words articulated by leaders matter a great deal and have a profound impact on domestic as well as foreign publics. At home, they impact the capacity of citizens to imagine new relationships predicated on commonality instead of fear and resentment. Overseas, these words are interpreted and reinterpreted by media analysts and political figures seeking signals of underlying national intentions and purposes.

To commence movement from isolation and antagonism toward new relationships, politicians, academics, journalists, religious personalities, and other public figures need to become more aware of alternatives to the narrow "story of confrontation" that has dominated narratives about Islamic-Western relations in recent years. Public discourse can have a constructive impact only if it transcends one-sided accounts of negative encounters such as the Crusades, Muslim conquests, Western colonialism, and the contemporary "war on terror," and begins to reframe relations by taking into account patterns of cultural, economic, and technological exchange. Stories of compatibility and complementarity (see Chapter 2) are well suited for this challenge. They are sensitive to the tragic consequences of destructive conflict, and identify sources of hope for reconciliation. Some leaders and activists may find it helpful to speak of a shared Judeo-Christian-Islamic or Abrahamic tradition that, though not monolithic, connects believers through common and complementary values.

If there is to be a prospect of breaking some of the negative cycles associated with Western-Islamic conflict, analysts and columnists will have to craft more nuanced constructs than the problematic "clash of civilizations" thesis, which fails to do justice to the many ways that Islamic or Western values and identities can be understood and embraced without exacerbating conflict. Because contemporary encounters among cultures and religions take place within a context of globalization, there is merit to Václav Havel's proposition that all of humanity now inhabits a single, "thin" global civilization defined by technology and pop culture, with diverse subcultures seeking to express or revive themselves within this shrinking global environment.[1] Such conceptualizations can assist academic researchers and policy planners in their efforts to take religious and cultural identities into account, without presuming that they can contribute only to war. Because civilizations are unavoidably pluralistic and poorly bounded units of analysis that do not act as coherent political actors, they are always at least partially "imagined communities," not monolithic or homogeneous entities.[2] To do justice to the open-ended nature of cultural life, analysts who seek to "bring culture back in" need to differentiate between overgeneralizations activated by fear and insecurity, and the far more complex realities behind these generalizations.

Just as symbolism can be used to divide, so too can it be used to affirm possibilities for coexistence. From the standpoint of confrontation narratives, the "other" is reduced to a symbol of values rejected by the "self." As a consequence, the presence of Muslims in the West and of Western influences in the Islamic world is regarded as a threat to cultural and religious purity. However, drawing attention to ways in which each cultural area has been enriched by the other can provide a powerful counterpoint to fear-predicated narratives. Likewise, giving greater media prominence to cultural exchanges and coexistence projects could encourage alternative readings of intercultural relations, within which difference becomes a source of complementarity and not solely a threat to security and other cherished values. While platitudes underscoring the political (as opposed to the cultural or religious) goals of counterterrorism efforts may have limited effectiveness at a time of war, it would be foolhardy for leaders in North America and Europe to cease emphasizing that extremists are never more than a small minority in every religion. Under no circumstances should counterterrorism efforts be likened to a cultural war or religious crusade.

New habits of thought and expression are vital not only for generating commitment to peacemaking at home, but also for conveying peaceful intentions to others. If the West is interested in communicating with the Islamic world that it is not fighting a religious war but rather seeks to counteract networks of radical fundamentalist violence, it must first demonstrate an interest in the concerns, fears, and grievances that have inspired these networks. The West need not recoil from Islamic symbols, as they are in no way reducible to anti-Western, antisecular, "irrational" extremism. Now that several years have passed since the events of September 11, 2001, the West should be secure enough to uncover the extent to which more mundane conflicts have been clothed in religious rhetoric, in order to defuse the mobilization potential of manipulated imagery and address root causes.

One of the most vitally important responsibilities of public figures, both in the West and in the Middle East, is to speak in a way that helps listeners discover coherence and possibility amid the complexity and insecurity of contemporary conflict. "With us or against us" simplifications are profoundly unhelpful, as they cast the concerns and reservations of other peoples in the worst possible light and seek to harness feelings of righteous indignation for the pursuit of predetermined conflict objectives. In contrast, mature public discourse refuses to allow powerful political emotions to sabotage dialogue about issues that fuel conflict, and rejects nationalistic sensationalism. In the present context, such discourse probes underlying sources of unrest, from Middle Eastern misgivings about the long-term presence of US troops in the region, to Western oil dependency, Palestinian suffering, and frustrated demands for social change. Seeking coherence in such a manner need not presuppose "moral equivalency" or trivialize "our side's" rightful claims. All that it requires is a genuine effort to help one's audience make sense of opposing views and consider the experiences behind them. Where discourse that escalates conflict magnifies that which appears strange, incomprehensible, and threatening in an adversary's conduct, constructive political discourse explores differences in light of shared humanity, interdependent futures, and the pursuit of solutions that respect the basic needs and interests of all concerned parties—even those who are tempted to support extremism.

By consistently adopting constructive forms of public discourse and eschewing pessimistic oversimplifications and easily misunderstood slogans (for example, a "long war against Islamofascism"), leaders in the West as well as in the Islamic world can set the stage for effective responses to current insecurities. By refusing to exploit popular stereotypes, they can encourage their audiences to suspend polarizing habits of thought and perception, empathize with the historical and cultural experiences of other peoples, and envision more equitable and life-enhancing forms of intercultural cooperation.

Strategize for Conflict Transformation, Not Escalation

As US intelligence agencies have acknowledged, excessive militarization of the "war on terror" (and particularly the choice to invade Iraq) has increased the appeal of radicalism in many parts of the Muslim world.[3] Overconfidence in the utility of military force in resolving contemporary problems of nonstate political violence has brought increasing turbulence not only to the Middle East, but also to increasingly diverse Western societies. War appears highly ineffective for destroying the "taproot" of terrorism, particularly insofar as it reinforces the "us versus them" dynamic of identity conflict and gives an undeserved advantage to rhetoric stressing the "ancient origins" of present strife.

Because the resort to military force feeds perceptions of injustice and legitimizes popular resistance, war is an ultimately self-defeating mechanism for defeating Middle Eastern radicalism. It is simply not possible to impose upon the Islamic world a set of political, cultural, and economic solutions that are viewed as inauthentic and humiliating. Attempts to do so have negative consequences not only for nonviolent democratization projects in the Middle East, but also for interreligious and intercultural relations in North America and Europe. The transnational character of Islamic identity ensures that at least some members of diaspora communities will view distant conflicts through Middle Eastern lenses, an outcome nurtured in no small part by the climate of fear and suspicion that war engenders.

The fact that the "war on terror" framework for responding to our present insecurity has increasingly become the subject of debate suggests a need to revisit strategic doctrine, especially but not exclusively in the United States. Writing in the *New York Times Book Review,* Samantha Power has proposed that the "war on terror" framework has obscured more than it has clarified: "As with the war on drugs and the war on crime, the invocation of 'war' initially seemed metaphorical (we do not send the 82nd Airborne into downtown Detroit to combat street crime). But in the terrorism context, war proved less a rhetorical frame than a strategic assertion that armed conflict (that is, ground and air invasions of other countries) was the main tool the United States should employ to neutralize terrorism."[4]

Though the idea of a war on terrorism is effective for driving home the point that great effort should indeed be devoted to preventing mass-casualty international terrorism, using the "war on terror" concept to justify actual wars has undermined other efforts to foster international security. With respect to the narratives explored in Chapter 2, application of the "war on terror" concept has reinforced the story of confrontation in the Islamic world and the West alike, together with the idea that incompatible doctrines and values are the root problem. Such thinking increases the risk of highly undesirable future scenarios, such as a postmodern, intercultural Thirty Years War sustained by the pursuit of a decisive cultural or religious "victory."

For better results, US and Western leaders could derive considerable benefit from policies that attempt not so much to "contain" adversaries as to de-escalate and transform conflicts in the Middle East and other Muslim-majority regions. Recent US proposals to revive or recalibrate a Cold War "containment" framework[5] presuppose a distanced relationship between the United States and the conflicts that motivate extreme Muslim political groups and movements. Though superior to more militarized prescriptions, such proposals fail to offer effective means for engaging Muslim populations and addressing the problems that fuel extremism—among the more important of which is the widespread impression that the United States is actively colluding with narrowly based, allied governments to thwart legitimate Muslim aspirations for self-determination, political autonomy, popular participation, and social justice. Enduring Western-Islamic peace can only be achieved by taking these realities into account, and recognizing their resonance with central preoccupations of Islamic "peace through equity" thinking (see Chapter 5).

Strategizing to transform conflicts in the Middle East and other regions of the Islamic world will ultimately require greater Western involvements in regional conflict resolution efforts than has been the case in recent years, together with willingness to engage with Islamic movements seeking a stake in the political process. Working to integrate religious movements into negotiation frameworks does not preclude the expression of strong criticism with respect to past actions taken by revisionist groups. Critics who argue that this amounts to "compromise with extremists" could be answered by recalling that, however distant the Reformation era may seem, now-mainstream Protestant religious movements began with passionate involvement in political controversy.[6] What were once "radical" movements willing to fight for their convictions have evolved into powerful, "mainline" vehicles for expressing humane religious sentiments. Humility and historical perspective—but not world-weary resignation—are vital qualities as Western leaders seek collaborative responses to internationally salient conflicts.

In an international system that has become far too polarized, there is a profound need for strong voices of sanity—voices that offer constructive ways to fulfill the values and protect the identities invoked by extremists. To amplify these voices, we cannot afford to remain in our traditional comfort zones as scholars, citizens, or practitioners in the field of international affairs. Westerners in particular should not miss opportunities to engage directly the religious and cultural dimensions of conflict and to accept a measure of collective responsibility for past involvement in the affairs of the Middle East and other regions. Over the long term, one of the most crucial tasks for peacebuilding is depriving violent extremism of legitimacy. Diverse parties can support the realization of this objective through religiously and culturally informed approaches to diplomatic engagement and to conflict resolution within and between societies.

Strengthen "Diplomatic Preparedness"

Although government institutions in most Western countries already possess (sometimes underutilized) expertise on Middle Eastern and Islamic issues, efforts to develop more proactive and effective policies for engaging the Muslim Middle East could nonetheless benefit from programs designed to augment cross-cultural diplomatic capacity and deepen specialization. As argued in a recent report from the Washington, D.C.–based Center for Strategic and International Studies, traditional Western thinking about the role of religion in international affairs has often hindered the development of a more dynamic approach to engagement with religious dimensions of conflict and peacemaking: "Both secular caution and threat-focused analyses of religion can prevent positive engagement with religion's potential for resolving conflict. . . . Current US government frameworks for approaching religion are narrow, often approaching religions as problematic or monolithic forces, over-emphasizing a terrorism-focused analysis of Islam and sometimes marginalizing religion as a peripheral humanitarian or cultural issue."[7]

Efforts to cultivate positive change in the Muslim Middle East and in Islamic-Western relations depend on diplomatic and government personnel who have developed knowledge of appropriate languages and Islamic culture. Cultural and religious literacy are essential in the diplomatic corps, and Western governments interested in augmenting their role in the Middle East should continue bolstering professional education programs designed to provide deeper historical context for current events, as well as information about multiple voices and political currents in the Islamic world. For pertinent historical background information, courses for diplomatic personnel could make use of excellent video resources such as the series *When the World Spoke Arabic: The Golden Age of Arab Civilization.*[8]

Because it is crucial for officials to have a well-informed, street-level perspective on the complex mix of political frustration and intercultural alienation that feeds radicalization within the region, additional steps could also be taken to enhance embassy relations with civic and religious leaders in Middle Eastern countries, and to maintain open channels of communication between appropriately knowledgeable diplomatic personnel and decisionmakers in executive and legislative branches of government. Ensuring that Middle Eastern diaspora communities are appropriately heard within government policymaking processes and recruited to public service is another important way to enhance governmental expertise and outreach capability.

Understanding the historical dynamic and state of the Islamic world today is essential if the West is to communicate a message of peace to Arabs and to Muslims more generally. Middle Eastern Muslims today find themselves engaged in a profound struggle at a crucial juncture in their history. They feel cut off from the past, and faced with a present characterized by authoritarianism, poverty, and humiliation, with no viable or desirable prospects for creating their own future. These are realities that the West must address when proposing new terms of engagement and conveying an image of a more positive future. Assurances of Western commitment to a stable, democratic, and prosperous region are invaluable, particularly if supplemented with gestures demonstrating respect for Middle Eastern cultural resources (including the Islamic peace paradigms presented in this book) that will be needed during the transition process.

Diplomatic discourse intended to win trust in the Middle East should give increased weight to multilateralism, cultural pluralism, respect, inclusion, consensus building, and conflict resolution. To communicate respect, new emphasis could be given to the idea of an emergent "global ethic" (forged through interreligious and intercultural dialogue) and to the many (past and present) Islamic contributions to Western culture.[9] By granting greater weight to these themes, Western diplomacy could more effectively convey a vision that people in many parts of the Muslim world can relate to and affirm. Connecting policy principles to a search for shared values might prove particularly useful in relating national interest to regional concerns and priorities.

Adopt a Multilateral, Human Security Framework

The events of recent years demonstrate that the United States and other Western countries have an interest in working through United Nations institutions whenever possible to address security concerns. Abstention from both involvement in and rhetorical support for military actions that have not received United Nations approval would be a wise and prudential policy for combating the sense of international lawlessness that feeds radicalization and supports terrorist recruitment.

A multilateral approach to international security based on respect for international institutions can be greatly enriched by applying an integrative "human security" approach to the problems of terrorism and political violence. This framework has a number of virtues: it recognizes that radicalization festers in situations of repression and protracted conflict; it places a strong emphasis on law enforcement, development, and protection of civilian populations rather than on large-scale (and deeply polarizing) military campaigns; and it affirms the importance of efforts to work toward a uniform standard of human rights, understood to include not only civil and political but also economic, social, and cultural rights. It redirects policy from a narrow focus on empowering state security and military apparatus toward a broader concern with protecting individual human beings from harm and deprivation.

In the search for common ground on issues of international security, Western politicians should take pains to resist polarizing conceptual frameworks (e.g., "war for civilization," "axis of evil," combat against "enemies of democracy," demonization of Islamic movements and parties). The stance taken by the US, Canadian, and some other governments on the tragically counterproductive Israel-Hezbollah war of 2006, like their perceived hypocrisy with respect to Hamas's victory in Palestinian elections the West had pressed for, have resulted in further loss of political capital for the West (not to mention credibility for democracy) in the Arab Middle East. Western influence and ability to mediate effectively in regional conflicts depend on acting in ways that thoughtful members on both sides in the region's painful conflicts can recognize as principled or at least fair-minded. Care needs to be taken to develop credibility through consistent appeals to international criteria for legitimacy (such as international human rights law and United Nations resolutions) as well as through constructive diplomacy. One-sided stands make little sense in complex Middle Eastern conflicts where no party is blameless.

Western governments would benefit by attending carefully to the messages sent by both words and deeds. Although it is not possible to control how one's actions will be construed, becoming keenly aware of regional perceptions can help to reduce cultural and political miscommunication. Policies that demonstrate steady commitment to the principles of human rights, human security, and international law (including *jus in bello*) are likely to be viewed with far greater favor than policies toward regional conflicts that appear opportunistic or inconsistent. Organizations that monitor human rights—intergovernmental as well as nongovernmental—may be able to provide helpful guidance in this regard. Whether the problem is the Arab-Israeli conflict, treatment of detainees in counterterrorism operations, or repression and counterviolence between Arab governments and opposition movements, working to cultivate international consensus on "fair" standards is far more desirable than staking out positions that may appear arbitrary or hostile to regional stakeholders.

Insist on Negotiated Solutions

Though Western governments may not wish to trumpet a willingness to engage with nonstate armed groups (be they active adversaries, as in the cases of Iraq and Afghanistan, or irregulars engaged with the governments of Middle Eastern states), negotiation with insurgent forces is often the only way to put an end to civil and regional wars. Denying "radical" groups a chance to develop a stake in the political process can make things worse, not better.

Because radicalism feeds on unresolved conflict, patient efforts to bridge divides are a necessity if more moderate political dynamics are to have a chance of succeeding in the Middle East. In seeking to reduce the overall amount of political stress in the region, there is a wide range of regional conflicts that US and Western diplomacy can address, whether in a public manner or through quiet efforts to foster dialogue. These conflicts include the Arab-Israeli conflict, the ongoing violence in Iraq, hostilities between Palestinian refugees and the Lebanese government, tensions between Kurdish minorities and the states within which they live, conflicts between states and Islamic movements, racialized ethnic conflict in Sudan, ethnoreligious tensions in Lebanon and Egypt, and the long-standing dispute over the status of the Western Sahara. Obvious linkages between Middle Eastern conflicts and ongoing events in Afghanistan and Pakistan are also worthy of attention.

By actively practicing dialogue and negotiation, Western governments will be in a much better position to advise Middle Eastern governments on the need to seek accommodation and reduce reliance on repressive measures. Creative Western policies might also include efforts to enhance regional conflict resolution capacity, by encouraging the Arab League and the Organization of the Islamic Conference to devote institutional resources to mediation training and to the development of improved mechanisms for dispute resolution and conciliation. Constructive proposals emanating from the region, such as the 2002 Saudi and Arab League peace initiative for the Israeli-Palestine conflict, merit diplomatic encouragement. By working together on such proposals and nurturing an interreligious "second track" for dialogue and negotiation, Western and Islamic leaders might make significant contributions to peace by reframing the conflict over Israel-Palestine as a feud within the Abrahamic family rather than as an interreligious collision, "crusade" (as seen by Muslims), or "defense of democracy" (as seen by Washington).

Given that Westerners still possess significantly more existential security than most inhabitants of majority-Muslim countries, it is vitally important for representatives of the West to take the initiative in efforts to convey peaceful intentions and a desire to partner with local actors to foster the emergence of a more prosperous and satisfactory future. Willingness to engage with Islamic movements can give enhanced credibility to Western demonstrations of respect for Islamic identity, and can help to ease Muslim perceptions of security threat. Calls to address the root causes of conflict without being distracted by manipulated imagery are also essential. Through their choices, Westerners have the power to respond to Middle Eastern conflicts in ways that either mobilize anti-Western sentiment or bolster the cause of moderation and mutual adjustment.

At the present moment, US efforts to negotiate a solution to the Iranian nuclear crisis could open new opportunities for broader regional peacemaking initiatives, while also sending a significant symbolic message. In addition, it is worth pointing out that while some grievances of Islamic movements are widely shared, others are highly localized. We should not repeat the errors of the Cold War by painting all movements with the same brush or adopting a totalizing agenda of ideological confrontation. Instead, the goal should be to disaggregate and address multiple contributing factors in a number of regional conflicts, and thereby reduce the appeal of transnational extremism.

Western policy toward the Middle East should not target Islamic revivalism (which, like Reformation-era movements in the West, is experienced as a process of internal renewal) or Islamic fundamentalist reactions to perceived external threats. Rather than seek to manipulate intraregional rivalries such as the Arab-Persian and Sunni-Shia divides, Western policy might generate more lasting contributions to security by calling for collaborative efforts to redress grievances used to justify terrorism—for example, the suffering of Palestinians and Iraqis, the maldistribution of resources, and the absence of legitimate and genuinely participatory political authority.

Foster Greater Inclusion of Muslims in North American and European Public Life

To support democratic change and human rights abroad effectively, Western countries should take a strong interest in practicing what they preach on matters pertaining to cultural and religious diversity. Domestic commitment to cultural and religious inclusion gives diplomats an important resource that can be utilized in the effort to engage Middle Eastern publics, so long as national policies remain free from anti-Muslim or Western exclusivist rigidities.

Because diaspora links are strong, a visitor to the Middle East should not be surprised to meet taxi drivers, businesspeople, and middle-class professionals who have relatives in Chicago, Toronto, or Frankfurt, and who may well have developed a positive view of the West insofar as relatives abroad have encountered economic and educational opportunity, rule of law, and freedom of religious expression far more consistently than prejudice, exclusion, or corruption. Though US foreign policies are indeed a source of grievance and concern, the importance of immigrant experiences in shaping Muslim perceptions of the West should not be underestimated. Recruiting more Muslims to career paths in government service would not only send a positive message to foreign publics, but also provide an invaluable reality check during domestic and foreign policy formulation processes.

Given the importance of domestic example for relations with predominantly Muslim societies, new steps should be taken to ensure inclusion of Muslims in Western societies. Special efforts could be made to utilize the resources of university systems, and to encourage multifaith projects that express shared religious values in the public sphere. The status of the United States and Canada as immigrant societies gives these countries unique assets in the effort to engage Muslim societies; there is a need, however, to ensure that the commitment to pluralism continues. To prevent moves toward retrenchment and anti-Muslim prejudice, advocates of cultural pluralism need to be articulate about the values underlying their efforts. Cultural pluralism entails a principled openness to others and an engaged commitment to coexistence through mutual recognition and respectful dialogue. Respect for the "other" permits a more truly democratic approach to differences, and facilitates the pursuit of common standards.

Support "Change from Within" in the Islamic World

By contributing to the radicalization of young Muslim men, overmilitarization of the "war on terror" has done more to destabilize the Muslim Middle East than to cultivate a basis for sustainable peace. The result has been a troubled policy that enjoins democracy on the one hand, while collaborating with (and indeed participating in) practices of state-sponsored torture on the other.[10] Though some democratic reformers in the Middle East initially took heart at US president George W. Bush's acknowledgment of past complicity with oppressive states, disruption created by the Iraq War has made genuine transformation a more distant goal.

Despite these trends, fostering incremental "change from within" in the Middle East is among the most vital tasks facing Western nations as they seek to adjust and redefine relations with the region. The United States and other Western countries can best support positive internal developments by promoting political participation within structures appropriate to the needs and culture of the people, and not by unreflectively promoting the transplantation of Western models or supporting authoritarian regimes.

By shaping conditions within which internal debates proceed, Western policies have exerted a significant—but often unrecognized—impact on prospects for democracy in the Middle East. Insofar as past policies have turned a blind eye to repressive practices and to the suffering associated with major regional conflicts, Western powers have inadvertently helped to create conditions favorable to anti-liberal, reactive action. Some policies, such as the decision to arm and actively assist anti-Soviet insurgents in Afghanistan during the Cold War, have unintentionally contributed to the present strength of radical networks. More recent policies linking democratization to the Iraq War have been at least as problematic, fostering the impression that "democracy" is a Trojan horse for Western conquest and political manipulation.

This impression is quite damaging, as the only viable democratic projects in Muslim countries are those that take root in local soil and are nourished by the aspirations of citizens for a more hopeful future. Though regional democratic projects may derive important ideas and insights from Western practices of democracy, their language and forms of expression will reflect regional culture and Islamic values, shorn of traditional as well as modern baggage that is no longer experienced as life-giving. As Jeremy Jones has argued, democratic change will stand the best chance of success in the Middle East if it is conceived as a genuinely indigenous enterprise:

> Democracy in the Middle East may not only be possible, it may already be under construction. In the diverse institutions and conversations, the traditions and experiments with which the people of the region conduct their daily lives, manage their social relations and organize their politics there might be all kinds of practices that ought to be recognized as democratic in nature. It may be these practices, rather than those that have developed in the West . . . that will form the foundations for the further development of democratic political institutions.[11]

By becoming sensitized to ongoing experiments with democratic change in Middle Eastern countries, Western policymakers stand a much better chance of finding means to strategically nourish positive dynamics.

Despite their differing cultural and religious heritage, industrialized nations can indeed assist Middle Eastern efforts to develop authentic democratic forms that respect Islamic precepts. The exclusion of Muslim majorities from active participation in political life undermines political stability in the Middle East and the larger Islamic world, and ultimately threatens Western interests. By acknowledging the need for local control over processes that seek to construct a democratic and culturally authentic future, the West can reduce suspicions of a hidden agenda and "partner" in the reconstruction of an Islamic world that is nonviolent, stable, and productive.

For a new vision to be accepted, it cannot be imposed. Western and US support for what is universal in democracy, and support for its emergence within an Islamic context, would signal a profound change in the region. Traditionally, Middle Eastern governments have been more concerned with maintaining the privilege and power of elites than with broad consultation and participatory decisionmaking. The pursuit of Western interests has for too long excluded legitimate aspirations of Arabs and Muslims; support for nondemocratic regimes has delivered mixed messages in the region and the impression of hypocrisy. If Western powers wish to protect long-term interests, then it is time to find the energy, the willpower, and the diplomatic skill necessary to deal with the fundamental problems.

A stake in a shared future would diminish the growing attraction toward fundamentalism in the Middle East today. Muslims and Arabs, who after decades of hoping and longing for freedom and prosperity and seeing little hope for a future that reflects their social or cultural values, are faced with the choice between a stagnant present with too many despotic leaders and the promises of new charismatic leaders. These new leaders speak to deep fears and frustrations in the collective Muslim and Arab psyche. In the absence of a positive image of the future, Muslim and Arab masses are likely to remain the victims and to continue clutching at straws or tyrants. Articulating a vision of (1) democratic reform in the region and (2) a changing US role that is more unequivocally committed to international standards might help provide the hope that fuels long-term, peaceable efforts to address many of the latent underlying conflicts that have created the current atmosphere of repression, violence, and anger.

Use Public Diplomacy to Listen as Well as to Speak

In the United States after September 11, one of the more immediate concerns—beyond the tightening of security measures and the formulation of a military strategy—was to ensure that public diplomacy efforts were adequate to "sell" the United States and its policies overseas. This concern for marketing, however, was not accompanied by a comparable interest in the salability of the foreign policy product, or in the utility of public diplomacy for gaining deeper understanding of foreign publics and discovering their messages for Americans. Some public diplomacy programs were even premised on the notion that Middle Eastern Muslims know very little about the United States—an assumption that even a very short visit to the region would belie.

While Middle Eastern publics are not without their biases and blind spots vis-à-vis the United States, they tend to be much better informed about developments in American pop culture, sports, politics, technology, education, and lifestyles than many suspect. Negative opinions of the United States often have less to do with judgments about the reputed licentiousness of American culture than with genuine political disagreements. There is no easy substitute for addressing these disagreements head-on, in a manner that reflects openness to dialogue. Vigorous public relations packaging cannot by itself solve the problem.

At its best, public diplomacy is a valuable instrument that the United States and other Western nations can use to open channels of two-way communication with Middle Eastern societies. An effective public diplomacy strategy starts with actively listening to voices in the region[12]—not only to their words and ideas, but also to the emotions and experiences behind the words and ideas. Active listening, an invaluable skill for conflict resolution and the cultivation of sustained dialogue, can also be an indispensable tool of analysis. In listening, the United States and other Western countries may begin to appreciate why their intentions have often been doubted or misunderstood by Muslims.

The United States, for example, has voiced its support for democracy, but because of oil dependency it has also acted in ways that bolster repressive governments. While the United States has condemned nuclear proliferation with respect to Pakistan's "Islamic bomb," US policymakers have refused to address Israel's nuclear capacity. While the United States has historically encouraged international legal recourse, it has systematically vetoed United Nations resolutions seeking redress for Palestinians. More generally, US advocacy for human rights appears hypocritical in the face of new practices involving detention without trial, use of secret evidence in court, torture, and "extraordinary rendition." Although these policies are hotly disputed in US politics, Middle Eastern Muslims inevitably focus on the end result and perceive deep ironies and contradictions. The belief that US leaders will not listen to or acknowledge Muslim criticisms deepens attitudes of indignation and alienation, and increases resistance to US perspectives on problems in the Middle East. Without dialogue, Muslims will be unable to hear even the most powerful, accurate, and valid US insights and concerns about the governance problems of many Middle Eastern countries.

For the United States to reach the hearts and minds of Arabs and Muslims, expressing agreement with differing points of view is far less important than demonstrating respect and interest through practices of dialogue and engagement. If used for such purposes, public diplomacy can also provide a channel for building relationships of trust while signaling a commitment to reconciliation, and the development of visions in which Americans and Muslims cooperate to bring about a better future. By using public diplomacy as a forum for deliberation, Americans can explore sensitive questions in a search for new answers: How could democratic reforms move the region toward stability, peace, social reform, prosperity, and good neighborliness? What form of democracy would be appropriate to Middle Eastern cultural and religious contexts, and would speak to the life-affirming, inclusive principles of Islam? What could Arab-Israeli and Israeli-Palestinian peace look like, and how might it be realized?

Establishing an atmosphere of trust and mutual concern cannot be achieved by plowing over historical inconsistencies and mixed signals, dispensing with dialogue, and expecting Middle Eastern audiences to embrace a new message. The United States and other Western powers cannot afford to exclude Muslim publics and civic leaders from the process of formulating messages intended to enlist support in shared efforts to construct a viable future. Granted, the trust of Middle Eastern Muslims cannot be won overnight. Yet a carefully designed approach that responds directly and consistently to high priorities of citizens in the region is likely to earn significant dividends.

Foster Intercultural and Interreligious Dialogue

The grand scale of Islamic-Western identity conflict tends to invite either sweeping overgeneralizations about cultural differences or efforts to discount cultural analysis altogether. However, both "broad-brushstroke" and "culture-blind" approaches are inadequate. The existence of real patterns of cultural difference increases the degree of "opacity" in Islamic-Western relations, heightening risks of miscommunication, misattribution of motives, and psychological projection. As important as it is to analyze these differences (e.g., individualism versus collectivism, gender norms, conceptions of legitimate authority, role of religion in the public sphere, forms of communication and emotional expression), careful attention to the internal diversity of cultures and the politics of culture is equally vital. Within a context of ongoing political conflict with the "cultural other" (be it Western or Islamic), competition for leadership inevitably involves strategic manipulation of "authentic culture" and its symbols. Troubled historical relations between groups also add to the potential for polarization and for demagogic calls to remove aspects of "alien" culture from a given milieu. The Taliban's efforts to abolish all things "Western," from cassette tapes and videos to clean-shaven faces and professionally empowered women, represents an extreme in negative psychological and ideological responses to "otherness" that can also appear in the West, taking such forms as mosque vandalism and periodic racially motivated attacks on individuals who "look like Arabs."

As noted previously, there is a very real danger that Islamic-Western ideological contestation is replacing the oppositions of the Cold War era, and that complex, diverse societies around the world are becoming enmeshed in a clash of symbols.[13] Within this clash, multifarious interests are competing for resources and for the claim to cultural and political leadership; in many cases, relatively self-serving emotions and motivations are masquerading as sublime and noble sentiments. As in other intense intergroup conflicts, symbols and images projected by *others* (in the North American case, Islamic symbols, and in the Islamic world, Western symbols) are becoming reservoirs for in-group fear, loathing, and insecurity. Surges of religious nationalism are in evidence not only in the Middle East but also in the United States.

All too easily, symbols for sacred values and moral growth can become emblems to carry forward into combat.[14] So also can symbols of wholesome national aspirations (including frequently invoked values like "democracy" and "freedom") become battle flags, even as the resources of society become diverted more and more to causes having little do with traditional measures of national betterment. Taken together, recent setbacks in Islamic-Western relations graphically illustrate the charged symbolic nature of contemporary identity conflict. In addition to September 11 and the invasions of Afghanistan and Iraq—themselves powerfully symbolic events that prompted political mobilizations far beyond the borders of the affected lands—intense controversies surrounding offensive Danish cartoons, Pope Benedict's Regensburg address, and a disturbingly provocative Holocaust cartoon contest in Iran indicate that intercultural and interreligious relations have become highly volatile.

Whenever intergroup conflict is perceived in existential terms, as a struggle over ultimate ends such as the fate of religions or civilizations, the traditions in question can quickly become hollowed out with respect to their essential moral content. What means can one forgo in the defense of one's deepest identity, in the face of an evil and implacable foe? Ironically, the moral restraints built into religions and cultures can become increasingly tenuous when partisans seek to defend these traditions from a threatening "other."

For complex psychological reasons, many people in this world are willing to risk or even embrace martyrdom if they deem it necessary to redeem what they value most, especially to save an assaulted or humiliated core identity.[15] Such behaviors may arise most readily within disadvantaged and traumatized communities such as Sri Lankan Tamils and Palestinian Muslims, but the use of violence to defend a "sacred" sense of identity is not a rare phenomenon. Political desperation, when combined with a deep sense of fear or an existential condition of disempowerment, can easily give way to violence. Analyzing behaviors and conditions that evoke this sense of "existential threat"—in both Western and Islamic milieus—should be a top priority of contemporary conflict resolution efforts.

Although government-supported channels have a key role to play in enhancing communication between the West and the Muslim Middle East, independent civil society initiatives remain indispensable. Only through active engagement with each other can Muslims and Westerners come to understand the deeper meanings and implications of the emerging clash of symbols in which they have become entangled.

Active engagement permits us to understand and recognize the authentic expressions of human religiosity, and protects us from the politics of manipulated symbolism. It defuses the felt need to continually defend legitimate religious beliefs and institutions. Whereas healthy expressions of religiosity express a mature understanding of a faith tradition and a desire for correspondence between symbolism and substance, some individuals and groups misuse religion by applying its symbols to generate a system of confrontation. This system of confrontation becomes divorced from larger understandings of a religion that seek to discern and apply the guiding principles embedded in sacred texts through careful consideration of material circumstances and spiritual intents. Instead of tapping such traditional resources, the system of confrontation feeds on emotions of pessimism and fear—emotions that have begun to grow on both sides of the Islamic-Western divide. Those who are party to the system deploy sacred symbols in a manner that is driven by viscerally felt anxieties and grievances. Active engagement is needed to avoid entrapment in such systems of confrontation, moving beyond immediate negative reactions to discover human commonality, shared experiences, and compatible aspirations.

Only through active engagement is it possible to gain an authentic, nuanced "feel" for other cultures, as well as a taste for how authentic expressions of religious sentiment differ from extremist manipulations. The familiarity that comes with dialogue obviates the need for defensiveness, and makes frank, self-critical discourse about bridging the gap between symbol and substance possible. As capacity to discern between mature religiosity and manipulative use of symbolism increases, insight into underlying sources of confrontation also grows, preventing resignation to a conflict system that still possesses potential for higher levels of escalation. A process of de-escalation also becomes conceivable, through which mutual fears are recognized and each side begins to articulate ways it can assist the other through measures addressing basic human needs for dignity, security, and a hopeful future.

Visible partnerships across cultural, religious, and political divides are not a panacea, but they are an invaluable corrective for the sort of groupthink that led to damaging and counterproductive post–September 11 policies in the United States. Their mere existence helps to undermine the "us versus them" logic that threatens to shred the fabric of contemporary societies, with their deep-rooted cultural, ethnic, and religious pluralism. To advance such bridge-building efforts, Western governments should encourage and facilitate interreligious dialogue, multifaith projects, and coexistence initiatives—forms of encounter and engagement that provide positive roles for religion in public life but do not favor any one particular religious tradition or undermine pluralist democratic principles. It is not enough simply to condemn radical religion; people need positive examples of faith-based engagement that channel religious energies toward positive alternative visions. The popularity of the *Left Behind* book series in some North American quarters suggests that this need for hopeful visions applies to Western Christians as well as to Middle Eastern Muslims;[16] in both communities there is a need for initiatives that open channels of communication and demonstrate the viability of coexistence.

Given their historical experiences with the Crusades (in which material and political incentives were at least as important as professed religious devotion), and with internal conflicts over religious beliefs during the Reformation era, Western Christians may be able to understand how sacred symbols can be misused for personal gain or political vendettas. Reflecting on such experiences within a framework of sustained dialogue can lead to broader understandings of how material circumstances and diverse motivations can shape the use of religious symbolism in politics. This makes it easier to differentiate mature and substantive religious faith from forms of religiosity that are more psychologically reactive, superficial, or instrumental. Recognizing the historical, material, and political factors that enliven contemporary Islamic activism, for example, is essential if Western analysts are to avoid sweeping and counterproductive generalizations. It is also vital if they are to recognize the potential for cultural creativity amid the present ferment of ideas and movements.

Despite polarization caused by confrontational use of symbolism, sustained and active Western-Islamic engagement can help each side recognize that it is reacting to the other without deep knowledge or awareness of cultural meanings. It can lead to greater discernment and even to mutual appreciation of similar and complementary values. At the level of political practice, experience with dialogue can help leaders resist pressures to prematurely narrow policy options or cloud distinctions between those who are "innocent" and those who are "guilty."

Support Religious Peacemaking

Any viable intercultural peace in the twenty-first century will have to include a religious dimension. Fortunately, as noted in this study, religious cultures provide broad repertoires of historical experiences, narratives, and symbols, and are by no means static or closed. Narratives of confrontation draw on narrowly selected encounters and experiences. Drawing attention to this selectivity, as well as to distorted and misleading uses of history, is an essential basis for peacebuilding activity. So, too, are efforts to "demystify" symbolic conflict by pointing to dynamics that are not strictly cultural or religious in nature.

The starting point for any intercultural peacebuilding effort is the development of religious and cultural literacy. This means acquiring fluency in essential religious precepts, and developing an understanding of the many ways in which these precepts have been interpreted and applied. Religion is expressed and lived through cultural activity; what is essentially religious to one subgroup or faction may reflect a historical synthesis or inflection that another subgroup rejects.

Even when many of the motivations behind "religious" conflict are not particularly spiritual in nature, religiously based peacemaking activity can help to counteract misdirected forms of religious devotion. When specifically religious values are perceived to be at stake, and when religion is being used to galvanize confrontation and justify violence, peacemaking can be greatly assisted by engagement with the religious dimension of conflict. By taking the presence of religious factors seriously, it becomes possible to redirect religion and spirituality toward conflict transformation and peace (see Table 10.1).

There are many common errors in analysis of conflicts with strong intercultural or religious dimensions, but one of the more unhelpful approaches involves a reductionist tendency to posit "fundamentalism" as the *root cause* of conflict. Though this barrier to more comprehensive understanding is not exclusive to the Western context (during a recent trip to Egypt, one of this volume's authors was surprised by the number of books on Christian fundamentalism and the US Christian right lining the shelves of bookstores in Cairo), moving beyond the "fundamentalism" frame is especially important for North American and European analysts seeking ways to prevent or reverse radicalization processes in the Muslim world.

Table 10.1 Religion in Conflict and Peacemaking

Ways Religion Enters Politics	Ways Religion Can Accelerate Conflict	Ways Religion Can Contribute to Peacemaking
Religiously engaged actors (individuals and groups)	Actors using religion as a "power tool," "force multiplier," or barrier	Actors using religion as a bridge or as a source of empowerment for peaceful change
Religious symbols, identities, and narratives	Competitive polarization of identities, with narratives of rivalry or victimization ("us versus them")	Open religious identities and narratives with positive role for the "stranger"
Religious cultures and values	Exclusive understandings of goodness and virtue; strong in-group versus out-group biases	Inclusive understanding of spiritual values; commitment to social justice, nonviolence, and reconciliation
Religious texts and interpretations	Cutting off dialogue about interpretation; authoritarianism; emphasis on righteous or purifying violence	Affirmation of transcendent divine mystery, of immanent human responsibilities, and of an open-ended quest for understanding

Scholars and policymakers need to exercise great discernment when analyzing and diagnosing religiously justified conflict behaviors such as those of the Al-Qaida network. To be sure, "fundamentalist" religion—if by "fundamentalist" is meant "authoritarian and intolerant"—is indeed a problem. As we have noted previously, however, there is a need to differentiate between fundamentalism and revivalism on the one hand, and extremism and terrorism on the other. There is also a need to acknowledge the potential for nonreligious fundamentalism. In Islamic-Western relations, the fundamentalist tendency is visible not only among Muslims who feel overwhelmed by external cultural and political influences (like some extreme US Christians), but also among Westerners who insist that dialogue with Muslims must have a predetermined outcome or inflexible agenda, such as persuading Muslims to adopt a secularist worldview, or to support particular foreign and domestic policies. It is arguable that many contemporary Western writings—and not only Muslim religious tracts—exhibit such dogmatically polemical tendencies.[17]

In deeply fractured societies such as Afghanistan and Iraq, attributing ongoing political violence primarily to fundamentalism has limited analytical utility. After decades of war and violence fueled by external intervention and internal divisiveness, a majority of Afghans and Iraqis have redoubled their commitments to conservative strains of religious thought. Many can quite fairly be classified as revivalists who are seeking to reassert key tenets of a religious belief system, as a means of salvaging meaning and existential security from the situation in which they find themselves. Among those currently in rebellion against their respective, coalition-supported governments, some are actually less rigid in their religious commitments than individuals now holding major government portfolios. Religion undoubtedly plays a powerful role in the motivation of core constituencies (including leaders of the Taliban in Afghanistan and of various Sunni and Shia factions in Iraq), yet this motivation arises not from "fundamentalism" as such but from a particular strain of fundamentalist thought that has become conjoined with ethnic loyalties, nationalism (particularly in the case of Iraq), and a highly combative worldview. It is the conflict narratives that animate the Taliban and Iraqi resistance organizations—and not merely religious beliefs—that have inclined these movements to oppose a foreign military presence and support extremist measures, including those of Al-Qaida.[18]

To understand why the darkest and most confrontational conflict narratives sometimes prevail over less deeply polarizing possibilities, ethnoreligious radicalization needs to be recognized as an ongoing process. Both in Islamic-Western relations and in other conflict environments, ethnoreligious radicalization can be explained without resorting to reductionist simplifications. Analyses of radicalization have to be sophisticated and multidimensional, allowing us to see extremism and terrorism in the multiple contexts that shape them, and to understand the complex processes that lead adherents of particular cultural and religious systems to believe that their identities and sacred values are under attack. We have to ask, "What went wrong?"—not only with radicalized groups but in the relations of these groups with their adversaries.

Applying this principle—analysis of multiple contexts—to explain the appeal of religiously justified conflict behavior can greatly expedite efforts to escape entrapment in escalating confrontations. Current problems in Islamic-Western relations did not develop overnight, and there is a history of rivalry that is selectively remembered on both sides. But we need not go back all the way to the early Islamic conquests or to the Crusades to account for present difficulties. Highlighting the formative impact of the modern colonial and Cold War experiences provides a menu of problems that continue to affect peoples' daily lives, and that can still be addressed constructively by religious as well as secular initiatives.

The ultimate aim of most religiously and culturally competent peacebuilding initiatives is to foster movement toward reconciliation, albeit in incremental motions, through the construction of alliances and networks. In some cases peacebuilding networks may be largely monocultural and religiously homogeneous, while in other cases they may be intercultural and interreligious. A long-term goal of religious peacebuilding is to develop a constituency for peace; short-term goals include confidence building, conflict prevention, and the resolution of local disputes that might otherwise escalate. Active, grassroots religious peacebuilding is itself an effort to prefigure the possibility of peace.

To empower religious peacebuilding efforts, scholars and practitioners can provide vital support by taking inventory of religious peace resources. A nongovernmental organization involved with peacebuilding and development work in Lebanon, Iraq, or Afghanistan, for example, would be well served if its foreign members were familiar with "Islamic peace paradigms" such as those explored in this volume, as well as with local practices and traditions that, though not explicitly rooted in Islamic sources, are implemented through use of an Islamic idiom. Traditional modes of conflict resolution and cooperative decisionmaking, including *sulha* (Arab world) and *shuras* and *jirgas* (Afghanistan), would have to be included in this inventory—not merely because they are still in use, but also because their symbolism and principles might be adapted in the service of *salam* (peace). Peace-workers and development professionals might also wish to become acquainted with Islamic exemplars of right conduct and reconciliation. Peacebuilding in most regions of the Islamic world must involve respect for principles from the Quran and *hadith.* Conversance with the achievements and beliefs of modern figures who are nonetheless recognized as Muslim peacemakers, such as the Pashtuns' great nonviolent leader, Abdul Ghaffar Khan (see Chapter 7), would also be useful.

Working to establish complementarity between "generic" and indigenous frameworks for peacebuilding—as well as between practices rooted in different religious traditions—is one of the most essential bases for empowering local actors and helping them develop effective, culturally legitimate practices.

In the past, international nongovernmental orgnizations and UN personnel working to support conflict resolution capacity development in the Gaza Strip found it useful to partner with local change agents who made imaginative linkages between contemporary practices such as "peer mediation" and traditional Arab roles such as that of the village headman *(mukhtar).* The result was a significant educational program that gave expression to traditional values in an innovative yet culturally resonant manner. Another intriguing model for interreligious peacemaking partnerships can be found in the example of Christian Peacemaker Teams, whose Iraq-based team encountered enthusiasm for nonviolent peace advocacy and human rights documentation work among Muslims. In joint Muslim-Christian workshops, team activists described their methods and religious motivation; Muslim participants shared their own religious sources for nonviolent activism, and elected to form an autonomous "Muslim Peacemaker Team" dedicated to building a more peaceful Iraq through adherence to Islamic principles.[19]

Developing locally grounded, culturally competent approaches to peacebuilding in zones of religious conflict can be a challenging process, and often requires the identification and amplification of suppressed peace resources and narratives. Where conflict involves religious diversity, protagonists of change may also find themselves toggling back and forth between the primary religious language of one group and that of another, or between primary religious languages and a second-order language that is shared (for example, the language of human rights). When organizing initiatives premised on interreligious or intercultural cooperation, special care often needs to be taken to gain support for localized partnership efforts from authorities operating at higher levels of religious and national organization.

Producing culturally appropriate peace education materials is vitally important for sustained peacebuilding efforts—ideally materials that make use of both traditional and innovative concepts, and that can be integrated into the curricula of primary, secondary, and postsecondary educational institutions. These materials can be used to explain the rationale for religious peacebuilding to skeptical parties, to inform readers about past instances of peace and coexistence, and to promote awareness of current peacemaking activities through various local and national media. Key contributions to social discourse can often be made through the dissemination of religiously informed rationales for tolerance, coexistence, peacemaking, political pluralism, and the defense of human rights. Given current trends, religious groups both in North America and in traditionally Islamic countries should no doubt be encouraged to produce high-quality study documents on these themes. Foundations and government development agencies would be wise to foster studies of religiously based peacemaking efforts, documenting hitherto unknown cases, promoting reflection about how such efforts might be evaluated and developed further, and disseminating knowledge about Islamic approaches to peacebuilding. One Middle Eastern initiative that has received international publicity in recent years involves a Yemeni judge who practices Quranic debate with religious extremists.[20] Anecdotal evidence suggests the possibility of a model with broader relevance, yet additional research would no doubt be valuable.

One of the more important challenges in contemporary interfaith peacebuilding efforts is moving beyond the introductory stages of dialogue toward more enduring partnerships and coalitions. Such partnerships and coalitions need not be formalized in independent organizations, but shared commitment to dialogue and public education efforts over an extended period of time would appear vital for the consolidation of deeper understanding, as well as for the full development of problem-based explorations and "people-to-people" activities. The "people-to-people" aspect of interfaith peacebuilding provides invaluable contact between people of faith who inhabit markedly different social and cultural realities; more focused activities can address challenges that religious communities share in defining their approaches to issues such as citizenship, pluralism, peace, hunger, poverty, ecology, and development.

Identify and Implement Intercultural Confidence-Building Measures

In previous chapters we noted the impact of unequal power relations on cultural contact between Muslims and Westerners. Unequal power has led to a situation in which genuine cultural differences are experienced simultaneously with serious political and economic disputes. The results have often been quite painful. Imagine, for example, how Iranian-US relations might have developed if not for Cold War geopolitics, and Western fears of Soviet control over Iranian oil resources in the event of a feared (but unlikely) communist takeover. In the absence of such concerns, Anglo-US support for a pro-monarchy coup might never have manifested in 1953, putting the West on a collision course with Iranian secular and religious nationalists. We cannot reverse history, yet there is cause for remorse at the unfortunate and unanticipated outcomes of past decisions and events.

If there is to be a new beginning, humility will be required of all parties. Within the West, there is a need to acknowledge that great powers such as England, France, and now the United States have often used their influence in ways that have dramatically reduced the capacity of Middle Eastern Muslims to control their own cultural and political destiny. At the time of their own breakthroughs in modern economic and political development, these Western powers competed with one another but faced no comparable obstacles to self-determination and self-respect. Becoming more cognizant of such issues through Western cultural empathy has become vital for international peace. However, placing all responsibility for change on the shoulders of Western powers is undesirable, because it denies the role contemporary Muslims can play by trusting in the enduring strength of their own values, which are no doubt quite capable of absorbing the shocks of Western intrusions while providing a principled basis for integrating and adapting those Western ideas and practices that can complement an ongoing revitalization of Islamic culture. "Sobriety" and "humility" are vital watchwords for Westerners and Muslims as they seek to avoid the perils of ideological hubris, and work to develop intercultural confidence-building measures.

Since Muslim support for political violence often correlates with the belief that Islam is under attack, Western powers need to seriously reconsider policies that feed this perception. To access Muslim perceptions of Western policies, policymakers should continue consulting with "moderate" and progressive Muslims, while also broadening the circle of conversation to gain exposure to other views. Muslims who have achieved a positive integration of Islamic and Western values in their own lives (e.g., "modern, democratic, and Muslim") will continue to have a valuable role to play in intercultural dialogue, particularly when they are able to maintain credibility in their own communities by practicing "multiple critique"—that is, by demonstrating a capacity for thoughtfully critiquing the practices of Muslim groups as well as Western states, and thereby acting as bridge-builders and as catalysts of self-reflection on both sides of the macro-cultural divide. Western policymakers should exercise a measure of caution with respect to those interlocutors who seem too eager to please (take, for example, the case of those who promised a hero's welcome to US soldiers upon arrival in Iraq), while remaining in active communication with regionally based Middle Eastern civil society activists, who can provide valuable feedback on attitudes toward Western policies in the region.[21]

The logic of "multiple critique" can also be applied in North America and Europe within Christian, Jewish, and secularist communities. In any conflict situation, it is all too easy to fall into defensive, self-serving habits of thought by comparing one's own idealized values to another people's practices, without allowing oneself to be challenged by another person's ideal (be it similar to or genuinely different from one's own). Practicing greater intellectual circumspection should not detract from an attitude of healthy self-respect, for considerable self-confidence is often required to "hear" criticism from others and to magnanimously respect the truths that others bear. Such magnanimity would seem particularly desirable given that, both objectively and in comparison to most Middle Eastern Muslims, the average Westerner still enjoys impressive security and prosperity.

Through their choices, Westerners have the power to respond to Islam in ways that either mobilize anti-Western sentiment or bolster the cause of moderation and mutual adjustment. Western demonstrations of respect for and genuine interest in Islam—which for so many Middle Easterners is the very core of their identity and sense of self—can help to ease Muslim perceptions of security threat. Calls to address the root causes of conflict are also essential if pathology and anti-Western extremism are not to be mistaken for the essence of the second-largest world religion. Affirming Islamic identity while also working for consensus to address outstanding political disputes can help Muslims shift away from a defensive stance and toward a more creative response to modern problems of development, participation, and social justice.

Contact between Middle Eastern Muslims and Westerners can and should be institutionalized to support regular interaction and mutual learning. In addition to public diplomacy and greater effort on the part of diplomats in the field to make contact with social leaders, governments and nongovernmental groups can promote youth exchanges, intercontinentally linked classrooms, and even sister city programs. The establishment of Western and Middle Eastern endowments to fund cultural events that use visual and performing arts to celebrate coexistence would also be welcome. Existing initiatives such as the Alliance of Civilizations at the United Nations can play an important role by mapping out the issues that divide Islamic and Western societies as a prelude to rapprochement based on reciprocity as well as "preemptive" conciliatory measures.

Harness the Potential of Universities and Civil Society Organizations

As policymakers consider ways of revitalizing public diplomacy and expediting "people-to-people" linkages, scholars and university administrators should consider ways that research and education can be directed toward goals of interreligious and intercultural peace. Promoting university-to-university partnerships could prove useful in this regard, as would resource centers and centers of excellence in interfaith relations, public policy, and peacebuilding.

With their diverse and highly international student bodies, universities are living laboratories for intercultural dialogue and experiential learning. In addition to their functions in the domain of research and knowledge dissemination, universities have the potential to become laboratories for Islamic-Western peacebuilding efforts, as well as forums for convening policy dialogues and fostering skill development. Universities can make vital contributions to contemporary peace efforts, both as catalysts of domestic and transnational relationship building and as institutions that equip future professionals with the tools they need to engage interculturally and interreligiously as they pursue career paths in development, conflict resolution, public policy, and diplomacy, as well as engineering, law, environmental protection, and medical research.

There may be a valuable niche in peacebuilding and development policy for initiatives that link universities and other civil society institutions (e.g., nongovernmental organizations, professional organizations in areas such as law and journalism, and international academic associations) for research and intercultural engagement on issues pertaining to world-order values (e.g., human security, peaceful conflict resolution, international justice, ecological sustainability, and human rights). Efforts to support the field of conflict resolution in regions such as the Middle East and South Asia through university-to-university partnerships may bear more fruit than those sponsored directly by government-affiliated foundations. Additional partnerships could address issues related to development, human rights documentation, preparation for government service, human security, international law, refugee support (Iraqi as well as Palestinian), cluster bomb removal (particularly in Lebanon, Afghanistan, and Iraq), "common ground" journalism, sustainable agriculture, regional security systems, social development, and interfaith dialogue. Such programs would underscore the importance of intercultural communication and cooperation in a world that needs principled bases for action by members of diverse groups.

Giving Life to the New Story

A central theme of this book has been that the path to peace in the Middle East and in the broader context of Islamic-Western relations is a path that runs through—and not around—Islam. This idea diverges from much conventional wisdom, which regards moderation and commitment to peacemaking as character traits that emerge *despite* rather than *through* commitment to Islamic values. In contrast, we have proposed that Islam plays many roles in Muslim politics, providing languages of justification not only for destructive conflict but also for justice-seeking and nonviolent behaviors. Although Islam has often been understood in ways that conceive of peace narrowly as an "absence of war" secured by a powerful and assertive governing authority, a strong foundation exists in Muslim thought for conceptions of peace that are linked to social justice, communal solidarity, and coexistence with non-Muslim communities. Efforts to engage Muslim peoples that take into account the "peace through equity," "peace through conciliation," "peace through nonviolence," and "peace through universalism" paradigms are likely to be far more productive than approaches that seek only to combat radicalism and shore up political authority structures.

Taking Muslim aspirations toward social justice and a more equitable international system seriously can generate new energy in Middle Eastern and Islamic-Western peacemaking. By affirming Islamic identity and deeply held ideals in a wide range of forums, from political speech and diplomacy to civil society dialogues, Westerners have the potential to reduce anxieties surrounding the perceived need to defend Islam. They can also help build sufficient trust for more wide-ranging discussions of how Islamic values can play a role in conflict resolution, nonviolent social change strategies, and development of a climate of relations among the world's religions in which mutuality and appreciation prevail rather than fear and recrimination.

Like the West and its constituent religious traditions, the Islamic tradition is internally rich with interpretations, practices, and meanings. Humbly and respectfully engaging Muslims and expressing curiosity about these internal resources can help to activate them. However, Muslim leaders should not hesitate to begin their own dialogue and confidence-building initiatives, while proactively applying Islamic peacebuilding resources to the problems of Middle Eastern societies. The events of recent years provide ample evidence that radicalism grows when insulting an adversary's values and "fighting fire with fire" become default responses to conflict; a time has come for new experiments in intercultural, interreligious, and international relations premised on mutual invitations to come to the table and seek common terms of understanding.

The possibility of fostering a "new story"[2] of complementarity between the West and the Muslim Middle East is a function of deep changes in the character of global politics. The inexorable dynamics of modern history rule out pretensions by any one group of finding a "separate peace" or establishing worldwide hegemony. We have moved from a humanity that experienced its collective life as fragments of the whole to a humanity that must experience itself as whole—a humanity that must embrace realities of interdependence in the spheres of economics, ecology, culture, and politics. Security is no longer the private good of a particular state and nation that may be purchased at the expense of others, but a public good that can be achieved only through the cultivation of consensus and collaboration within a framework of dialogue and reciprocity.

The new story of complementarity exists only in the form of a working outline, and can begin with the simplest of acknowledgments: Islam and the West are "stuck" with each other, and have no choice but to learn to coexist. Islam and the West are truly between stories—between the stories of the past, and the story that they must now create together. All who identify with Islam and with the West can become coauthors of this new story, and not merely those who reside in the Middle East and North America. We are all heirs of the story of conflict. If we leave aside tired generalizations and seek to know one another, we can become the architects of a truly new order of cooperation.

Notes

Some material in this chapter has been adapted from Funk, "Transforming Islamic-Western Identity Conflict," 2007.

1. Capps, "Interpreting Václav Havel," 1997.
2. Anderson, *Imagined Communities,* 1991.

3. Office of the Director of National Intelligence, "Declassified Key Judgments of the National Intelligence Estimate," 2006.
4. Power, "Our War on Terror," 2007, p. 8.
5. Thompson, "A War Best Served Cold," 2007; Shapiro, *Containment,* 2007.
6. The revolutionary religious and political projects pursued by Oliver Cromwell and the English Puritans are exemplary. See Walzer, *The Revolution of the Saints,* 1969.
7. Center for Strategic and International Studies, *Mixed Blessings,* 2007, p. 3.
8. Films for the Humanities and Sciences (Princeton, 1999).
9. Morgan, *Lost History,* 2007; Saliba, *Islamic Science and the Making of the European Renaissance,* 2007.
10. Mertus, *Bait and Switch,* 2004.
11. Jones, *Negotiating Change,* 2007, pp. 5–6.
12. Center for Strategic and International Studies, *Mixed Blessings,* 2007, p. 17.
13. Funk and Said, "Islam and the West," 2004, pp. 20–21.
14. Appleby, *The Ambivalence of the Sacred,* 2000.
15. Lindner, *Making Enemies,* 2006.
16. Frykolm, *Rapture Culture,* 2004.
17. See, for example, Hitchens, *God Is Not Great,* 2007.
18. For Iraqi Shia organizations, of course, Al-Qaida remains a mortal foe.
19. Muslim Peacemaker Team, "About MPT," 2006. For more on Christian Peacemaker Teams in Iraq, see Brown, *Getting in the Way,* 2005.
20. Brandon, "Koranic Duels Ease Terror," 2005.
21. Lynch, "Taking Arabs Seriously," 2003.

Bibliography

Abdalla, Amr. "Principles of Islamic Interpersonal Conflict Intervention: A Search Within Islam and Western Literature." *Journal of Law and Religion* 15, nos. 1–2 (2000–2001): 151–184.

Abdul Rauf, Feisal. *What's Right with Islam: A New Vision for Muslims and the West.* New York: HarperCollins, 2004.

Abou El Fadl, Khaled. *The Great Theft: Wrestling Islam from the Extremists.* New York: HarperCollins, 2005.

———. *Speaking in God's Name: Islamic Law, Authority, and Women.* Oxford, England: Oneworld, 2001.

Abu-Nimer, Mohammed. "Conflict Resolution Approaches: Western and Middle Eastern Lessons and Possibilities." *American Journal of Economics and Sociology* 55, no. 1 (1996): 35–53.

———. "A Framework for Nonviolence and Peacebuilding in Islam." *Journal of Law and Religion* 15, nos. 1–2 (2000–2001): 217–265.

———. *Nonviolence and Peacebuilding in Islam.* Gainesville: University of Florida Press, 2003.

Abu-Nimer, Mohammed, Amal I. Khoury, and Emily Welty. *Unity in Diversity: Interfaith Dialogue in the Middle East.* Washington, DC: US Institute of Peace, 2007.

Abu Zahra, Mohammad. "International Relations in Islam." *The First Conference of the Academy of Islamic Research.* Cairo: Al-Azhar Academy for Academic Research, 1968.

Abul-Fadl, Mona. "Community, Justice, and Jihad: Elements of the Muslim Historical Consciousness." *American Journal of Islamic Social Sciences* 4, no. 1 (1987): 13–30.

———. "Contrasting Epistemics: *Tawhid,* the Vocationist, and Social Theory." *American Journal of Islamic Social Sciences* 7, no. 1 (March 1990): 15–38.

AbuSulayman, 'AbdulHamid. *The Islamic Theory of International Relations: New Directions for Islamic Methodology and Thought.* Herndon, VA: International Institute of Islamic Thought, 1987.

Ackerman, Peter, and Jack DuVall. *A Force More Powerful: A Century of Nonviolent Conflict.* New York: Palgrave, 2000.

Ackerman, Peter, and Christopher Kruegler. *Strategic Nonviolent Conflict: The Dynamics of People Power in the Twentieth Century.* Westport: Praeger, 1994.

al-Ahsan, 'Abdullah. *OIC: The Organization of the Islamic Conference.* Herndon, VA: International Institute of Islamic Thought, 1988.

al-Ghazali, Abu Hamid. *The Incoherence of the Philosophers.* Translated by Michael E. Marmura. Provo, UT: Brigham Young University Press, 2002.

———. *The Niche of Lights.* Translated by David Buchman. Provo, UT: Brigham Young University Press, 1998.

———. *On the Duties of Brotherhood.* Translated by Muhtar Holland. London: Latimer, 1975.

al-Ghunaimi, Mohammad Talaat. *The Muslim Conception of International Law and the Western Approach.* The Hague: Nijhoff, 1968.

al-Haqq, Jad. "Fatwa Against the Iraqi Invasion of Kuwait." In *The Saddam Hussein Reader: Selections from Leading Writers on Iraq,* edited by Turi Munthe, pp. 246–250. New York: Thunder's Mouth, 2002.

al-Hibri, Azizah. "Islam, Law, and Custom: Redefining Muslim Women's Rights." *American University Journal of International Law and Policy* 12, no. 1 (1997): 1–44.

Ali, Tariq. *The Clash of Fundamentalisms: Crusades, Jihads, and Modernity.* London: Verso, 2002.

Ambler, Rex. *Global Theology: The Meaning of Faith in the Present World Crisis.* Philadelphia: Trinity International, 1990.

Anderson, Benedict. *Imagined Communities: Reflections on the Origin and Spread of Nationalism.* 2nd ed. London: Verso, 1991.

Ansari, Zafar Ishaq, and John Esposito, eds. *Muslims and the West: Encounter and Dialogue.* Islamabad: Islamic Research Institute, 2001.

Appleby, R. Scott. *The Ambivalence of the Sacred: Religion, Violence, and Reconciliation.* Lanham: Rowman and Littlefield, 2000.

Arberry, A. J., ed. *Persian Poems: An Anthology of Verse Translations.* Tehran: Yassavoli, 2005.

Arinze, Cardinal Francis. *Meeting Other Believers: The Risks and Rewards of Interreligious Dialogue.* Huntington, IN: Our Sunday Visitor, 1998.

Arkoun, Mohammed. *Rethinking Islam: Common Questions, Uncommon Answers.* Boulder: Westview, 1994.

Armstrong, Karen. *Holy War: The Crusades and Their Impact on Today's World.* New York: Anchor, 1991.

———. *Jerusalem: One City, Three Faiths.* New York: Ballantine, 1997.

———. *Muhammad: A Biography of the Prophet.* New York: HarperCollins, 1992.

Aslan, Reza. *No God but God: The Origins, Evolution, and Future of Islam.* New York: Random House, 2005.

Augsburger, David. *Conflict Mediation Across Cultures: Pathways and Patterns.* Louisville, KY: Knox, 1992.

Avruch, Kevin. *Culture and Conflict Resolution.* Washington, DC: US Institute of Peace, 1998.

Ballen, Kenneth. "The Myth of Muslim Support for Terror." *Christian Science Monitor,* February 23, 2007.

Barnett, Michael N. *Dialogues in Arab Politics: Negotiations in Regional Order.* New York: Columbia University Press, 1998.

Bayrak, Tosun, trans. *Divine Governance of the Human Kingdom.* By Ibn 'Arabi. Louisville, KY: Fons Vitae, 1997.

Bennett, Brad. "Arab-Muslim Cases of Nonviolent Struggle." In *Arab Nonviolent Political Struggle in the Middle East,* edited by Ralph E. Crow, Philip Grant, and Saad E. Ibrahim, pp. 41–57. Boulder: Lynne Rienner, 1990.

Black, Anthony. *The History of Islamic Political Thought: From the Prophet to the Present.* New York: Routledge, 2001.

Boase, Roger, ed. *Islam and Global Dialogue: Religious Pluralism and the Pursuit of Peace.* Burlington, VT: Ashgate, 2005.

Bogle, Emory C. *The Modern Middle East: From Imperialism to Freedom, 1800–1958.* Upper Saddle River, NJ: Prentice Hall, 1996.

Boulding, Elise. *Cultures of Peace: The Hidden Side of History.* New York: Syracuse University Press, 2000.

Boylan, Michael. *Hafiz: The Dance of Life.* Washington, DC: Mage, 1998.

Bozeman, Adda. *Politics and Culture in International History.* Princeton: Princeton University Press, 1960.

Brandon, James. "Koranic Duels Ease Terror." *Christian Science Monitor,* February 5, 2005. http://www.csmonitor.com/2005/0204/p01s04-wome.html (accessed April 6, 2008).

Brown, Tricia Gates, ed. *Getting in the Way: Stories from the Christian Peacemaker Teams.* Scottdale, PA: Herald, 2005.

Brubaker, Rogers. *Nationalism Reframed: Nationhood and the National Question in the New Europe.* New York: Cambridge University Press, 1996.

Bulliet, Richard W. *The Case for Islamo-Christian Civilization.* New York: Columbia University Press, 2004.

Burton, John W. *Conflict: Resolution and Prevention.* New York: St. Martin's, 1990.

Bush, George W. "President's Remarks at the 2004 Republican National Convention." American Presidency Project, University of California at Santa Barbara. http://www.presidency.ucsb.edu/shownomination.php?convid=24 (accessed July 23, 2005).

Butterworth, Charles E., trans. *Alfarabi, the Political Writings: Selected Aphorisms and Other Texts.* Ithaca: Cornell University Press, 2001.

Capps, Walter H. "Interpreting Václav Havel." *Cross Currents* 47, no. 3 (1997): 301–316.

Casanova, Jose. "Civil Society and Religion: Retrospective Reflections on Catholicism and Prospective Reflections on Islam." *Social Research* 68, no. 4 (Winter 2001): 1041–1080.

Center for Strategic and International Studies. *Mixed Blessings: US Government Engagement with Religion in Conflict-Prone Settings.* Washington, DC, 2007.

Chittick, William. *The Sufi Path of Knowledge: Ibn al-'Arabi's Metaphysics of Imagination.* Albany: State University of New York Press, 1989.

Clark, Janine. "Canadian Interests and Democracy Promotion in the Middle East." In *Canada and the Middle East: In Theory and Practice,* edited by Paul Heinbecker and Bessma Momani, pp. 91–115. Waterloo, ON: Wilfrid Laurier University Press, 2007.

Coates, Peter. *Ibn 'Arabi and Modern Thought.* Oxford, England: Anqa, 2002.

Cohen, Anthony P. *The Symbolic Construction of Community.* New York: Routledge, 1985.

Combs-Schilling, M. Elaine. "Sacred Refuge: The Power of a Muslim Female Saint." *Fellowship* 60, nos. 5–6 (May–June 1994): 17.

Corbin, Henry. *Alone with the Alone: Creative Imagination in the Sufism of Ibn 'Arabi.* Princeton: Princeton University Press, 1997.

Cowan, James, trans. *Rumi's Divan of Shems of Tabriz.* Rockport, MA: Element, 1997.

Crow, Karim Douglas. "Nonviolence, Ethics, and Character Development in Islam." In *Peace and Conflict Resolution in Islam: Precept and Practice,* edited by Abdul Aziz Said, Nathan C. Funk, and Ayse S. Kadayifci, pp. 213–226. Lanham: University Press of America, 2001.

Dallmayr, Fred R. *Border Crossings: Toward a Comparative Political Theory.* Lanham: Lexington, 1999.

———. *Dialogue Among Civilizations: Some Exemplary Voices.* New York: Palgrave Macmillan, 2002.

Daly, Herman E., and John B. Cobb. *For the Common Good: Redirecting the Economy Toward Community, the Environment, and a Sustainable Future.* Boston: Beacon, 1994.

Daniel, Norman. *Islam and the West: The Making of an Image.* Oxford, England: Oneworld, 1993.

Deane, Claudia, and Darryl Fears. "Negative Perception of Islam Increasing: Poll Numbers in U.S. Higher Than in 2001." *Washington Post,* March 9, 2006.

Dekmejian, R. Hrair. *Islam in Revolution: Fundamentalism in the Arab World.* New York: Syracuse University Press, 1995.

Easwaran, Eknath. *A Man to Match His Mountains: Badshah Khan, Nonviolent Soldier of Islam.* Petaluma, CA: Nilgiri, 1984.

The Economist. "Hamas Won't Go Away." January 31, 2008. http://www.economist.com/opinion/displaystory.cfm?story_id=10608398&cfid=9255691&cftoken=f4f1ee3ebdf03cfe-315784cd-b27c-bb00-012bea62ca3765fd (accessed March 16, 2008).

Eickelman, Dale F. "Islam and Ethical Pluralism." In *Islamic Political Ethics: Civil Society, Pluralism, and Conflict,* edited by Sohail H. Hashmi, pp. 115–134. Princeton: Princeton University Press, 2002.

———. *The Middle East and Central Asia: An Anthropological Approach.* Englewood Cliffs, NJ: Prentice Hall, 1998.

Eickelman, Dale F., and James Piscatori. *Muslim Politics.* Princeton: Princeton University Press, 1996.

Eliade, Mircea. *The Sacred and the Profane: The Nature of Religion.* New York: Harcourt Brace, 1959.

Enayat, Hamid. *Modern Islamic Political Thought.* New York: Tauris, 1982.

Esack, Farid. *On Being a Muslim: Finding a Religious Path in the World Today.* Oxford, England: Oneworld, 1999.

———. *Quran, Liberation, and Pluralism: An Islamic Perspective of Interreligious Solidarity Against Oppression.* Oxford, England: Oneworld, 1997.

Esposito, John L. *Islam and Politics.* Syracuse: Syracuse University Press, 1987.

———. *The Islamic Threat: Myth or Reality?* New York: Oxford University Press, 1999.

———. *The Oxford Dictionary of Islam.* New York: Oxford University Press, 2003.

Euben, Roxanne L. *Enemy in the Mirror: Islamic Fundamentalism and the Limits of Modern Rationalism—A Work of Comparative Political Theory.* Princeton: Princeton University Press, 1999.

Fair, C. Christine, and Bryan Shepherd. "Who Supports Terrorism? Evidence from Fourteen Muslim Countries." *Studies in Conflict and Terrorism* 29, no. 1 (2006): 51–74.

Falk, Richard. "False Universalism and the Geopolitics of Exclusion: The Case of Islam." *Third World Quarterly* 18, no. 1 (1997): 7–23.

Fallaci, Oriana. *The Force of Reason.* New York: Rizzoli, 2006.

Fattah, Moataz A. *Democratic Values in the Muslim World.* Boulder: Lynne Rienner, 2006.

Fergani, Nader, et al. *The Arab Human Development Report 2002: Creating Opportunities for Future Generations.* New York: United Nations Development Programme, Regional Bureau for Arab States, 2002.

Fisher, Roger, William Ury, and Bruce Patton. *Getting to Yes: Negotiating Agreement Without Giving In.* 2nd ed. New York: Penguin, 1991.

Foltz, Richard C., Frederick M. Denny, and Azizan Baharuddin, eds. *Islam and Ecology: A Bestowed Trust.* Cambridge: Harvard University Press, 2003.

Fox, Jonathan, and Shmuel Sandler. *Bringing Religion into International Relations.* New York: Palgrave Macmillan, 2004.

Frykolm, Amy Johnson. *Rapture Culture: Left Behind in Evangelical America.* New York: Oxford University Press, 2004.

Fukuyama, Francis. *The End of History and the Last Man.* New York: Free Press, 1992.

Funk, Nathan C. "Transforming Islamic-Western Identity Conflict: A Framework for Strategic Engagement." *International Journal of Peace Studies* 12, no. 1 (Spring–Summer 2007): 23–51.

Funk, Nathan C., and Abdul Aziz Said. "Islam and the West: Narratives of Conflict and Conflict Transformation." *International Journal of Peace Studies* 9, no. 1 (Spring–Summer 2004): 1–28.

Galtung, Johan. *Peace by Peaceful Means: Peace and Conflict, Development and Civilization.* Thousand Oaks, CA: Sage, 1996.

Gerges, Fawaz A. *America and Political Islam: Clash of Cultures or Clash of Interests?* New York: Cambridge University Press, 1999.

———. *Journey of the Jihadist: Inside Muslim Militancy.* New York: Harcourt, 2006.

Gilpin, Robert. *War and Change in World Politics.* New York: Cambridge University Press, 1981.

Glassé, Cyril. *The Concise Encyclopedia of Islam.* New York: HarperCollins, 1989.

Gold, Rabbi Ben-Zion. "The Diaspora and the Intifada: The Responsibility of American Jews." *Boston Review* 27, no. 5 (October–November 2002). http://bostonreview.net/br27.5/gold.html (accessed March 16, 2008).

Goldberg, Jonah. "A New Cold War—With a Twist." *National Review Online*, October 26, 2001. http://www.nationalreview.com/goldberg/goldberg102601.shtml (accessed August 25, 2003).

Goolam, Hafiz Nazeem. "Gender Equality in Islamic Family Law: Dispelling Common Misconceptions and Misunderstandings." In *Understanding Islamic Law: From Classical to Contemporary*, edited by Hisham M. Ramadan, pp. 117–134. Lanham: AltaMira, 2006.

Gray, Elizabeth, trans. *The Green Sea of Heaven: Fifty Ghazals from the Diwan of Hafiz.* Ashland, OR: White Cloud, 1995.

Gregor, Thomas, and Leslie E. Sponsel, eds. *The Anthropology of Peace and Nonviolence.* Boulder: Lynne Rienner, 1994.

Gregorian, Vartan. *Islam: A Mosaic, Not a Monolith.* Washington, DC: Brookings Institution, 2003.

Guillaume, A., trans. *The Life of Muhammad: A Translation of Ibn Ishaq's Sirat Rasul Allah.* Karachi, Pakistan: Oxford University Press, 1990.

Guilmartin, John F., Jr. "Ideology and Conflict: The Wars of the Ottoman Empire, 1453–1606." *Journal of Interdisciplinary History* 18, no. 4 (Spring 1988): 721–747.

Hafez, Mohammed M. *Why Muslims Rebel: Repression and Resistance in the Islamic World.* Boulder: Lynne Rienner, 2003.

Halliday, Fred. *Islam and the Myth of Confrontation: Religion and Politics in the Middle East.* New York: Tauris, 1996.

———. *Two Hours That Shook the World: September 11, 2001—Causes and Consequences.* London: Saqi, 2002.

Hanafi, Hasan. "Alternative Conceptions of Civil Society: A Reflective Islamic Approach." In *Islamic Political Ethics: Civil Society, Pluralism, and Conflict*, edited by Sohail H. Hashmi, pp. 56–75. Princeton: Princeton University Press, 2002.

Harvey, John W., and Rudolf Otto. *The Idea of the Holy.* New York: H. Milford, 1928.

Harris, Rabia Terri. "Nonviolence in Islam: The Alternative Community Tradition." In *Subverting Hatred: The Challenge of Nonviolence in Religious Traditions,* edited by Daniel L. Smith-Christopher, pp. 95–114. Cambridge: Boston Research Center for the 21st Century, 1998.

Hashmi, Sohail H. "Interpreting the Islamic Ethics of War and Peace." In *The Ethics of War and Peace: Religious and Secular Perspectives,* edited by Terry Nardin, pp. 146–166. Princeton: Princeton University Press, 1996.

———. "Islamic Ethics and International Society." In *Islamic Political Ethics: Civil Society, Pluralism, and Conflict,* edited by Sohail H. Hashmi, pp. 148–172. Princeton: Princeton University Press, 2002.

———. *Islamic Political Ethics: Civil Society, Pluralism, and Conflict.* Princeton: Princeton University Press, 2002.

Havel, Václav. "The Divine Revolution." *Civilization* 5 (April–May 1998): 52.

Hegel, Georg W. F. *Hegel's Philosophy of Right.* Oxford, England: Clarendon, 1967.

Helminski, Edmund, trans. *The Ruins of the Heart: Selected Lyric Poetry of Jelaluddin Rumi.* Putney, VT: Threshold, 1981.

Herzog, Roman. *Preventing the Clash of Civilizations: A Peace Strategy for the Twenty-First Century.* New York: St. Martin's, 1999.

Hitchens, Christopher. *God Is Not Great: How Religion Poisons Everything.* New York: Allen and Unwin, 2007.

Hjarpe, Jan. "Historiography and Islamic Vocabulary in War and Peace: A Memento for Conflict Resolution in the Muslim World." In *Cultural Variation in Conflict Resolution: Alternatives to Violence,* edited by Douglas P. Fry and Kaj Bjorkqvist, pp. 115–122. Mahwah, NJ: Erlbaum, 1997.

Hodgson, Marshall G. S. *The Venture of Islam: Conscience and History in a World Civilization.* Vol. 1. Chicago: University of Chicago Press, 1974.

Hooglund, Eric. "The Other Face of War." *Middle East Report* no. 171 (July–August 1991): 3–7, 10–12.

Human Rights Watch. "Algeria: Amnesty Law Risks Legalizing Impunity for Crimes Against Humanity." April 14, 2005. http://hrw.org/english/docs/2005/04/14/algeri10485.htm (accessed July 27, 2007).

Hunter, Shireen. *Iran and the World: Continuity in a Revolutionary Decade.* Bloomington: Indiana University Press, 1990.

Huntington, Samuel P. "The Clash of Civilizations?" *Foreign Affairs* 72, no. 3 (Summer 1993): 22–49.

———. *The Clash of Civilizations and the Remaking of World Order.* New York: Simon and Schuster, 1996.

Hussein, Saddam. "Call for Jihad." In *The Saddam Hussein Reader: Selections from Leading Writers on Iraq,* edited by Turi Munthe, pp. 239–246. New York: Thunder's Mouth, 2002.

Ibrahim, Saad E. "Introduction: Why Nonviolent Political Struggle in the Middle East?" In *Arab Nonviolent Political Struggle in the Middle East,* edited by Ralph E. Crow, Philip Grant, and Saad E. Ibrahim, pp. 1–8. Boulder: Lynne Rienner, 1990.

Iqbal, Afzal. *Diplomacy in Early Islam.* 5th ed. New Delhi: International Islamic, 1992.

Irani, George E., and Nathan C. Funk. "Rituals of Reconciliation: Arab-Islamic Perspectives." *Arab Studies Quarterly* 20, no. 4 (Fall 1998): 53–73.

Ismael, Tareq Y., and Jacqueline S. Ismael. *The Iraqi Predicament: People in the Quagmire of Power Politics.* London: Pluto, 2004.

Izutsu, Toshiko. *Sufism and Taoism: A Comparative Study of Key Philosophical Concepts.* Berkeley: University of California Press, 1983.

Jabbour, Elias. *Sulha: Palestinian Traditional Peacemaking Process.* Montreat, NC: House of Hope, 1996.

James, William. *The Varieties of Religious Experience: A Study in Human Nature.* New York: Modern Library, 1929.

Johansen, Robert, C. "Radical Islam and Nonviolence: A Case Study of Religious Empowerment and Constraint Among Pashtuns." *Journal of Peace Research* 34, no. 1 (1997): 53–71.

Johnston, Douglas, ed. *Faith-Based Diplomacy: Trumping Realpolitik.* New York: Oxford University Press, 2003.

Johnston, Douglas, and Cynthia Sampson, eds. *Religion: The Missing Dimension of Statecraft.* New York: Oxford University Press, 1994.

Jones, Jeremy. *Negotiating Change: The New Politics of the Middle East.* New York: Tauris, 2007.

Juergensmeyer, Mark. *The New Cold War? Religious Nationalism Confronts the Secular State.* Berkeley: University of California Press, 1993.

Kadayifci-Orellana, S. Ayse. "Religion, Violence, and the Islamic Tradition of Nonviolence." *Turkish Yearbook of International Relations* 34 (2004): 23–62.

———. *Standing on an Isthmus: Islamic Narratives on Peace and War in Palestinian Territories.* Lanham: Lexington, 2007.

Kazemi, Farhad. "Perspectives on Islam and Civil Society." In *Islamic Political Ethics: Civil Society, Pluralism, and Conflict,* edited by Sohail H. Hashmi, pp. 38–55. Princeton: Princeton University Press, 2002.

Keddie, Nikki R. *Modern Iran: Roots and Results of Revolution.* New Haven: Yale University Press, 2003.

Kelman, Herbert. "Social-Psychological Dimensions of International Conflict." In *Peacemaking in International Conflict: Methods and Techniques,* edited by I. William Zartman and J. Lewis Rasmussen, pp. 191–237. Washington, DC: US Institute of Peace, 1997.

Khadduri, Majid. *War and Peace in the Law of Islam.* Baltimore: Johns Hopkins Press, 1955.

Khalidi, Rashid. *Resurrecting Empire: Western Footprints and America's Perilous Path in the Middle East.* New York: Tauris, 2004.

Khalidi, Tarif. *Arabic Historical Thought in the Classical Period.* New York: Cambridge University Press, 1994.

Khan, M. A. Muqtedar. "Islam as an Ethical Tradition of International Relations." *Islam and Christian-Muslim Relations* 8, no. 2 (1997): 177–192.

———. *Islamic Democratic Discourse: Theory, Debates, and Philosophical Perspectives.* Lanham: Lexington, 2006.

———. "Radical Islam, Liberal Islam." *Current History* 102, no. 668 (December 2003): 417–421.

King, Mary E. *A Quiet Revolution: The First Intifada and Nonviolent Resistance.* New York: Nation, 2007.

Kishtainy, Khalid. "Violent and Nonviolent Struggle in Arab History." In *Arab Nonviolent Political Struggle in the Middle East,* edited by Ralph E. Crow, Philip Grant, and Saad E. Ibrahim, pp. 9–24. Boulder: Lynne Rienner, 1990.

Kiser, John. *The Monks of Tibhirine: Faith, Love, and Terror in Algeria.* New York: St. Martin's, 2002.

Korten, David C. *When Corporations Rule the World.* West Hartford, CT: Kumarian, 1995.

Kung, Hans, and Karl-Josef Kuschel, eds. *A Global Ethic: The Declaration of the Parliament of the World's Religions.* London: SCM, 1993.

Kurzman, Charles. "Islamic Statements Against Terrorism." 2008. http://www.unc.edu/~kurzman/terror.htm (accessed March 15, 2008).
———, ed. *Liberal Islam: A Source Book.* New York: Oxford University Press, 1988.
Labidi, Kamel. "Amnesia Is the Price of Algerian Peace and Reconciliation." *Daily Star* (Lebanon), April 1, 2006. http://www.dailystar.com.lb/article.asp?edition_id=10&categ_id=5&article_id=23419# (accessed July 27, 2007).
Lambton, Ann K. "Islamic Mirrors for Princes." *Probelmi Attuali di Scienza e di Cultura* no. 160 (1971): 419–442.
Lang, Sharon D. *Sharaf Politics: Honor and Peacemaking in Israeli-Palestinian Society.* New York: Routledge, 2005.
Lapidus, Ira, M. *A History of Islamic Societies.* New York: Cambridge University Press, 1988.
Laue, James H. "Contributions of the Emerging Field of Conflict Resolution." In *Approaches to Peace: An Intellectual Map,* edited by W. Scott Thompson and Kenneth M. Jensen, pp. 299–332. Washington, DC: US Institute of Peace, 1988.
Lawrence, Bruce, ed. *Messages to the World: The Statements of Osama bin Laden.* New York: Verso, 2005.
Lederach, John Paul. "The Mediator's Cultural Assumptions." In *Mediation and Facilitation Training Manual: Foundations and Skills for Constructive Conflict Transformation.* 3rd ed., edited by Jim Stutzman and Carolyn Schrock-Shenk, pp. 80–83. Akron, PA: Mennonite Conciliation Service, 1995.
———. *The Moral Imagination: The Art and Soul of Building Peace.* New York: Oxford University Press, 2005.
Lerner, Michael. *Healing Israel/Palestine: A Path to Peace and Reconciliation.* San Francisco: Tikkun, 2003.
Lewis, Bernard. "Islam and Liberal Democracy." *Atlantic Monthly* 271, no. 2 (1993): 89–98.
———. "The Roots of Muslim Rage." *Atlantic Monthly* 266, no. 3 (1990): 47–60.
———. *What Went Wrong? The Clash Between Islam and Modernity in the Middle East.* New York: Perennial, 2003.
Lewis, Franklin D. *Rumi: Past and Present, East and West: The Life, Teaching, and Poetry of Jalal al-Din Rumi.* Oxford, England: Oneworld, 2000.
Lindner, Evelyn G. *Making Enemies: Humiliation and International Conflict.* Westport: Praeger, 2006.
Linzer, Dafna. "Poll Shows Growing Arab Rancor at U.S." *Washington Post,* July 23, 2004.
Lowney, Chris. *A Vanished World: Medieval Spain's Golden Age of Enlightenment.* New York: Free Press, 2005.
Lynch, Marc. "Taking Arabs Seriously." *Foreign Affairs* 82, no. 5 (2003): 81–94.
Maalouf, Amin. *The Crusades Through Arab Eyes.* New York: Schocken, 1984.
MacDonald, Robert W. *The League of Arab States: A Study in the Dynamics of a Regional Organization.* Princeton: Princeton University Press, 1965.
Mafi, Maryam, and Azima Melita Kolin, trans. *Rumi: Hidden Music.* New York: HarperCollins, 2001.
Malaysian National News Agency. "Declaration on Palestine." April 22, 2004. http://www.bernama.com/events/ext_oic2004/palestine.php (accessed August 15, 2005).
Mamdani, Mahmood. *Good Muslim, Bad Muslim: America, the Cold War, and the Roots of Terror.* New York: Pantheon, 2004.
Martin, Richard C. *Encyclopedia of Islam and the Modern World.* New York: Macmillan, 2004.

Mathews, Dylan. *War Prevention Works: 50 Stories of People Resolving Conflict.* Oxford, England: Oxford Research Group, 2002.
Mazrui, Ali. "Islamic and Western Values." *Foreign Affairs* 76, no. 5 (September–October 1997): 118–132.
Meacham, Jon, and Sally Quinn. "The Many Meanings of Jihad to 2 Prominent Muslims." *Washington Post,* July 28, 2007.
Menocal, Maria Rosa. *The Ornament of the World: How Muslims, Jews, and Christians Created a Culture of Tolerance in Medieval Spain.* Boston: Little, Brown, 2002.
Mertus, Julie. *Bait and Switch: Human Rights and US Foreign Policy.* New York: Routledge, 2004.
Milton-Edwards, Beverley, and Peter Hinchcliffe. *Conflicts in the Middle East Since 1945.* New York: Routledge, 2001.
Moisi, Dominique. "The Clash of Civilizations Is Really One of Emotions." *Daily Star* (Beirut), March 27, 2006. http://www.dailystar.com.lb (accessed March 27, 2006).
Moore, Oliver. "Working to Rid Afghanistan of Land Mines a 'Kind of Jihad.'" *Globe and Mail,* April 1, 2008.
Morgan, Michael H. *Lost History: The Enduring Legacy of Muslim Scientists, Thinkers, and Artists.* Washington, DC: National Geographic Society, 2007.
Morrow, Lance. "The Case for Rage and Retribution." *Time,* September 12, 2001.
Moussalli, Ahmad S. "An Islamic Model for Political Conflict Resolution: *Tahkim* (Arbitration)." In *Conflict Resolution in the Arab World: Selected Essays,* edited by Paul Salem, pp. 44–71. Beirut: American University of Beirut Press, 1997.
———. *Moderate and Radical Islamic Fundamentalism: The Quest for Modernity, Legitimacy, and the Islamic State.* Gainesville: University of Florida Press, 1999.
Muhaiyaddeen, Bawa. *Islam and World Peace: Explanations of a Sufi.* Philadelphia: Fellowship, 1987.
Munthe, Turi, ed. *The Saddam Hussein Reader.* New York: Thunder's Mouth, 2002.
Murata, Sachiko. *The Tao of Islam: A Sourcebook on Gender Relationships in Islamic Thought.* Albany: State University of New York Press, 1992.
Murata, Sachiko, and William C. Chittick. *The Vision of Islam.* New York: Paragon, 1994.
Muslim Peacemaker Team. "About MPT." 2006. http://www.mpt-iraq.org/?q=node/3 (accessed April 7, 2008).
Nagler, Michael N. *Is There No Other Way? The Search for a Nonviolent Future.* Berkeley: Berkeley Hills, 2001.
Nasr, Seyyed Hossein. *The Heart of Islam: Enduring Values for Humanity.* New York: HarperCollins, 2002.
———. "Islam, the Contemporary Islamic World, and the Environmental Crisis." In *Islam and Ecology,* edited by Richard C. Foltz, Frederick M. Denny, and Azizan Baharuddin, pp. 85–105. Cambridge: Harvard University Press, 2003.
———. *Sufi Essays.* New York: State University of New York Press, 1973.
———. *Traditional Islam in the Modern World.* New York: Routledge and Kegan Paul, 1987.
Neumann, Iver B. *Uses of the Other: "The East" in European Identity Formation.* Minneapolis: University of Minnesota Press, 1999.
Newby, Gordon D. *A Concise Encyclopedia of Islam.* Oxford, England: Oneworld, 2002.
Nicholson, Reynold A., trans. *The Tarjuman al-Ashwaq: A Collection of Mystical Odes by Muhyi'ddin Ibn al-'Arabi.* Wheaton, IL: Theosophical, 1978.
Northrup, Terrell A. "The Dynamic of Identity in Personal and Social Conflict." In *Intractable Conflicts and Their Transformation,* edited by Louis Kriesburg, Terrell

A. Northrup, and Stuart J. Thorson, pp. 55–82. Syracuse: Syracuse University Press, 1989.

Nuland, Sherwin B. *Maimonides*. New York: Schocken, 2005.

Nyang, Sulayman. "Scriptural Faith and Ethnicity: Some Lessons from the Islamic Experience." In *Abrahamic Faiths, Ethnicity, and Ethnic Conflicts,* edited by Paul Peachey, George F. McLean, and John Kromkowski, pp. 237–248. Washington, DC: Council for Research in Values and Philosophy, 1997.

Office of the Director of National Intelligence. "Declassified Key Judgments of the National Intelligence Estimate—'Trends in Global Terrorism: Implications for the United States' Dated April 2006." Washington, DC. http://www.dni.gov/press_releases/declassified_nie_key_judgments.pdf (accessed March 28, 2008).

Otto, Rudolph. *The Idea of the Holy: An Inquiry into the Non-Rational Factor in the Idea of the Divine and Its Relation to the Rational.* Toronto: Oxford University Press, 1929.

Paige, Glen D., Chaiwat Satha-Anand, and Sarah Gilliatt, eds. *Islam and Nonviolence.* Honolulu: Center for Global Nonviolence Planning Project, 1993.

Panikkar, Raimon. *Cultural Disarmament: The Way to Peace.* Louisville, KY: Knox, 1995.

Payne, Richard J. *The Clash with Distant Cultures: Values, Interests, and Force in American Foreign Policy.* Albany: State University of New York Press, 1995.

Perry, Whitall N. *A Treasury of Traditional Wisdom.* New York: Simon and Schuster, 1971.

Peters, Rudolph. *Islam and Colonialism: The Doctrine of Jihad in Modern History.* Berlin: Mouton de Gruyter, 1979.

Pew Global Attitudes Project. "Global Opinion Trends 2002–2007: Rising Tide Lifts Mood in Developing Countries—Sharp Decline in Support for Suicide Bombing in the Muslim Countries: 47-Nation Pew Global Attitudes Survey." Washington, DC: Pew Research Center, 2007. http://pewglobal.org/reports/pdf/257.pdf (accessed July 28, 2007).

Piscatori, James P., ed. *Islamic Fundamentalisms and the Gulf Crisis.* Chicago: University of Chicago Press, 1991.

Power, Samantha. "Our War on Terror." *New York Times Book Review,* July 29, 2007.

Rahman, Fazlur. *Islam and Modernity: Transformation of an Intellectual Tradition.* Chicago: University of Chicago Press, 1982.

———. *Revival and Reform in Islam: A Study of Islamic Fundamentalism.* Oxford, England: Oneworld, 2000.

Ramadan, Tariq. *In the Footsteps of the Prophet: Lessons from the Life of Muhammad.* New York: Oxford University Press, 2007.

———. *To Be a European Muslim: A Study of Islamic Sources in the European Context.* Leicester, UK: Islamic Foundation, 1999.

Rehatsek, Edward. *The Rose Garden (Gulistan): Sa'di.* North Fitzroy, Australia: New Humanity, 1990.

Reiss, Hans, ed. *Kant: Political Writings.* New York: Cambridge University Press, 1991.

Ross, Marc Howard. "The Political Psychology of Competing Narratives: September 11 and Beyond." In *Understanding September 11,* edited by Craig Calhoun, Paul Price, and Ashley Timmer, pp. 303–320. New York: New Press, 2002.

Sachedina, Abdulaziz Abdulhussein. *The Islamic Roots of Democratic Pluralism.* New York: Oxford University Press, 2001.

Sádiki, Larbi. "Popular Uprisings and Arab Democratization." *International Journal of Middle East Studies* 32 (2000): 71–95.

Saeed, Abdullah, and Hassan Saeed. *Freedom of Religion, Apostasy, and Islam.* Burlington, VT: Ashgate, 2004.

Safa, Oussama. "Lebanon Springs Forward." *Journal of Democracy* 17, no. 1 (January 2006): 22–37.

Safi, Louay M. *Tensions and Transition in the Muslim World.* Lanham: University Press of America, 2003.

———. "War and Peace in Islam." *American Journal of Islamic Social Sciences* 5, no. 1 (1988): 29–57.

Said, Abdul Aziz, Mohammed Abu-Nimer, and Meena Sharify-Funk, eds. *Contemporary Islam: Dynamic Not Static.* New York: Routledge, 2006.

Said, Abdul Aziz, and Nathan C. Funk. "The Role of Faith in Cross-Cultural Conflict Resolution." *Peace and Conflict Studies* 9, no. 1 (2002): 37–50.

Said, Abdul Aziz, Nathan C. Funk, and Ayse S. Kadayifci, eds. *Peace and Conflict Resolution in Islam: Precept and Practice.* Lanham: University Press of America, 2001.

Said, Abdul Aziz, Charles O. Lerche Jr., and Charles O. Lerche III. *Concepts of International Politics in Global Perspective.* 4th ed. Englewood Cliffs, NJ: Prentice-Hall, 1995.

Said, Abdul Aziz, and Meena Sharify-Funk. *Cultural Diversity and Islam.* Lanham: University Press of America, 2003.

Said, Edward. "The Clash of Ignorance." *The Nation,* October 22, 2001. http://www.thenation.com/doc/20011022/said (accessed March 8, 2008).

Saliba, George. *Islamic Science and the Making of the European Renaissance.* Cambridge: Massachusetts Institute of Technology Press, 2007.

Salutin, Rick. "Muslims 'R' Us, Not Them." *Globe and Mail,* February 10, 2006.

Sands, Kristin Zahra. *Sufi Commentaries on the Qur'an in Classical Islam.* London: Routledge, 2006.

Satha-Anand, Chaiwat. "Muslim Communal Nonviolent Actions: Minority Coexistence in a Non-Muslim Society." In *Cultural Diversity and Islam,* edited by Abdul Aziz Said and Meena Sharify-Funk, pp. 195–207. Lanham: University Press of America, 2003.

———. "The Nonviolent Crescent: Eight Theses on Muslim Nonviolent Action." In *Arab Nonviolent Political Struggle in the Middle East,* edited by Ralph E. Crow, Philip Grant, and Saad E. Ibrahim, pp. 25–41. Boulder: Lynne Rienner, 1990.

———. *The Nonviolent Crescent: Two Essays on Islam and Nonviolence.* Alkmaar, Netherlands: International Fellowship of Reconciliation, 1996.

———. "The Politics of Forgiveness: Islamic Teachings and Gandhi's Teachings." In *The Nonviolent Crescent: Two Essays on Islam and Nonviolence,* by Chaiwat Satha-Anand, pp. 9–24. Alkmaar, Netherlands: International Fellowship of Reconciliation, 1996.

———. "Transforming Terrorism with Muslims' Nonviolent Alternatives?" In *Contemporary Islam: Dynamic Not Static,* edited by Abdul Aziz Said, Mohammed Abu-Nimer, and Meena Sharify-Funk, pp. 189–211. New York: Routledge, 2006.

Schimmel, Annemarie. *Deciphering the Signs of God: A Phenomenological Approach to Islam.* New York: State University of New York Press, 1994.

———, trans. *Look! This Is Love! Poems of Rumi.* Boston: Shambhala, 1991.

———. *Mystical Dimensions of Islam.* Chapel Hill: University of North Carolina Press, 1975.

Schleifer, S. Abdullah. "Jihad and Traditional Islamic Consciousness." *Islamic Quarterly* 27, no. 4 (1983): 173–203.

———. "Understanding Jihad: Definition and Methodology." *Islamic Quarterly* 27, no. 3 (1983): 117–131.

Scimecca, Joseph A. "Conflict Resolution in the United States: The Emergence of a Profession." In *Conflict Resolution: Cross-Cultural Perspectives,* edited by Kevin Avruch, Peter Black, and Joseph A. Scimecca, pp. 19–39. Westport: Greenwood, 1991.

Senturk, Recep. "Sociology of Rights: Inviolability of the Other in Islam Between Universalism and Communalism." In *Contemporary Islam: Dynamic Not Static,* edited by Abdul Aziz Said, Mohammed Abu-Nimer, and Meena Sharify-Funk, pp. 24–49. New York: Routledge, 2006.

Segesvary, Victor. *Dialogue of Civilizations: An Introduction to Civilizational Analysis.* Lanham: University Press of America, 2000.

Shah-Kazemi, Reza. *The Other in the Light of the One: The Universality of the Qur'an and Interfaith Dialogue.* Cambridge, England: Islamic Texts Society, 2006.

———. *Paths to Transcendence: According to Shankara, Ibn Arabi, and Meister Eckhart.* London: World Wisdom, 2006.

Shapiro, Ian. *Containment: Rebuilding a Strategy Against Global Terror.* Princeton: Princeton University Press, 2007.

Sharabi, Hisham. *Nationalism and Revolution in the Arab World.* Princeton: Van Nostrand, 1966.

Sharp, Gene. *The Politics of Nonviolent Action: Part Two—The Methods of Nonviolent Action.* Boston: Porter Sargent, 1973.

———. *The Politics of Nonviolent Action: Part Three—The Dynamics of Nonviolent Action.* Boston: Porter Sargent, 1973.

———. *There Are Realistic Alternatives.* Boston: Albert Einstein Institution, 2003. http://www.aeinstein.org/organizations/org/tara.pdf (accessed February 23, 2008).

Shirazi, Muhammad. *War, Peace, and Non-Violence: An Islamic Perspective.* Elmhurst, NY: Tahrike Tarsile Qur'an, 2001.

Sirriyeh, Elizabeth. *Sufis and Anti-Sufis.* Richmond, UK: Curzon, 1999.

Smith, Charles D. *Palestine and the Arab-Israeli Conflict.* 3rd ed. New York: St. Martin's, 1996.

Smith, Daniel L. "The Rewards of Allah." *Journal of Peace Research* 26, no. 4 (1989): 385–398.

Sponsel, Leslie E., and Thomas Gregor, eds. *The Anthropology of Peace and Nonviolence.* Boulder: Lynne Rienner, 1994.

Steele, James. *An Architecture for People: The Complete Works of Hassan Fathy.* New York: Whitney Library of Design, 1997.

Stein, Janice Gross. "Image, Identity, and the Resolution of Violent Conflict." In *Turbulent Peace: The Challenges of Managing International Conflict,* edited by Chester A. Crocker, Fen Osler Hampson, and Pamela Aall, pp. 189–208. Washington, DC: US Institute of Peace, 2001.

Suhrawardy, Abdullah al-Mamun. *The Sayings of Muhammad.* New York: Citadel, 1990.

Sulha Peace Project. "Our Vision." 2008. http://www.sulha.com/showitem.asp?itemid=vision (accessed April 5, 2008).

Taha, Mahmoud Mohamed. *The Second Message of Islam.* Syracuse: Syracuse University Press, 1996.

Tavakoli-Targhi, Mohamad. "Frontline Mysticism and Eastern Spirituality." *ISIM Newsletter* (International Institute for the Study of Islam in the Modern World) (January 2002): 13, 38.

Teasdale, Wayne. *The Mystic Heart: Discovering a Universal Spirituality in the World's Religions.* Novato, CA: New World Library, 2001.

Tehranian, Majid, and David W. Chappell. *Dialogue of Civilizations: A New Peace Agenda for a New Millennium.* New York: Tauris, 2002.

Thackston, W. M., trans. *Signs of the Unseen: The Discourses of Jalaluddin Rumi.* Putney, VT: Threshold, 1994.

Thomas, Scott. *The Global Resurgence of Religion and the Reconstruction of International Relations.* New York: Palgrave Macmillan, 2005.

Thompson, Nicholas. "A War Best Served Cold." *New York Times,* July 31, 2007.

Trimingham, John Spencer. *The Sufi Orders in Islam.* New York: Oxford University Press, 1998.

US Institute of Peace. "Support for Terrorism Linked to Feelings of Threat." *PeaceWatch* 12, no. 1 (January–February 2006): 14–15.

Voll, John O. *Islam: Continuity and Change in the Modern World.* 2nd ed. Syracuse: Syracuse University Press, 1994.

Wachtel, Paul L. *The Poverty of Affluence: A Psychological Portrait of the American Way of Life.* Philadelphia: New Society, 1989.

Walker, Christopher J. *Armenia: The Survival of a Nation.* 2nd ed. New York: St. Martin's, 1990.

Walzer, Michael. *The Revolution of the Saints: A Study in the Origins of Radical Politics.* New York: Atheneum, 1969.

Weber, Max. *The Protestant Ethic and the Spirit of Capitalism.* New York: Routledge, 1930.

Wehr, Paul, and John Paul Lederach. "Mediating Conflict in Central America." *Journal of Peace Research* 28, no. 1 (February 1991): 85–98.

Weiss, Bernard G. *The Spirit of Islamic Law.* Athens: University of Georgia Press, 1998.

Winslade, John, and Gerald Monk. *Narrative Mediation: A New Approach to Conflict Resolution.* San Francisco: Jossey-Bass, 2000.

Zakaria, Fareed. "How to Save the Arab World." *Newsweek,* December 24, 2001.

Zunes, Stephen. *Tinderbox: US Foreign Policy and the Roots of Terrorism.* Monroe, ME: Common Courage, 2003.

Index

About the Book

Islam and Peacemaking in the Middle East begins with a set of provocative questions: How, for example, do Muslims conceive of peace? To what degree do differences in the interpretation of Islam affect the ways in which peace is sought in the contemporary Middle East?

Through analysis of regional trends and case studies, the authors explore various Islamic ideas of peace and their bearing on difficult ethnic, nationalist, and civic conflicts. The result widens the parameters for serious discussion of Islam's contributions—real and potential—to ongoing negotiations.

Nathan C. Funk is assistant professor of peace and conflict studies at the University of Waterloo, Canada. **Abdul Aziz Said** is professor of international peace and conflict resolution and founder of the Center for Global Peace at American University.